Coming of Age in
Popular Culture

Coming of Age in Popular Culture

Teenagers, Adolescence, and the Art of Growing Up

DONALD C. MILLER

GREENWOOD™

An Imprint of ABC-CLIO, LLC
Santa Barbara, California • Denver, Colorado

Library of Congress Cataloging-in-Publication Data

Names: Miller, Don (Donald C.) author.
Title: Coming of age in popular culture : teenagers, adolescence, and the art
   of growing up / Donald C. Miller.
Description: Santa Barbara : Greenwood/ABC-CLIO, [2018] | Includes
   bibliographical references and index.
Identifiers: LCCN 2018008781 (print) | LCCN 2018031216 (ebook) | ISBN
   9781440840616 (eBook) | ISBN 9781440840609 (hardcopy : alk. paper)
Subjects: LCSH: Teenagers—United States—History—20th century. | Popular
   culture—United State—History—20th century.
Classification: LCC HQ799.U65 (ebook) | LCC HQ799.U65 M55 2018 (print) | DDC
   306.0973/0904—dc23
LC record available at https://lccn.loc.gov/2018008781

ISBN: 978-1-4408-4060-9 (print)
       978-1-4408-4061-6 (ebook)

22 21 20 19 18   1 2 3 4 5

This book is also available as an eBook.

Greenwood
An Imprint of ABC-CLIO, LLC

ABC-CLIO, LLC
130 Cremona Drive, P.O. Box 1911
Santa Barbara, California 93116-1911
www.abc-clio.com

This book is printed on acid-free paper ∞

Manufactured in the United States of America

This book is dedicated to Bob and Morrie for their patience and kindness to me while I wrote it.

Contents

Acknowledgments

As anyone who has ever tackled a significant project knows, there is strength in numbers. I was fortunate enough while writing this book to have a stellar research assistant: Aaron Tomey. His help throughout the process was invaluable and much appreciated. Thanks also to Jay and Lesley for their proofreading skills!

Introduction

As one can imagine, pulling together a representative sample of various media presentations designed to represent a segment of any population can be challenging. The focus of this book is on the coming-of-age of youths in popular culture across six decades: the 1950s through the 2000s. Twenty-five entries (including decade overview) are included in each chapter, wherein an effort was made to be inclusive of all types of media: television, theatrical films, music, and literature. In more recent decades, two popular video games (*Call of Duty* and *Grand Theft Auto*) were included in order to represent that media category.

The approach to discussing the subjects is done largely through a media literacy lens. Rather than simply summarizing the various films, books, movies, and TV shows with superficial information, an effort has been made to deconstruct much of the content in an attempt to learn more about the "why." In order to do this, many of the entries discuss the role of the media communicator relative to his or her product. Nothing exists in a vacuum, and, to have a more appreciative understanding of any media content, it's often important to know the background, experiences, and sometimes ideologies of the communicator. For example, when analyzing the popular young adult novel series *Twilight,* does the author Stephenie Meyer's Mormon background influence her writing in terms of story lines or themes? Some are more obvious than others, but this information can many times supplement our understanding of meaning and help with context.

Although the life stage that occurs between adolescence and adulthood has been in existence forever, it wasn't until the 1950s that the actual term "teenager" was created and used to define a specific segment of the population. Much of what drove this was economics. Advertisers and marketers suddenly realized the potential profitability of a previously untapped target market with disposable income for goods and services. With that newfound knowledge, media producers created films, books, movies, and music that would appeal to this group.

An explanation of the criteria used in selecting the various chapter entries follows.

1950s

Music may have been the most influential medium on teenagers in this decade. With the introduction of rock and roll to the country, teens suddenly had an outlet that spoke to their feelings of being misunderstood and their need to rebel against authoritarianism. Since this period was one of social conservatism within America, many teens gravitated toward a new type of music that was considered lewd and even dangerous by parents and other adult figures. Four "teen idols" are covered in this chapter: Elvis Presley, Pat Boone, Bobby Darin, and Frankie Avalon. Though each one was unique in his style and material, they all reaped the benefits of teen popularity and significantly influenced what teens listened to and bought.

The 1950s were not without controversy. Two of the most shocking novels of the time were both released during this decade: William Burroughs's *Naked Lunch* and Vladimir Nabokov's *Lolita*. Although the former didn't deal directly with teen characters, its shocking depictions of drug use and sexual behaviors intrigued young readers. *Lolita*'s title character is an adolescent, and although the book wasn't intended for teenagers, they found this novel hard to resist as well, given its focus on the sexual relationship between a young girl and much older man.

Classic novels such as *Lord of the Flies* and *The Catcher in the Rye* were included due to their iconic status in high school literature courses and their teen-centered plots and themes. Ralph Ellison's landmark novel, *Invisible Man*, examined race relations in America via the perspective of a black man. Television shows like *Leave It to Beaver, Father Knows Best*, and *The Adventures of Ozzie & Harriet* are cultural representations of what many people wanted others to think the 1950s were like. On closer examination, however, they were largely sanitized and carefully constructed fictions of family life during that time. A series like *The Many Loves of Dobie Gillis*, though, seemed to be a bit more self-aware of what teenagers were thinking about and doing at school and with their friends and families.

Other entries for this period analyze themes of teen sexuality (*A Summer Place*), juvenile violence in schools (*Blackboard Jungle*), and even abortion (*Blue Denim*).

1960s

Perhaps the most politically volatile of the decades examined in the book, the 1960s were a period of significant social change and upheaval. Teens continued consuming media, but a new social consciousness was developing that would significantly influence many of their media choices. Growing vocal dissatisfaction among women and other minorities and a polarizing war in Vietnam increased political activism and challenged the status quo. Artists like Bob Dylan directly spoke to the rising counterculture at the time while other singers like Janis Joplin, Joni Mitchell, and Jimi Hendrix generally avoided making overt political statements and focused more on the highs and lows of personal relationships.

Supergroups like the Beatles and the Rolling Stones enjoyed phenomenal success during the 1960s as their careers flourished. The Beach Boys and the Monkees also appealed to teenage listeners, thought their musical styles were vastly different from one another. Topics covered in film included date rape (*Where the Boys Are*), the impact of educators on their young students (*To Sir, with Love*), and teen gangs and violence (*A Clockwork Orange*). Popular television series featuring female teen leads included *Gidget* and *The Patty Duke Show*.

Relevant novels from this decade that appealed to teen readers tackled topics like depression and suicide (*The Bell Jar*) and the trajectory of careers and personal lives for a group of female college friends (*The Group*). S. E. Hinton's *The Outsiders* was a breakthrough teen novel that continues to be popular with young readers today. Examining issues of social class and family among a group of young boys, the novel spoke to a generation about relevant socioeconomic impacts on their daily lives.

1970s

Drug usage escalated in this decade, and there was a growing movement away from larger cultural issues and toward a more "me centered"–approach to life. This wasn't because minority issues didn't still exist or that equality had been achieved for all, but there was a societal shift that seemed to impact an overall sense of priorities.

Relevant teen films from this period addressed bullying via a horror film (*Carrie*), the coming-of-age of a group of American high schoolers (*American Graffiti*), and debauchery and class warfare between college fraternities (*National Lampoon's Animal House*). *Cooley High* was a milestone film with its depiction of black coming-of-age youths. The first blockbuster film was released in 1975 (*Jaws*), which forever changed the way that Hollywood would make, market, and distribute big-budget films. Popular television series included the high school–based comedy *Welcome Back, Kotter* and the family drama *Little House on the Prairie*. Other popular shows with teens included *The Six Million Dollar Man* and *Charlie's Angels,* which featured a trio of female sleuths solving a variety of crimes undercover.

Teen themes were examined in novels like *Go Ask Alice,* which was intended to be a cautionary tale about drug use, and *The Chocolate War*, a story about conformity versus individuality at an elite private boy's school.

The 1970s saw the rise of "arena rock" bands like Led Zeppelin and Queen. Attending concerts was now a significant social event for teens, and the cost of doing so increased as venues became larger and bands and their promoters became more fixated on material wealth and physically distancing themselves from fans. The 1970s also experienced "disco mania" as groups like the Bee Gees and singers like Donna Summer had young people flocking to dance clubs to dance and socialize. Another musical genre that gained traction in this decade was punk rock. Bands like the Clash and the Sex Pistols would influence not only music but fashion and politics as well.

1980s

This was the decade of material wealth and a fixation on class and status. Teens were now full-fledged consumers, and just as obsessed with designer name goods as their parents. Perhaps the greatest impact on popular culture was the introduction of a 24-hour cable channel that played music videos: MTV. Truly revolutionary, it would influence music, fashion, and even film. It launched the careers of countless new artists and breathed new life into the staying power of already established singers and groups. Cyndi Lauper, Madonna, Boy George and Culture Club, and Duran Duran all benefited significantly from this platform.

Teen comedies reaped significant box office success with films like *Risky Business, Revenge of the Nerds*, and *Say Anything . . . .* While all included romantic elements, they also analyzed (to varying degrees) issues of social class and wealth. Not everyone in the 1980s enjoyed financial success, and this inequity was felt among a lot of American families. Arguably, the most effective and insightful films about the teen experience from the decade were made by John Hughes. *Pretty in Pink* and *The Breakfast Club* especially examined the pain of romantic love and rejection, as well as the influence of social status and economics on interpersonal relationships. Other popular teen-based films included *Back to the Future, Fast Times at Ridgemont High,* and *Less Than Zero,* a dark tale of drug abuse and nihilism among rich teens in Los Angeles, California, based on the novel by Bret Easton Ellis.

Popular teen television shows included *The Facts of Life, The Wonder Years*, *The Cosby Show*, and *Saved by the Bell.* While *The Facts of Life* was heavy-handed with its moral lessons, *The Wonder Years* attempted to be less contrived. It focused on universal teen experiences and allowed the audience to many times draw their own conclusions. *The Cosby Show* was revolutionary in its depiction of a black American family, and remains iconic despite the tarnished legacy of Bill Cosby. *Saved by the Bell* was generally regarded as mindless and clichéd, but it was popular nonetheless and also attempted to relay social messages to its audience.

Popular teen novels in the 1980s included *Flowers in the Attic,* a melodramatic family saga with a focus on siblings who are imprisoned in a home by their abusive grandmother. *Sweet Valley High* was a slick series of stories about West Coast twins Jessica and Elizabeth Wakefield and their endless social and romantic challenges. The reigning master of horror, Stephen King, also appealed to teen readers with his epic tale of evil clown terror, *It.*

1990s

Though teen-based films were made in this decade, television was the preferred format for much media content among the youth market. Female-fronted shows like *Charmed* and *Buffy the Vampire Slayer* were incredibly popular and attracted cultlike followings. Both shows featured young and independent-minded women who successfully fought malevolent forces. Even Nickelodeon's *Clarissa Explains It All* featured a female lead character whose worth or existence wasn't tied to that of a boyfriend or male figure.

Freaks and Geeks and *That '70s Show* took a nostalgic look back at an earlier decade. Although the former only lasted one season on NBC, it developed a cult following and is now thought to be an underappreciated gem that wasn't supported or marketed properly by the network. The latter was successful and ran for eight seasons. Both covered familiar teen terrain in different styles.

The evolution of "girl power" also swept across music and film. Recording artists like Alanis Morissette sang about broken relationships from a distinctive female perspective, and Salt-N-Pepa broke down gender barriers within the rap and hip-hop community with their songs about female empowerment and sexual freedom. And, of course, the United Kingdom's influence via the Spice Girls drove discussion and dialogue about a new wave of feminism. The proliferation of boy bands also exploded in the 1990s with the success of groups like the Backstreet Boys.

At the box office, teen-centric horror was rebooted with the smash hit, *Scream.* Both reinforcing and reinventing teen slasher movie tropes from earlier decades, the film featured smart female lead characters who were able to thwart evil without male assistance. Teen horror film *I Know What You Did Last Summer,* on the other hand, embraced previous incarnations of the genre, failing to provide any new spin on the material. Teen sex comedies showed no signs of relenting, and much of that can be attributed to the breakout success of *American Pie,* a raunchy look at a group of male high schoolers desperate to lose their virginity.

The 1990s brought grunge music into the mainstream as bands like Nirvana and Pearl Jam enjoyed enormous commercial and critical acclaim. Both groups had strong teen appeal, but Nirvana especially seemed to resonate with angst-ridden youth who seemed to find a musical messiah in lead singer Kurt Cobain. Green Day blasted into the music scene with their debut album, *Dookie.* They would later capitalize on political divisions during the George W. Bush era with their concept album, *American Idiot.*

The growing popularity of the next generation of video games was also important in this decade. Offerings like the *Grand Theft Auto* series raised serious questions and triggered debate about the negative impacts of video game violence on players.

2000s

In a new digital era, teens had more access to more media than ever before. Two significant themes emerged in this decade: tales of the supernatural and a fixation on dystopian futures. In literature, the *Twilight* series of novels featured a tormented love story between a human woman, Bella, and her vampire boyfriend, Edward. The books and film adaptations within the series were wildly successful. Both *The Hunger Games* and the *Divergent* series of novels were also popular with teen readers and both featured strong female protagonists.

The Sisterhood of the Traveling Pants was a teen-centered story that accentuated positive relationships among a group of female friends. Unlike many media representations that pit women against one another, this series of books focused on the supportive and nurturing relationships that existed among a group of longtime friends.

The "mean girls" trope featured prominently in film, television, and young adult books, including *Mean Girls, Pretty Little Liars,* and *Gossip Girl.* Hoping to capitalize on the staggering success of *Twilight,* television offered *The Vampire Diaries,* tweaking the familiar and legendary story of the undead and updating it for a young modern audience. *Glee* attracted a cultlike following in its first few seasons as viewers tuned in weekly to follow the stories of their favorite fictional students at McKinley High. The show tackled a variety of topics including teen bullying, sexual orientation, and romantic relationship challenges. *One Tree Hill* and *Friday Night Lights* offered three-dimensional teen characters with real and relatable problems and tackled issues of homophobia, racism, and drug usage.

In the world of music, female pop superstars like Rihanna, Britney Spears, Miley Cyrus, and Taylor Swift dominated radio play and record sales. Teen angst and despair was echoed in the music of My Chemical Romance, and Avril Lavigne was marketed successfully as the anti–Britney Spears with her grungy tomboy image and her songs that focused on relationships (minus the sexual innuendos).

The film *Juno* cleverly tackled both teen pregnancy and the pain of first-time love while *The Princess Diaries* reinforced existing gender stereotypes about girls while pretending to subvert them superficially.

Applying Media Literacy to Media Presentations

After reading this book, try using media literacy tools to analyze some of your favorite TV shows, movies, music, and books. One approach is to take an "oppositional reading" of the text. When watching a TV show or movie, be more active and less passive in how you absorb the content. Ask questions as to why characters behave in a certain way. Is it largely based on gender role expectations? How are minority characters presented? Are they typically secondary players whose primary purpose in the narrative is to move the main character's story line along successfully? Are their story lines important? Do they even have a story line outside of their supporting role to the main character? If you are curious about the media communicator, research more about that person or group. What are their values or beliefs? What are their backgrounds? How does that inform the content and context of what they have created?

Doing this will not lessen your enjoyment of the content. If anything, it will enhance knowledge and many times increase appreciation of media presentations. And on those occasions when you disagree with how an issue or theme is presented, your opinion is better informed when using these evaluative tools.

The 1950s

DECADE OVERVIEW

The 1950s was an era of unparalleled economic growth. On the heels of World War II, government spending was at an all-time high and significant amounts of money were being invested in the nation's roads and highways. More importantly, thanks to the GI Bill, war veterans received money for education and low-cost loans to buy new homes. With this newfound economic security, household appliances were heavily marketed toward wives and mothers as part of an idealistic vision of what the lifestyle of middle-class Americans looked like. Women were encouraged to quit their jobs since the war had ended, and husbands and fathers had returned home to once again be the "breadwinner" for their families.

Although things looked good on the surface, racial tensions were simmering. Because the majority of new home construction took place outside of urban areas, hordes of families moved into the suburbs, causing a significant white flight from large metropolitan areas. Additionally, minority groups were growing more assertive about their right to equal access to public education, decent and affordable housing, and basic civil rights. The unrest and dissatisfaction felt by much of the population, but especially among women and minorities, were barely contained during much of this decade. However, in the decade to come the tension would boil over.

In popular culture, movie stars like John Wayne, Bob Hope, and Jimmy Stewart were among the highest-paid actors. The top-grossing film of 1950 was *King Solomon's Mines* with *All about Eve* a close second. Nat King Cole's single "Mona Lisa" reached the number one position on *Billboard*, and best-selling nonfiction books of the decade included *Betty Crocker's Picture Cook Book; Betty Crocker's Good & Easy Cook Book,* and *Better Homes and Gardens Barbeque Book.*

The term "teenager" was coined in the 1950s. Although this life stage had always existed, advertisers now recognized that teenagers were a viable consumer segment. The wealth that middle-class parents accumulated was now extended to their children. Teens were using their allowances (and, in some cases, money from part-time jobs after school) to purchase records, magazines, and other goods. However, the prevalent socially conservative values and ideals of the decade stifled many teenagers that felt oppressed by their parents, teachers, and other adult figures of authority. One way they dealt with this was through their musical choices.

The creation and rise of rock-and-roll music is generally attributed to the 1950s, though its origins have roots in the mid- to late 1940s. Although several hit records came out before it, Bill Haley's "Rock Around the Clock" had the most significant cultural impact on the new genre of music—a genre that widely and wildly appealed to American youth. Although the majority of rock-and-roll artists were black, it took the spending power of a predominantly white teen audience to make it commercially successful. The dichotomy of black artists performing for middle-class white teens while not being able to attend the same schools or sit at the same lunch counters as them underscored the significant inequalities that existed in America at this time.

The 1950s also saw the rise of Communism and the ever-present threat from the Soviet Union. The Red Scare swept through America, fomenting fear and distrust among its own citizens. The U.S. government began formal hearings in response to alleged "un-American" activities, and accused numerous individuals of secretly plotting communist activities designed to destroy the country.

This pervasive sense of unease and insecurity influenced popular media via a plethora of horror and science-fiction films. These movies were viewed as allegories for the anti-Communism hysteria that enveloped the nation. Movies like *Creature from the Black Lagoon* (1954), *The Abominable Snowman* (1957), *Attack of the Giant Leeches* (1959), and others followed a formula where an outside force gains strength and power and attempts to dominate or control humanity. The simple plots of these productions appealed to teen audiences, and, because they were inexpensive to make, most were able to turn a profit.

By the mid- to late 1950s, Hollywood films were focusing more on the teenage experience and offering more thought-provoking fare that included *Rebel without a Cause* (1955), *Blackboard Jungle* (1955), *Peyton Place* (1957), and *A Summer Place* (1959). And by 1959, tastes in literature were evolving as novels like *Lady Chatterley's Lover* and *Lolita* topped best-seller lists.

The 24 entries in this chapter are a cross-section of 1950s popular culture. Each of them highlights a significant aspect of the decade, from the glut of teen idols to looming cultural anxieties, from new rebellions against the status quo to idealized domesticity. The TV shows, films, books, and bands covered show readers how popular media portrayed life during the decade and heralded the changes to come in the future.

Further Reading

Giordano, Ralph. 2017. *Pop Goes the Decade: The Fifties*. Santa Barbara, CA: Greenwood Press.

Halberstam, David. 1994. *The Fifties*. New York: Fawcett.

Hollings, Ken. 2014. *Welcome to Mars: Politics, Pop Culture, and Weird Science in 1950s America*. Berkeley, CA: North Atlantic Books.

Young, William H., and Young, Nancy K. 2004. *The 1950s: American Popular Culture through History*. Westport, CT: Greenwood Press.

ADVENTURES OF OZZIE AND HARRIET, THE

ABC sitcom *The Adventures of Ozzie and Harriet* (1952–1966), along with shows *Leave It to Beaver* and *Father Knows Best*, depicted the idealized nuclear family in American culture after World War II. The popular series had its roots in radio.

Real-life married couple Ozzie and Harriet Nelson appeared on *The Baker's Broadcast* (1933–1938) and later *The Red Skelton Show*. They had multiple guest appearances on other radio programs until Ozzie created his own show in 1944. The popularity of radio began to wane as television ownership and usage increased, and the couple transitioned their show to network television. Before that decision was finalized, a theatrical film, *Here Come the Nelsons* (1952), was released in movie theaters to test the popularity of the material on screen. It served as the pilot for the series.

The show revolved around the Nelson family: parents Ozzie and Harriet, and sons David and Ricky. The exterior of the family's real-life home was shown on the series, and a soundstage was developed to replicate the interior of the family's home. As with its television counterparts listed previously, a typical episode featured a minor conflict or issue that was easily resolved within 30 minutes (minus commercials). The focus was on home life, and it wasn't ever really clear what Ozzie's job was in the show. Similar to June Cleaver on *Leave It to Beaver*, Harriet was generally seen performing domestic chores and caring for the children. Her appearance was always impeccable.

After World War II ended, military men returned home. Many of them quickly married and formed families. Because of the increased ability for those in the military to purchase homes due to the GI Bill that offered service members affordable house loans, construction expanded at a rapid pace. Most of this took place in suburban areas rather than in cities. American men had new roles as husbands, fathers, and breadwinners. Culturally, this was an era of conformity. Men and boys were expected to be strong both physically and emotionally and women were expected to be nurturers. Husbands worked outside of the homes while most wives' primary duties were housekeeping and child rearing. These societal roles were mirrored in the real lives of Ozzie and Harriet Nelson as well. Ozzie was a perfectionist and a workaholic when it came to the TV show. In addition to creating and producing the show, he was its head writer. He was involved to some degree in almost every aspect of the production.

Where this show differed significantly from both *Leave It to Beaver* and *Father Knows Best* was in its blurring of the real with the fictional. The biological Nelson family was also the television Nelson family. Where did one end and the other begin? As mentioned already, even the staging of the show was meant to replicate the Nelsons' actual home in real life. The Nelson TV family was meant to offer a template of what an "average" American family looks and acts like. The children on the show were also meant to depict the ideal obedient offspring that adhered to expectations of their role within the household and within society relative to respecting authority figures.

The real life Nelsons, however, didn't fit that model as much as many believed at the time. Ozzie Nelson had a reputation as a task master and perfectionist. The family image was very carefully cultivated, so this wasn't necessarily common knowledge outside the inner circle of people who worked on the show. He is alleged to have prevented or at least discouraged both sons from attending college or seeking careers in order to devote their energies to the TV show. Harriet had a reputation for partying and enjoying her freedom before she met and married Ozzie. She also had a career in vaudeville and performing in nightclubs before she settled down to become a real-life mother and housewife and then emulated that persona on the series.

The Nelson family member who best personified this conflict between the personal and the professional was son Ricky. Although he was a talented musician as an adult, he was never able to fully shed the homogenized and squeaky clean image that he'd perfected on *The Adventures of Ozzie and Harriet*. He would spend much of his adult life attempting to divest himself from that persona up until his death in a 1985 plane crash. Ricky had become a teen idol with hits like "Be-Bop Baby" and "Poor Little Fool." Over the course of his musical career, he had more than 50 songs on the Billboard Hot 100. Although this success added to the draw of the TV show and his appeal to a teen demographic, it limited his reach as an adult artist.

A TV documentary about the Nelsons ripped open a lot of old wounds for remaining members of the family. Older son David expressed disappointment in the way that the documentary portrayed his late father, but he admitted that the show had taken its toll on all of them, perhaps no one more so than Ricky. *The Adventures of Ozzie and Harriet* was never in the top 10 rated Nielsen shows during its run, but it is still the longest running live action sitcom ever broadcast on network television.

See also: 1950s: *Father Knows Best*; *I Love Lucy*; *Leave It to Beaver*; 1960s: *Patty Duke Show, The*; 1970s: *Happy Days*; 1980s: *Cosby Show, The*; *Family Ties*; *Full House*; *Wonder Years, The*; 1990s: *Boy Meets World*; *Clarissa Explains It All*; *7th Heaven*; 2000s: *Friday Night Lights*

Further Reading

Bashe, Philip. 1993. *Teenage Idol, Travelin' Man: The Complete Biography of Rick Nelson*. New York: Hyperion.

Faucette, Brian. 2012. "Televising Masculinities: The Sitcom Dad in the 1950s on *The Adventures of Ozzie and Harriet*." *This Was Television*, November 26. https://thiswastv.com/2012/11/26/televising-masculinities-the-sitcom-dad-in-the-1950s-on-the-adventures-of-ozzie-and-harriet/.

Hinckley, David. 2011. "David Nelson Defined by Brother Ricky Nelson, 'Ozzie and Harriet' Co-Star, Teen Idol." *New York Daily News*, January 12. http://www.nydailynews.com/entertainment/tv-movies/david-nelson-defined-brother-ricky-nelson-ozzie-harriet-co-star-teen-idol-article-1.153734.

AMERICAN BANDSTAND

The most successful music/dance-oriented show in television history, *American Bandstand* (1957–1987) was a teen-oriented production that featured the most popular music of the day. The nationally syndicated program began locally in Philadelphia under the name *Bandstand* in 1952. The show moved to ABC in 1957 and ran Monday through Friday for its first six seasons on the network. It was hosted by Dick Clark, often referred to as "America's Oldest Teenager."

On the surface, the show appeared to be a simple dance show. Top 10 hits and other songs were played while teenagers showcased the latest dance moves. Popular singers and groups appeared on the show (almost always lip-synching) to promote their latest music. Various segments such as "Rate a Record" asked teen audience members to critique songs and then explain the rationale for their ratings. There was also a segment where slower songs played and the visual focus was on the couples dancing.

Because of the growing demographics of the teen population, the show was actually a phenomenal success in its marketing and advertising of non-music products that appealed to its young viewers. Teen-targeted products included soda, snack foods and candy, acne medicine, and more. Advertisers had a captive audience as this was the only show of its type on TV at the time, and, of course, this was decades before the advent of cable television and the internet. Although these products may not have been directly linked to music, they were (and still are) linked to many teenage lifestyles.

Many think that product placement is a relatively new advertising gimmick. One can look at shows like *America Idol*, *The Voice,* and countless other reality television programs and see stars drinking specific soft drinks or using specific brands of products in an effort to "plug" that brand. *American Bandstand* was doing this in the 1950s and after. An example of this is the show's promotion of the soft drink 7-Up. In addition to an actual commercial for the beverage, the show featured host Dick Clark handing out bottles of the soda to teen dancers before a musical segment happened. During the song, the camera cut back and forth between dancing teens and the group of teens drinking 7-Up.

Music, of course, was being sold as well. The primary reason for playing the popular songs and having musical artists on the show was to sell records. Given the money paid by the advertisers and the fact that the record companies either paid the artists for their appearances or simply made it part of their contract agreements, the cost of producing the show was relatively cheap—no paid actors, no scriptwriters, and no locale shoots outside of the studio. Dick Clark recognized the commercial opportunities of the show and viewed it mainly as a vehicle to profit from.

At the time of *American Bandstand,* the black community—especially teens—had no real visibility on television. Their exposure to popular music came from the radio. Until the show moved production to Los Angeles in 1964, it featured only white teens. Once it was moved to a more racially diverse geographic area, the decision was made to include black and other minority teens. The film (both the original and musical version) and Broadway musical *Hairspray* is a thinly veiled critique of these events. The story line of *Hairspray* features an overweight white teen girl whose dream is to force a local teen dance program to integrate its dancers, in part so that she and her racially diverse friends can all participate and be shown on live television. The format of the show and its "all American" optics (white) are eerily similar to the early days of *American Bandstand.*

The show's origins are deeply embedded in the status quo and focused on a majority (white) segment of American teens. In an arguably misguided effort to include more diversity, the network alternated between *American Bandstand* and a new program called *Soul Unlimited*. Its target market gave a lukewarm response, primarily because the show was not conceived and produced by black Americans. Shortly after Jesse Jackson and Don Cornelius expressed their dissatisfaction with the program, it was canceled.

American Bandstand's phenomenal success is reflected not just in its longevity and place within American popular culture but also in its influence on shows such as *Soul Train*, the origins of MTV (Music Television), and even modern shows like *American Idol* and *The Voice*.

Artists from all genres appeared on the show to perform and promote their music. In 2004, there were plans to revive the show with host Ryan Seacrest. Although that never materialized, the current show *So You Think You Can Dance* stemmed from an effort to produce an ongoing national dance contest televised on network TV. The show's coproducer is listed as Dick Clark Productions. After an ongoing series of health issues, Dick Clark died of a heart attack in 2012 at the age of 82.

See also: 1970s: *Grease*; 1980s: MTV

Further Reading

Delmont, Matt. 2012. "'They'll Be Rockin' on Bandstand, in Philadelphia, PA': Dick Clark, Georgie Woods, and the Value of Rock 'n' Roll." *Journal of Popular Music Studies* 24 (4): 457–485.

Jackson, John. 1997. *American Bandstand: Dick Clark and the Making of a Rock 'n' Roll Empire.* Oxford: Oxford University Press.

Maurantonio, Nicole. 2013. "The Nicest Kids in Town: American Bandstand, Rock 'n' Roll, and the Struggle for Civil Rights in 1950's Philadelphia (Book Review)." Rhetoric and Communication Studies Faculty Publications, http://scholarship.richmond.edu /rhetoric-faculty-publications/41/.

AVALON, FRANKIE

Although teen idols had been around for a while before the emergence of Frankie Avalon (1940–), this singer-actor is one of the best-known teen idols from the 1950s. Between 1958 and 1962, he scored 31 hit singles, including "Venus," "Why," "Just Ask Your Heart," and "Boy without a Girl." Producers believed he had crossover appeal because of his musical popularity and good looks, so he was cast in several films starting in 1957, the first being a brief part in *Jamboree*. It was common at the time to include younger pop stars in films with more established actors in order to generate additional box office revenues.

The 1950s saw the emergence of the teenager as a powerful economic force with significant purchasing power. Teenagers had disposable income and were happy to spend it on records and movies. Additionally, the invention of the portable record player played a significant role in the convenience and transportability of music. Teens could carry the device to a friend's house where they could listen to new and popular songs.

When rock-and-roll music first came onto the American music scene, parents and other authority figures were panicked by it. The images and sounds of artists like Elvis Presley, Little Richard, and Jerry Lee Lewis were jarring to them; these performers thrilled and titillated their teen fans with their passionate and sensual singing styles and dancing. But unlike the simmering sexuality and potential danger of those artists, Avalon portrayed a clean-cut image that was attractive to many young girls. Perhaps more importantly, he was nonthreatening to adults, who many times decided what their children could buy with their money or allowances. He looked to these adults like a young man that they could imagine their daughters dating and even marrying. The rawness of some earlier performers—especially people of color—had been sanitized and repackaged into a safe product.

Although Avalon was a certified star on his own, his foray into a series of movies with Annette Funicello would heighten his popularity and appeal even more and forever link his and Funicello's names to the subgenre of beach party movies. Beach party movies arose from the desire to make teen-centric films without the interfering parent component that existed in predecessor films. The strategy was to tease target audiences with implications of sex but never actually deliver any in the content. The first in the original series of these films was simply titled *Beach Party*. The plot is nonsensical and involves an anthropologist who wants to study the physical interactions of teen surfers in Southern California. It was an excuse to feature a beautiful locale and lots of half-clad young men and women. The movie was shot in less than a month and on a shoestring budget. The film grossed nearly 10 times what it cost to make at the box office, and a franchise was born.

Six sequels (all produced in the 1960s) followed: *Muscle Beach Party* (1964), *Bikini Beach* (1964), *Pajama Party* (1964), *Beach Blanket Bingo* (1965), *How to Stuff a Wild Bikini* (1965), and *The Ghost in the Invisible Bikini* (1966). The plots varied slightly, but the formula stayed the same: some external force threatens the group's ability to have fun at the beach, but they are able to thwart it and get back to their love of sun, surf, and sand. Once the beach party genre dried up, Avalon attempted success in other types of movies, but none matched the success he had enjoyed with Annette Funicello as his costar. He did make a cameo appearance in the hit film *Grease* (1978) in the role of Teen Angel.

Avalon and Funicello reunited in the 1987 film, *Back to the Beach*. The movie is a harmless spoof about a married Midwestern couple en route to a Hawaiian vacation. They stop in California to visit their daughter and become entangled in some melodrama involving their daughter's surfer boyfriend. Avalon's character is able to prove to himself and others that his youthful skills and talents as a former surfer are still intact. In the years since then, Avalon has branched out into selling his own line of health and beauty aids on Home Shopping Network (HSN). He also wrote an Italian cookbook and starred in various stage productions of both *Grease* and *Tony n' Tina's Wedding*. In a nutshell, Frankie Avalon embodied the role of the boy next door in his beach party movies and through his popular hit songs that offered an alternative to the perceived bad influences of the rock-and-roll era.

See also: 1950s: Boone, Pat; Darin, Bobby; 1960s: Beach Boys, The; Beatles, The; 1970s: Osmonds, The; 1980s: Gibson, Debbie; Lauper, Cyndi; Madonna; 1990s: Backstreet Boys; Spice Girls; 2000s: Cyrus, Miley; Spears, Britney; Swift, Taylor

Further Reading

Liebenson, Donald. 2017. "Remembering *Back to the Beach*, the Beach Party Movie's Last Hurrah." *Vanity Fair*, August 7. https://www.vanityfair.com/hollywood/2017/08/beach -party-back-to-the-beach-anniversary-frankie-avalon-annette-funicello.
Lisanti, Thomas. 2012. *Hollywood Surf and Beach Movies: The First Wave*. Jefferson, NC: McFarland.
McEvoy, Blaine. 2013. "Eight Classic Beach Party Movies." *Rolling Stone*, June 19. https:// www.rollingstone.com/movies/news/eight-classic-beach-party-movies-20130719.
Shapiro, Marc. 2013. *Annette Funicello: America's Sweetheart*. New York: Riverdale Avenue Books.

BLACKBOARD JUNGLE

Blackboard Jungle, a 1955 coming-of-age film, served as a precursor to an impending teen rebellion. The story focuses on white teacher Richard Dadier (Glenn Ford) who accepts a position at North Manual High School in order to support himself and his pregnant wife. Dadier soon discovers that rampant rumors about the inner-city school's violent reputation are indeed accurate. When Dadier attempts to control his class with disciplinarian methods, racial tensions escalate with black student leader, Gregory Miller (Sidney Poitier), whom Dadier suspects as the ringleader of the group. Subsequently, it is discovered that the instigator of the conflicts is a white student named Artie West (Vic Morrow) and not Miller. The film had wide appeal to its target teen audience, and the makers of the film were painstaking about production elements that would connect with and attract this demographic. This was especially true with respect to selecting the right "sound" for the film in terms of music.

Race relations in the 1950s were seriously strained. Blacks and other minorities struggled financially and were victims of unfair housing practices under the Federal Housing Administration. Unable to receive low-income loans like their white counterparts, poverty-stricken families remained in economically challenged areas in many regions of the United States. Shortly before the film's release in 1954, the Supreme Court's ruling on *Brown v. Board of Education* was made. In that landmark decision, the issue of racial segregation within the public school system was deemed unconstitutional.

At the time of its release, *Blackboard Jungle* was considered shocking to audiences. No major feature film before it had tackled the issues within urban schools in such a gritty and straightforward manner. The film's writer-director, Richard Brooks, edited the film significantly to appease concerns of the studio executives

Movie poster for *Blackboard Jungle*. The film shocked audiences with its edgy depiction of violent youth within a public school setting. (Redferns /Getty Images)

who were concerned that filmgoers would flinch at the realistic portrayal of an educational system in turmoil. When the film originally premiered in theaters, riots broke out in several cities. This wasn't confined to the United States; young men at a southern London theater destroyed seats and danced in the aisles. Further mayhem broke out across other theaters in England when the film was screened.

The movie also served to catapult a song released a year earlier to staggering sales and popularity. Bill Haley and His Comets' "Rock around the Clock" played over the film's opening credits and during an extended sequence in the middle of the film. Suddenly the song became immensely popular and served as a symbol of teen unrest and discontent within society's status quo.

The sensationalized film was based on source material from deceased writer Evan Hunter, better known under his pen name of Ed McBain, author of a series of police procedurals centered on the fictional 87th Precinct. Evan's novel, *The Blackboard Jungle*, was more focused on serious issues facing urban schools in the 1950s than it was on dramatic showdowns between students and teachers or school violence. Hunter based the story largely on his own brief experience as a school teacher. After graduating from Hunter College, Hunter took a position at a vocational technical school in the Bronx. He found the experience so unnerving and dissatisfying that he resigned from the position after only one term. Although he was not involved in physical altercations during his time teaching, he did experience dealing with students who were woefully unprepared for learning, some even illiterate. When he decided to use the experience as the basis for his novel, he did laborious research and consulted with educational experts in an effort to be as authentic as possible.

The novel was serialized in the *Ladies Home Journal* in 1954. Predictably, it was met with shock and even fear. Literary reviews of the books were overwhelmingly positive, and some hoped that it would spark not just conversation and debate but action on the topic. Not much happened after the initial effect wore off. Part of the problem was that many educators and administrators downplayed the deplorable conditions described by Hunter in the book. Some even outright dismissed them, insinuating that the author had greatly embellished or invented the conditions in order to sell books. Hunter was also admittedly less interested in education reform than he was in nurturing a writing career.

Blackboard Jungle and its themes of juvenile delinquency, violence in school, and the unwavering dedication and commitment of many teachers (especially in the public school system) inspired future films such as *Dangerous Minds* that explored similar terrain decades later. The term "blackboard jungle" became a descriptor for general school violence across the country. The film was nominated for four Academy Awards as well as a Directors Guild of America award and a Writers Guild of America award (the latter both for Richard Brooks).

See also: 1960s: *Explosive Generation, The*; *Room 222*; *To Sir, with Love*; 1970s: *Cooley High*; *Welcome Back, Kotter*

Further Reading

Benton, Steve. 2013. "Two Heads Are Better Than One (and Three Are Better Than Two): Challenging the Individualist Ethos of the Educator-Hero Film." *Journal of Popular Film and Television*, June 18. http://dx.doi.org/10.1080/01956051.2013.787354.

Faw, Leah, and Daniel Perlstein. 2015. *American Education in Popular Media: From the Blackboard to the Silver Screen*. Basingstoke: Palgrave Macmillan.

Gabler, Jay. 2015. "'Blackboard Jungle' Turns 60: Revisiting the Movie That Marked the Beginning of the Rock and Roll Era." *The Current*, March 19. https://blog.thecurrent.org/2015/03/blackboard-jungle-the-movie-that-marked-the-beginning-of-the-rock-and-roll-era-turns-60/.

Hunter, Evan. 2017. *The Blackboard Jungle*. New York: Ishi Press.

BLOB, THE

The Blob, a 1958 low-budget horror film, starred an as yet unknown actor named Steve McQueen in a tale of a menace from outer space that terrorizes a small town in Pennsylvania. The formula for *The Blob* and any number of 1950s horror/science-fiction films was the same: an unknown threat arrives with the intent to destroy the country and maybe even the planet. Whether this threat comes in the form of mutant insects (*Them!*) or a hybrid land-sea entity (*Creature from the Black*

Lagoon), it is depicted as a menace that must be obliterated. In *The Blob,* the source of evil is not from this planet but rather from outer space.

The film opens with teen couple Steve Andrews (Steve McQueen) and girl-friend, Jane Martin (Aneta Corsaut), parked in a car and kissing. They witness what appears to be a meteorite crash into a hillside not too far from where they are and decide to investigate. An elderly man who pokes the meteorite with a stick is its first victim as a gelatinous liquid oozes from the rock and begins to consume his arm. Steve and Jane rescue the man and take him to the local doctor for assistance. The amorphous blob continues to grow in size as it devours the old man. Both the nurse and the doctor fall prey to it as well. As Steve and Jane recruit their friend Tony for help, explaining what is happening within the town, the blob continues to devour people, including a local mechanic.

An interesting element of *The Blob* is its portrayal of teens as the rational and level-headed ones who quickly realize the threat and seek a solution to destroy it. Adults in the film mainly are suspicious of what they are told by Steve and Jane and appear largely ineffective. This may have been an attempt to appeal more to the target audience of the film, but the fact that authority figures in the film aren't seen as being resourceful or proactive is noteworthy given the rampant authoritarianism of the decade in which the film was made. Additionally, in most science-fiction films of the era, the role of science is viewed in two different but related ways: scientists are usually depicted as both the villains who created (or had a role in creating) the monster and the potential heroes in controlling or even destroying it once its malevolent nature becomes evident. They are typically portrayed as intelligent, but there is a downside to this intellectual curiosity as it is many times the driving force behind creating or enabling the creature or monster to attack humans.

The teens find themselves trapped in the walk-in freezer of a diner where they hide from the murderous blob. An ill-fated effort is made by police to electrocute the mass, but it has no effect on it. The blob seems to recoil from cold when it slithers under the door of the freezer, and Steve is able to communicate this to the police over the phone. Townspeople arrive en masse armed with fire extinguishers and are able to drive the blob away from the diner. The Air Force intervenes, and, at the conclusion of the film, they freeze the blob and airlift it to the Arctic, where it is dropped and presumably thwarted.

Science-fiction films were incredibly popular in the 1950s. Part of this popularity was due to the fact that they were frequently produced very cheaply and appealed to a teenage demographic that was willing to lay down their money for entertainment. A more significant reason for the proliferation of these films during the 1950s, however, had to do with the ongoing Cold War between the United States and the Soviet Union. After World War II, tensions between America and the Soviet Union were palpable. Americans viewed Communism with outright disdain and saw it as a direct threat to the democracy and freedom of the United States. In addition, after successful testing of atomic weapons had been completed by the Soviets, the reality of a nuclear holocaust existed and terrified Americans.

Although the government tamped down any public criticism or outcry on these matters, filmmakers were free to pursue them in the world of fiction.

The function of a movie like *The Blob* beyond its entertainment value is to reinforce a cultural message or agenda. Using aliens or monsters to symbolize a more real terror was an effective method of spreading propaganda under the guise of entertainment. The films subconsciously reinforced existing negative beliefs about Communism and a more overarching fear of "the other" while simultaneously celebrating the unity and collective efforts of the citizenry banding together to vanquish whatever nefarious force threatened the safety of civilization.

The film, which was made on a budget of slightly more than $100,000, grossed approximately $4 million at the box office and has gone on to achieve cult movie status. Low-budget horror and science-fiction films were immensely popular with teens during the 1950s and often were viewed as perfect "date movies" for young couples.

A low-budget 1972 sequel entitled *Beware! The Blob* fared poorly with critics and at the box office. In the 1988 remake of *The Blob*, the story line remains largely true to the original. In this version, though, it is the government who creates the blob as part of an experiment after the Cold War. This is a significant revision because it reflects growing distrust of the government that grew and flourished in the 1960s and 1970s. The remake was a financial disappointment, but because of technological advances within the film industry, the special effects were singled out as effective and much more realistic than its predecessor's.

See also: 1950s: *I Was a Teenage Werewolf*; 1960s: *Twilight Zone, The*; 1970s: *Carrie*; 1980s: *It*; 1990s: *I Know What You Did Last Summer*; *Scream*

Further Reading

Brand, Keith. 2008. "'The Blob' Marks 50th Anniversary." *NPR*, September 10. https://www.npr.org/templates/story/story.php?storyId=94486445.

Lambie, Ryan. 2015. "The Strange History of *The Blob* movies." *Den of Geek!* January 29. http://www.denofgeek.com/us/movies/the-blob/243202/the-strange-history-of-the-blob-movies.

McGee, Mark Thomas, and R. J. Robertson. 2013. *You Won't Believe Your Eyes: A Front Row Look at the Sci-Fi/Horror Films of the 1950s*. Albany, GA: BearManor Media.

Warren, Bill. 2016. *Keep Watching the Skies! American Science Fiction Movies of the Fifties, the 21st Century Edition*. Jefferson, NC: McFarland and Company.

BLUE DENIM

Based on a 1958 play of the same, *Blue Denim* is a 1959 theatrical film that deals with a taboo topic in the 1950s: abortion. Set in the Midwest, Arthur Bartley (Brandon deWilde) is a sheltered teen with overly protective parents. He hangs out with his friends Ernie (Warren Berlinger) and Janet Willard (Carol Lynley), not realizing that Janet has romantic feelings for him. The two have sex and Janet becomes pregnant. Unable to get support from their parents, they turn to Ernie, who had bragged about helping another friend with the same problem.

The play and film both tackled a serious issue, but they did so very differently. In the play version of *Blue Denim*, Janet has the abortion. In the film version, she does not. Instead, parents intervene and stop the planned procedure from happening. This critical change to the story line is very telling. Abortion was illegal in the United States until 1973. Prior to that, it was only legal in some states, and only under very specific circumstances and conditions. Because of this, Hollywood producers were adamant that all references to abortion be removed from the screenplay for the movie and that the plot be changed dramatically. In the play, Janet and Arthur discuss the abortion afterward and their feelings for one another, realizing how their naïveté caused the situation to become dire. In the film version, the two go off together to be married and stay with one of Janet's relatives until the baby is born.

Although the film created a controversy at the time of its release, an examination of the content reveals that it adheres strongly to the social values and ideologies of the time in which it was made. Arthur's father Major Malcolm Bartley (Macdonald Carey) is a strict authoritarian and retired military major who makes decisions for his son. He shields him from the difficult situations that a young person transitioning into adulthood often has to make. For example, the family dog is ill and needs to be euthanized. Rather than involving Arthur in that decision and action, it's done while he's at school, thereby shielding him from unpleasantness. Major Bartley views Janet's pregnancy in much the same way. He sees it as a problem for Arthur that will change the course of his life. However, he expends little or no concern as to how this affects Janet and her future.

In short, the film is a coming-of-age story about Arthur, and less so about Janet. This is perplexing given that the dramatic event in the story—the pregnancy and planned abortion—affect Janet much more directly than Arthur. In the end, Arthur's father and Janet's parents make arrangements for a hasty retreat for her from town. Arthur musters the emotional strength to challenge his father on this and leaves with Janet so that they can be together. When Arthur goes against his father and decides to make a life with Janet, the audience is meant to identify with him. He becomes the central focus, and again his story arc is given more relevance than Janet's.

Although the film was made in the 1950s, movies about abortion that focused more on male characters than female characters continued to be made long after the decade ended. Later films such as *The Cardinal* (1963) and *Cider House Rules* (1999) also focus primarily on the men in those stories. In the former, an ambitious priest refuses the procedure for his sister that would likely save her life; in the latter, a young man must decide whether he will inherit an abortion clinic that provides safe procedures for women. Hollywood has a long history of making heroes out of the men in these stories but neglecting or minimizing the role of the women. Oftentimes, men are shown as the ones who "arrange" the procedures and/or get the funding for the abortions. They are the ones swooping in to fix the "problem."

In other films, they assign blame to the women. In *Blue Denim*, friend Ernie tells Janet and Arthur that abortion is murder, even though earlier he'd bragged about helping a friend secure one. The focus is on helping the male friend so that he isn't inconvenienced by being forced to marry the girl whom he impregnated. One deviation from this trend, however, is *Dirty Dancing* (1987), which centers upon women in the plot.

Blue Denim is able to avoid the ugly reality of abortions in the 1950s. At that time, only women with access to money could be afforded the luxury of safe procedures. An estimated 200,000 to 1 million illegal and unsafe abortions were performed in that decade. Women who tried to self-abort used methods ranging from the ingestion of bleach and turpentine to the insertion of items like knitting needles and coat hangers (Grimes 2015).

Blue Denim was a moderate box office success and earned one Golden Globe nomination for Carol Lynley as "Most Promising Newcomer."

See also: 1960s: *Group, The*; 1980s: *Dirty Dancing*

Further Reading

Grimes, David A. 2015. "The Bad Old Days: Abortion in America before *Roe v. Wade*." Huffington Post, January 15. https://www.huffingtonpost.com/david-a-grimes/the-bad-old-days-abortion_b_6324610.html.

Leibman, Nina C. 1995. *Living Room Lectures: The Fifties Family in Film and Television*. Austin: University of Texas Press.

Mitchell, Charles P. 2004. *Filmography of Social Issues: A Reference Guide*. Westport, CT: Greenwood Press.

BOONE, PAT

Unlike James Dean and Elvis Presley, singer-actor Pat Boone (1934–) is known as a 1950s icon with a "squeaky clean" image and lifestyle. At a time when peers like Frank Sinatra and Dean Martin were notorious for partying and womanizing, the self-identified Christian performer was vocal about his religious values and beliefs. However, Boone's career has some obvious parallels with Presley's. He began his singing career with a record label in 1954. He also recorded a number of songs previously recorded by black artists such as Fats Domino and Nat King Cole. Boone soon began appearing on TV, most notably on ABC's *Ozark Jubilee* and as spokesperson for Chevrolet, a long-term contract that capitalized on his all-American persona. Although Boone appeared in close to a dozen films during his career, he was selective and cautious about the roles he accepted, ensuring that they aligned with his moral convictions and ideals.

Pat Boone reflected 1950s mainstream culture with an adherence to gender conformity and a patriarchal mind-set with respect to the roles played by men and women. This worldview remained constant as time passed. In a 1973 interview with *The Saturday Evening Post,* Boone commented, "Another thing I would like to mention is the domesticity that has happened in the last two years. Shirley now is doing all our cooking, most of the housekeeping, tending to her grandmother, and running around taking care of the children" (Boone 1973).

It's a cultural misconception that 1950s rock and roll was exclusively about teen rebellion against the status quo. Although that may have been a driving force behind its origins, artists like Pat Boone were also immensely popular and reflected rather than opposed the decade's cultural climate. Boone appealed to a large demographic of young white teenagers, and one of his practices was to change the lyrics in some of his cover songs in order to sanitize them for his audience. Many view this as both cultural appropriation and antithetical to the integrity of the original artist. However, there is also an argument to be made on the monetary side of this issue. Keeping in mind the segregation of audiences at that time, it's doubtful that many Pat Boone fans would proactively seek out music by black recording artists. When Boone changed the lyrics to songs like "Tutti Frutti" and "Ain't That a Shame," many of his listeners then sought out the originals by Little Richard and Fats Domino. This theory is supported when reviewing sales data for the period. Although covers of original songs may have been popular early in the decade, by the mid-1950s, originals were topping the charts. Singer Fats Domino even joked in front of an audience once that Boone's cover of one of his songs is what enabled him to buy an expensive ring.

The entire Boone family—Pat and his wife and their four daughters—became emblematic of the Jesus movement in the late 1960s and early 1970s. Growing out of the hippie counterculture, the Jesus movement focused on a return to "basics" within the Christian faith. This was the origin of today's evangelical Christians and was an early influence on contemporary Christian music genres such as Christian rock and Christian metal.

In the late 1990s, Boone released an album of heavy metal rock covers entitled *In a Metal Mood: No More Mr. Nice Guy.* The recording created disharmony between the singer and some in the Christian community, but it had no long-lasting negative effect on his relationship with religious groups as he explained that the move was meant to be a self-parody. Many of his former teen fans, now adults like him, remained faithful followers to the entertainer.

Pat Boone's daughter Debby Boone recorded one of the biggest hit records of the late 1970s. "You Light Up My Life" was a Billboard smash hit and remained in the number one chart position for 10 weeks. It also scored her a Grammy Award for "Best New Artist" in 1977 and an American Music Award for "Favorite Pop Single." Although she released a few other pop songs later, nothing matched the success of this one.

More recently, Boone's right-wing political ideology has overshadowed his career in entertainment. He has made several controversial statements about LGBT people. Additionally, he is part of the "Birther" movement that questioned the legitimacy of Barack Obama's presidency based on a belief that the president was not born in the United States.

In 2011, the entertainer received a Lifetime Achievement Award from the Conservative Political Action Conference. He was also inducted into the Gospel Music Hall of Fame in 2003.

See also: 1950s: Darin, Bobby; Presley, Elvis; 1960s: Beach Boys, The; Beatles, The; Dylan, Bob; 1970s: Osmonds, The; 1980s: Gibson, Debbie; 1990s: Backstreet Boys; 2000s: Swift, Taylor

Further Reading

Boone, Pat. 2006. *Pat Boone's America: 50 Years.* Nashville: B&H Publishing.

Interview with Pat Boone. 1973. *The Saturday Evening Post.*

Schlueter, Roger. 2017. "White Singers Paid the Fees, but Black Singers Didn't Get the Money." *Belleville News-Democrat*, February 23. http://www.bnd.com/living/liv-columns -blogs/answer-man/article134070984.html.

Swayne, Matthew. 2017. "How the 1950s Made Pat Boone a Rock Star." *Futurity*, February 3. http://www.futurity.org/rock-n-roll-history-1350552-2/.

CATCHER IN THE RYE, THE

Iconic 1951 novel *The Catcher in the Rye* by J. D. Salinger (1919–2010) features one of the most recognized characters in modern-day literature: Holden Caulfield. The book tells his story via first-person narrative, so the reader is privy to all of Holden's thoughts and sometimes rambling stream of consciousness. The book begins with Holden being temporarily suspended from school for academic failure in a history class. Holden writes a note to the professor who failed him and even visits the man in a gesture of goodwill. The teacher, Mr. Spencer, proceeds to read Holden's paper aloud, causing the teen to feel ashamed and humiliated.

Holden also fights with his roommate, Stradlater, over a girl he has feelings for, but who Stradlater may have seduced. Feeling alienated and confused about the world around him, Holden journeys to New York City. He checks into a dingy hotel where he observes the antics of "perverts" across the hall. This prompts him to begin examining his own sexuality. After a disappointing evening spent dancing with three older women who he finds to be very superficial, he calls a prostitute to come to his room. Once there, he decides that he simply wants companionship. The girl gets upset and leaves after Holden has paid her. She then returns to his room with her pimp, who demands additional cash and then physically assaults him.

When the novel was initially released, it was met with positive reviews. Though originally intended as an adult novel, the work resonated more strongly with adolescents and has gone on to become one of the most popular books in the young adult genre. However, it was also met with a lot of criticism for both its profanity and its exploration of issues considered taboo at the time, including drinking, smoking, and sexual promiscuity.

Holden's parents are largely absent from the story, and what little mention they are given is colored by his distrust of authority figures in general. He has a younger sister, Phoebe, with whom he enjoys a close relationship, but the death of his younger brother, Allie, haunts him. In addition, his parents' action to prevent him from attending the funeral of his sibling creates emotional stress and confusion that contributes to his problems.

As with many works of art that become widely popular, the book has often generated a firestorm of controversy. Between 1961 and 1982, *The Catcher in the Rye* was the most banned book in both schools and libraries in America. Critics leveled a multitude of charges at the book, accusing it of promoting teenage rebellion and lax morality. Of course, this also piqued the curiosity of many young people who perhaps otherwise would not have been interested in reading it. This in turn helped the novel remain both a best seller and a relevant discussion point in the American cultural landscape.

The book's title originates from a fantasy Holden has about overseeing children who are playing in a wheat field. He imagines himself as their protector, able to prevent them from falling off ("catching" them) a fictional cliff at the end of the field.

A common interpretation of the novel is that it's a spiritual and coming-of-age journey for the main character. Holden is disillusioned with the world around him. He sees adults as phony and as irresponsible caretakers. Additionally, at some level, Holden Caulfield is emblematic of all teenagers in terms of their struggle for self-identity. Although some of the specific events and traumas in the book may be enhanced for dramatic purposes and impact, the central themes of loneliness, confusion, and seeking purpose in life are universal, especially for young people.

Although the topic of depression among teenagers has become fairly commonplace in today's young adult literature landscape, this wasn't the case in the 1950s. In terms of where the field of psychiatry was at this time, it's relevant to note that the DSM (*Diagnostic and Statistical Manual of Mental Disorders*) wasn't published until 1952, and much of the content in it by today's standards seems reactionary and regressive. In the book, Holden makes multiple references in the novel to feeling depressed. The extent of his depression is unclear, but he is in a mental institution at the beginning of the novel. Given the various traumas that he endures throughout the book, it seems more likely than not that he has serious and unresolved issues that plague him. He is resistant to counseling, though. Several times throughout the narrative, he scoffs at the idea of therapy or the potential value it may offer him.

Anxiety is also an ongoing issue in the book. Holden makes multiple references to being nervous or anxious about a variety of situations. He alleges that this constant turmoil and stress has turned his hair prematurely gray and has caused him to suffer from constipation and diarrhea. He becomes consumed with thoughts of death, and even contemplates suicide a few times.

Even though *The Catcher in the Rye* never won any book awards, it is considered one of the most culturally influential novels ever written. Its issues and themes are easily traced to other popular novels including *Ordinary People* (1976), *The Bell Jar* (1963), and *The Perks of Being a Wallflower* (1999). Modern Library included the novel in its list of "The 100 Best English Language Novels of the 20th Century."

See also: 1960s: *Bell Jar, The*; 1970s: *Chocolate War, The*; *Go Ask Alice*; Updike, John; 1980s: *Less Than Zero*; 1990s: *Dazed and Confused*; *Kids*

Further Reading

Jen, Gish. 2010. "Why Do People Love 'Catcher in the Rye'?" *New Republic*, January 27. https://newrepublic.com/article/72860/why-do-people-love-catcher-the-rye.

Kirshner, Lauren. 2016. "The Age of Anxiety: On *The Catcher in the Rye*." *Hazlitt,* July 20. https://hazlitt.net/feature/age-anxiety-catcher-rye.

Pinsker, Sanford, and Ann Pinsker. 1999. *Understanding* The Catcher in the Rye*: A Student Casebook to Issues, Sources, and Historical Documents*. Westport, CT: Greenwood Press.

Salinger, J. D. 1951. *The Catcher in the Rye*. Boston: Little, Brown.

DARIN, BOBBY

Although his eponymous, first hit record came out in 1958, Bobby Darin's (1936–1973) musical and acting career blossomed in the 1960s. Born Walden Robert Cassotto, Darin's childhood has all the earmarks of a made-for-television movie. He grew up in East Harlem and was raised by his grandmother. His birth mother, Vanina Juliette "Nina" Cassotto, pretended to be his sister. Because of the culture at the time, a 17-year-old unwed mother was fodder for scandal, and the plan was to provide Bobby with as "normal" of a childhood as possible. Musically gifted at a young age, Darin learned how to play several instruments including guitar, piano, and drums.

Although Darin thought of himself as more of an actor and entertainer, the path to success that opened up for him was that of a professional singer. He confessed in several early interviews that his voice wasn't nearly as strong as that of some of his musical peers. Many critics agreed. However, they also noted that he did have an appeal that was elusive.

Pop singer and teen heartthrob, Bobby Darin. The singer-actor struggled with issues of self-esteem and authenticity throughout his career. (Bettmann/Getty Images)

Unlike other popular singers at the time, such as Frank Sinatra, Darin rarely held back his opinions or feelings when speaking to the media. What insiders knew to be low self-confidence and angst over his childhood and formative years was misconstrued as arrogance by reporters. Given the false bravado he exhibited when dealing with the press, it's easy to see how this could happen. He often compared himself to other established singers when his career was just getting started, and much of this was met with derision and dismissal.

Anyone doubting Darin's innate talent or ability might be persuaded to think otherwise when learning that he wrote the song "Splish Splash" in roughly 30 minutes. That single sold over 1 million copies. He'd also written hit songs prior to that for popular recording artist Connie Francis.

The song that established Bobby Darin as a pop superstar was "Mack the Knife" in 1959. The original version of the song was recorded by Louis Armstrong two years earlier. The tune comes from *The Threepenny Opera* and seemed an unlikely choice for a radio friendly pop song. Darin initially had serious reservations about even releasing it as a single, so, of course, it went on to become a smash hit and a song that he was inextricably linked to for the remainder of his career.

A recurrent theme throughout much of Darin's career and personal life was this struggle with self-identity and authenticity. Going as far back as his days at the Bronx High School of Science, he spoke of his feelings of inadequacy when compared to other students who were more gifted academically. He referred to times when he was mocked or ridiculed by some of his peers for this alleged deficit.

Other pop hits in Darin's catalog of work include "Dream Lover" and "Beyond the Sea." The latter had such an influence on now-disgraced actor Kevin Spacey that he used it as the title for his 2004 biopic of Bobby Darin, *Beyond the Sea*, in which he portrayed the conflicted entertainer.

Darin's hit singles made him a bona fide teen idol. On the set of the 1961 film *Come September*, he met his costar Sandra Dee, whom he later married. Dee was also a teen idol and appeared in several hit movies that connected with young audiences, for instance, *A Summer Place* and *Gidget*. They kept their marriage a secret from the public for several years even while appearing in several more films together. They divorced in 1967.

Darin may have found his authentic self—or at least a kernel of it—with the recording of his 1966 song, "If I Were a Carpenter." More of a folk than a pop tune, this choice may have been a small but significant sign of a new direction in the star's life. His appeal to teens during this phase of his career remained, but it connected more with socially aware teens than the larger and broader demographic he had previously enjoyed. A year later, he commented to the press that he would now focus on making music that pleased him artistically, a clear swipe at some of his earlier choices. More importantly, he became politically active and campaigned for Robert Kennedy's presidential bid in 1968. After Kennedy's assassination and the revelation that the woman he always believed to have been his sister was in fact his mother, Darin retreated to privacy and stayed out of the public eye for a period of reflection.

In 1969, he released the album *Commitment*. The songs were more socially and politically aware than anything he'd done previously. The sound was also a radical departure from his trademark crooning style. Unfortunately, it was a critical and commercial failure. As many artists learn when they attempt to change direction musically or reinvent themselves artistically, the general public likes the familiar. They are not typically inclined to go along with an artist on a journey of self-discovery. His older fans wanted the music from him they'd loved as teenagers. Darin realized the necessity of "giving the people what they want" in order to financially survive and remain a viable commodity within the entertainment industry. He returned to Las Vegas and pleased audiences with the standards that he was known for; he and his fans pretended that his brief artistic detour had never taken place.

In addition to writing and recording multiple hit songs, Darin won a Golden Globe Award for his acting in *Come September* (1961). The following year, he was nominated for "Best Performance by an Actor in a Motion Picture—Drama" in *Pressure Point* (1962). Bobby Darin died from complications after heart surgery at the age of thirty-seven. He was posthumously inducted into the Rock and Roll Hall of Fame in 1990.

See also: 1950s: Boone, Pat; 1960s: Beach Boys, The; Beatles, The; *Gidget*; 1970s: Osmonds, The; 1980s: Gibson, Debbie; Lauper, Cyndi; Madonna; 1990s: Backstreet Boys; Spice Girls; 2000s: Cyrus, Miley; Spears, Britney; Swift, Taylor

Further Reading

Hajdu, David. 2005. "Chameleon with a Toupee." *The Atlantic,* January/February. https://www.theatlantic.com/magazine/archive/2005/01/chameleon-with-a-toupee/303677/.
Raymer, Miles. 2015. "On *Commitment*, Bobby Darin Became a Folkie Radical." *AV Club,* December 22. https://music.avclub.com/on-commitment-bobby-darin-became-a-folkie-radical-1798287583.
Starr, Michael Seth. 2011. *Bobby Darin: A Life*. Boulder: Taylor Trade.

DEAN, JAMES

Perhaps no one media figure represents the rebellion and angst of 1950s youths better than actor James Dean (1931–1955). Although the immensely popular film star died in a car accident at the age of 24 after making only three films, his influence and legacy remain strong even today. He is the only actor to ever have been nominated posthumously for two Motion Picture Academy Awards. Dean was born in Indiana but moved to California with his parents and eventually landed in New York after switching college majors from prelaw to theater. He studied at the prestigious Actors Studio under Lee Strasberg and secured small roles on several TV shows until he was noticed in Hollywood after an impressive performance in the play, *The Immoralist* in 1954. For his first major film role in 1955's *East of Eden*, Dean was selected for the part of Cal Trask by *Eden*'s author, John Steinbeck.

Dean's real-life persona paralleled the chaos and charisma of characters he played on screen. Alienated from his father after choosing the pursuit of acting over law, he eventually dropped out of college and took a series of menial jobs to support himself while he auditioned for roles. Recognized for his physical traits and sensuality, the actor's sexual orientation garnered widespread speculation in a socially conservative time among Hollywood insiders and later among the general population. Although some close to him denied it, many believed him to be gay or at least bisexual based on revelations from former colleagues and confidants.

Dean is best known for his role as Jim Stark in 1955's *Rebel without a Cause*. The film tells the story about teenage alienation and disillusionment when a young Stark (James Dean) moves to a new town and must prove his toughness via knife fights and dangerous and even deadly games of "chicken" in speeding cars. During a decade of heightened turmoil and generational culture clashes, the actor seemed to embody the feelings of being an outsider more effectively than his other media peers.

Closer analysis of *Rebel without a Cause* actually reinforces the very dominant culture of the 1950s that it pretends to question or challenge. Jim Stark is depicted as an angry and confused teen who doesn't conform to expected standards of behavior. His father, Frank (Jim Backus) constantly argues with his mother Carol (Ann Doran). Frank is portrayed as a weak-willed individual who allows his wife to control him. Jim is frustrated with his father and wants him to stand up to his mother, but his pleas go ignored. To visually reinforce this stereotype of a hen-pecked husband and father, Frank is shown wearing an apron and making a meal for his wife at home in a scene where Jim calls home in desperate need of parental guidance. The only adult who seems to understand him is police officer Ray Fre-mick (Edward Platt), an authority figure whose demeanor is more closely aligned with expected gender roles during this period.

Because Jim feels so alienated at school and home, his friends John "Plato" Crawford (Sal Mineo) and Judy (Natalie Wood) become his de facto family of choice. During an altercation at an abandoned mansion where the three are stay-ing, Plato fights off three intruders and ends up shooting one of them. Despite Jim's attempts to calm him, Plato continues to be combative. Jim removes the bullets from Plato's gun but the police shoot him when he comes out of the home, not realizing that the gun is unloaded. In the final scene, Jim's parents arrive on the scene. Jim introduces them to Judy, whom he now has a romantic interest in. Mrs. Stark begins to make a comment but is silenced by Mr. Stark. Jim places his arm around Judy's shoulder, and Mr. Stark does the same with his wife. Rather than Jim Stark changing or fighting the system, he is changed in order to "fit in" with the system and the status quo. At the end of the film, order is restored as prescribed gender roles are fulfilled.

Dean's third and final film was the critical and commercial hit *Giant* (1956), based on a best-selling novel about the lives of a family living on a Texas ranch. The popular film costarred Rock Hudson and Elizabeth Taylor and was nominated for 10 Academy Awards. Dean and Hudson both were nominated for "Best Actor in a Leading Role."

James Dean's iconic status remains evident even today. The self-confidence he exuded (whether genuine or not) coupled with his physical appeal continue to intrigue and excite new generations of young fans. The image of him in a white T-shirt and black leather jacket with an ever-present cigarette is visually embedded within our cultural psyche. Most merchandised images of the actor are taken from *Rebel without a Cause;* this signifies that rare occurrence when an actor is so uniquely identified with a specific role that one cannot be imagined without the other.

Dean's pervasive influence is partly evidenced by use of his name in popular songs. "James Dean" is referenced by more than 100 artists ranging from the Goo Goo Dolls and Hilary Duff to Scouting for Girls and Taylor Swift. Merchandise sales (posters/postcards/etc.) from his estate topped $3 million in 2002, more than 47 years after his tragic death.

See also: 1960s: *Outsiders, The*; 2000s: Swift, Taylor

Further Reading

Canote, Terence Towles. 2015. "The Lasting Appeal of James Dean." *Silhouette Magazine*, September 30. https://learningandcreativity.com/silhouette/james-dean/.

Dalton, David. 2001. *James Dean: The Mutant King—A Biography*. Chicago: Chicago Review Press.

Rawlins, Justin Owen. 2013. "Over His Dead Body: Hedda Hopper and the Story of James Dean." *Velvet Light Trap: A Critical Journal of Film and Television* (71) 27.

Spoto, Donald. 1996. *Rebel: The Life and Legend of James Dean*. New York: HarperCollins.

Winkler, Peter, and George Stevens Jr. 2016. *The Real James Dean: Intimate Memories from Those Who Knew Him Best*. Chicago: Chicago Review Press.

FATHER KNOWS BEST

1950s sitcom *Father Knows Best* (1954–1960) started as a radio show in 1949, where it aired for six seasons before being adapted for television. The show focuses on the middle-class Andersons and their coming-of-age children who live in the town of Springfield. The main characters are Jim (Robert Young), Margaret (Jane Wyatt), and children Betty (Rhoda Williams), Bud (Ted Donaldson), and Kathy (Norma Jean Nilsson). Jim is an insurance agent and Margaret is a housewife and mother. In the original radio play, Jim was a sarcastic individual who often made rude and insulting remarks about his children. When the material was adapted for television, lead actor Robert Young was very vocal about his desire to reengineer the show and make it more of a family- and relationship-oriented comedy. He wanted to soften his character and suggested that the show be recast entirely.

In many ways, the Andersons are the ideal of the "typical" American nuclear family, certainly so during the 1950s. The father is the breadwinner and the mother oversees all of the domestic tasks. As with other 1950s media productions, home is the centerpiece of life. Family meals, especially dinner, are held in the dining room and everyone in the family is in attendance. This is usually where the parents discover what the children are doing and may uncover some sort of conflict or issue in need of resolution.

It was common in most 1950s media representations for women to stay at home, and *Father Knows Best* was no different. Gender roles are clearly predefined and adhered to in the show: Jim is the provider, and Margaret is the nurturer. Margaret functions as a domestic angel—always cooking, cleaning, and attending to whatever her husband or children need. Although the two may have discussions about dealing with and even disciplining the children, it is always left to the male authority figure to make the final decision. Even the title of the show reinforces where the balance—or imbalance—of power lies.

In a typical *Father Knows Best* episode, some conflict or challenge is identified and resolved via intervention of the title character. For example, in a Season Two episode entitled "Ten Dollar Question," Jim is frustrated with the children asking for money for various activities and items. He's also upset with all of the "snitching" that they do on one another, so he makes them an offer: whoever can refrain from snitching on their siblings will receive $10. He places the money in a drawer and it disappears. He confronts the children at breakfast and asks the guilty party to come to his office to confess. Betty, Bud, and Kathy each come individually and confess to taking the money, obviously "covering" for whichever one of them is the guilty party. By the conclusion of the episode, it's revealed that Margaret found the money while cleaning and put it back in her husband's wallet. Roberts takes the family out for dinner and says that he's learned a valuable lesson about making assumptions.

How does a 1950s sitcom like *Father Knows Best* compare to a contemporary sitcom in terms of depicting the "all-American" family? One popular show that provides an apt comparison is popular ABC sitcom *Modern Family*. On the show, Phil and Claire Dunphy (Ty Burrell and Julie Bowen) are parents to daughters Haley (Sarah Hyland) and Alex (Ariel Winter) and son Luke (Nolan Gould). Phil is a real estate agent and Claire is a stay-at-home mother (for many of the seasons until she goes to work for her father). Unlike the Anderson household, Phil is not the primary decision maker when it comes to family issues. To the contrary, he is often presented as a dimwitted and many times irresponsible authority figure. He is often more concerned that his kids find him "cool" than meting out punishment or repercussions for any transgressions they commit.

In an episode entitled "The Bicycle Thief," Phil buys Luke a new bicycle. Later, he finds an abandoned bike that looks just like the one he bought Luke, so he assumes it's his. He plans on returning the bike to Luke but gets distracted helping a neighbor inside, and when he comes back outside, the bike is gone. Returning home, he discovers that Luke has had his bike the whole time and that he never abandoned it. He goes to the bike store to buy a replacement for the bike he took (and that was subsequently stolen outside of the neighbor's home), only to discover that it was placed safely inside a garage when a passerby noticed it lying on the curb. The episode showcases Phil's constant anxiety about looking foolish in front of his family, especially his wife.

Much has changed culturally and socioeconomically in the decades since the Andersons were on television, representing a "typical" American family. Women's role in society has changed dramatically. Along with this demographic shift bringing more women into the workplace, parenting is now largely viewed as a dual effort and dual responsibility. Roles and responsibilities that historically were assigned to mothers are now increasingly taken on by fathers as well.

In a typical episode of *Modern Family*, the main conflict or issue is also usually resolved within 30 minutes. However, in comparison to *Father Knows Best*, getting there is much messier. Unlike TV parents of the 1950s, neither Claire nor Phil believes they have all the answers. What is evident, though, is that the male authority figure is not inherently more qualified to deal with crises than his female counterpart. Many episodes in *Modern Family* showcase the ability of the children, especially the two girls, to manipulate or deceive Phil in order to get what they want or to get away with something they've done.

One thing that has remained constant in these types of sitcoms, however, is the economic stability of these middle-class families. External factors or influences rarely seem to affect their financial well-being. Neither the Andersons nor the Dunphys are ever forced to deal with severe economic challenges. And while it can be argued that sitcoms are supposed to be lighthearted, not delving into the harsher aspects of life, many sitcoms of the 1970s did just that. They did not lose popularity for it, either.

Father Knows Best represented what 1950s popular culture strived to reinforce as the status quo: nuclear families headed by married parents. They followed a strict code of conduct both within the family unit and in society. The father was the unchallenged authority figure, and the mother served an important but secondary role whose task was to satisfy the needs and wants of her family.

Modern Family represents a family of the new millennium where gender roles are often nontraditional. Children don't fear their parents; they're bemused by them. The father figure is seen as a lovable clown rather than a respected authoritarian.

During the course of its run, *Father Knows Best* was nominated for 18 Primetime Emmy Awards and won 9 of them. Lead actors Robert Young and Jane Wyatt won trophies and other actors from the show received nominations.

See also: 1950s: *Adventures of Ozzie and Harriet, The*; *I Love Lucy*; *Leave It to Beaver*; 1960s: *Patty Duke Show, The*; 1970s: *Happy Days*; 1980s: *Cosby Show, The*; *Family Ties*; *Full House*; *Wonder Years, The*; 1990s: *Boy Meets World*; *Clarissa Explains It All*; *7th Heaven*; 2000s: *Friday Night Lights*

Further Reading

Genzlinger, Neil. 2012. "The Mother of All Bad TV Moms." *New York Times*, May 11. http://www.nytimes.com/2012/05/12/arts/television/jane-wyatt-on-father-knows-best.html.

LoBrutto, Vincent. 2018. *TV in the USA: A History of Icons, Idols, and Ideas*. Santa Barbara, CA: Greenwood Press.

Shales, Tom. 2010. "Tom Shales Reflects on 'Father Knows Best' and His Real-Life Margaret." *Washington Post*, February 23. http://www.washingtonpost.com/wp-dyn/content/article/2010/02/22/AR2010022204782.html.

FROM HERE TO ETERNITY

Released in 1953, *From Here to Eternity* is based on a best-selling novel by James Jones, an American author. The film follows the activities of a group of soldiers stationed on a military base in Hawaii prior to the attack on Pearl Harbor that triggered World War II. The central character, Robert E. Lee Prewitt (Montgomery

Clift), is bullied and harassed by a group of fellow soldiers at the behest of Captain Dana Holmes (Philip Ober), who lives at the base with his wife, Karen (Deborah Kerr). The captain is infuriated with Prewitt's refusal to participate in team boxing; since Prewitt is notorious for his skills in the sport, Holmes believes that his athletic abilities will advance Holmes's own military career.

As with many novels that are adapted to the big screen, alterations were made to the story line. This is not an uncommon practice in Hollywood; studio executives work to keep their product nonthreatening and familiar in order to maximize profits. With *From Here to Eternity*, however, many of the changes were made because of government censorship. The Department of Defense and the Breen Office were concerned with several issues and themes in the film, most notably its depiction of prostitution and adultery, and its less than kind portrayal of Army leadership. In the novel, Prewitt finds himself attracted to a prostitute (Lorene) he meets in a brothel. In the movie adaptation, the character of Lorene (Donna Reed) is changed to that of a hostess, and there is no insinuation that anything sexual ever happens between Prewitt and Lorene. Additionally, in the film, the affair between Karen Holmes (Deborah Kerr) and Sergeant Warden (Burt Lancaster) ends, whereas in the novel it's ongoing. Yet another difference is that in the book, the protagonist is killed by fellow Army members. Government officials wanted him to be killed in the film by the Japanese. The filmmakers refused to accommodate this request, but they did compromise by not having him in his Army clothes in the scene. This presumably softened the visual image of an American soldier dying at the hands of his comrades.

Another example of the government's unease with the story's depiction of Army life dealt with the rewarding of incompetence at the leadership level. The mean-spirited and unethical Captain Holmes is promoted to the rank of major in another military company in the novel. Government officials adamantly protested the notion that poor leadership within the armed forces would be rewarded, so the compromise was that the character in the film resigns, the implication being that order is restored and dignity of the military as an institution is maintained. In making the concessions and compromises, the director of the film did receive authorization both to shoot scenes in Schofield Barracks and to use actual soldiers rather than Hollywood extras in scenes showing military exercises. The Department of Defense did not approve of the final cut of the film, however; they still felt its characterization of the military was overtly negative.

The melodrama within *From Here to Eternity* holds universal appeal regardless of its setting. Although not targeted at a teen demographic, most films that focus on military life attract young male viewers. Even when the story line is critical of the government or specific branches of the service, young men still tend to gravitate toward the material. This was especially true for war films in the pre–Vietnam era of the 1950s. The camaraderie among the service members is appealing and evokes feelings of patriotism. Additionally, the romantic elements of the story attracted female teen viewers that otherwise might not be interested in the film. Another reason that teens may have had interest in the film was for its infamous beach scene that featured Karen Holmes and Sergeant Warden. Though tame by today's cinematic standards, at the time, it was considered provocative and sexually daring.

James Jones, the author of the novel and cowriter of the adapted screenplay, spent time in the military until his honorable discharge in 1944. The book was almost unanimously praised for its raw storytelling and unbridled criticism of the military as an institution. Jones went on to write several other popular books, including *The Thin Red Line* in 1962.

From Here to Eternity was both a commercial and critical success despite the deviations from the novel. It was nominated for 13 Academy Awards and won 8, including Best Picture, Best Director (Fred Zinnemann), Best Adapted Screenplay, Best Supporting Actor (Frank Sinatra), and Best Supporting Actress (Donna Reed). The material inspired a 1979 television miniseries starring Natalie Wood and William Devane, and a short-lived TV series the following year.

A musical play version of *From Here to Eternity* premiered in London in 2013. It was based on the uncensored version of the novel, which was released in 2011. The musical contained references to gay sex within the military and also included profanity—elements that the 1953 film version omitted. Although the musical was praised for its grittiness in dealing more candidly with the issues than its earlier film version did, overall, most critics did not see the need for it. Given the time that has lapsed since the story took place, audiences no longer are shocked by military tales of abuse and cover-ups or the fact that there were closeted gay men in the armed forces. The musical closed in March 2014 after a six-month run.

See also: 1960s: *Catch-22*

Further Reading

Bosman, Julie. 2011. "Author's Heirs Uncensor a Classic War Novel." *New York Times,* April 4. http://www.nytimes.com/2011/04/05/books/james-joness-from-here-to-eternity-is-uncensored.html.

Cameron, Kate. 1953. "'From Here to Eternity' Is a Realistic Look into Peacetime Army Life." *New York Daily News*, August 6. http://www.nydailynews.com/entertainment/movies/eternity-peacetime-army-life-article-1.2085463.

Jones, James. 1951. *From Here to Eternity*. New York: Scribner's.

Sternberg, Claudia. 1994. "Real Life References in Four Fred Zinneman Films." *Film Criticism* 18: 108–126.

I LOVE LUCY

I Love Lucy, an iconic 1950s sitcom (1951–1957), centers on the antics of spouse and mother Lucy Ricardo (Lucille Ball), a frustrated housewife whose husband Ricky (Desi Arnaz) is a successful nightclub performer. Most of the episodes take place in a New York City apartment where Lucy and Ricky live. In 1950, the Ricardos welcomed a son, Little Ricky (Richard Keith), whose birth on the show coincided with the birth of Ball and Arnaz's son, Desi Arnaz Jr. Lucy's best friend Ethel Mertz (Vivian Vance) also lives in the building where she and her husband

Fred (William Frawley) serve as landlords. The show had a major impact on coming-of-age viewers in the 1950s.

The "situation" in this situational comedy is simple: Lucy is a frustrated performer who feels limited and even restricted by her expected domestic lifestyle. She longs to perform at Ricky's nightclub, The Tropicana. The issue, besides Ricky forbidding her to do so, is that Lucy's talents are mediocre at best. That, however, does not deter her efforts. The bulk of the show's episodes showcase the zany and unorthodox efforts of Lucy to convince Ricky that she is worthy of performing to an audience.

One of the many blurred lines on the show between reality and fiction was the real-life marriage of actress Lucille Ball to actor Desi Arnaz. It was unconven-

Actress and comedian Lucille Ball. While her hit TV show *I Love Lucy* was not geared toward teens, its zany plotlines and physical humor had wide appeal and drew in viewers of all ages. (Library of Congress)

tional to have a real-life married couple play a fictional married couple on television. It's not always easy for viewers to differentiate the actor from the role, and the fact that these two were playing characters fairly closely aligned to their own personas may have been part of the appeal. They also had enormous creative control over the show, exercising casting and other production choices on a regular basis.

Initially, CBS was interested in Ball but did not want to cast Arnaz because of his race and thick accent. They felt that viewers would not accept that he was the husband of a white American woman. However, Ball refused to do the show without him, and eventually the network gave in. Ball and Arnaz were pioneers in this regard and arguably changed how interracial marriage in America was perceived among its viewers, especially those who were coming of age.

Modern-day viewers may find some aspects of the show jarring, such as the depiction of gender roles. Ricky is a strict authoritarian. He clearly lays down the rules for what his wife is "allowed" to do and not do. As with many 1950s housewives, Lucy is financially dependent on her husband. Although Lucy is free-spirited to some degree, she is at a distinct disadvantage with regard to power in the relationship: she has none. But this premise cleared the way for Lucy's relentless schemes to find a way into the show at the Tropicana. Arguably, underlying these (mostly) futile attempts is a steadfast desire for some level of independence.

The gender roles of Fred and Ethel Mertz also fall along similar lines. Fred is a former military man and is frugal to a fault. Ethel is a former vaudeville performer and model who is invariably dragged into Lucy's harebrained schemes to trick Ricky into allowing her to perform.

The show also reflected society in its depiction of mass consumerism in the 1950s, which was all-consuming and inescapable. The dream of that all-American lifestyle was easily categorized and defined by "things." Having a new car and new appliances was a worthwhile goal that people strived to attain. This fascination with material things was personified by the merchandise created and sold that was directly tied to the show. Clothes, dolls, and all sorts of items were hugely popular with fans. Even today, these and other items are available in shops and online. The mass marketing of *I Love Lucy* and Lucille Ball has not abated in the time since the show originally aired.

I Love Lucy didn't cater specifically to a teen audience, but teenagers would watch the show along with their family members; it was a show that the entire family could watch together. Because so much of the humor was physical, younger children and teens could view it and understand and appreciate many of the jokes and sight gags. For example, two of the most popular episodes in the show's history relied heavily on visuals for humor: "Job Switching" and "Lucy's Italian Movie." In "Job Switching," Lucy and Ethel get jobs at a candy factory while their husbands stay home to do housework. Predictably, things go very badly when the conveyor belt speeds up and the two friends cannot keep up with the pace. They begin stuffing the chocolates into their mouths as quickly as possible and eating them. In "Lucy's Italian Movie," the famous redhead ends up in the only nonautomated part of a winery and has to stomp the grapes with her feet. Coming-of-age viewers appreciated this humor as much as their parents did.

Lucille Ball is iconic. Although her early days in Hollywood were a mixed bag of roles that never quite captured her essence, this show solidified her place within American pop culture. She was the beloved trickster who excelled at physical comedy and won the loyalty of millions of fans. *I Love Lucy* was a Nielsen's ratings hit and remained in the top-three-rated television shows through its sixth and final season. The show was nominated for and won several Primetime Emmy Awards including Best Comedy (or Situational Comedy) in 1953 and 1954. Ball herself won for "Best Actress in a Comedy" in 1956, and costar Vivian Vance won "Best Supporting Actress in a Comedy" in 1954. In 2012, *I Love Lucy* was chosen as the "Best TV Show of All Time" in a joint survey conducted by ABC News and *People* magazine. The show is also noteworthy for being the first television comedy shot before a live audience on 35-millimeter film.

See also: 1950s: *Adventures of Ozzie and Harriet, The*; *Father Knows Best*; *Leave It to Beaver*; 1960s: *Beverly Hillbillies, The*; *Patty Duke Show, The*; 1970s: *Happy Days*; 1980s: *Cosby Show, The*; *Facts of Life, The*; *Family Ties*; *Full House*; *Wonder Years, The*; 1990s: *Boy Meets World*; *Clarissa Explains It All*; *7th Heaven*; 2000s: *Friday Night Lights*

Further Reading

Ball, Lucille. 1996. *Love, Lucy*. New York: Putnam.

Bor, Stephanie. 2013. "Two Babies: Framing the First Televised Depiction of Pregnancy." *Media History* 19 (4): 464–478.

Egge, Sarah. 2015. "'I Love Lucy' Confronts the 1950s American Housewife Ideal." *Norton Center for the Arts*, February 2. http://nortoncenter.com/2015/02/02/i-love-lucy-confronts-the-1950s-american-housewife-ideal/.

Grigsby Bates, Karen. 2014. "Love in Technicolor: Interracial Families on Television." *NPR*, February 15. https://www.npr.org/sections/codeswitch/2014/02/15/276526212/love-in-technicolor-interracial-families-on-television.

White, Rosie. 2016. "Funny Peculiar: Lucille Ball and the Vaudeville Heritage of Early American Television Comedy." *Social Semiotics* 26 (3): 298–310.

I WAS A TEENAGE WEREWOLF

This low-budget 1957 horror film has become synonymous with cheaply made exploitation movies and has been referenced in countless TV shows ranging from *The Dick Van Dyke Show* to *SpongeBob Square Pants*. The first major motion picture to use the word "teenage" in its title, *I Was a Teenage Werewolf* follows the struggles of high school student Tony Rivers (Michael Landon), who has a penchant for losing his temper and getting into fights with fellow classmates. After witnessing one particularly rough fight between Tony and peer Jimmy (Tony Marshall), Detective Donovan (Barney Phillips) advises Tony to seek professional counseling. Resistant at first, Tony does end up seeing Dr. Alfred Brandon (Whit Bissell) after he gets into another brawl and realizes how terrified his schoolmates are of him.

In the film, Tony is a rebel—a troublemaker. He doesn't like to be touched and is overly sensitive to perceived insults or slights. Tony doesn't play well with others and doesn't follow the rules. Once under the care of hypnotherapist Dr. Brandon, Tony becomes an unwilling guinea pig in a science experiment testing the efficacy of scopolamine serum, a drug that affects the brain and disinhibits primal behavior. After a few sessions, the doctor plants the thought in Tony's mind that he was once a wild animal. Shortly thereafter, Tony's friend Frank (Michael Rougas) is murdered while walking home through the woods late at night. A police station janitor sees the crime photos and attempts to convince the police chief that this is the result of a werewolf attack, pointing out the unique marks on the victim's body.

Triggered by a loud school bell, Tony again transforms into a werewolf and kills a cheerleader who is practicing drills in the gymnasium. Even in his altered physical state, he is recognized because of his clothes, particularly his athletic letterman jacket. A local news reporter speaks with Tony's father and girlfriend as well as her parents in an attempt to locate him. With police closing in, Tony manages to evade capture but kills a dog that surprises him in the process.

The underlying issues of alienation and the loss of self-control resonate strongly with teenagers. The transition from childhood to adulthood is fraught with a multitude of challenges and disappointments. On a social and emotional level, teenagers are navigating new ground during this period as well. 1950s teens and their actions were especially under the "microscope" by parents, teachers, police, and other authority figures. The antisocial behavior depicted by Tony during his transformation, while frightening, was also thrilling. He was acting out in an exaggerated and violent manner, but he was in some ways rebelling against order and authority as well, and that theme connects deeply with teenagers. Additionally, the physical transformation of Tony is in some ways similar to what happens when young men go through puberty. While not as dramatic or deadly as Tony's change, it's still a physical and emotional change.

Teenagers were viewed with suspicion by many adults in the 1950s. Given the rigid social and political landscape of the decade, it was expected that teens would conform and adhere to societal norms. A large part of that meant obeying authority figures and following the rules of institutions like the government and the church.

On its surface, *I Was a Teenage Werewolf* can be viewed as a fairly standard horror film. Given the time in America's history when it was made, however, it lends itself to analysis and dissection. Although the wave of anti-Communism and McCarthyism from the late 1940s and 1950s had largely dissipated by 1957, the sting of it was still felt by Americans. During that time frame, the country was besieged by political fervor via accusations directed at anyone suspected of anti-American activities. Senator Joseph McCarthy and FBI director J. Edgar Hoover drove much of this under the premise that they were protecting America from Communism. Thousands of government workers lost their jobs for suspicion of being involved with Communist groups or organizations; the government went after many in Hollywood and ruined the careers of various writers, actors, and other film workers that were accused of this activity.

I Was a Teenage Werewolf was produced by American International Pictures (AIP). They were famous for making "cheapie" films accompanied with over-the-top advertising designed to lure in viewers. In addition to this film, they also made *I Was a Teenage Frankenstein* (1957) and *How to Make a Monster* (1958). These films also relied heavily on teen audiences to buy tickets. *Blood of Dracula* (1957) is another film in their series, and this was a female retelling of the story (with vampires). It featured teens with behavioral issues and doctors bent on manipulating the crisis for their own professional benefit.

Critics largely dismissed the film, although Landon was recognized for a solid performance as an explosive teen. Although labeled as a campy film today, *I Was a Teenage Werewolf* was considered shocking and edgy at the time because it featured a teen being scientifically morphed into a killer animal. The ending of the film, wherein Tony begs Dr. Brandon to reverse the experiments, goes badly for all involved. The doctor, who attempts to film the transformation, injects Tony with the serum. A bell once again triggers Tony, who wildly attacks the doctor and his assistant, killing them both. Police break in and shoot and kill the werewolf as it advances on them. Now dead, the werewolf transforms back into Tony. The police suspect that Dr. Brandon was to blame for the mayhem, but since the camera is destroyed during the attack, there is no record of the experiment and its outcome. This plotline has since been used in numerous films and TV shows.

I Was a Teenage Werewolf has become an iconic media production for its camp value and its nostalgia factor. Without its success, there may not have been follow-ups like *An American Werewolf in London* (1981), the Michael J. Fox comedy *Teen Wolf* (1985), or the gory MTV series (2011–2017) of the same name. The original film was extensively paid homage to in the Michael Jackson music video *Thriller* (1983).

See also: 1950s: *Blob, The*; 1960s: *Addams Family, The*; *Twilight Zone, The*; 1970s: *Carrie*; 1980s: *It*; 1990s: *Buffy the Vampire Slayer*; *I Know What You Did Last Summer*; *Scream*

Further Reading

Clement, Priscilla Ferguson, and Jacqueline S. Reinier, eds. 2001. *Boyhood in America: An Encyclopedia*. Santa Barbara, CA: ABC-CLIO.

Heffernan, Kevin. 2004. *Ghouls, Gimmicks, and Gold: Horror Films and the American Movie Business 1953–1968*. Durham: Duke University Press.

McMahon-Coleman, Kimberley, and Roslyn Weaver. 2012. *Werewolves and Other Shape-shifters in Popular Culture: A Thematic Analysis of Recent Depictions*. Jefferson, NC: McFarland.

INVISIBLE MAN

Invisible Man, a 1952 novel by Ralph Ellison (1914–1994) examines the life of a nameless black man living in America during a time of deep racial strife and division. The title of the book refers to the main character's feeling of "invisibility" to white society. The story is told in first-person voice, which allows the author to control the narrative from start to finish. The novel opens with the protagonist literally living underground, hidden away from the world. The story traces his experiences from his time in the South during the late 1920s and early 1930s through a series of harrowing and demeaning events that eventually lead him to his subterranean dwelling as a place of refuge.

Invisible Man examines many issues, but the most significant clearly is that of race and subjugation in a society dominated by whites. Many critics believe that the novel is largely Ellison's negative response to Communism, a cause that he and others in his circle initially embraced as a possible solution to race and class conflicts within America. This change of attitude and belief were exemplified in a letter written by Ellison to fellow black writer Richard Wright. In the letter, Ellison conveyed his frustration and anger with the Communist Party in what he felt was its betrayal of the lower class and minorities with respect to advancing the cause of equality.

The impact of the Housing Act of 1949 and its effects on urban (primarily black) residents parallels events in the novel. The protagonist at one point ends up in Harlem and becomes involved with a group of young black men known collectively as the "Brotherhood." Taking up their cause of addressing social inequality, he begins working at a paint factory until he's injured in an explosion at the workplace. This section of the book analyzes the displacement of many black Americans within Harlem due to "urban expansion." Although the concept sounds harmless, it was not uncommon for white landlords to evict their black tenants due to their inability to pay rent. Because of severe economic downturns, many jobs traditionally done by blacks were now done by whites. This, of course, had a domino effect on new investments in areas like Harlem and on the ability of its residents to stay afloat financially.

After a serious betrayal by members of the Brotherhood, the protagonist watches as Harlem descends into chaos via riots and property destruction. The message is quite clear: the movement he was a part of sacrificed the security and shelter of its members and those they were supposedly fighting for in order to gain long-term political ground. Key leaders in the Brotherhood purposefully incite the riot and the ensuing lawlessness to make way for urban renewal and redevelopment. They literally destroy and burn neighborhoods to enable modernization of the area, but because of their actions, the elderly and families are displaced with nowhere to go.

Although the book was praised for its literary merits and its unflinching look at racial issues within Western society, it also received harsh criticism from some of Ellis's colleagues and peers. Irving Howe and James Baldwin both took aim at Ellis and accused him of failing to capture the "true" experience of the black man at that time in history. Ellison responded to this in the essay, "The World and the Jug," in which he contends that there are a wide array of black experiences and not all of them fit a narrow and prescribed narrative of anger, rage, and victimization.

Prior to *Invisible Man*, most books by young black male writers followed a theme of civil protest, focusing exclusively on the subjugation of their community by white authority. Although Ellison surely understood discrimination and all the issues associated with it, he also felt it was important to discuss positive cultural influences on the community and even on himself, such as jazz music and poetry. He felt restricted by the notion that all of his creative efforts should be solely focused on one issue.

Invisible Man connects with teenagers because it examines themes of race and class and the experience of being an outsider within society. Many media vehicles that focus on minorities and issues of struggle and oppression resonate with younger audiences because they are relatable in a very general way. Teens often feel alienated and alone and can connect with characters and stories that reflect this. They are also more receptive to messages of inclusion with respect to other races and ethnicities than older audiences.

Given the central theme of the book, it is ironic that it has also received heavy criticism from feminists for what they feel is the treatment of female characters in the story. Carolyn Sylvander and Ann Stanford claim that female characters in *Invisible Man* are relegated to roles of being objectified or dismissed. They feel this treatment of women in the novel lessens the strength of its attention on the second-class status of black Americans, specifically men. Some of this objection has been countered with an alternate reading that this portrayal is intentional—that is, it is used to demonstrate the invisibility of all minorities and how culture perpetuated this during that period.

Regardless of controversies, *Invisible Man* is a significant piece of work. Ellison received the National Book Award in 1953, and the novel appeared in *Time* magazine's list of the 100 Best English Language Novels from 1923–2005. The book has been a staple in high school literature courses for decades and continues to be regarded as an important cultural and political tale. Although Ellison died in 1994, his unfinished novel was published under the name *Three Days before the Shooting* in 2010.

See also: 1950s: *Blackboard Jungle*; 1960s: *To Kill a Mockingbird*; *To Sir, with Love*; 1970s: *Cooley High*; 1980s: *Cosby Show, The*

Further Reading

Ellison, Ralph. 1952. *Invisible Man*. New York: Random House.

Mason, John Edwin. 2016. "Gordon Parks and Ralph Ellison: How a Man 'Becomes Invisible.'" *Time*, May 20. http://time.com/4328189/gordon-parks-and-ralph-ellison-how-a-man -becomes-invisible/.

Rampersad, Arnold. 2008. *Ralph Ellison: A Biography*. New York: Vintage Books.

Vitale, Tom. 2014. "Ralph Ellison: No Longer the 'Invisible Man' 100 Years after His Birth." *NPR*, May 30. https://www.npr.org/sections/codeswitch/2014/05/30/317056807/ralph -ellison-no-longer-the-invisible-man-100-years-after-his-birth.

LEAVE IT TO BEAVER

The title character in *Leave It to Beaver* (1957–1963) is an adolescent prone to getting into mischief on a regular basis. Theodore "The Beaver" Cleaver (Jerry Mathers) is a good-natured but curious boy who is easily led astray by friends and foes. Although father Ward Cleaver (Hugh Beaumont) is never shown physically punishing his sons, the threat of corporal punishment is always simmering beneath his soft-spoken facade. June Cleaver (Barbara Billingsley) is the model of a devoted mother and wife; she rarely questions her husband's judgment, and, when she does, it is Ward's decision that almost always prevails.

Beaver is naive and shy when it comes to girls. His brother Wally (Tony Dow) is a jock who is popular with both boys and girls. Two bullies on the show serve as central antagonists: Eddie Haskell (Ken Osmond) and Lumpy Rutherford (Frank Bank). There is no issue so complicated that it cannot be resolved within a 30-minute episode, and unlike sitcoms of subsequent decades, the issues addressed on *Leave It to Beaver* remain rooted in the narrow and immediate and never stray into larger societal woes. The focus of the show was on Beaver and his brother and friends, so their misadventures and exploits were the appeal for young viewers. Unlike sitcoms in later decades, parents were not depicted as mock-worthy.

In *Leave It to Beaver*, the typical plotline involves Beaver going against his instincts and committing an act of defiance or disobedience to his parents, teachers, and other authority figures. Inevitably, his transgression is discovered and he is punished in some fashion. The message to children watching the show could not be more clear: going against authority figures is a bad idea and will generally result in negative outcomes.

The show presented the American family as an idealization of all that is perfect in the world—at least on the surface. Sitcoms prior to this focused more on young married couples and their adjustment to being newlyweds and taking on more adult responsibilities. Suddenly, the creation and maintenance of the family unit became the central focus. There was also a shift in the function of the lead female character. In sitcoms like *I Love Lucy*, the female lead was often the source of most of the antics. She was frequently portrayed as overreactionary and even hysterical, and, more times than not, her "level-headed" husband was forced to rein her in to restore dignity to the situation and presumably to society in general.

Leave It to Beaver also reinforced traditional gender roles and authoritarianism within the family unit and beyond. This was after World War II, when many women had ventured outside of the home to aid in the war effort, many of them taking factory jobs helping to build warplanes and other military weapons and devices. But June doesn't work outside of the home, and this was typical and largely representative of American women at the time. The Cleaver home is antiseptically clean, and June performs housework in a dress and pearl necklace. In the suburban landscape of *Leave It to Beaver*, women function as an integral part of the *family* unit but not necessarily beyond that.

The 1950s was a period of strong economic growth and the middle class grew and thrived. Materialism and its significance to the family household was evident in both the creation of appliances and the way in which they were advertised during this decade. As women were spending most of their time inside the home, a wave of kitchen appliances hit the market and targeted housewives and mothers as their primary consumers. This explains why women in many TV productions at the time are shown within the household primarily as individuals whose focus is on keeping an immaculate home and well-groomed and well-behaved children.

Another common theme in 1950s sitcoms that stemmed from the postwar experience was that of order and control. In most presentations, the husband and father had been in the military prior to starting a family. Because discipline and order is paramount to success within the military institution, these beliefs and practices were supplanted into the household after the war. Father ruled the home with the proverbial iron fist. As mentioned earlier, though, violence or at least the threat of violence was always present. Both wives and children feared repercussions and with good reason. In one episode of *Leave It to Beaver*, Beaver refuses to come down from a tree that he had climbed because he is afraid that his father will hit him. Ward begins to acknowledge this reality as he starts to remove his belt. All that prevents him from using it is the now gathering crowd that surrounds him.

Expectations of ideal masculine behavior are also conveyed in the show. Another episode of *Leave It to Beaver* depicts Beaver as frightened of visiting the dentist. In the office with his father, he is encouraged to be a "good soldier." This advice operates on two levels: it discounts Theodore's concerns and reinforces the notion that boys don't get scared, and, if they do, they need to conceal it. Additionally, it reminds the viewer of the role and importance of the military with regard to developing "strong" men. This reinforced established stereotypes and expected behaviors for young men based solely on gender.

Though *Leave It to Beaver* never won any major awards, it has remained popular in reruns many decades after it went off the air. More importantly, it has become an iconic American television series due to its longevity and influence on popular culture. It was also included in *Time* magazine's list of "The 100 Best Shows of All-Time."

See also: 1950s: *Adventures of Ozzie and Harriet, The*; *Father Knows Best*; *I Love Lucy*; 1960s: *Beverly Hillbillies, The*; *Patty Duke Show, The*; 1970s: *Happy Days*; 1980s: *Cosby Show, The*; *Family Ties*; *Full House*; *Wonder Years, The*; 1990s: *Boy Meets World*; *Clarissa Explains It All*; *7th Heaven*; 2000s: *Friday Night Lights*

Further Reading

Mathers, Jerry. 1998. *And Jerry Mathers as the Beaver*. New York: Berkeley Boulevard.

Murray, Noel. 2011. "Leave It to Beaver, 'The Last Day of School.'" *AV/TV Club*, June 9. https://tv.avclub.com/leave-it-to-beaver-the-last-day-of-school-1798226148.

Osmond, Ken, Christopher Lynch, and Jerry Mathers. 2014. *Eddie: The Life and Times of America's Preeminent Bad Boy*. Los Angeles: Christopher J. Lynch.

Rosenblum, Gail. 2017. "Generation in Flux. Younger Millennials Pine for '50s families." *Star Tribune*, April 9. http://www.startribune.com/generation-in-flux-younger -millennials-pine-for-50s-families/418558093/.

LOLITA

Lolita, a 1955 novel by lauded novelist Vladimir Nabokov (1899–1977), is one of the most controversial books ever published. The central character, Humbert Humbert, is a middle-aged literature professor. The title character is a 12-year-old named Delores Haze. Humbert rents a room from Delores's mother, Charlotte, primarily in an attempt to get closer to Delores. Humbert and Delores engage in a sexual relationship, something that Humbert has fantasized about doing for many years. He begins journaling his thoughts and fantasies about Delores, whom he refers to as Lolita.

Although a story line like this would raise eyebrows even today, publishing a novel in the 1950s about pedophilia was utterly shocking. The tale is told from Humbert's point of view, and this is almost as troubling as the topic itself to many people. By having Humbert as the narrator, he is in control of the narrative. He can tell the reader as much or as little as he wants them to know. This style deprives Delores, a young girl, from having a voice and sharing her thoughts and feelings about events. Some argue that by giving Humbert this control, he is able to shape the narrative in a way that attempts to normalize pedophilia.

Nabokov knew that the subject matter was explosive, and he initially planned to publish it under a pseudonym. After being rejected by several large publishers and even a few lesser-known ones, he opted to have it published in France by Olympia Press—the same company that published the controversial *Naked Lunch* by William Burroughs. After famed author Graham Green penned a positive review of the book in a British newspaper, followed by a heated written response from an editor at another publication, the book was banned in England. Customs officers were instructed to remove it from anyone entering the country, and France soon took the same action.

The novel was released in the United States by G. P. Putnam's Sons in 1958 and became an instant best seller. It sold approximately 300,000 copies in less than one month.

As the story develops, Charlotte falls in love with Humbert. The feelings are not reciprocal, but he knows that he must stay in her favor in order to be in close proximity to Delores. He marries Charlotte and briefly contemplates murdering her so that he can take guardianship of Delores. Later, Charlotte discovers Humbert's diary and threatens to mail detailed letters about his sexual obsession that she has written to family and friends. Then, she is hit and killed by a passing car.

Humbert kidnaps Delores and plans to molest her after giving her a mild sedative. The plan fails, but she later confesses to him that she's had sex with a boy from camp. She then convinces him to have sex with her. This element of the story is problematic for many critics. They along with some readers believe that Nabokov, by having the young girl initiate the sexual encounter, deflects blame from the protagonist for his actions. The argument follows that even if Delores did "seduce" him, she is a child and he is an adult.

Another part of the story line that attempts to normalize Humbert's sexual obsession involves his childhood sweetheart, Annabel Leigh. The two never consummate their relationship as teens, and Annabel dies shortly after moving away with her family. This apparently keeps Humbert in a state of arrested development; he is fixated sexually on young girls under the age of 14 due to his unresolved grief.

After Humbert tells Delores about her mother's accidental death, the two of them begin traveling by car across the country. He keeps her content by buying her gifts. They eventually end up in a small New England town where he enrolls her in an all girl's school. But during a stop in Texas, Delores is taken ill to a hospital. When Humbert arrives to pick her up, she is gone, and he is told that a relative paid her bill and took her to stay with her grandfather. Knowing that she has no other immediate family, Humbert realizes that someone else has kidnapped her.

When he finally tracks her down, she is married, pregnant, and broke. She reveals that a male friend of her mother's named Quimby retrieved her from the hospital and attempted to force her into pornography. When she refused, he kicked her out with no money. She met a man while waitressing and the two got married. Humbert begs her to leave with him but she refuses. He gives her money and then goes in search of Quimby for revenge. He locates him, and the two fight. Humbert shoots and kills Quimby, and at the end of the story, Humbert is arrested by police.

Lolita was clearly not a book that was intended for a teen audience, but its salacious subject matter opened it up for controversy and analysis. Although most people categorize it as an "erotic" novel, others view it more as an ironic and sarcastic novel that is surreal and not to be taken at face value. Regardless of interpretation, its presence in the world of literature has generated endless arguments and debates about intention. The name "Lolita" exists in the American lexicon still today and refers to a sexualized tween or teenage girl.

The novel has been adapted into a musical and a play and twice as a movie. The 1962 film adaptation directed by Stanley Kubrick was critically lauded and is considered a classic in the world of film. It starred James Mason, Shelley Winters, and 14-year-old Sue Lyon in the title role. It was nominated for five Golden Globes (Sue Lyon won for "Most Promising Newcomer") and an Academy Award for Nabokov for Best Adapted Screenplay. Due to tight ratings restrictions at the time, Kubrick was forced to significantly tamp down much of the erotic content. He later commented in an interview that had he known just how much he would have to edit the source material, he most likely never would have made the film.

A 1997 theatrical remake of *Lolita* was a critical and box office failure.

See also: 1950s: *Naked Lunch*

Further Reading

Connolly, Julian W. 2005. *The Cambridge Companion to Nabokov*. Cambridge: Cambridge University Press.

Connolly, Julian. 2005. *A Reader's Guide to Nabokov's "Lolita."* Brighton, MA: Academic Studies Press.

Johnston, Bret Anthony. 2006. "Why 'Lolita' Remains Shocking, and a Favorite." *NPR*, July 7. https://www.npr.org/2006/07/07/5536855/why-lolita-remains-shocking-and-a-favorite.

Metcalf, Stephen. 2005. "Lolita at 50: Is Nabokov's Masterpiece Still Shocking?" *Slate*, December 19. http://www.slate.com/articles/arts/books/2005/12/lolita_at_50.html.

Nabokov, Vladimir. 1955. *Lolita*. Paris: Olympia Press.

Nabokov, Vladimir, and Alfred Appel Jr. 1991. *The Annotated Lolita: Revised and Updated*. New York: Vintage.

Pifer, Ellen, ed. 2002. *Vladimir Nabokov's Lolita: A Casebook*. New York: Oxford University Press.

LORD OF THE FLIES

Required reading even today in many high schools, 1954 novel *Lord of the Flies* by British writer William Golding (1911–1993) examines issues such as groupthink versus autonomy and independent reasoning, power struggles, masculinity, and the disintegration of society when the foundation of rules collapses. On its surface, *Lord of the Flies* is an adventure tale that follows the activities of a group of British schoolboys stranded on a desert island after a plane crash. Ralph and "Piggy" are the only survivors of one plane crash but soon meet boys from a choir group who are also marooned on the island. Alliances are formed as the boys live together and attempt to survive until help can arrive. Even though Ralph assumes a leadership role, the other members of the group become embroiled in a power struggle. The overweight and eyeglass-wearing Piggy becomes the object of cruelty and humiliation as the rules of civility break down and the boys display savage and destructive behavior.

Lord of the Flies invites all sorts of analysis relative to the themes and ideas in the novel. There has been much discussion and even debate about what the different characters and events are meant to portray or symbolize. Some insight can be gained by studying the author's background. For example, Golding's father, Alec, was a socialist and science teacher at the school that William and his brother attended. Additionally, William served in the Royal Navy in 1940 and saw combat at Normandy. These facts helped shape the events that play out in the novel.

One possible interpretation of the novel focuses on the effects of war on children—specifically the evacuation of British school children during air raid attacks in World War II. A recurring "character" in the novel is referred to simply as "the beast." Although none of the boys ever actually sees the animal, it is a cause of great turmoil, fear, and nightmares. Author Joyanta Dangar believes that the beast is a representation of the trauma surrounding the evacuation of children during the war; he points to numerous references in the book where the boys experience recurring dreams while on the island. In these dreams, they are pursued by a faceless beast or monster. Other possible or even additional stressors that may cause the nightmares involve the witnessing of death and destruction during aid raids and the psychological impact of children being separated from their parents during wartime.

The novel is rife with symbolism, and one of the most analyzed and discussed symbols is the conch shell. It is intended to represent order. It is used to alert the boys to the need for a meeting because of its loud sound. More importantly, though, it denotes order in the sense of a democracy; only the person holding the conch during a meeting is allowed to speak. Anyone wishing to share ideas and opinions is given the conch. This prevents the boys from talking over and interrupting one another. It is significant that Piggy is the character who discovers the conch because he is the one most concerned with upholding order and establishing rules of behavior for the group.

As discussed earlier, the beast is ever present within the story and represents collective fear and the worst traits that are triggered by paranoia and fear of the unknown. The first time that discussion of the beast occurs, it is described as reptilian in appearance. This may be a reference to the serpent from the Bible described in Genesis. The story of Adam and Eve centers on the concept of original sin and temptation that originates from Satan in the Garden of Good and Evil. This can be seen as an allegory dealing with the initial trait of innocence within the boys and the subsequent violence and cruelty that ensue when order breaks down and primal urges overpower rational thought and civility.

This is especially applicable to teen boys during their formative years when physiological changes are taking place via increased testosterone. Many times, impulse control is a serious challenge and conflicts tend to be solved through physical aggression. The novel also examines the effects of peer pressure and the vulnerability—especially of children—to succumb to gang mentality when there is a lack of order and supervision and threats to individualism.

Even the dead pilot whom the boys stumble upon is initially believed to be the beast. They eventually sacrifice a pig in an effort to appease what they believe are the supernatural powers of the sinister predator. Animal sacrifices, of course, have a strong historical context within religion where certain rituals were performed in attempts to ward off evil spirits or curry favor with gods.

When *Lord of the Flies* was initially released, it sold poorly (fewer than 3,000 copies). It went on to become a best-selling book and has received several noteworthy mentions on various lists such as *Time* magazine's 100 Best Novels released between 1923 and 2005 and on Modern Library's 100 Best Novels. The work has inspired artists such as horror writer Stephen King and popular rock group U2 and has been adapted to film three times (one being a Filipino all-female cast) and also to various stage productions.

See also: 1960s: *Outsiders, The*; 1970s: *Chocolate War, The*

Further Reading

Berlatsky, Noah. 2017. "There's Already a 'Female Lord of the Flies,' and It's about How Civilization Is the Real Horror." *Slate,* September 1. http://www.slate.com/blogs /browbeat/2017/09/01/joanna_russ_we_who_are_about_to_is_the_real_female _lord_of_the_flies.html.

Golding, William. *Lord of the Flies.* 2016. London: Penguin.

Olsen, Kirstin. 2000. *Understanding Lord of the Flies: A Student Casebook to Issues, Sources, and Historical Documents.* Westport, CT: Greenwood Press.

Whittle, Matthew. 2016. "Why 'Lord of the Flies' Speaks Directly to the Turbulent World of 2016." *Newsweek,* December 8. http://www.newsweek.com/lord-flies-balthazar -getty-william-golding-christmas-2016-literature-529695.

MANY LOVES OF DOBIE GILLIS, THE

The Many Loves of Dobie Gillis (1959–1963), though lasting only four seasons, is a significant media artifact for several reasons. The show was the first television situational comedy to feature a group of teenagers as the main characters. The standard formula of the time centered on families with much of the action taking place within the household. This show flipped that format on its head by zeroing in more on what was happening within high school. The main character, Dobie Gillis (Dwayne Hickman) is a teen boy obsessed with the opposite sex. A below average student, Dobie fixates on multiple girls, hoping that he will find "the one" and enjoy blissful romantic love. The main object of his affection is the gorgeous but unattainable Thalia Menninger (Tuesday Weld). Thalia is quite candid about her priorities—she needs someone with money to take care of her and her family. A recurring gag on the show is Thalia explaining that the money she needs is never for her; she is being altruistic in order to help her ailing father and sister, who is allegedly married to someone with no ambitions. Dobie doesn't believe this, but it also doesn't dissuade him from pursuing her.

Dobie's parents run a grocery store, and much of the comedy and tension come from the frustration that the father, Herbert (Frank Faylen), feels toward his son. Herbert is a no-nonsense World War II veteran who frequently expresses his anger and disappointment in Dobie's laziness. His mother Winnifred (Florida Friebus) is shown as more compassionate and forgiving of her son's shortcomings. As with most sitcoms of the 1950s, the father and husband is seen as an unyielding authoritarian with a rigid set of values and beliefs.

The source material for the show was a series of short stories written by Max Shulman. The locale in those stories was college and not high school. The stories were adapted into a musical comedy film that starred Debbie Reynolds and Bobby Van in the title role. Though the film was not a success, Shulman felt that it had potential as a TV series. In order to move forward with his idea, producers mandated that the age of the title character be changed from 19 to 17. They felt that featuring a high school character held more mass appeal than a college-aged one. Given that less than half of all high school graduates at this time were transitioning to college, it made sense from a business perspective given their target demographic.

Another noteworthy aspect of *The Many Loves of Dobie Gillis* is its examination of class and capitalism during the time frame in which it takes place. Dobie realizes that in order to attract and retain a woman, he needs money. He needs to offer financial security to his potential mate. Whether this is primarily due to his desire for Thalia is unclear, but Dobie wishes to be rich and popular even if he isn't quite certain how to get there.

Dobie's best friend is beatnik Maynard G. Krebs (Bob Denver). Maynard rejects authoritarianism and capitalism. He winces at the mere mention of the word "work." Though played largely for laughs, this character is relevant in a bigger sense. Krebs's antiestablishment worldview was a precursor of what was coming in the 1960s: the civil rights movement, a fervent antiwar effort during Vietnam, and roots of what would later become equal rights movements for women and even the LGBT community.

Comparing a show like this to any one of today's teen-based TV shows may seem futile at face value, but on closer inspection and keeping in mind when the series took place, there were seeds of rebellion within it. Interestingly enough, both Dobie and Maynard despise physical labor, though Dobie longs for the rewards that work often brings with it. Ironically (or maybe not), neither of them seems to understand or care about the important role that formal education often plays in career development and monetary success.

Another character on the show that may be viewed as a trailblazer of sorts is Zelda Gilroy (Sheila Kuehl). Where Dobie relentlessly pursues scores of young girls, Zelda has her sights set on only one boy: Dobie. Although Dobie insists he is not attracted to her and routinely rebuffs her advances, she continues her campaign to win him over. Although this type of sitcom character can easily be discounted as the annoying pursuer, viewing this through the lens of gender roles at the time can provide a different reading. Zelda is undeterred. She knows what— or who—she wants and goes after it. Women were not expected to be socially aggressive in the 1950s. Zelda doesn't feel compelled or obligated to adhere to societal expectations with regard to her behavior in pursuit of Dobie. The actress who played Gilroy, Sheila Kuehl, shared in an interview with the *New York Times* that she got letters from female viewers of the show when it originally aired. Many of them thanked her for portraying a strong-willed female character at a time when they were in short supply.

The Many Loves of Dobie Gillis featured two actors who would go on to significant success in Hollywood with feature films: Warren Beatty and Tuesday Weld. Beatty left the show after only five episodes, but Weld stayed for the entire first season and even returned in guest spots in later seasons. Several unsuccessful attempts to reboot the series happened in the late 1970s and 1980s with the characters now as adults. In the 1988 TV movie, Dobie has married Zelda and the two run his parents' former grocery store, which also now includes a pharmacy.

See also: 1960s: *Where the Boys Are*; 1970s: *Cooley High*; *Happy Days*; 1980s: *Saved by the Bell*; *Sweet Valley High*; *Wonder Years, The*; 1990s: *Boy Meets World*; *Clarissa Explains It All*; *Freaks and Geeks*; 2000s: *Glee*; *One Tree Hill*

Further Reading

Adams, Erik. 2014. "Dobie Gillis Found a Winner by Making Its Lead a Loser." *AV/TV Club,* April 14. https://tv.avclub.com/dobie-gillis-found-a-winner-by-making-its-lead -a-loser-1798267808.

Genzinger, Neil. 2013. "The Many Rebellions of Dobie Gillis." *New York Times,* June 28. http://www.nytimes.com/2013/06/30/arts/television/the-many-rebellions-of-dobie -gillis.html.

Hickman, Dwayne, and Joan Roberts Hickman. 1994. *Forever Dobie: The Many Lives of Dwayne Hickman*. New York: Birch Lane Press.

NAKED LUNCH

This 1959 novel by author William S. Burroughs (1914–1997) created a whirlwind of scandal and controversy for its profane language and graphic depictions of drug usage, violence, and bizarre sexual activities. The book is nonlinear in structure and follows the exploits of its protagonist, junkie William Lee. Time shifts back and forth within the book as bizarre incidents take place that involve warring political factions. Orgies, decapitations, heavy drug use, and a story line involving a police pursuit of the protagonist also occur within the novel, although the narrative thread does not necessarily tie any of them together coherently.

This is a media creation that is impossible to analyze or discuss without a solid understanding of its creator's history. Burroughs came from a wealthy Midwestern family. He was educated at Harvard and enlisted in the army but was ultimately

American writer William Seward Burroughs, author of the cult novel *Naked Lunch*. Although he wrote other books, Burroughs is best known for this sexually explicit and gruesome tale that stirred controversy and received extensive negative attention upon its American publication. (Evening Standard/Getty Images)

rejected for service. He developed a serious drug addiction shortly thereafter that remained with him throughout his life. After moving to New York City in the early 1940s, he became friends with fellow scribes Allen Ginsberg and Jack Kerouac. The three writers are attributed as founding fathers of the Beat generation, a counterculture movement that gained traction in the 1960s. Because of their rejection of the status quo and embrace of unconventional lifestyles, stories by and about members of the Beat generation intrigue teenagers.

Burroughs allegedly wrote most of what later became *Naked Lunch* under a haze of drugs. He penned a series of unconnected events ("contingencies") that were later somewhat strung together to form a semicohesive narrative. Burroughs knew that, due to the explicit language and content of the book, it had slim possibility of being published in the United States. He was elated when *The Chicago Review* agreed to print excerpts of the book in their publication in 1958. After passages were included in the spring and fall volumes of the publication with little fanfare, a newspaper article outlining its obscenities prompted the University of Chicago's (the publisher) chancellor to squash further excerpts from being printed in subsequent volumes of the journal.

It's difficult to say exactly what inspired Burroughs to write the novel, but the political atmosphere in the country during the 1950s almost certainly contributed to its origins. In a 1950 document that is part of congressional records from the government, references to the threat of homosexuality to the country's sense of well-being are made several times. Words and phrases including "putrid" and "fetid" are peppered throughout the document. Fear and hysteria about the threat of Communism were rampant at this time, and the issue of homosexuality among government employees was tied to this and lumped in as a serious security threat. Material that is labeled as controversial or subversive many times connects strongly with younger audiences. There is a curiosity factor that can trigger intense interest in consuming media that has been deemed "forbidden."

Naked Lunch features a wide assortment of gay characters, and the majority of them are presented as monstrous. This seems odd given that Burroughs was openly gay and must have been affected by pervasive vitriol and efforts to rid the government of gay employees. This panic, of course, spread throughout the citizenry and painted a degenerate and worthless picture of the gay community, already a disenfranchised group at that time.

It's important to remember, however, that he was also a drug addict and was usually under the influence of drugs when creating his work. It's also possible that the representation of gays in the book served the stylistic purpose of writing in a Gothic fashion. The lurid depictions of sexual violence and the physical descriptions of creatures in the book adhere to earlier works designed to shock audiences. Additionally, the "monstrous" elements of the novel can be viewed as the equally monstrous language and actions aimed at denigrating American gays and lesbians, and those suspected of being Communist or Communist sympathizers. Teens—especially teenage men—often gravitate toward explicit gore and sex within media productions. A fascination with morbidity and bodily functions drives much of this.

Burroughs finally found an American publisher for the book: Grove Press. The small publisher had been successful in the niche area of publishing paperback novels that were commercially successful. Media attention from overseas helped pique the public's curiosity about the novel, and it finally went on sale in the United States in 1962. Extensive efforts were made to limit potential legal actions. The publisher created and distributed a pamphlet for booksellers with highlights from the work so they would be knowledgeable about potential areas of objection. The book jacket also featured accolades from several prominent authors and magazines that would hopefully legitimize the novel as art and not mere pornography.

The book was banned in Boston the year it was published. The legal reasoning behind this was that it violated existing obscenity laws for its inclusion of child murder and pedophilia. This decision was overturned four years later by the Massachusetts Supreme Court who found that there was some redeeming social value within the novel, and therefore it wasn't exclusively a prurient work of obscenity.

Naked Lunch is significant for its unconventional structure, excessive use of profanity, graphic violence, and explicit sex. It's a polarizing work that divides readers even now in terms of its literary value. It's also inextricably linked to its author, William Burroughs, in terms of defining him as both a writer and an individual. *Time* magazine included *Naked Lunch* in its list of the "100 Best English-Language Novels from 1923 to 2005."

See also: 1950s: *Lolita*; *On the Road*; 1960s: *Clockwork Orange, A*

Further Reading

Burroughs, William S. 1959. *Naked Lunch*. Paris: Olympia Press.

Flood, Alison. 2016. "How William Burroughs's Drug Experiments Helped Neurology Research." *The Guardian,* July 21. https://www.theguardian.com/books/2016/jul/21/how-william-burroughss-drug-experiments-helped-neurology-research.

McCarthy, Mary. 2013. "Mary McCarthy on William S. Burroughs's 'The Naked Lunch.'" *New York Times Review of Books*, January 9. http://www.nybooks.com/articles/2013/01/10/mary-mccarthy-william-burroughs-naked-lunch/.

Wilson, Meagan. 2012. "Your Reputation Precedes You: A Reception Study of Naked Lunch." *Journal of Modern Literature* 35 (2): 98–125.

Woodard, Rob. 2009. "Naked Lunch Is Still Fresh." *The Guardian*, April 16. https://www.theguardian.com/books/booksblog/2009/apr/16/naked-lunch-william-burroughs.

ON THE ROAD

The 1957 novel *On the Road* by Jack Kerouac (1922–1969) largely defined and is associated with the Beat generation of the 1950s. The Beat movement comprised young artists and authors whose negative reaction to post–World War II consumerism was evident in their style of dress and mannerisms but most important in their writing and poetry. The foundation of this movement was based on the notion that American life had become meaningless and superficial since the end of the war. Beat followers advocated a lifestyle of carefree adventures rather than a structured existence with all of the rules and responsibilities attached to it.

On the Road follows the cross-country road trip of its two central characters: Sal Paradise and Dean Moriarty. The book is divided into five sections and takes place in locales ranging from New York City to Colorado to San Francisco. The plot of the novel spans a period of three years during which Sal and Dean drift back and forth between various locations. Dean is very impulsive and his love for travel sparks interest in Sal who is trying to move forward after a divorce.

Rejecting the mainstream values and norms of the 1950s, Sal and Dean represented growing frustration and disillusionment among many young people who felt stifled creatively, sexually, and personally. At the same time, the novel failed to represent women in any meaningful way outside of their sexual appeal to men. Marylou, Dean's wife, is often neglected while Dean sexually pursues other women. The two young men spend much of their time partying and doing drugs. At one point in the novel, they leave Texas with another friend, Stan, and cross over into Mexico where they have sex with prostitutes. As the story progresses, a growing rift between the two main characters becomes more evident as their lives diverge.

The story line and themes examined in *On the Road* appeal to teens for a variety of reasons. Given the rigid cultural norms of the decade, the simplified and responsibility-free lifestyle enjoyed by Sal and Dean must have seemed revolutionary. Their sexual promiscuity especially may have enticed teenage boys into reading the book. Beyond that, there was a strong sense of impending societal change evident in the worldview of the characters and the Beat generation in general. On a more global level, the novel connects with coming-of-age readers especially because it's about the search for meaningfulness. It questions the acceptance of a prescribed existence that depends on material wealth, marriage, and children to constitute happiness or self-fulfillment.

Critical reaction to the book was initially mixed with accusations that the story had plotlines that were left unresolved. To some, it seemed that the style *was* the substance. A more significant criticism of the book was its seeming lack of depth in its portrayal of African American jazz musicians and singers. Kerouac and his peers were fascinated with jazz and this was reflected by their use of the music during poetry readings. Although they voiced admiration and respect for many of these artists, there seemed to be a lack of understanding or empathy for the social issues that fueled much of this music. Kerouac never indicated any sort of recognition of racial and social injustices that were rampant during 1950s America. It's probable that the strong attraction and even identification with these artists was driven by mainstream culture's distaste and even rejection of the Beat movement. So, although Kerouac and his peers may have felt they shared an "outsider" status with this group, the larger socioeconomic and racial issues that kept them separate and still divided were ignored.

The sexual passages in the novel were censored by the publisher. In the book, there is an ample supply of recreational sex, both heterosexual and homosexual. In the release of the 50th edition of the book in 2007, the unedited version contained those passages. In the opening pages, Sal hears Dean and another man having sex as Sal muses that this activity doesn't interest him in the least. Another passage in the book involves an interaction between Dean and a male hustler.

Even though the author had well-known friendships with gay authors such as Allen Ginsberg and William Burroughs, his descriptions in the novel of gay men is derogatory; gay slurs are prevalent throughout these sections. Whether or not this was merely a reflection of popular opinion during that time or indicative of Kerouac's beliefs is unclear. Several books written about the author since his death allege that he had sexual encounters with other men, but his religious upbringing and oppressive family background prevented him from ever pursuing these relationships beyond the physical.

Joyce Johnson, a friend of Kerouac's, was with him when the *New York Times* review of the book came out. She believed that the sudden notoriety of the book overwhelmed him. He went from relative anonymity to the voice of a generation, even though that was never his intention. Kerouac was incredibly uncomfortable with his success and all that came with it. By the time other Beat writers such as Ginsberg were enjoying success with their take on the Beat movement, Kerouac had little interest in it. He never reached this level of success or acclaim again after *On the Road,* and he died in 1969 at the age of 47 from liver disease.

The novel has sold over 3 million copies, and it continues to be a popular book choice in college-level English courses. Its influence has been seen in artists ranging from Jim Morrison of the Doors to the Beastie Boys. Ironically, Kerouac was featured in ads for retail clothing chain the Gap in the 1990s. Given the author's disdain for Western consumerism and corporate ideology, some of his still living peers lament the hyperfocus on name brand fashion and materialism currently displayed in American culture. A line of clothing that used his name was also launched in America in 1995.

Kerouac's name and his history still connect with many who feel a sense of being an outsider or being unhappy with the status quo. *On the Road* was chosen by *Time* magazine as one of the 100 best English-language novels published between 1923 and 2005. After decades of stalled film adaptations, the novel was translated to film in 2011 and starred Kristen Stewart and Sam Riley.

See also: 1950s: *Naked Lunch*; 1960s: Doors, The; 1970s: *Breaking Away*

Further Reading

George-Warren, Holly. 1999. *The Rolling Stone Book of the Beats: The Beat Generation and the American Culture*. New York: Hyperion.

Ginsberg, Allen, Bill Morgan, and Anne Waldman. 2017. *The Best Minds of My Generation: A Literary History of the Beats*. New York: Grove Press.

Kerouac, Jack. 1957. *On the Road*. New York: Viking Press.

Lanzetta, Danny. 2012. "In Defense of Jack Kerouac and Other Flawed Literature." Huffington Post, August 17. https://www.huffingtonpost.com/danny-lanzetta/defending -jack-kerouac-an_b_1797698.html.

Lounsbury, Lynnette. 2016. "I Loved the Beat Generation. Then I Realised It Has No Place for Women." *The Guardian*, April 4. https://www.theguardian.com/books/2016/apr/04 /beat-generation-writers-no-place-for-women.

PRESLEY, ELVIS

If James Dean was the poster boy for the rebellion and angst of the 1950s, then Elvis Presley (1935–1977) was the personification of strained race relations in the country—especially in the Deep South—during the same decade. Presley was born in Tupelo, Mississippi, but moved with his parents to Memphis, Tennessee, in 1948. His poverty-stricken surroundings exposed Presley to black culture, especially that of black churches and choirs. During his teen years, he and his family routinely attended worship services where singers and choir members emphasized physical movement and uninhibited dancing during performances.

Presley's singing career began in 1954, and, within two years, he was an international superstar. His provocative style of dancing excited his younger fans, but many adults and other authority figures found it shocking and even obscene. His 1956 appearance on the *Ed Sullivan Show* cemented his status as both a skilled singer-musician and as a sex symbol. His first appearance on the show reached almost 83 percent of the TV-viewing audience. During his third appearance on the program, camera operators filmed him from the waist up and used close-ups to avoid showcasing the singer's gyrating lower-body movements. Presley's physical appeal to teenage girls especially cannot be understated. His swagger and sexual charisma contained an element of danger that thrilled younger fans and incensed many of their parents.

His songs covered familiar terrain—romantic love and romantic struggles—and attracted and retained a cult-like following among teens: "Heartbreak Hotel," "Don't Be Cruel," and "Love Me Tender" were among his number one hits that solidified his status as a sex symbol and teen icon. Presley's appeal with teens was so strong that an Elvis Teen Idol doll was manufactured and sold. Mattel also made an Elvis in *Blue Hawaii* doll and Elvis Presley "The Army Years" one as well.

When Presley was drafted for military service in 1958, many of his young fans were distraught. Though given an option to avoid the possibility of experiencing battle, he declined an offer within the Special Services branch to entertain troops. This decision gained him newfound respect from many of his fans' parents who had criticized him previously. He actively served in the Army for two years until his official discharge in 1960.

Although some viewed Presley's success as a validation of the skills and talents of the black artists whom he was inspired by, others perceived it as the co-opting of their culture. One thing that could not be disputed, however, was the effect he had on breaking down social barriers. Because of his low-income background and experiences as an outcast during his youth, he seemed to relate to many black Americans on a personal level and was able to bridge some of the racial strife within the culture simply by the company he kept. Black Panther leader Eldridge Cleaver argued that he "dared to do in the light of day what America had long been doing in the sneak thief anonymity of night—consorted on a human level with the blacks" (Gregory 1992, 110).

In addition to his phenomenal success as a recording artist, Presley also enjoyed success as a film star. He starred in 33 feature films, most of which were financially successful. He fared better in vehicles that highlighted his singing and dancing abilities rather than his few forays into more dramatic material. His most financially successful film was 1964's *Viva Las Vegas* costarring Ann-Margret.

Although Presley's popularity remained high throughout the 1960s and 1970s, his unhealthy eating habits coupled with alleged drug abuse began taking a toll on both his physical appearance and his ability to perform in front of crowds. The former slender heartthrob became obese and suffered from a variety of afflictions, including high blood pressure, liver damage, and severe gastrointestinal problems. These years are often referred to as the "Vegas" years when Presley performed regularly to huge crowds in Las Vegas. The actor-singer played to sold-out crowds there for seven years. Many of his previous teen fans happily followed him into this next (and final) phase of his career.

After accumulating 14 Grammy nominations (and 3 wins), selling over 180 million albums in the United States, and becoming one of the most iconic pop cultural icons of all time, Elvis Presley died on August 16, 1977. Although a drug overdose was suspected by many, a coroner ultimately ruled in 1994 that the cause of death was most likely a sudden violent heart attack.

The popularity of "Elvis" continues through today. According to *Parade* magazine, close to 600,000 fans visit Graceland (Elvis's primary residence) every year. The only home that attracts more visitors than this is the White House in Washington, D.C. Pretax earnings for "The King" via merchandising and various licensing monies exceeded $25 million in 2016. Widow Priscilla Presley has appeared in movies such as *The Naked Gun* and its sequels along with television shows such as *Dallas* and *Melrose Place*. Daughter Lisa Marie Presley has recorded several albums and more notably was briefly married to pop superstar Michael Jackson in 1994. The marriage lasted less than three years before the couple divorced.

Elvis Presley remains one of the most popular and beloved entertainers even today; his legacy within music and popular culture is significant.

See also: 1950s: Boone, Pat; Darin, Bobby; Dean, James; 1960s: Beach Boys, The; Beatles, The

Further Reading

Gregory, Janice, and Neal Gregory. 1992. *When Elvis Died: Media Overload and the Origins of the Elvis Cult*. New York: Pharos.

Guralnick, Peter. 1994. *Last Train to Memphis: The Rise of Elvis Presley*. Boston: Little, Brown.

Vincent, Alice. 2017. "The Sex Symbol and the Schoolgirl: When Elvis Presley Married Priscilla." *The Telegraph*, May 1. http://www.telegraph.co.uk/music/news/sex-symbol -schoolgirl-elvis-presley-married-priscilla/.

Williamson, Joe. 2014. *Elvis Presley: A Southern Life*. Oxford: Oxford University Press.

PUBLIC SERVICE ANNOUNCEMENTS—SEX EDUCATION IN THE 1950s

Your Body during Adolescence (1955) is but one "sex ed" film that was created for school systems in the 1950s. The film begins with a group of high school boys and girls preparing for a class picture. The narrator begins discussing the more obvious physical differences between them: some are overweight while others are thin, some are taller while others are shorter, and so on. The narrator then segues into the topic of puberty and discusses the physical changes that occur between boys and girls during this stage of life. The narration is clinical in nature, a biology lesson on the sex glands and how these affect both men and women. Information on the development of breasts and pubic hair growth is discussed as well as details on how semen is formed and discharged.

The history of sexual education in the United States provides strong insight into societal or cultural norms at the time information was being formally provided or distributed. Pre–World War I efforts to create and utilize sexual education curriculum within American school systems were not successful. The first official attempt at this took place in Chicago schools in 1913. The initiative failed after the Catholic Church took both notice of and action against it, resulting in its demise and the resignation of the superintendent of the school district that offered it.

Because of an increase in sexually transmitted diseases (STDs) during wartime, Americans began to view them as a public health issue that needed attention. The government passed the Chamberlain-Kahn Act in an attempt to educate soldiers and hopefully lessen the number of STDs transmitted within the ranks. The American Sexual Health Association (ASHA)—an outgrowth of the social hygiene movement—was formed in 1914. The name alone communicates the focus on what the main goal was to be. *Damaged Goods* is the name of the first official "sex ed" film that was produced for the military. It's a melodramatic depiction of the consequences of a soldier who contracts syphilis. He has sex with a prostitute and then passes along the disease to his wife on their wedding night. The effort was well received and a subsequent push was made to begin educating men in the armed forces earlier in school before they transitioned into service.

ASHA then produced a film that addressed the "evils" of masturbation. *The Gift of Life* vilified self-gratification and warned young men that the act was selfish and would impede their development into manhood.

Over the next few decades, sexual education became more standardized with an emphasis on film over written materials, though an abundance of pamphlets were created to address all types of sexual issues. It wasn't until the 1940s and 1950s that college courses were offered on the subject. Teachers and educators could now specialize in the area of study and bring their knowledge into the classroom.

The emphasis of sexual education content in the 1950s operated on a few assumptions: young men and women should wait until marriage before engaging in sex, and the primary if not sole purpose for sexual intercourse was procreation. This ignored basic human instincts and the fact that both men and women during their teenage years are experiencing both physiological and emotional needs relative to sexuality. One way that school systems avoided or lessened the chances of parental outrage and controversy was to frame "sex ed" within the context of family life. Classes stressed this in tandem with issues like financial responsibility, character development, and, of course, child rearing. Sexual activity for pleasure alone was not discussed as an option.

Another sex ed film created during this decade was 1957's *As Boys Grow.* This one focuses on a group of high school boys and their physical education teacher, referred to as "Coach." It covers issues like hair growth and shaving and height and weight increases during puberty. It then moves into the discussion of male hormones and the development of sperm. Each time that sperm is discussed, it is connected directly to procreation. One of the boys brings up having a "wet dream," which is referred to by the narrator as a "nocturnal emission."

One important thing to remember when viewing these historical artifacts through a modern lens: birth control pills were not approved for contraceptive use in the United States until 1960. Although the FDA had approved them three years earlier, they were to be prescribed and used only for instances of severe menstrual pain and cramping. Women were still expected to become wives and mothers and for these roles to be their primary ones in life.

Sexual education materials in the 1950s were a reflection of our society's expected norms and customs. It wasn't until 1957 that William Masters and Virginia Johnson began what would become groundbreaking research and subsequent publications on human sexuality. The married couple delved into issues that had previously been considered taboo: self-gratification, homosexuality, and sexual behaviors of prostitutes. Prior to this extensive research, educational media surrounding human sexuality was very basic and conventional as evidenced by the creation and use of the sexual education films discussed previously.

Viewing a sex education film like *Your Body during Adolescence* may elicit unintentional laughs during modern times, but the makers of the film and the overall effort to curb sexual activity among teens and young men and women was concerted and serious.

See also: 1960s: *Explosive Generation, The*

Further Reading

Cornblatt, Johannah. 2009. "A Brief History of Sex Ed in America." *Newsweek*, October 27. http://www.newsweek.com/brief-history-sex-ed-america-81001.

Cueto, Emma. 2013. "The 1950s and '60s Pretty Much Take the Cake for Worst Sex Ed Ever." *Bustle*, September 4. https://www.bustle.com/articles/4604-the-1950s-and-60s -pretty-much-take-the-cake-for-worst-sex-ed-ever.

Moran, Jeffrey. 2002. *Teaching Sex: The Shaping of Adolescence in the 20th Century*. Cambridge, MA: Harvard University Press.

SUMMER PLACE, A

The 1959 melodrama *A Summer Place* was based on a best-selling novel by author Sloan Wilson (1920–2003). At the time of its release it was considered shocking due to its frank depiction of marital infidelity and teenage sexual desires. At the close of an era that was defined by conservative social values and authoritarianism, the subject matter of a film like *A Summer Place* telegraphed the impending higher divorce rates and increased sexual activity among teenagers that would occur in the 1960s and 1970s. The film follows two unhappily married couples and their respective children over the course of a year. Ken (Richard Egan) and Helen (Constance Ford) Jorgensen are miserable. They endure a sexless marriage and presumably avoid divorce because of the negative example it would set for their young daughter Molly (Sandra Dee). Ken is a self-made millionaire who grew up poor, and Helen is fixated on keeping their daughter a virgin for as long as possible.

Sandra Dee and Troy Donahue holding hands in *A Summer Place*. The portrayal of young love and teen sexuality on screen was considered shocking at the time of the film's release. (John Springer Collection/Corbis via Getty Images)

Much of the tension in the film comes from arguments between Ken and Helen, who each have very different ideas of how to help their daughter understand and cope with her blossoming sexuality. Helen views Molly's physical development and interest in boys as a harbinger of doom that will destroy her morality. Ken wants his daughter to understand that her desires are a normal part of transitioning into adulthood. Helen can be viewed as a symbol of the 1950s with her obsession about keeping up appearances and always behaving in a ladylike manner. This, of course, adhered to the social customs of that decade, which relegated women to second-class status and defined their role as that of nurturers and domestic caretakers. Ken symbolized changing values and mores relative to the changing gender roles and emphasis on sexual liberation that would sweep across the county in the following decade.

In the film, Ken and Helen and Molly take a vacation to Pine Island off the coast of Maine. There, Bart and Sylvia Hunter (Arthur Kennedy and Dorothy McGuire), the owners of a decrepit inn, are financially struggling to stay afloat. Bart and Ken were childhood acquaintances when Ken was a lifeguard on the island as a teenager. Ken and Sylvia have a romantic past, but she ultimately rejected him because of his economic status at the time. Both of them ended up marrying for reasons other than love. Not too long after settling in at the inn, Ken and Sylvia rekindle their romance, knowing that it will ultimately be destructive to their respective families. To further complicate matters, the Hunters' son, Johnny (Troy Donahue), is immediately attracted to Molly. This, of course, is an example of history repeating itself as two potential mates are separated by issues of class and wealth.

The 1950s saw an explosion of what is now referred to as pulp novels. These were mass-produced paperbacks typically written by unknown authors and covering a wide variety of subjects. The one thing they all had in common were their outrageous titles and taglines. Examples include: *Love Fever*, *Shriek with Pleasure*, *Office Hussy*, and *Lesbo Wife*. Although *A Summer Place* is based on a mainstream novel, it is by today's standards quite melodramatic and even hyperbolic. A novel with this subject matter wouldn't have been as popular without the evolution of pulp fiction that preceded it. Those books weren't written or marketed as serious literature, but they contained adult story lines focused on sex, adultery, homosexuality, and other topics that were considered scandalous at the time. The popularity and financial success of these stories enabled books like *A Summer Place* and the equally salacious *Peyton Place* (1957) to be written and published by reputable book publishers. Because of the oppressive sexual norms of the decade, these types of books were largely regarded as "guilty pleasures" with little to any redeeming artistic value.

Both couples in the film eventually divorce. Molly becomes even more estranged from her mother after Helen forces her to endure a physical examination after spending the night with Johnny; Helen suspects that the teens had sex even though her daughter assures her they did not. The results of the exam prove that Molly has told the truth.

Johnny and Molly do end up having sex later, and Molly becomes pregnant. Even after the laborious efforts of trying to keep them apart, it becomes obvious to Helen that they are determined to be together, and, by the film's end, they are married. Ken and Sylvia, who are now reunited as well, offer support to the young couple. Bart is a bitter alcoholic who is hospitalized for his drinking by the end of the film and refuses to give his blessing.

The message of *A Summer Place* seems fairly obvious: although teens are expected to obey their parents, they will resist their demands and interference, especially when hypocrisy is involved. The film was a commercial success but received very mixed reviews from critics. The theme music from the film became a huge success in 1960 when Percy Faith rearranged and recorded it from the original score. "Theme from *A Summer Place*" reached the number one *Billboard* position and stayed there for nine consecutive weeks.

See also: 1960s: *Parent Trap, The*; 1970s: Blume, Judy; 1990s: McDaniel, Lurlene; 2000s: *Gossip Girl*

Further Reading

Lopez, Kristen. 2013. "A Summer Place." *Journeys in Classic Film,* May 24. https://journeysinclassicfilm.com/2013/05/24/a-summer-place-1959/.

Menard, Louis. 2013. "Pulp's Big Moment." *The New Yorker*, January 5. https://www.newyorker.com/magazine/2015/01/05/pulps-big-moment.

Sweeney, R. Emmet. 2013. "Heat Waves: A Summer Place." *Streamline,* July 23. http://streamline.filmstruck.com/2013/07/23/heat-waves-a-summer-place/.

Wilson, Sloan. 1958. *A Summer Place*. New York: Simon and Schuster.

The 1960s

DECADE OVERVIEW

The 1960s began on a hopeful note with the election of John F. Kennedy as president of the United States. His plan was one of unification and equality for all. Hoping to remedy the socioeconomic inequities of preceding decades, Kennedy spoke of a "New Frontier" that would be created via legislation aimed at establishing equal rights for minorities, both economically and socially.

In popular culture, the top-grossing film of 1960 was *Spartacus,* and the most popular book in the country was James Michener's sprawling saga, *Hawaii.* Of the top five watched television programs in that year, four of them were westerns—*The Andy Griffith Show,* ranked at number four, was the outlier. The top three spots on the Billboard record charts were occupied by the Kingston Trio, *The Sound of Music* cast recording, and "Theme from *A Summer Place.*"

The promises of President Kennedy stalled in late 1963 when he was assassinated. Replacing him as commander-in-chief was Lyndon B. Johnson, who moved quickly to enact Medicare in 1965. This important government program—which also included Medicaid—enabled elderly citizens over 65 years of age and poor families to qualify for federal health insurance.

The country experienced waves of protests and resistance from its citizenry in response to the racial and social injustices that were still endemic throughout the country. Student activists increased in number and took to the streets to demand change. This, in part, spurred the 1964 Civil Rights Act, which ended the common practice of segregation based on race. This landmark legislation was later extended in the Voting Rights Act of 1965.

Three civil rights icons were assassinated in 1968: Martin Luther King Jr., Malcolm X, and Robert F. Kennedy, brother to President John F. Kennedy. These losses devastated an already divided country. At the same time, intense debate about America's role in the Vietnam War continued to escalate; its impact on young people especially was significant. This is because many young people fought and died in the conflict. Many of those who fought came back wounded physically and mentally and were confronted with a hostile public that still questioned the legitimacy of the conflict. Many more died or went missing, presumably prisoners of war. Additionally, some young men evaded the draft by fleeing to Canada.

A youth counterculture evolved in the 1960s: hippies demonstrated their anger and disillusionment with the status quo by "dropping out" of society. Some formed communes where they lived with other like-minded individuals. A free love movement started that challenged traditional ideas about monogamy and commitment. Young people rebelled against parents, teachers, and other authority figures in acts of defiance. Casual drug usage escalated with an increasing number of people smoking marijuana. Psychedelic drugs such as LSD also became popular during this decade.

Another watershed moment happened at the end of the 1960s that changed the world of music: Woodstock. This infamous 1969 outdoor music festival in upstate New York drew more than 400,000 revelers who gathered together in a celebration of music, peace, and community. Its name would become part of the American lexicon and its symbolism inextricably linked to the decade of social protest.

Societal chaos and an ongoing fight for equality in this decade culminated in the Stonewall riots of 1969. After repeated harassment from law enforcement, a group of gay bar patrons fought back and a violent riot ensued. The aftermath of this spawned the development of gay activist organizations in New York City that fought for the basic civil rights of its LGBT community.

It is during this time of societal upheaval and change that young people came of age, and the pop culture of the era reflects many of the trials and tribulations teenagers faced. The entries in this section cover 26 of the books, movies, television shows, and musicians who simultaneously shaped and reflected the adolescent experience of the 1960s. As gender roles shifted and racial tension simmered, writers, bands, and actors documented it all.

Further Reading

Farber, David. 1994. *The Age of Great Dreams: America in the 1960s*. New York: Hill and Wang.

Gitlin, Todd. 1993. *The Sixties: Years of Hope, Days of Rage*. New York: Bantam Books.

Reilly, Edward J. 2003. *The 1960s: American Popular Culture through History*. Westport, CT: Greenwood Press.

Ward, Brian, ed. 2009. *The 1960s: A Documentary Reader*. Malden, MA: Wiley-Blackwell.

ADDAMS FAMILY, THE

The Addams Family only lasted for two seasons on network television, but its impact on popular culture is significant. The sitcom debuted in 1964 on ABC at the same time that *The Munsters* debuted on CBS. Both shows featured an unconventional family, most of whom appeared to have supernatural traits. Gomez (John Astin) and wife Morticia Addams (Carolyn Jones) are a loving couple and nurturing parents to their children Wednesday (Lisa Loring) and Pugsley (Ken Weatherwax). Gomez is wealthy and very attentive to his wife. Morticia has a very calm demeanor and dresses all in black. She has the ability to light candles with her fingertips and sometimes emits smoke from her body. Neither Wednesday nor Pugsley explicitly demonstrate supernatural powers, but they have bizarre hobbies such as raising spiders as pets and playing with dangerous fireworks. Other characters include Uncle Fester (Jackie Coogan) and Grandma (Blossom Rock). Their servant Lurch (Ted Cassidy) and cousin Itt (Felix Silla) add to the bizarre family dynamic. The

Addams Family source material comes from a series of black and white cartoons by illustrator Charles Addams. They were featured in the *New Yorker* magazine.

The impetus for a show like *The Addams Family* can be traced to the explosion of cheaply made horror films from the 1950s. After the real-life horrors of World War II had ended, they made their way into our collective subconscious through the creation of monster movies. These films usually had shoddy production values and rarely featured recognizable film stars, but they appealed to teenagers and typically made a profit due to their low production costs. The source of terror in these movies ranged from the familiar (*Dracula* and *Frankenstein*) to the unfamiliar (*Creature from the Black Lagoon* and *The Thing from Another Planet*). The films that focused on mutations and science run amok stemmed from real-life events such as the creation and use of the atomic bomb and also from a Communist threat that pervaded the American psyche after the end of World War II.

The source of humor in the show comes from interactions of the family with outsiders. Invariably someone would enter the Addams home under some pretense and become traumatized after exposure to them. The end result was the visitor many times fleeing the country, switching professions, or even being admitted to a psychiatric clinic for treatment. The Addams were usually baffled by reactions from others since they viewed themselves as quite normal and their lives as uneventful.

This same story line played out on *The Munsters*. That show was helmed by married couple Herman Munster (Fred Gwynne) and Lily Munster (Yvonne De Carlo). The Munsters resided at 1313 Mockingbird Lane, and the family included son Eddie Munster (Butch Patrick), Grandpa (Al Lewis), and niece Marilyn (Beverley Owen and Pat Priest).

As with the Addams, the Munsters were nonthreatening and didn't harm others. Interlopers would often attempt to infiltrate their home or lives and were met with disastrous consequences. Herman Munster's physical appearance resembled that of Frankenstein, and Lily and Grandpa appeared more as classic vampires. Eddie resembled a werewolf and even carried a doll named Woof Woof that looked like the classic movie werewolf. Marilyn was the "normal" family member on the show. She was physically attractive but was convinced by Lily and the others that she was odd and needed to be more like them. A running gag on the show was Marilyn meeting a young man and then inviting him to her home to meet the family. He, of course, would become terrified after encountering them and would quickly escape. Marilyn would be despondent after this, and Lily would express sadness that Marilyn had once again scared another potential suitor away.

The Addams Family was adapted into a 1991 theatrical film. The plot centered on the efforts of a con man to swindle the family out of their money. It was a box office success and also received mostly favorable reviews. The sequel *Addams Family Values* was released in 1994 and played up the role of Wednesday (Christina Ricci) in a subplot featuring her nonconformist behavior at Camp Chippewa. She and brother Pugsley (Jimmy Workman) are mocked by both fellow campers and the overbearing married couple that run the camp. The main plot features murderous nanny Debbie (Joan Cusack) who is out to marry and then murder Uncle Fester (Christopher Lloyd) for his money.

A musical version of *The Addams Family* debuted on Broadway in 2010 after a premier in Chicago, Illinois. It won both a Drama League Award and Drama Desk Award. Nathan Lane and Bebe Neuwirth played the roles of Gomez and Morticia in the original Broadway version. *The Addams Family* was a short-lived television series, but its popularity and staying power is evidenced by the success of both the theatrical and the live stage reboots the show has prompted.

See also: 1950s: *I Was a Teenage Werewolf*; 1990s: *Buffy the Vampire Slayer*; *Charmed*; *Harry Potter*; 2000s: *Twilight*; *Vampire Diaries, The*

Further Reading

Blevins, Joe. 2016. "50 Years Ago Today, *The Addams Family* Lurched Off TV Forever." *AV Club*, April 8. https://news.avclub.com/50-years-ago-today-the-addams-family -lurched-off-tv-fo-1798246156.

Cardin, Matt, ed. 2017. *Horror Literature through History: An Encyclopedia of the Stories That Speak to Our Deepest Fears*. Santa Barbara, CA: Greenwood Press.

Chilton, Martin. 2014. "The Addams Family v The Munsters." *The Telegraph*, December 9. http://www.telegraph.co.uk/culture/tvandradio/11102649/The-Addams-Family-v -The-Munsters.html.

BEACH BOYS, THE

In contrast to the British Invasion of the 1960s, the arrival of the Beach Boys to the American music scene in 1962 served as a reminder that there was still ample room in the pop cultural landscape for this homegrown West Coast band with enormous appeal. Perhaps no other band in modern history embodied the California lifestyle of the 1960s more than the Beach Boys. Their early songs and biggest hits focused on elements of a distinctive American teenage dream that included surfing, driving fast cars, and, of course, teen romance and longing at its most basic level. Although only one of the founding band members (Dennis) surfed on a regular basis, the group embraced and embodied the surfer lifestyle in a series of hit songs that include "Surfin' Safari," "Surfin' USA," and "Surfer Girl."

Founding members of the band were three brothers: Brian (lead vocals and bass guitar), Carl (guitar), and Dennis Wilson (drums), along with cousin Mike Love (vocals) and childhood friend Al Jardine (guitar). Although the band became more innovative and experimental as their careers progressed, initially they were reminiscent of earlier all-male bands of the 1950s, focusing on smooth harmonies and guitar riffs as centerpieces of their work.

As with most bands, a leader soon emerged. Brian Wilson quickly became the artistic soul of the band and is largely responsible for much of its success. He is credited with penning most of their hit songs and also for taking risks in the studio as he voiced his desire to take the band further artistically with new sounds and approaches to music. In terms of top hit songs written between 1963 and 1966, Wilson is in third place, right after John Lennon and Paul McCartney.

The band's most ambitious record was released in 1966 to mixed results. *Pet Sounds* produced only three Top 40 hits (fewer than their previous releases) and only achieved "gold status" 30 years after its release. In terms of its musical significance and legacy, however, it's important to note that Paul McCartney and a producer of the Beatles mentioned years later in an interview how *Pet Sounds* influenced their album *Sgt. Pepper's Lonely Hearts Club Band*.

The lyrics of many of the Beach Boys songs appear on the surface to deal with frivolity, especially the frivolity of youth. Although this may be true to an extent with their first few hits and albums, *Pet Sounds* doesn't contain even one song that references surfing or racing cars. It's no coincidence that the album is now considered a classic and arguably the best musical effort put forth by the band, largely due to Brian Wilson's innovation and risk taking with respect to both the songwriting and the production. Even in what is considered some of their most commercial songs, there is an underlying wistfulness, even sadness, to the lyrics. In the song "In My Room," the singer refers to a room where he can go and hide away from all of his worries and fears. There are references to darkness and being alone that seem remarkably different from the carefree activity celebrated in the surfing songs.

Although the band continued to record music and tour, the 1970s failed to yield any significant hits. The 1980s were largely filled with professional disappointments as well, with one notable exception: the song "Kokomo" from the Tom Cruise hit movie *Cocktail* (1988). The song climbed to number three on the Billboard charts and ultimately became the group's biggest selling single ever.

As with many creative individuals, Brian Wilson's personal life was far from ideal. His father was both physically and mentally abusive to him as a child. In the late 1960s and into the early 1970s, Wilson largely withdrew from the public and isolated himself in an attempt to do more writing and producing.

Incidents involving Wilson and therapist Eugene Landy during the 1980s are detailed in the 2015 film *Love & Mercy*. The film chronicles both childhood and adult experiences of Wilson, but much of the emphasis is on the controlling nature of the relationship of the doctor over the musician and how this impacted both his professional and personal life.

Band member changes due to illnesses and personal issues hampered the group significantly in the 1990s and beyond. Many of their record releases in the early 2000s were reissues of previously recorded material.

The Beach Boys hold the Billboard/Nielsen Soundscan record for top-selling American bands for both singles and albums. They were inducted into the Rock-and-Roll Hall of Fame in 1988, and in 2001, the group received a Grammy Lifetime Achievement Award. Their songs have been used to solid effect in Hollywood films including *American Graffiti* (1973), *Teen Wolf* (1985), and *Boogie Nights* (1997). Brian Wilson shocked many by touring to celebrate the 50th anniversary of the release of *Pet Sounds*. He added many dates to his calendar in 2017, thrilling long-time fans of his and the band.

See also: 1950s: Boone, Pat; Darin, Bobby; Presley, Elvis; 1960s: Beatles, The; Monkees, The; Rolling Stones, The; 1970s: *American Graffiti*; Bee Gees, The; Led Zeppelin; Osmonds, The; Queen; 1980s: Blondie; 1990s: Backstreet Boys; Spice Girls

Further Reading

Morgan, Johnny. 2015. *The Beach Boys: America's Band*. New York: Sterling.

Unterberger, Andrew. 2016. "The Beach Boys' 'Good Vibrations' at 50: A Masterpiece of Emotion as Much as Science." Billboard, October 10. https://www.billboard.com/articles/columns/pop/7534270/beach-boys-good-vibrations-50th-anniversary.

Wilson, Brian. *Wouldn't It Be Nice: My Own Story*. New York: HarperCollins.

Wilson, Carl. 2015. "The Beach Boys' Brian Wilson: America's Mozart?" *BBC*, June 9. http://www.bbc.com/culture/story/20150608-is-this-americas-mozart.

BEATLES, THE

No other musical group in history is more well-known than the Beatles. The band comprises John Lennon (1940–1980), Paul McCartney (1942–), George Harrison (1943–2001), and Richard Starkey, better known as Ringo Starr (1940–). The names of the members, their song titles, and lyrics of most of their songs are instantly recognizable by a large portion of the Western population. The Beatles enjoyed unprecedented success when they burst onto the U.S. musical scene in 1964 with an appearance on *The Ed Sullivan Show*. Although the group already had a number one single here with "I Wanna Hold Your Hand," their guest spot on this TV show catapulted them into superstardom. Already a modest success in the United Kingdom, the Beatles' Western popularity was uncanny in both its breadth and depth.

Their early songs appeared to be "safe," and were aimed primarily at a young female audience. Catchy lyrics accompanied with a fast tempo, these songs caused throngs of young girls to swoon at the band at live concerts—and, of course, to buy lots of records. The level of their popularity was so impressive that the term "Beatlemania" was coined. Hordes of young fans, mainly female, gravitated toward the band with unprecedented fervor. Their appearances on the *Ed Sullivan Show* are iconic, featuring images of young girls crying and screaming while the group performed. Merchandising of the band became a cottage industry with everything from T-shirts to hats to cookies being peddled to eager fans.

The Beatles of this early period were sexually nonthreatening. Unlike Elvis and some other popular entertainers, the four young men dressed conservatively in suits and ties and had androgynous hairstyles. Parents worried less about their influence on their daughters than they did about more overtly sexual entertainers.

Recreational drug usage and Eastern influences changed the direction of their music. But because of their talent, originality, and ability to be technically innovative, their young fans went along for the ride. They even gained new fans as the music took a more analytical and reflective route than it did before. Their appearances changed during this time as well. No longer the clean-cut boys from Liverpool, England, the members adopted colorful wardrobes and hairstyles that were more in line with the culture of the mid-to-late 1960s.

Rejecting the standard path that many pop bands took at that time, the Beatles began writing and recording their own songs in favor of recording songs written by other artists. Members Paul McCartney and John Lennon penned most of these songs, although there was and continues to be some debate about who wrote what when the band was still together.

The release of the album *Rubber Soul* in 1965 marked a clear change in direction for the group. Although still wildly popular, the toll of touring and several high-profile media controversies prompted the group to stop officially touring in 1966. Their studio success continued unabated. Complex arrangements and musical experimentation propelled them to create critically heralded albums such as *Sgt. Pepper's Lonely Hearts Club Band* and *The White Album*. Internal struggles within the band eroded their cohesion, and, in 1970, the Beatles officially broke up and went their separate ways.

Although the casual listener may only be aware of the Beatles through their more commercially popular songs, their legions of fans are intimately familiar with most or all of their songs. Specifically, casual listeners may recognize some of their more lighthearted work, such as "Yellow Submarine," "I Wanna Hold Your Hand," or even songs with more reflective lyrics such as "Let It Be" or "The Long and Winding Road."

The Beatles transcended the pop music genre. It's evident from the shift in their music starting with *Rubber Soul* that they embraced the evolution of being artists, and all of the growth and change that implies. They experimented with new sounds (most notably the sitar, a musical instrument that George Harrison became interested in while studying and traveling in the East) and created memorable songs and images that still seem fresh today.

The longevity and undying popularity of the group is evidenced by the 2016 Ron Howard documentary, *Eight Days a Week*. The film focuses on the early days of the Fab Four, concentrating on their skyrocketing fame within the United States, their iconic appearance on the *Ed Sullivan Show*, and the mania unleashed by female fans during U.S. concerts.

Sadly, John Lennon was murdered outside of his New York City apartment in 1980. George Harrison died from cancer in 2001.

Ringo Starr continues to record music and released an album in 2015. Paul McCartney continues to record albums and does concert tours.

See also: 1950s: Boone, Pat; Darin, Bobby; Presley, Elvis; 1960s: Beach Boys, The; Monkees, The; Rolling Stones, The; 1970s: Bee Gees, The; Clash, The; Led Zeppelin; Osmonds, The; Queen; 1980s: Blondie; 1990s: Backstreet Boys; Green Day; Nirvana; Smashing Pumpkins, The; Spice Girls; 2000s: My Chemical Romance

Further Reading

Burrows, Terry. 2017. *The Beatles: The Band That Changed the World.* London: Carlton.
Guesdon, Jean-Michel, and Philippe Margotin. 2013. *All the Songs: The Story behind Every Beatles Release.* New York: Black Dog and Leventhal.

Miguel, Luis, et al. 2016. *The Long and Winding Road: The Greatest Beatles Story Ever Told.* Toronto, Canada: Fanreads.

Sheffield, Rob. 2015. "50 Years of 'Rubber Soul': How the Beatles Invented the Future of Pop." *Rolling Stone,* December 3.

BELL JAR, THE

The Bell Jar, a harrowing novel of a woman's spiral into depression, is the only novel ever written by poet/author Sylvia Plath (1932–1963). Originally released in 1963 under a pseudonym (primarily in order to protect, and not hurt, her parents), the novel was rereleased in 1966 under her real name to great acclaim and has become a literary classic. The novel deals with a young woman's attempts at independence in patriarchal 1950s society and her dissent into mental illness. Based largely on Plath's own life events, the book examines the detrimental effects of a culture that forces stereotypical gender roles onto women—especially young women—and then punishes them when they refuse to accept those predetermined paths and seek something more meaningful.

The novel's protagonist, Esther Greenwood, is completing an internship at a popular women's magazine called *Ladies' Day*. She has always been an exemplary student and is hoping this may lead to a career in writing or journalism. She is also hoping for another scholarly opportunity that involves a prestigious writing program, but on a return trip home she discovers she wasn't accepted into that program. Feeling both societal and family pressure to conform to the status quo by either finding a suitable man to marry or accepting unrewarding work as a way to be financially independent, Esther becomes depressed. Her depression worsens and her mother arranges psychiatric treatment. Esther's therapist is shallow and self-absorbed. After the doctor administers electroconvulsive therapy (ECT), Esther refuses to continue seeing him.

Plath's life partially paralleled that of her literary character. Plath completed an internship with *Mademoiselle* in 1953. Just as her character was disillusioned with the experience and disheartened with career aspects of merit for young women at that time, Plath experienced clinical depression throughout her brief adult life. Other connections between Plath's life and Esther's include their East Coast origins and suicide attempts.

An interesting aspect of the novel and of Plath's own personal experience involves the nature of internships. Although these are common nowadays and often provide college students with an opportunity to gain valuable experience within the workplace, the history of this generates troubling insight into labor practices. Magazines in the 1950s and 1960s were dominated by men. Female employees largely performed subservient or support roles, for instance, as secretaries and clerks. Management was exclusively white men. Although several high-profile class action lawsuits against publishers would come almost two decades after Plath's internship experience, women had to fight for both pay and position parity.

The temporary position that Plath enjoyed at *Mademoiselle* was somewhat prestigious in that she was given a guest editorship. This allowed her to gain some experience managing deadlines and other authors, but more importantly, it allowed her to have some of her writing featured in the publication. Plath apparently realized how fortunate she was in her temporary role, but she also might have seen how difficult a career position would be to obtain and keep in a male-dominated profession.

Another troubling element of women's magazines during the time that Plath worked for *Mademoiselle* was mixed media messages. Examining articles from this time period proves a puzzling and perplexing exercise in inconsistencies and even contradictions. The tagline for the publication was "the magazine for smart young women." However, it was not uncommon to run stories encouraging women to attend college or travel the world right alongside articles or advertisements that stressed the importance of family over career or the inherent pitfalls of choosing work over domesticity. What message is communicated to women when placement of ads about finding the right bra or selecting the perfect china pattern pepper a magazine that claims to celebrate women's choices and opportunities? How are women supposed to differentiate and navigate these seemingly conflicted narratives? Is this simply inherent in publications that largely depend on advertising dollars to operate?

Several noted scholars feel that Plath's internship significantly influenced the views and experiences she communicates through Esther in *The Bell Jar*. The character in the novel is conflicted about the "proper" way for a young woman to behave. It's never clear what path is the right one for her. This directly corresponds to both explicit and implicit media messages within some of these women's magazines, specifically *Mademoiselle*. It's noteworthy that many of these same mixed messages exist in some publications today that are aimed at younger women.

The ending of *The Bell Jar* is cautiously optimistic as Esther finds comfort in a new female therapist, Dr. Nolan, who administers doses of insulin as well as ECT—but this time, it's administered properly. Her life changes and she appears to be ready to leave the psychiatric hospital, where she has been staying, at the story's conclusion.

Sylvia Plath committed suicide in 1963. *The Bell Jar* has been a mainstay of high school literature courses for decades and was adapted to film in 1979. The movie was neither a commercial nor a critical success. Actress Kirsten Dunst announced plans to make her directorial debut with an adaptation of the novel for a 2018 scheduled release.

See also: 1950s: *Catcher in the Rye, The*; 1970s: *Go Ask Alice*

Further Reading

Latson, Jennifer. 2015. "Why Some Blamed Poetry for Sylvia Plath's Death." *Time*, February 11. http://time.com/3695332/sylvia-plath-blame/.

McLaren, Leah. 2013. "Plath's Bell Jar, 50 Years On: A Powerful Look at Mental Illness." *The Globe and Mail*, February 8. https://www.theglobeandmail.com/arts/books-and-media/plaths-bell-jar-50-years-on-a-powerful-look-at-mental-illness/article8385163/.

Plath, Sylvia. 1963. *The Bell Jar*. Portsmouth: Heinemann.

Plath, Sylvia, and Karen V. Kukil, ed. 2000. *The Unabridged Journals of Sylvia Plath*. New York: Anchor Books.

BEVERLY HILLBILLIES, THE

The Beverly Hillbillies (1962–1971) followed the misadventures of the Clampett family as they are transplanted from the poverty of a rural existence into the glamorous setting of Beverly Hills, California. Patriarch Jed Clampett becomes a millionaire when he sells swampland that is rich with untapped oil to a petroleum company. After much coercion from a relative, he uproots and moves his family to the land of "swimming pools and movie stars." Most of the humor from the series relies on the culture clash between the Clampetts and the various wealthy individuals with whom they have contact. The antagonist of the show is Mr. Drysdale (Raymond Bailey), the family's banker. His sole purpose as a character is to retain the Clampett's money in his financial institution. He is kept in check many times by his conflicted assistant, Jane Hathaway (Nancy Kulp). She abides by her boss's demands, but she frequently gets frustrated with his greedy machinations and often resolves conflicts for him with little to any display of gratitude.

The term "hillbilly" has its roots in rural America, specifically within the Appalachia area and the Ozarks. Hillbillies were economically deprived individuals who struggled to keep up with advancements in technology and social progress in other areas of the country after the Civil War. In an effort to improve their financial status, many hillbillies relocated to industrialized cities to find work and keep their families intact. Today, the modern connotation of the hillbilly is primarily a negative one. Although they are attributed with traits such as perseverance and independence, they are also viewed with disdain and mistrust. They are often perceived as being direct and lacking social skills in their interactions with others.

The Beverly Hillbillies played on these beliefs and capitalized on their comedic potential. The show played with the "rags to riches" myth by introducing a group of unsophisticated and uneducated individuals and plopping them down in the epicenter of wealth and luxury. What they lacked in etiquette they compensated for in common sense and strong personal values such as honesty and fairness.

For a show like this to work, it has to operate successfully on several levels. Of course, it must be humorous since it's a situational comedy. More importantly, though, that humor derives from the audience's buy-in to existing stereotypes and myths. The viewer must believe that certain beliefs and behaviors are authentic on the part of the characters. This relies on preexisting knowledge and acceptance of cultural stereotypes.

Jed Clampett (Buddy Ebsen) is depicted as a very simple man who deals with individuals honestly and expects the same in return. Although wary of his newfound wealth and all of the complications it brings, he attempts to make the best of the situation.

Granny Clampett/Daisy May (Irene Ryan) is Jed's mother-in-law. She is loud and opinionated and intensely dislikes pretentiousness and dishonesty. She frequently is seen cooking "vittles" in the kitchen and also has an affinity for her shotgun, which she uses in several episodes when she feels threatened or is extremely agitated. She has an inherent distrust of authority and governmental institutions. Since Jed's wife in the show is deceased, Granny assumes the role of matriarch and a motherly figure who oversees many of the domestic chores within the home.

Elly Mae Clampett (Donna Douglas) is Jed's daughter. She is physically attractive and loves caring for animals. Portrayed as

Cast of the TV sitcom, *The Beverly Hillbillies*. The show capitalized on the inherent distrust between the "haves" and the "have nots" and frequently portrayed the "backwards" country clan as more sensible than their "big city" counterparts. (CBS/Courtesy of Getty Images)

a tomboy, Elly Mae is often pursued by young Hollywood actors. Perpetuating female stereotypes, Elly Mae is often on the receiving end of jokes about her poor culinary skills. The implication is that she should excel at this because she is a woman, and when she fails at this, her overall worth is discounted.

Jethro Bodine (Max Baer Jr.) is Jed's cousin. The running gag with Jethro is his dimwitted persona and inability to be successful in any number of jobs that he takes on; this runs the gamut from telephone lineman to sculptor to restaurant owner. He also struggles with making romantic connections with women. Miss Hathaway has personal feelings for Jethro, but nothing ever transpires between the two of them.

Mrs. Drysdale (Harriet E. MacGibbon) abhors the Clampetts and all that they represent. She especially detests Granny, and they frequently battle on the show. She and her husband are meant to symbolize the shallow and money-hungry culture of Beverly Hills. They are frequently outwitted by the Clampetts much to their dismay.

The Beverly Hillbillies was a smash hit for CBS. It was in the top 20 Nielsen ranked shows for every one of its seasons but the last. A made-for-television movie aired in 1981: *Return of the Beverly Hillbillies*. It was produced by the show's original creator. A theatrical version of the show was released in 1993 and starred Jim Varney as Jed Clampett. The house that was used to portray the Clampett mansion is located in the Bel-Air area of California. It went up for sale in 2017, and listed at $350 million. At the time, it was the most expensive house listing in the United States.

See also: 1950s: *I Love Lucy; Leave It to Beaver*

Further Reading

Greene, Doyle. 2007. *Politics and the American Television Comedy: A Critical Survey from* I Love Lucy *through* South Park. Jefferson, NC: McFarland.

Gross, Matt. 2017. "'Beverly Hillbillies' Mansion Is Priciest in U.S. at $350 Million." *Seattle Times*, August 9. https://www.seattletimes.com/business/real-estate/beverly-hillbillies -mansion-is-priciest-in-us-at-350-million/.

Harkins, Anthony. 2004. *Hillbilly: A Cultural History of an American Icon*. Oxford: Oxford University Press.

CATCH-22

Catch-22 (1961), a huge critical and commercial success by author Joseph Heller (1923–1999), is considered a classic American novel and was named, by *Time, Newsweek,* and *The London Observer*, one of the best novels ever written. Not many novels have such an impact on popular culture that they originate a term that becomes embedded within our daily vernacular. *Catch-22* is defined as "a frustrating situation in which one is trapped by contradictory regulations or conditions." The book's protagonist, John Yossarian, is a U.S. Air Force bombardier stationed in a fictionalized island in the Mediterranean during World War II. Although the book starts off in 1944, the timeline is not linear, and the reader follows Yossarian through a series of events that ultimately lead him to the inescapable resolution that war truly is hell.

Even though the work is largely viewed as satire, the tone—especially in the last two-thirds of the novel—turns somber as the lead character sees several fellow soldiers killed in combat. Throughout the story, Yossarian witnesses not just the brutality of combat but also the structural incompetency and self-serving interest of leadership within the armed forces. The novel is antiwar and can be viewed primarily as a form of protest literature. *Catch-22* connected with young readers in part because of this. Many teenagers question authority, and a book that criticizes a government's war efforts and portrays the experiences of a soldier in this manner resonates with young readers; it reflects many of the same concerns and issues they may feel toward the subject matter.

The turning point of the novel occurs when Yossarian finally recovers the full memory of seeing fellow bombardier Snowden dying. Throughout the book, Yossarian remembers fragments of the death, but it isn't until near the end that he remembers it completely and then acts on it. This recovered memory is as important to the reader as it is to the character. This subject of trauma relates to Sigmund Freud's studies on the topic. He believed that trauma survivors relive damaging events (or parts of them) over and over until something finally triggers them into action. Yossarian experiences revulsion once he can see Snowden's death fully and within context; he is then able to process all of the other events of the book in relation to this and make a conscious decision that he will not be part of the machinery of war.

Though the book was published in the 1960s, it was written during the 1950s. This is key to understanding some of the themes and observations put forth by the protagonist. The 1950s was marred by a patriotic fervor fueled by rising anti-Communist sentiment. Much of this was orchestrated by Senator Joseph McCarthy, a congressman who accused sitting members of Congress and many in the entertainment business of being secretly aligned with the Russian enemy. These accusations triggered hearings within Congress, and many individuals' lives and careers were seriously damaged or even ruined, all due to conjecture and faulty assumptions.

At least one interpretation of the novel compares Yossarian's journey to that of Dante's in Hell. Yossarian for much of the book is unaffected directly by what unfolds around him. The brutality, cruelty, and violence that has become commonplace in his environment also seems and feels exterior. But when he ventures into Rome to try and save the life of a young girl, he is plunged into an underworld that is all too real. He witnesses cruelty against both humans and animals and sees a weary resignation in civilians who have given up hope for a peaceful and safe existence. Although he physically survives this expedition, it depletes his soul and leaves him numb.

Much debate surrounds the book relative to its central theme. Is it antiwar? Anti-God? Both? There is an argument to be made that the scope exceeds that of antiwar. The atrocities seen by Yossarian seem irreconcilable to those who claim that an all-knowing and (more importantly) all-loving God can allow them to happen.

As with most media messages, much insight can be gained from the creator and his or her background. Heller grew up in an immigrant household in Brooklyn, New York. After high school, he began doing government work that eventually led to his enlistment into the Air Force as a bombardier. After flying approximately 60 missions, he left the military and took advantage of the GI Bill, obtaining a college degree. He published some short stories prior to the release of *Catch-22*, but it was this novel that eventually catapulted him to fame and worldwide recognition within literature.

The novel was adapted to film in 1970 and directed by Mike Nichols (1931–2014). It received mixed reviews and failed to garner any noteworthy awards. In his review of the movie, film critic Roger Ebert lambasted the lazy approach of telling the complex story in overly simple and clichéd terms. Ebert admits that taking a widely acclaimed novel like this and translating it on the screen is fraught with potential disaster. But he felt the director played it safe and simply made yet another war movie that lulled viewers in with laughs, and then viciously turned the tables on them with violence and gore designed to hammer home the message that war is hell.

See also: 1950s: *From Here to Eternity*; 1960s: *Clockwork Orange, A*; *Slaughterhouse-Five*; 1970s: *Six Million Dollar Man, The*

Further Reading

Daugherty, Tracy. 2011. *Just One Catch. A Biography of Joseph Heller.* New York: St. Martin's Press.

Heller, Joseph. 1961. *Catch-22.* New York: Simon and Schuster.

Neary, Lynn. 2011. "'Catch-22': A Paradox Turns 50 and Still Rings True." *NPR*, October 13. https://www.npr.org/2011/10/13/141280833/catch-22-a-paradox-turns-50-and-still -rings-true.

CLOCKWORK ORANGE, A

Given the excessive violence permeating films, books, and TV shows currently, it's difficult to imagine that a novel written more than 50 years ago by Anthony Burgess (1917–1993) contains imagery and ideas that still have the potential to shock (to some degree) some readers unfamiliar with its content. *A Clockwork Orange* (1962) tells the story of a violent teenager named Alex. He and his friends spend their evenings assaulting strangers, gang raping women, and wreaking havoc on the general population where they live. The story takes place in England and is divided into three sections: (1) Alex's World, (2) The Ludovico Technique, (3) After Prison.

Alex and his three young companions Georgie, Pete, and Dim commit criminal acts on a routine basis. Before setting out on their nightly missions, the trio hangs out at the Korova Milk Bar, where hallucinogenic drugs are mixed with milk and served to patrons. The drugs heighten the thrill of the violence, but Alex and his cohorts show little to no morality or conscience even when they are not in a chemically altered state. The apathy among these characters taps into the disillusionment and dissatisfaction felt by many youth.

After one particular home invasion and attack where their victim dies after sustaining serious injuries, Alex is betrayed by his colleagues and ends up in police custody. In prison, Alex commits yet another violent attack and is selected for an experiment that uses the Ludovico Technique. This method of rehabilitation forces the offender to watch ultraviolent images while nausea-inducing drugs are administered to him. Posttherapy, Alex is physically confronted by someone, and, rather than retaliate, the very notion of violence causes him to collapse and remain passive. This is viewed as a tremendous success by the authorities in the government who sanctioned the experiment, and Alex is deemed worthy of release into society.

It's important to note that Alex has been failed by the family support system. His parents do not provide the guidance, love, and security that is required to set positive examples for children while they develop their sense of self. Alex supplants his biological family with his friends. On the surface, there seems to be a bond among them—albeit one based on warped values and disregard for the welfare of others. When they betray him later, Alex then becomes the ward of the state.

The authoritarianism displayed in prison is anything but nurturing, but those in charge feel that they have finally "cured" Alex of his affliction.

When Stanley Kubrick (1928–1999) directed the film adaptation of Burgess's novel, one of the most notable changes—or additions to be precise—in the film was the set design or decor featured in the interiors. In the novel, most of Alex's narration focuses on action as opposed to detailed descriptions of objects. But, in the film, visuals are conspicuous. More specifically, works of art are featured in several of the violent scenes where attacks and rapes occur. In the home invasion scene, the occupant is killed with a piece of art—it is literally used as a weapon against her.

Scholars have made several different interpretations of the display of art and its importance to the film. Some believe it was to show the contrast between the beauty of art and the ugliness of violence. Others, however, believe that Kubrick was making

English writer Anthony Burgess wrote more than fifty books, including the modern classic novel *A Clockwork Orange*. The book was brought to the screen by director Stanley Kubrick in 1971. (Sophie Bassouls/Sygma via Getty Images)

an oppositional statement: that art and violence both come from the same place. Both are expressions of individuality and of a need to challenge the status quo. This theory creates even more discomfort for those offended by the actual violence and amoral behavior of the protagonist in the film because this viewpoint makes the viewer ask difficult questions about motives, ego, and baser instincts.

Even Alex's love of classical music (art) is linked with violence when his favorite composition—Beethoven's Fifth Symphony—is played during the horrific images shown to him during implementation of the Ludovico Technique. Pictures of Nazis and their brutal acts are predominant during his "treatment." The theme of government control over its citizens is one that often connects with teens as they rebel against institutions of authority during this life stage.

The book and film examine violence and its embrace by young men as a tool of power. The sadistic exploits of the gang reinforce notions of testosterone-fueled aggression and the tendency toward destructive behavior exhibited by these individuals.

The third section of the novel focuses on Alex's transition back into society. In the pre-1986 American edition and in Kubrick's film adaptation, the story ends on a dark note as Alex pretends that he has been cured after a botched suicide attempt, but, in reality, his violent yearnings remain. The American edition of the novel that was rereleased after 1986 contains the original final chapter in which Alex finds redemption and longs for a normal life. Many critics including Kubrick found that ending incompatible and unrealistic.

The overriding theme of free choice permeates the story. Even though Alex exists within a dysfunctional universe, he makes conscious choices to act out in violent and destructive ways. The gift and power of free choice is taken away from him by the government after his treatment. Ironically, the one thing that apparently brings him pleasure—classical music—now coexists with the aversion to violence and nauseates and repels him.

The novel was banned from at least two American schools and removed from two libraries due to "objectionable language." It appears on the *Guardian's* list of the Top 100 Best Novels and also was selected by *Time* magazine as one of the 100 best English-language books released between 1923 and 2005. The 1971 film was nominated for four Academy Awards, including nods to Kubrick for both direction and screenplay adaptation. It also received three Golden Globe nominations, including one for Malcolm McDowell for Best Actor.

See also: 1950s: *Naked Lunch*; 1960s: *Catch-22*; *Outsiders, The*; 1990s: *Kids*

Further Reading

Amis, Martin. 2012. "The Shock of the New 'A Clockwork Orange' at 50." *New York Times*, August 31. http://www.nytimes.com/2012/09/02/books/review/a-clockwork-orange -at-50.html.

Burgess, Anthony. 1962. *A Clockwork Orange*. London: Heinemann.

Robey, Tim. 2016. "A Clockwork Orange: The Look That Shook the Nation." *The Nation*, February 3. http://www.telegraph.co.uk/film/what-to-watch/a-clockwork-orange -stanley-kubrick-controversy/.

DOORS, THE

American rock band the Doors is as synonymous as Janis Joplin and Jimi Hendrix with the counterculture of the 1960s. The band consisted of vocalist Jim Morrison (1943–1971), keyboardist Ray Manzarek (1939–2013), guitarist Robby Krieger (1946–), and drummer John Densmore (1944–). Lead singer Morrison quickly gained attention as the sensual and sensitive band member. He generated significant controversy with his onstage antics that included overtly sexual movements and several tense encounters with police during concerts.

The group's self-titled debut album was a success, but it wasn't due to the original single that was released. "Break on Through" was expected to become a hit single, but it failed to connect with listeners. A second single was released, "Light My Fire." It reached number one on the Billboard chart and sold a million copies. They performed on several TV variety shows to promote the album and toured a variety of clubs.

Jim Morrison had been anointed a sex symbol shortly after the release of the band's debut album. The media, especially female reporters, routinely made references to his physicality and appearance. Morrison was well aware how important image was to the success of a band, and he utilized that as a way to promote the Doors. Print references to him included "King of Orgasmic Rock" and "leather tiger." There were several photo shoots done by professional photographers Gloria Stavers and Joel Brodsky that further cemented his sex symbol status, and he appeared in several teen magazines that played up his appeal to young girls.

The attention to Morrison's slim physique and sexual allure helped to perpetuate the sex symbol status and later added to the mythic figure that he would become after his death in 1971 at the age of 27. Morrison's signature look consisted of tight leather pants, no shirt, and thick, wavy hair. Many young men at the time wore their hair longer, and, although some of this was for style, much of it was a political statement against cultural norms relative to male appearance. Long hair on men was also viewed many times as a statement against the Vietnam War and military rigidity and rules in general.

Of course, there was also the music. The lyrics of many of the group's songs are steeped in mystery and seduction, such as the second verse of "Light My Fire" which proclaims, "Try now we can only lose / and our love become a funeral pyre." Morrison was a poet and found inspiration from the works of Arthur Rimbaud, a French poet who heavily influenced modern literature. Rimbaud was also a libertine; he placed heavy importance upon the pleasures of the senses and didn't feel bound to societal customs or norms with respect to sexuality or monogamy. Given Morrison's reputation as being sexually promiscuous and his reluctance to marry or strive for conventional romantic relationships with any number of women he met, this affinity for the French poet and his worldview makes sense.

Morrison has the notoriety of being the first rock singer ever arrested by police during a concert. Prior to going onstage in New Haven, Connecticut, he was allegedly maced by an officer for refusing to vacate an area. During the performance, he began singing a stream of consciousness song about the experience, hurling profanities at the law enforcement officers surrounding the stage for his and the band's protection. He was dragged offstage and arrested on charges of public indecency, although charges were later dropped due to insufficient evidence. Another fiasco followed in 1968 when Morrison was again arrested during a performance for lewd behavior that included simulated masturbation. His disdain for institutional authority was well known and documented and resonated with his young fans, both male and female.

Even though specific events like the Vietnam War were happening during this time, Morrison was never overtly political. He never proclaimed allegiance to a particular political party or candidate, but, in many of his lyrics, he expressed global concerns about the integrity of the planet and the harm done to others by evil men. His rebellious reputation seemed more rooted in his sexual confidence and defiance of authority figures and institutions.

Morrison had an interest in mysticism, which can be traced to a car accident he witnessed when he was four years old; a truck carrying Native Americans had overturned on the road. As he got older, he began using more and more drugs, believing that they opened up his mind to a wealth of experiences and knowledge that would feed his art. He also became increasingly obsessed with the topic of death. Accounts vary on the degree to which these issues affected his relationship with other band members, but tensions certainly existed.

Famed Hollywood director Oliver Stone attempted to bring all of this to life in his 1991 film, *The Doors*. Stone had become intrigued with Morrison and the Doors and desperately wanted to translate the mystique of the brooding icon to film. Val Kilmer played the role of Morrison, and although his performance received decent reviews, the film overall was not received well by critics nor was it a commercial success.

As with many popular artists, Morrison achieved mythic status after his death. The combination of his sexual magnetism, defiant attitude, and dark analysis of the world via his artistry still intrigues people today.

The Doors officially disbanded in 1973, but their music has continued to sell even four decades later. They were inducted into the Rock and Roll Hall of Fame in 1993, and, during their career, they sold millions of albums and were named by *Rolling Stone* magazine as one of the "100 Greatest Artists of All Time."

See also: 1960s: Hendrix, Jimi; Joplin, Janis; Mitchell, Joni; Rolling Stones, The; 1970s: Led Zeppelin; 1980s: Boy George; Duran Duran; Madonna; 1990s: Green Day; Morissette, Alanis; Nirvana; 2000s: My Chemical Romance

Further Reading

Densmore, John. 2013. *The Doors: Unhinged*. North Charleston, SC: Percussive Press.

Majstorovic, Dunja. 2017. "A Young Lion, the Lizard King, and Erotic Politician: Tracing the Roots of Jim Morrison's Mythical Image." *Journal of Communication Inquiry* 41 (2).

Riordan, James, and Jerry Prochnicky. 1991. *Break on Through: The Life and Death of Jim Morrison*. New York: William Morrow.

Weiss, Jeff. 2012. "Surviving Doors Members Speak on Jim Morrison's Substance Abuse." *LA Weekly*, February 16. http://www.laweekly.com/music/surviving-doors-members -speak-on-jim-morrisons-substance-abuse-2401843.

DYLAN, BOB

It's an overused term, but Bob Dylan (1941–) truly was the "voice of a generation." No other musical artist of the 1960s is more closely associated with civil and social unrest in the United States than this iconic figure. Dylan, born Robert Allen Zimmerman, showed an intense interest in music in his late teens and early 20s. Although he never finished college, he began performing songs in local coffeehouses and signed his first record contract at the age of 20. Dylan would go on to define the rebellious nature of 1960s youths and become a symbol of the decade's turmoil and upheaval.

The music of Dylan is complex on several levels. Although he achieved commercial success to some degree, his music and lyrics were far from superficial and many times analyzed both social and personal issues and their symbiotic relationship with one another. Many of Dylan's early songs expressed a strong desire for Utopia and denial or resistance of material wealth and possessions. This reflected the feelings and attitudes of many teens as they grappled with issues like the Vietnam War and changing attitudes about sexual freedom and gender roles in the aftermath of the 1950's social and political conservatism. Additionally, while Dylan wrote and sang of romantic love, most times it was only part of a broader tapestry related to self-realization or self-actualization; Dylan didn't reject it, but there was an underlying theme of striving for pure relationships that were not based on insecurities and possessiveness. In these songs, self-reliance came first and only with a strong sense of self and broader purpose was love realized. Songs like "I'm Not There" and "If You Gotta Go, Go Now" embody this philosophy of fleeing emotionally unfulfilling or draining personal relationships.

Although he is most closely associated with folk music, Dylan has proven that his musical tastes and ambitions are diverse, and he has never been interested in conforming to narrow or categorical expectations. His origins may have aligned with the folk music movement, but after his first few albums, Dylan shifted gears musically, and many of his fans were not pleased with the transformation. On his fifth album, *Bringing It All Back Home* (1965), the artist switched from acoustic guitar to electric, and this created an avalanche of criticism from many of his fans who accused him of abandoning the folk music movement in favor a more commercial ("safer") route to success. When he played to a huge crowd in 1965 at the Newport Folk Festival, he was booed by audience members when he began playing the acoustic guitar.

Dylan was crowned a social justice hero barely after starting his career. This, of course, came with expectations. When he failed to live up to those expectations either through his songwriting or his stance on social issues, many of his early advocates and fans turned against him. As Dylan's "sound" evolved into more of that of a rock star and less of a folk singer relying on acoustic protest songs, he lost ground with some of his original fans. Editorials were written in several New York–based publications that accused the artist of selling out and putting his own ambitions and career ahead of a bigger social justice movement.

It became evident that Dylan felt confined by the limitations of being identified solely as a folk singer. In an ongoing attempt to branch out musically and personally, Dylan took notice of other artists and their successes creating nonfolk music. The Beatles influenced Dylan and vice versa. Dylan allegedly introduced the band to drugs while on tour in the United Kingdom in 1964. This is attributed—at least partially—to their foray into newer and more exotic sounds and lyrics as their songwriting and instrumentation evolved. Likewise, the widespread popularity and acceptance of the Beatles certainly paved the way for Dylan to conceive and deliver songs that had wider appeal.

The 1965 anthem, "Like a Rolling Stone" became his most commercially successful single and quickly became the rallying cry of a cynical generation that questioned the significance placed on material wealth in Western society. Although Dylan may have distanced himself from the label of "political activist," his fans latched onto the song and it too became a symbol of youthful resistance and protest. Additionally, "Like a Rolling Stone" originally had little chance of ever getting airplay. Its original length was over six minutes and its lyrics fairly confrontational—not exactly ingredients for a hit record. The song has endured in popularity and relevance for decades. It has been covered by artists ranging from Jimi Hendrix to John Cougar Mellencamp to Green Day.

In October 2016, Bob Dylan was awarded the Nobel Peace Prize for Literature. This unusual choice as a recipient for the honor received a lot of criticism. Dylan took his time even responding to the accolade, but, when he did, he declined the invitation to the actual ceremony. This reinforced his roots as an individual who typically rejected mainstream acceptance and was in line with his rebellious persona from the decade that made him a folk hero. Regardless of opinions on his worthiness for the award, the choice of Dylan for this recognition signifies his iconic status within popular culture.

Bob Dylan has won 12 Grammy Awards (his most recent in 2016) and both an Academy Award and a Golden Globe Award for Best Original Song, "Things Have Changed" from *The Wonder Boys*.

See also: 1960s: Hendrix, Jimi; Joplin, Janis; Mitchell, Joni; 1990s: Green Day

Further Reading

Barnes, Tom. 2015. "5 Bob Dylan Songs That Actually Changed the Course of History." *Mic*, March 20. https://mic.com/articles/113316/5-bob-dylan-songs-that-actually-changed-the-course-of-history#.ISkgX2OGT.

Dylan, Bob. 2005. *Chronicles: Volume One*. New York: Simon and Schuster.

Marshall, Scott M. 2017. *Bob Dylan: A Spiritual Life*. Washington, D.C.: BP Books.

Smith, Larry David. 2005. *Writing Dylan: The Songs of a Lonesome Traveler*. Westport, CT: Praeger.

EXPLOSIVE GENERATION, THE

The same year that Disney released the hit comedy *The Parent Trap* (1961), another film was released that was a serious attempt at examining shifting social attitudes and behaviors toward sex. *The Explosive Generation* isn't a well-known film, but it deserves attention because of its subject matter and the manner in which it is handled. The story focuses on the repercussions of a questionnaire that is distributed to students in a civics class after one of them indicates a desire to discuss sex in the classroom. Instructor Peter Gifford (William Shatner) is polling his students in order to compile a list of their concerns. He assumes that issues such as getting accepted into a good college and developing solid study habits will be at the top of this list. Student Janet Sommers (Patty McCormack) contends that what is on most of their minds is the issue of sex. Gifford initially deflects this and encourages his students to have those private conversations with their parents. He then realizes that most of his class doesn't feel comfortable discussing the topic at home, so he agrees to include it for classroom discussion via the results of a questionnaire completed by his students.

What triggers this conversation are events that take place the night prior to the class. Janet (Patty McCormick), Lee (Dan Carlyle), Bobby (Billy Gray), and Margie (Suzi Carnell) all spent the night at a beach house after a party. Although the viewer isn't privy to any details of what happened during or after the party, it's implied that there might have been sexual activity. Janet is visibly flustered in class when she expresses concern about exactly "how far" a girl should go to show a boy that she likes him.

News of the survey and plans to discuss its results reach parents and school administrators. The outrage is predictable and passionate. Parents demand that the survey be squashed, but Mr. Gifford is reluctant to do so even after it's clear that he may lose his job over the issue.

What begins as a drama centered on the sexual attitudes and ideas of teens in the early years of the 1960s takes a turn halfway through and becomes a lesson plan on effective student protest. When Gifford refuses to apologize to the parents, he is suspended. The student body responds with displays of support. They protest in silence and demand that their teacher be reinstated even as angry parents continue to make noise about the "incident." The students refuse to attend classes until Mr. Gifford gets his job back, which he does by the end of the film.

Sexual education programs in the early 1960s were still mainly focused on sexual hygiene and knowledge about pregnancy. Soon, however, things began to change societally and there was a need for more detailed and topical information. With the availability of the birth control pill and emerging new attitudes about sexual freedom, teens found themselves grappling with their own sexuality while absorbing cultural messages of abstinence and sex that was tied inextricably to marriage.

The sexual revolution of the late 1960s and early 1970s was still years away when the film was released. Educators were operating under assumptions that didn't take into effect the growing number of teenagers who were having premarital sex. It wasn't until 1964 that the Sexuality Information and Education Council of the United States (SIECUS) was founded by physician Mary Calderone. The need for the organization stemmed from the restrictive culture and influence of the American Social Hygiene Association. The first governmental grant to aid in the development of sexual education curriculum came in 1968, seven years after *The Explosive Generation* was released.

What makes the film so interesting from a cultural and historical perspective is that the very mention of sex in a high school classroom could cause such disruption and extreme reactions from parents and even some educators. The film can be seen as a foretelling of what was to come as the women's movement and other efforts that were growing in the country opposing patriarchal domination. It's very telling that Janet, at one point later in the film, reveals that nothing sexual happened at the party after all. Had the story line revealed that consensual sex had in fact happened, one can only imagine the volatile reaction from parents.

The Explosive Generation is a film that is very defined by the era in which it was made, and although the sexuality theme falls flat, the unexpected protest element is quite effective.

See also: 1950s: *Blackboard Jungle*; Public Service Announcements; 1960s: *Parent Trap, The*; *To Sir, with Love*; 1970s: *Cooley High*; *Welcome Back, Kotter*; 1980s: *Fast Times at Ridgemont High*

Further Reading

Brooks, Victor. 2012. *Last Season of Innocence: The Teen Experience in the 1960s.* Lanham, MD: Rowman and Littlefield.
Rabin, Nathan. 2011. "The Explosive Generation." *AV Club,* August 29. https://film.avclub .com/the-explosive-generation-1961-1798227187.

GIDGET

Gidget is a fictional creation penned by author Frederick Kohner (1905–1986), a screenwriter who immigrated to Hollywood in the 1930s due to the rise of Nazism in his homeland, Germany. The first novel *Gidget, The Little Girl with Big Ideas* (1957), is based on Kohner's daughter, Kathy Kohner-Zuckerman (1941–). Kohner was inspired to write the novel when he noticed how consumed Kathy was in the burgeoning "surf" culture of Malibu, California. As with most sports, surfing was dominated by men when it first originated. In the 1950s, it was noteworthy when a woman, let alone a teen girl, ventured into areas controlled almost exclusively by men. The novel became popular, largely due to its teen heroine. It was adapted into a theatrical film with the shortened title of *Gidget* in 1959. Although popular actress Sandra Dee portrayed the main character in this film, two sequels were later released, *Gidget Goes Hawaiian* (1961), and *Gidget Goes to Rome* (1963), and each featured a different actress in the title role. It also spawned a television sitcom in the mid-1960s.

There are a few different ways to read the text of *Gidget*. One potential reading is that of a feminist who was a trailblazer for young women. Gidget's character showed what a teen girl could do during that era, and that included surfing. Some considered it revolutionary that a young woman could join young men and perform alongside them in a very physical sport. Gidget "kept up with the boys" during the day, and then dated some of them in the evenings. This may seem quaint or even unremarkable by today's standards, but, in the historical context of the 1950s and early 1960s, it was outside of the status quo. It certainly challenged societal norms with respect to gender. Gidget can even be viewed as a precursor to the more independent and vocal young women coming of age in the 1960s—women who created awareness about gender inequality and shifting roles of women within our culture.

An oppositional reading, however, is that, while Gidget ventured into a traditional man's world, she was not taken seriously. She ultimately served to reinforce the existing gender stereotypes of women who need guidance from male authority figures in order to make their way successfully in the world. In other words, Gidget's ability to compete in a male-dominated activity is contingent on the patriarchal guidance of a male figure.

In the television series, *Gidget* (Sally Field), the primary focus is on the relationship between Gidget and her father, UCLA professor Russ Lawrence (Don Porter). A typical episode of *Gidget* features the young heroine attempting to help an individual or a cause. Despite her good intentions, she almost always fails at her endeavors and ends up needing moral instruction from her father. This reinforces two worldviews that were prevalent in the 1950s: that teenagers need constant attention and guidance and are seldom able to figure out things on their own, and that young women especially need supervision and authority from father figures.

Another stereotype present in many of the TV episodes is that of the "bumbling" and awkward girl. Although Gidget is presented as physically attractive and perennially cheery, she cannot seem to complete tasks without disastrous results. This ranges from situations as innocuous as waitressing in order to buy her father a surprise birthday gift (she screws up orders and spills drinks on customers), to giving her friend a makeover to help attract romantic prospects (the girl ends up looking worse than before the makeover happened).

Some scholars have also noted that the TV series reinforces paternal stereotypes of a father's role in the social and romantic life of his daughter. In the show, Mr. Lawrence is widowed (a change from the source material and the films). His preoccupation with Gidget's romantic life can be viewed as normal given the traditional roles and responsibilities of parents, or it can be viewed as overreaching, maybe even intrusive. Gidget gravitates toward older men, possibly reinforcing the notion of being a "daddy's girl." Regardless of the quandary she finds herself in, Daddy always seems to know best and is able to remedy the situation. Furthermore, it is insinuated in at least one episode that the inevitable outcome of Mr. Lawrence's meddling in his daughter's romantic life will result in neither of them ever finding love or suitable mates. This, of course, is rejected by Gidget's father who deems it "baloney."

Although the series lasted for only one season, the cumulative media impact of Gidget is undeniable. In addition to the novel, theatrical films, and TV series, Gidget also found life in several made-for-television movies: *Gidget Gets Married* (1972), and *Gidget's Summer Reunion* (1985). The character of Gidget undeniably triggered interest in surfing, especially for girls, and broadened its appeal beyond California. The novel was rereleased in 2001 and was promoted by the real-life Gidget, Kathy Kohner-Zuckerman. The nostalgia factor helped sell copies, especially among families in surfing communities where the link to the well-known character is strong. The TV series also launched the career of Oscar-winning actress Sally Field, who went on to star as *The Flying Nun* for the same network.

See also: 1950s: Darin, Bobby; 1960s: Beach Boys, The; *Group, The*; *Where the Boys Are*; 1970s: Blume, Judy; 2000s: *Sisterhood of the Traveling Pants, The*

Further Reading

Gillogly, Brian L. 2011. "Happy 54th, Gidget!" *Journal of Popular Culture* 44 (4): 681–683.
Ionata, Kathryn. 2014. "'Just a Doll in Dungarees': Revisiting *Gidget*." *The Toast*, July 24, 2014. http://the-toast.net/2014/07/16/just-doll-dungarees-revisiting-gidget/.
Kohn, Sally. 2014. "How *Gidget* Broke the Rules in '60s TV." *CNN*, August 24, 2014. http://www.cnn.com/2014/05/29/opinion/kohn-tv-women-60s-gidget/index.html.
Nash, Ilana. 2006. *American Sweethearts: Teenage Girls in Twentieth Century Popular Culture*. Bloomington: Indiana University Press.

GROUP, THE

Mary McCarthy (1912–1989) penned *The Group* (1963), a best-selling and influential novel that has had a lasting impact and influence on American culture relative to the roles of women within Western society. The book follows the lives of eight Vassar graduates in the late 1930s: Kay Strong, Mary Prothero ("Pokey"), Dottie Renfrew, Elinor Eastlake ("Lakey"), Polly Andrews, Priss Hartshorn, Helena Davison, and Norine Schmittlapp. These characters deal with a range of issues involving the men in their lives: alcoholism, extramarital affairs, career challenges, child rearing, and sexuality. Although published as fiction, many have attributed the novel as a thinly veiled account of the author's own life, primarily due to the fact that she also graduated from Vassar. The book is known for speaking about women's issues honestly and authentically at a time where many of these topics were taboo.

At a time when women were still primarily viewed as best suited to be mothers and housewives, the young college grads in McCarthy's novel had other ideas. Most of them had career aspirations and refused to be confined by prescribed gender roles. More shockingly, though, the author wrote about a very private issue that had never been featured in popular fiction previously: birth control. One chapter in the book that centers on Dottie opens with the infamous line, "Get yourself a pessary," a pessary being a diaphragm. This might seem silly or nonsensical by contemporary standards, but it was quite shocking at the time. The notion that an unmarried woman could have sex with a man in the 1930s was daring enough, but a reference to birth control was revolutionary.

The relevance of the media communicator here is significant. Mary McCarthy liked writing about topics and issues that were generally considered private at the time, and women's sexuality was one of those issues. It's important to remember that, although this novel was published in the early 1960s, it took place in the 1930s, decades before what is commonly referred to as "the women's movement." The very notion of sexually active women who were unmarried seemed scandalous to many. But McCarthy was no stranger to controversy. Her 1941 short story, "The Man in the Brooks Brothers Shirt," features a single woman who has a sexual encounter with a man on a train. This was shocking to many for two reasons: the sexual activity occurs in a public place, and it was a woman who wrote about it. Clearly McCarthy was unafraid to write about women and sexuality. Although she later revealed that writing about a woman experiencing carnal pleasure on public transportation caused her initially to blush, it was this sort of realism and honesty that she later was most proud of in her work.

Predictably, much of the criticism of *The Group* came from male reviewers and authors. Some, such as Norman Mailer, felt that the story worked more as a sociopolitical work than as a novel. Others simply felt that the material was too graphic and inappropriate. However, it connected with its intended audience. Female readers largely felt as though their stories and their lives were being realistically portrayed in McCarthy's writing. The mention of the diaphragm was so much more than a simple plot point. Reproductive rights were and remain a topic of relevance even in Western society today. McCarthy has noted that *The Group* is told exclusively from a female perspective, and that can make some men uncomfortable or even defensive when analyzing its content.

The type of "confessional" that McCarthy is now known for writing is more commonplace within the world of literature today. Autobiographical to a point, she uses characters, some of which closely resembled her, to make points and criticisms about women's experiences and issues. Many decades after its publication, for example, she revealed the true life identity of "The Man in the Brooks Brothers Shirt." She provides his name and other damning data about the married man who apparently had a tryst with her and served as the inspiration for the short story. Not everyone appreciates this type of "outing," though, as there has been a tradition of debate about the ethics involved in revealing this type of information when it previously lived only in the realm of fiction.

Many of McCarthy's stories and themes connected with young women who related to the lives of the female characters in her work. McCarthy wrote about sexually active women who (many times) were also career focused. This was noteworthy at the time and signified the vacuum of female-driven stories that featured three-dimensional characters.

The Group was a *New York Times* best seller and stayed on that list for two years. It was also adapted into a 1966 theatrical film directed by Sidney Lumet. Its cultural effect has extended for decades, and it is the inspiration for the highly successful HBO series, *Sex and the City*.

See also: 1950s: *Blue Denim*; Public Service Announcements; 1960s: *Gidget*; *Where the Boys Are*; 1970s: Blume, Judy; 1980s: *Dirty Dancing*; *Sweet Valley High*; 1990s: *Clarissa Explains It All*; 2000s: *Gossip Girl*; *Mean Girls*; *Pretty Little Liars*; *Sisterhood of the Traveling Pants, The*

Further Reading

Begley, Sarah. 2013. "Mary McCarthy's 'The Group' Was the Original 'Sex and the City.'" *Newsweek*, July 31. http://www.newsweek.com/2013/07/31/mary-mccarthys-group -was-original-sex-and-city-237810.html.

Day, Elizabeth. 2009. "The Group by Mary McCarthy." *The Guardian*, November 28. https:// www.theguardian.com/books/2009/nov/29/the-group-mary-mccarthy.

Jacobs, Laura. 2013. "Vassar Unzipped." *Vanity Fair*, July. https://www.vanityfair.com /culture/2013/07/vassar-sex-single-girl-ivy-league-mary-mccarthy.

McCarthy, Mary. 2010. *The Group*. London: Virago.

HENDRIX, JIMI

Another musical artist whose name is synonymous with the 1960s is guitarist Jimi Hendrix (1940–1970). Although his career was relatively brief, the impression he left on music and popular culture is undeniable. When any discussion centers on relevant musicians of the 1960s, Hendrix is named alongside artists like Janis Joplin, Joan Baez, and Jim Morrison of the rock group the Doors. With no formal musical training, Hendrix gravitated toward an interest in playing guitar from an early age. He joined his first band at the age of 16; shortly thereafter, he received an electric guitar and moved on to his second group, the Rocking Kings.

Hendrix even formed a band when he was in the military. During his time as an Army paratrooper, Hendrix formed the band the King Casuals. After a medical discharge due to a parachuting injury, he went on to work as a session guitarist, and, by the mid-1960s, he was playing with well-known acts like Ike and Tina Turner, Sam Cooke, and the Isley Brothers.

Gaining insight into Jimi Hendrix requires at least a cursory understanding of the cultural and musical history of the guitar itself. Up until the 1940s and 1950s, acoustic guitars were the standard. Music played on these is by nature "soft" and melodic. With the invention of the electric guitar, the sound of music changed dramatically. With the advent of this new technology, people began to draw a clear distinction between "noise" and "musical sound." This transition was met with notable opposition and criticism. An argument was made that acoustic guitars were more orthodox (read: respectable) for musical venues. The electric guitar was viewed by some as an impersonal or even "cold" instrument.

Electric guitars by nature are able to emit different sounds than acoustic guitars. In addition to the feedback noise emitted from electric guitars, artists began to use them to more viscerally represent the artist's feelings and emotions associated with certain songs. In the 1960s, it became commonplace among some musicians to extend or elongate a song simply by "riffing" on the strings during a performance. More importantly, some artists recognized the emotional connection between their playing and the reception of their young audiences to this new and arguably more expressive sound. Unlike his predecessors, Hendrix now had access to technology that dramatically broadened his ability to communicate through music. On stage, he personified an artist who was "in the moment" and unimpeded.

In the recording studio, however, it was much different. Hendrix began work on a recording studio several years before his death. He named it Electric Lady, and, when he recorded there, people saw another side to him. He was fascinated with possibilities of new technology, especially the effects and sounds emitted from the electric guitar. He reportedly spent hours trying to perfect a single note or sound. In multiple interviews throughout his career, he referenced what he believed to be the healing and unifying power of the electric guitar; Hendrix strongly argued that it had the power to bring people together and transcend issues of race, gender, and politics.

Iconic musical artist Jimi Hendrix performing on stage. Along with artists like Janis Joplin and Joan Baez, his music helped to define a generation during the tumultuous 1960s. (David Redfern/Redferns/Getty Images)

Another artist who took the electric guitar into new realms of expression and aggression was Pete Townshend of the rock group, the Who. Townshend began smashing his guitar during or sometimes after performances. This action was viewed as one of protest, anger, and a direct resistance to the status quo. Hendrix's action involved fire. He began setting his guitar on fire while playing it. This ritual contained elements of sacrifice but also of protest.

Although Hendrix is not identified as a strong critic or protester of the Vietnam War, his music arrived at a time when even ambivalent lyrics and messages seemed to be flavored with politics. Both folk and rock artists created many songs in response to the war. At first, many of these were delivered via traditional folk singers, many of whom used acoustic guitars. Singers such as Buffy Sainte Marie ("Universal Soldier") and Peter, Paul, and Mary ("Leaving on a Jet Plane") offered songs that questioned the morality of the war while still being mainstream enough in both sound and lyric to attract a fairly wide audience. Although folk songs aimed at criticism of the war tended to be less angry or explicitly combative, rock songs—both in sound and content—seemed less concerned with not offending or even alienating listeners. Still, many songs of this period can be read in a variety of ways. Were the songs really protests of the war or were they equally protests of how government infringed or was believed to infringe on the carefree lifestyle adopted by so many in the 1960s? Both?

Sexual liberation and the demand that women be afforded the same rights as men in both the boardroom and the bedroom certainly drove some of the counter-culture resistance and defiance of the status quo. This movement manifested itself in the form of marches, sit-ins, and other activities designed to draw attention to vocal demands for a new generation. The politics of gender and sexuality were and are inextricably linked to the essence of rock music.

Hendrix was a very sexual performer. His intimate relationship with the electric guitar was communicated through physical movement and an expression of bliss that many found if not overtly erotic, at least sensual and seductive. During a 1969 performance of the Chuck Berry hit, "Johnny B. Goode," Hendrix kept the guitar at crotch level for a prolonged period of time, stretching out a lengthy and distorted note while grimacing as if in the throes of orgasm.

The staying power of Hendrix's musical legacy is evident by the archival release of *People, Hell and Angels*, in 2013, which easily debuted in Billboard's Top 10 list of albums for that week.

See also: 1960s: Doors, The; Joplin, Janis; Mitchell, Joni; 1970s: Led Zeppelin; 1990s: Nirvana

Further Reading

Blake, John. 2014. "How Jimi Hendrix's Race Became His 'Invisible Legacy.'" *CNN*, October 18. http://www.cnn.com/2014/10/18/showbiz/jimi-hendrix-invisible-legacy/index.html.
Hendrix, Jimi. 2014. *Starting at Zero: His Own Story*. New York: Bloomsbury.
Tate, Greg. 2003. *Midnight Lightning: Jimi Hendrix and the Black Experience*. Chicago: Chicago Review Press.
Watts, Simon. 2013. "Kathy Etchingham: Life as Jimi Hendrix's 'Foxy Lady.'" *BBC*, February 3. http://www.bbc.com/news/magazine-21292762.

JOPLIN, JANIS

Few artists leave such an indelible legacy that they are instantly recognized by their first names: Elvis, Aretha, and Prince to name a few. Janis Joplin (1943–1970) is part of that elite group. During her short life, she created a unique musical sound and style that helped define a generation. As with many talented artists, Joplin was an outsider during her formative years. Not popular with classmates, she gravitated toward art and music. Influenced heavily by African American singers Bessie Smith and Big Mama Thornton, Joplin's earthy and throaty delivery of lyrics earned her an iconic place in the history of music.

As with Elvis Presley's "Hound Dog," Joplin took a lesser-known song—in this case, Big Mama Thornton's "Ball and Chain"—and turned it into a smash hit. Her rendition of Thornton's song, which she performed at the 1967 Monterey Jazz Festival, resurrected interest in Thornton, who went on to do some international touring in her middle-aged years.

The parallels between Bessie Smith and Joplin are significant and extend significantly beyond music. Both were openly bisexual. Both were considered by many to be lewd and loud—perceptions not held in high esteem by their respective generations. Smith was looked down on not only by white culture; she was treated with disdain by many African Americans who were socially mobile in the 1920s. Smith's appearance, her heavy drinking, and her penchant for getting into loud (sometimes violent) fights were viewed as harmful and reinforcing of negative stereotypes. Some blacks, even within the arts community, found her demeanor and attitude vulgar. Part of this stemmed from the belief that Jazz music in general embodied crude sentiments and behavior.

Joplin was also viewed as abrasive and overly sexualized. She embodied the casual drug culture of the era; her drinking and drug use were legendary as were her one night stands with both men and women. Unlike Smith, she never married but was engaged three times. She seemed to enjoy defying labels, and, even though she presented herself as heterosexual, she never denied her gay relationships. One of her female sexual partners, Peggy Caserta, coauthored a memoir *Going Down with Janis*, claiming that she and Joplin had a stormy but long-term relationship. Caserta accompanied Joplin to the Monterey Pop Festival in 1968 and to Woodstock in 1969. Caserta was still linked with Joplin at the time of Joplin's death.

Joplin confounded many in the LGBT community who felt she used substance abuse (especially the use of heroin) as a mask to repress her homosexual tendencies. It's important to remember that the "acceptance" of Janis's same-sex conquests was granted only in conjunction with her heterosexual activities that she frequently bragged about. It's highly doubtful that an openly lesbian artist would have been embraced at the time that Janis was in the public spotlight.

Joplin strongly connected with her young audience based on her talent, her projected self-confidence, and her representation of female sexuality during the early stages of the women's rights movement. Her hit singles "Piece of My Heart" and "Me and Bobby McGee" especially connected with listeners as they alternately highlighted the raw and authentic emotions of the singer and her ability to draw in the listener and feel a personal connection to her.

The link between sexuality and blues music is an important one. Since the lyrics in many of these songs can be applied to either gender ("babe," "baby"), it allows the performer to sing the song and express feelings of sexual desire without identifying the object of lust as either male or female. These coded performances enabled artists to passionately identify their feelings without having to explicitly reveal their own sexual identity and/or orientation. This holds especially true for singers like Bessie Smith, who already had to navigate through a male-dominated system where both her gender and her race placed her not just at a disadvantage but opened her up to potential physical harm.

It is noteworthy that Joplin, unlike many other popular female artists at the time, showed little to any self-restraint in her performances. She visibly inhabited her songs, writhing around onstage, sweating, and allowing herself to look "messy." Her inhibitions were—or at least seemed—nonexistent when she was performing for an audience. Contrary to the gentle "Earth Mother" persona projected by some of her peers at the time, Joplin owned the intensity of her emotions just as most of the male jazz/rock performers did. This refusal to conform to gender norms was noteworthy. At a time when male rock performers were expected to display overtly sexual mannerisms while performing for live crowds, it was still quite shocking to see a female artist do this.

Joplin's final album, *Pearl,* was released after her death in 1970. The album was a commercial and critical success. She was inducted into the Rock and Roll Hall of Fame in 1995 and is listed at #28 by *Rolling Stone* magazine in their 2008 list of the 100 greatest singers of all time. Several musicals about Joplin have been produced throughout the years, including the 2013 production entitled *A Night with Janis Joplin.* The star was given her own star on the Hollywood Walk of Fame in 2013. Actress Michelle Williams is currently in negotiations to play the title role of Janis in a theatrical biographical film.

See also: 1960s: Doors, The; Hendrix, Jimi; Mitchell, Joni; 1970s: Led Zeppelin; Summer, Donna; 1980s: Blondie; Boy George; Lauper, Cyndi; Madonna; 1990s: Nirvana; Morissette, Alanis; 2000s: Rihanna; Spears, Britney

Further Reading

Ali, Lorraine. 2015. "Review 'Janis: Little Girl Blue' Reveals What Drove, and Haunted, Janis Joplin." *Los Angeles Times,* December 3. http://www.latimes.com/entertainment /movies/la-et-mn-janis-joplin-review-20151204-story.html.

Ayele, Tia. 2012. "The Life of Janis Joplin: A Look into Dismantling Patriarchy." *Georgia Political Review*, December 18. http://georgiapoliticalreview.com/the-life-of-janis-joplin -a-look-into-dismantling-patriarchy/.

Friedman, Myra. 1973. *Buried Alive: The Biography of Janis Joplin.* New York: William Morrow.

MITCHELL, JONI

Canadian-born folk pop icon Joni Mitchell (1943–) made an indelible impact on the American music scene in the 1960s, 1970s, and beyond. Given her place in the history of American popular music, it is surprising that her initial artistic inclinations were geared more toward drawing. As a child, Mitchell took piano lessons. Her teacher apparently was displeased that she showed much more interest in writing her own music than memorizing and playing the music of classical composers. Later in her career, she was recognized as an artist whose work echoed elements of classical music, and that is something she was very vocal about in interviews.

Mitchell isn't easily labeled as a mere "folk singer." Although some of her earliest music may fit fairly comfortably into this genre, she always viewed the musical process as more comprehensive and complex than being pigeonholed into a single genre. Even to this day, many critics are confounded by her ability to not fit easily into a single musical category. Mitchell expressed on many occasions that she didn't want to be limited in her musical ambitions and work, but, even in the 1960s, record companies still wanted to market and package artists and groups that fit a specific target.

Mitchell's private life certainly lent itself to introspection. Pregnant at the age of 20, she left with the father of her unborn child and fled her hometown. She was abandoned shortly thereafter and was then confronted with the harsh reality of being poor and having to care for a baby. Although she ended up meeting and marrying folk singer Chuck Mitchell, it proved incompatible both personally and professionally, and the two divorced after a brief partnership of touring together as a duo. She later gave up the child for adoption.

To explore Mitchell's appeal and impact on popular music, it's necessary to place her work within the context of the late 1960s and early 1970s. Unlike the 1950s, a new sense of sexual freedom existed within the country. With the British Invasion in full swing and a burgeoning new sense of sexual autonomy, young women were now freer to at least think about sexual activity without overt guilt and shamefulness. And while music from the 1950s certainly addressed romance and sexual attraction, it did so from a conservative worldview and largely within the confines of marriage or the end goal of marriage; a dominant message in love songs of the 1950s was that of virginity and fidelity. Girls were encouraged to "save themselves" for the wedding night and not to be too aggressive when pursuing the boy or man of their dreams. Sex in 1950s pop songs—at least from a female perspective—was also tame in terms of physicality. The popular song "Leader of the Pack" only includes a kiss as a gesture of affection and longing, for example.

In her first album, *Blue,* Mitchell explored various journeys of young women who were sexually active and not married. Although this may seem unimportant by modern standards, it was a significant departure from 1950s song narratives. The song "Cactus Tree" focuses on a young women who has many sexual partners. Much to the chagrin of her suitors, she is rarely available to them as much as they would like. This isn't her leading them on or "playing hard to get." Instead, this is the song about a woman who is independent and autonomous, and though she certainly enjoys the company of men, she doesn't feel obligated to give up her freedom in order to please them.

The song "My Old Man" rejects the traditional notion that marriage is what signifies the validity and value of a man–woman relationship. Mitchell doesn't just discount the worth of a legal marriage in terms of its value to a relationship, she dismisses it. A line of the song proclaims, "We don't need no piece of paper / from the city hall" in order to validate their union. Again, this was quite a provocative stance in the 1960s given existing gender roles and conformity at that time.

Remember that during this time in the record industry itself, women were still largely occupying subservient positions—clerks and secretaries, primarily. So although there was a burgeoning (and successful) movement of independent women writing and recording their own songs, managerial and executive positions were still held by men. When interviewed by popular magazines, reporters placed an undue emphasis on the physical appearance and sexuality of female performers. During an interview with popular singer Carly Simon, for example, a reporter from *Rolling Stone* magazine remarked on how lucky the singer's infant son was to have access to her breasts for feeding. Mitchell was also put off by this sort of treatment when the same publication named her "Old Lady of the Year" in 1971, zeroing in on her as an object of affection from the male perspective.

Sexualization of women was still rampant regardless of how far they had come personally or professionally, but Mitchell and fellow female artists certainly set the tone and paved an opening for women artists to speak honestly through their craft about dreams and ambitions that weren't all tethered to the notion of finding a man. Joni Mitchell won Grammy Awards in 1969, 1974, 1995, 2000, and 2007.

See also: 1960s: Dylan, Bob; Joplin, Janis; 1970s: Summer, Donna; 1980s: Blondie; Boy George; Lauper, Cyndi; Madonna; 1990s: Morissette, Alanis; 2000s: Rihanna; Spears, Britney; Swift, Taylor

Further Reading

Marom, Malka. 2014. *Joni Mitchell: In Her Own Words*. Toronto, Canada: ECW Press.
Peters, Alexa. 2017. "The 16 Best Joni Mitchell Songs." *Paste*, January 20. https://www
    .pastemagazine.com/articles/2017/01/the-16-best-joni-mitchell-songs.html.
Weller. Shelia. 2008. *Girls Like Us: Carole King, Joni Mitchell, Carly Simon—And the Journey
    of a Generation*. New York: Atria.
Yaffe, David. 2017. *Reckless Daughter: A Portrait of Joni Mitchell*. New York: Sarah Crichton
    Books.
Zoladz, Lindsay, 2017. "Joni Mitchell: Fear of a Female Genius." *The Ringer*, October 16.
    https://www.theringer.com/music/2017/10/16/16476254/joni-mitchell-pop-music-canon.

MONKEES, THE

Decades before the terms "boy band" and "reality television" existed in the American lexicon, pop group the Monkees was introduced to television audiences. The band was created as an American response to the wildly popular British band the Beatles. Like the boy bands that became popular in the 1980s and 1990s, the Monkees were created by producers in order to make money, capitalizing on the spending power of teenagers and young adults. Upon seeing the phenomenal success of the Beatles' film, *A Hard Day's Night*, producers Bob Rafelson and Bert Schneider decided that they could create an American equivalent and successfully market it on a network television show. Originally conceived as a vehicle for the pop group Lovin' Spoonful, the idea evolved into what would later become a business formula for boy bands of later decades: assemble a cast of members with good looks and musical talent, and turn them into revenue machines.

With the exception of British born actor-singer Davey Jones (1945–2012), the original members of the Monkees had limited commercial experience. The original group lineup consisted of Davey Jones, Micky Dolenz (1945–), Michael Nesmith (1942–), and Peter Tork (1942–). Using a template that future producers would employ, an advertisement was published in an effort to recruit band members. It was important that, in addition to being able to sing, members be required to have personalities that would appeal to the audiences of the small screen. During auditions, sometimes the applicants would be asked silly questions or even ignored to see what their reactions would be. Producers made it clear that they weren't looking for professionally trained actors; their focus was on comedic timing and the ability to improvise. Once hired, the group went through an improvisational boot camp to prepare for filming.

The irony of putting together an act like this is fairly obvious: producers seek band members with innate talent and authenticity, even though the band is an artificial construct from the start. The band members were literally selected based on a checklist. To exacerbate this, the Monkees initially had very limited creative control over both the music and the content of the show. The producers oversaw the writing of music and lyrics, and the group was expected to simply sing the songs they were given. The inability to become more directly involved with the show frustrated the four performers and also fed into a growing criticism of the inauthenticity of the show itself. Both this and their participation in what they felt was ultimately a "sham" energized the group to go public with their dissatisfaction. As a result, Don Kirshner, the music industry heavy hitter who managed all creative aspects of the TV show, was fired.

While tensions were indeed high on the set of the show, the Monkees still proved that they could sell records. Weeks before the first show was broadcast, the band's first single, "Last Train to Clarksville," was released. It became a hit single, and their self-titled debut album was a smashing success. It sold millions of copies and stayed on the Billboard charts for more than a year and a half. Additionally, the band was actively marketed to a teen audience, appearing in youth-oriented publications like *Teen Beat* and *Tiger Beat*. Special attention was given to their style and looks in these magazines, and less so on their musical abilities.

After Kirshner's dismissal, the group gained considerable control over the music and content of the show. Criticism continued, however, of the show's artificial construct. Rather than fight back, the group ultimately satirized themselves in the film *Head,* which was made after the series was canceled. Made by the show's former producer Bob Rafelson and actor Jack Nicholson, the movie mocked the artificiality of the show and its creative origins. Although the film was a box office failure, it did serve one purpose: the Monkees distanced themselves from the show and created a significant rift between themselves and Rafelson.

The Monkees continued to record music after the show ended. Their hit singles include "Pleasant Valley Sunday," "Daydream Believer," and "I'm a Believer." They ultimately went on to sell approximately 75 million records and influenced countless other bands that copied elements of their musical stylings. Additionally, many artists have covered the band's songs, from Linda Ronstadt to pop-rock group Smash Mouth, whose cover of "I'm a Believer" was prominently featured in the animated film *Shrek*. The Monkees' single "I'm Not Your Stepping Stone" has been covered several times by groups as diverse as the Sex Pistols and thrash metal band Intruder. Another interesting factoid about the Monkees is that many people credit them for the creation of the music video that MTV popularized in later decades. They are similar to videos that were featured on the Monkees' television show.

The group has enjoyed renewed popularity on the touring circuit. The death of Davey Jones in 2012 triggered speculation that departed band member Michael Nesmith might rejoin the group, but that didn't transpire. The group has been referenced in the animated TV show *The Simpsons* and has received praise from modern rock groups such as U2 and REM. In 2016, the band released a 50th Anniversary album entitled *Good Times!*

See also: 1960s: Beach Boys, The; Beatles, The; 1970s: Clash, The; Osmonds, The; 1990s: Backstreet Boys, The

Further Reading

Jones, Davey. 2014. *They Made a Monkee Out of Me*. Fort Collins, CO: A Book's Mind.

Lawson, Mark. 2016. "From the Monkees to the Get Down: How Music and TV Try to Stay in Tune." *The Guardian*, August 11. https://www.theguardian.com/tv-and-radio/2016/aug/11/the-get-down-monkees-music-tv-drama.

Mills, Peter. 2016. *The Monkees, Head, and the 60s*. London: Jawbone.

Stanley, Bob. 2012. "Davy Jones and the Monkees: This Boy Band Never Monkeyed Around." *The Telegraph*, March 1. http://www.telegraph.co.uk/culture/music/9115591/Davy-Jones-and-The-Monkees-This-boy-band-never-monkeyed-around.html.

OUTSIDERS, THE

If Judy Blume is considered the reigning queen of young adult novels, fellow female author S. E. Hinton (1948–) can be called the originator of the genre. Prior to the publication of *The Outsiders* in 1967, few if any novels had been written for a teen audience—by an actual teenager. Written while she was still in high school, *The Outsiders* tells the tale of two rival groups that are divided by their socioeconomic status. One group, known as "Greasers," is composed of brothers Ponyboy, Sodapop, and Darry. The other group consists of the "Socs" (short for socialites), who are teenagers from upper-middle-class families.

The story begins with the narrator, Ponyboy, being assaulted by two boys from the Soc group. His brothers rescue him, but soon thereafter he again becomes a target when he is spotted with a young girl who is a member of the Soc group. An altercation leads to violence, and Ponyboy's friend Johnny accidentally stabs one of the perpetrators in an effort to protect Ponyboy. As a result, the boy dies. Fearing arrest, the two hide out in an abandoned church until things settle down.

More than just a simple class struggle played out between two warring groups of teenagers, *The Outsiders* addresses the two distinct types of teen groups that emerged after World War II: teens from blue collar or low-income families, who many times worked part-time jobs to assist with family expenses, and those who enjoyed the fruits of their parents' financial success. The first group was unable to actively participate in the consumerism that the second group was afforded. Remember that a whole new market existed in the 1950s: teens who had disposable income to spend. All sorts of new products were created for and marketed to this demographic.

In the novel, Sodapop and Darry both work instead of attending school. Darry also serves as Ponyboy's caretaker. All three of them function as a family unit, but they don't have biological parents active in their lives. Because of this, Darry must step into the role left vacant by their parents and oversee the health and welfare of Ponyboy (and, to a lesser degree, Sodapop) by providing both financial and psychological support. They aren't able to enjoy the pampered existence that other typical teenagers could. This, of course, serves as the foundation for the conflict between those who are privileged and those who are disenfranchised, the haves and the have-nots.

Hinton purposefully set out to write a realistic account of teenage life, at least for some teens. Prior to *The Outsiders,* most books that may have appealed to teens were based in fantasy. Beyond the surface abuses that the Greasers suffer at the hands of their rivals, other negative sentiments are brewing: alienation and malaise. A sense of doom or dread hovers over these characters because they see no viable way to get out of the situation into which they were born. This prevailing inability to change their circumstances in a meaningful way contributes to feelings of low self-worth and futility.

Due to their domestic situation, the brothers live in constant anxiety and fear of being split apart. Of primary concern is the role of the government in their future. With their parents dead, they know they must obey all laws and rules if they are to remain together; getting into any kind of trouble could draw attention to them, which would put them at risk of separation. This pressure strains the relationships among all three boys. Ponyboy feels like a burden to his older brothers, as if he's just another mouth to feed.

Johnny dies later after sustaining injuries he incurs when the church they are staying in catches fire. Darry's reaction to this in the hospital convinces his youngest brother that he truly does care about and love him. Ponyboy ends up in court, but the judge shows leniency and allows him to stay in the care of his oldest brother. Some measure of order is restored by the end of the book when Ponyboy returns to school. Failing English, he is offered a chance to redeem his grade by writing a story. The story he writes is *The Outsiders,* a recount of all that came before this within the novel.

The Outsiders originally created controversy with its gritty depiction of teens. It is #38 on the Top 100 Most Frequently Challenged Books of 1990–1999. Nowadays, however, it can be found on many middle school and high school reading lists. It is estimated to have sold more than 14 million copies. The book won accolades including the *New York Herald Tribune* Best Teenage Books List and the *Chicago Tribune* Book World Spring Book Festival Honor Book. Hinton went on to write several other well-received young adult novels including *That Was Then, This Is Now* and *Rumblefish.* A film version of the novel was released in 1983 and featured a number of popular young actors including Rob Lowe, Tom Cruise, Matt Dillon, and Patrick Swayze.

See also: 1950s: *Catcher in the Rye, The*; *Lord of the Flies*; 1960s: *Clockwork Orange, A*; 1970s: Blume, Judy; *Go Ask Alice*; *Grease*

Further Reading

Eby, Margaret. 2017. "Why "The Outsiders' Still Matters 50 Years Later." *Rolling Stone*, April 26.

Hinton, S. E. 2016. *The Outsiders: 50th Anniversary Edition*. New York: Penguin Group.

Michaud, John. 2014. "S. E. Hinton and the Y.A. Debate." *The New Yorker*, October 14.

PARENT TRAP, THE

The 1961 version of the Disney film *The Parent Trap* starred Haley Mills in the role of identical twins Susan Evers and Sharon McKendrick; Lindsay Lohan re-created the role in the 1998 remake. The story line follows twin sisters who end up at the same summer camp together. Identical in appearance, they start out as rivals; they play pranks on one another until they are forced away from the other campers and punished by being put into temporary isolation. There they discover that they are sisters whose parents divorced, each one taking one of the girls to live elsewhere. They are understandably angered, but they concoct a plan to reunite their father and mother. After quizzing each other tirelessly about likes and dislikes, and learning each other's mannerisms and behaviors, they switch places for the return trip home: Susan heads to Boston and Sharon to California, each girl pretending to be the other.

Divorce was a fairly new reality in the 1960s. With the introduction of "no fault" divorces in 1969, first in California and later in most other states, couples could now split much more easily than they could previously. Prior to that, divorces were not just more difficult to obtain, they were sought less often due to societal and religious disapproval. Seeking a divorce in the 1950s and earlier was fairly uncommon.

The results of divorce upon children have been covered in countless novels, television shows, and theatrical films. Some of these presentations have been comical and others dramatic. In *The Parent Trap,* it's played for laughs. This might explain why the topic of divorce itself and all of its implications are conveniently glossed over in the movie.

A tangible reason for the divorce of Susan and Sharon's parents isn't provided within the film. Mitch (Brian Keith) and Maggie (Maureen O'Hara) divorced almost immediately after the girls were born. There are no allegations of infidelity, mental or physical abuse, or even irreconcilable differences mentioned or alluded to—they simply decide to call it quits. This in and of itself seems odd but can be forgiven for the purpose of plot development. However, the subsequent action of separating the girls and keeping them apart—without ever telling either of them about the other—seems cruel even by today's standards.

Once installed in their new homes, Sharon informs Susan that Mitch has a girlfriend that he is planning to marry. The girls agree that this must be stopped and that they need to expedite their plans to reunite their parents before the wedding. They plan to do this by forcing a family camping trip. They promise that at the end of the trip, each will reveal her true identity and return to life with her designated parent. This, of course, doesn't happen. Susan and Sharon scare away the fiancée,

Vicky (Joanna Barnes), and Mitch and Maggie suddenly realize that they are meant to be together and live with their daughters as a family.

Just as no solid reason is ever provided for the divorce, the reasons for the reunion are equally as vague. Since the film begins with the parents already divorced and the children separated, there are no shared events for the viewer to experience. The girls have never met, so they have no shared memories either. It seems the sole reason for the reunion is to make the family unit cohesive. If the parents cannot even remember why they split, doesn't that make the split all the more questionable and even more cruel from the children's perspective?

The preferred reading of the text is that everything turns out for the best and the family lives happily ever after. The oppositional reading, however, poses several relevant questions. If Mitch and Maggie split so easily the first time, what's to prevent it from happening again? Why didn't they work out visitation arrangements rather than taking the drastic step of keeping sisters apart and with no knowledge of one another? Are the girls really better off now than they were previously?

The 1998 remake largely kept the story line intact. In this version, Mitch and Maggie are now Nick (Dennis Quaid) and Elizabeth (Natasha Richardson), and both are conspicuously wealthy. Nick owns a Napa Valley vineyard and Elizabeth is a successful wedding gown designer living in London. The twins put the same scheme into motion with the same results. At the end of the film, Nick and Elizabeth are remarried aboard the Queen Elizabeth II ship with Annie and Hallie (character names changed from the original film) as bridesmaids. The only noticeable difference in the remake is the material upgrades. Both parents live lavishly, which makes the viewer wonder again what the driving force was behind the split. Clearly, they have no financial woes. Also, in 1998, it seemed even more outlandish that modern-day parents would do this to their children.

The Parent Trap remake was a box office success and received overall positive reviews from film critics. It also solidified Lindsay Lohan's early career as a bankable child star.

See also: 1950s: *Summer Place, A*; 1960s: *Patty Duke Show, The*; 1980s: *Sweet Valley High*

Further Reading

Forman-Brunnel, Miriam, ed. 2005. *Girlhood in America: An Encyclopedia*. Westport, CT: Greenwood Press.

Hazel, Andy. 2016. "Why Isn't 'The Parent Trap' a Cult Classic?" *Vice*, July 21. https://www.vice.com/en_au/article/zn7yy5/why-isnt-the-parent-trap-a-cult-classic.

Kastner, Erich. 2015. *Lottie and Lisa*. Brooklyn, NY: Lizzie Skurnick Books.

PATTY DUKE SHOW, THE

The Patty Duke Show, which aired on ABC from 1963–1966, marked a significant milestone in television history by featuring a young female actress in the title role. The premise of the show focused on the exploits of two cousins: American teen

The Patty Duke Show was noteworthy in that it featured a young female star in the title role. At a time when television was dominated by male stars, actress Patty Duke proved that women also had mass appeal. (Bettmann/Getty Images)

Patty (Duke) and her Scottish cousin, Cathy (Duke). Playing a dual role, actress Patty Duke (1946–2016) relied primarily on the use of split screens, two distinct hairstyles, and the use of a slight accent for the foreign-born cousin to distinguish the characters for viewers. A double was used for Cathy, but, because of limited technology at the time, she was only ever seen from the back. In the show, Patty is the outgoing and at times mischievous twin while Cathy is reserved and sensible.

The show was built to showcase Duke's rising star within Hollywood. By the time *The Patty Duke Show* premiered, the teen actress had already been in four motion pictures and won an Academy Award for her supporting role as Helen Keller in the movie version of *The Miracle Worker*. The role originated on Broadway where Duke had also played the same part. In 1962, Duke was the youngest performer ever to win an Academy Award.

The idea for the show grew from a visit that Patty Duke had with the show's creator, Sidney Sheldon. On a visit with Sheldon and his family while brainstorming ideas for a sitcom, Sheldon noted that Duke seemed to have two very contrasting personalities. The role of both Patty and Cathy's fathers was played by actor William Schallert. When Sidney Sheldon made the observation about Duke's behavior, it may have been creative inspiration for the show, but the dark reality of her condition would not be known until many years later. It was not until 1982 that the actress was diagnosed with bipolar disorder. She remarked that after being placed on medication for the illness, she felt "normal" for the first time in her life.

Duke's childhood was chaotic. Duke's mother, raising her from an early age with her two brothers, suffered from depression. Her alcoholic father had been absent for some time after her mother kicked him out of the house. When she turned eight, she was left mostly with Ethel and John Ross, a married couple who were talent agents for her brother Ray. They became fixated on making her into a star. According to Duke, the Rosses were abusive toward her, and she has talked and written about it extensively in her adult years.

Duke won over fans with her portrayal as the twins on television. In an interesting marketing strategy, she was "encouraged" to record music while on the series. She recorded and released two albums during the time of the show: *Don't Just Stand There* (1965) and *Patty* (1966). The actress later remarked that she felt that she could never sing well, but several musical insiders who worked with her noted that her charm and energy compensated for lack of formal training.

The Patty Duke Show didn't necessarily break new ground in its portrayal of young women. However, the show, simply by featuring a young girl in the lead role(s), set the stage for the next wave of female-centric sitcoms. These included *That Girl!* (1966–1971) and *The Mary Tyler Moore Show* (1970–1977); both shows featuring unmarried and independent women who were as concerned with career goals as they were with romance. The plots in *The Patty Duke Show* may have been simplistic and formulaic, but the ability to appeal to a wide TV audience proved that women could attract viewers and garner ratings.

The show was still considered a hit when it was canceled in 1966. The primary reason for the cancelation had to do with state laws regarding child labor. The show was filmed in New York but intended to move production to Los Angeles, and California had much stricter labor laws for child actors than New York. There was also a push at the time to film TV shows in color, and *The Patty Duke Show* was filmed in black and white; production costs to make the conversion were apparently high.

Patty Duke went on to make several theatrical films and a number of TV movies. In addition to the TV show, she is best known for her role in the critically panned at the time (but later to become a cult classic) *Valley of the Dolls* (1967). She played the role of Neely O'Hara, a famous Hollywood actress who succumbs to alcoholism and drug addiction and is eventually admitted to a psychiatric hospital for treatment.

Duke won a Golden Globe Award and several Emmy Awards after the TV show ended. Perhaps more importantly, she became an advocate for mental health and established the Patty Duke Online Center for Mental Wellness in 2005. She felt that her celebrity status afforded her the opportunity to discuss mental health issues and increase awareness among the general population. She authored two books that dealt with mental illness: her autobiography, *Call Me Anna* (1987), and *Brilliant Madness: Living with Manic Depressive Illness* (1992). The actress-activist died in 2016 but left an indelible impression on TV, film, and beyond during her noteworthy career.

See also: 1950s: *Adventures of Ozzie and Harriet, The*; *Father Knows Best*; *I Love Lucy*; *Leave It to Beaver*; 1960s: *Parent Trap, The*; 1980s: *Sweet Valley High*

Further Reading

Duke, Patty. 1987. *Call Me Anna*. New York: Bantam Books.

Duke, Patty, and Gloria Hochman. 1992. *Brilliant Madness: Living with Manic Depressive Illness*. New York: Bantam Books.

King, Susan. 2013. "Remembering 'The Patty Duke Show' 50 Years Later." *Washington Post*, July 6. https://www.washingtonpost.com/entertainment/tv/remembering-the-patty-duke-show-50-years-later/2013/07/03/4e4513ae-df3c-11e2-b2d4-ea6d8f477a01_story.html?utm_term=.abd7d3c52ae8.

Lipton, Michael, and Liz McNeil. 2016. "From the People Archive: Patty Duke Opens Up about Her Battle with Bipolar Disorder." *People*, March 29. http://people.com/movies/patty-duke-opens-up-about-her-battle-with-bipolar-disorder/.

Rose, Jenn. 2016. "8 Times Patty Duke Was the Ultimate Feminist Film Icon." *Romper*, March 29. https://www.romper.com/p/8-times-patty-duke-was-the-ultimate-feminist-film-icon-7942.

ROLLING STONES, THE

The Beatles were not the only British musical group to burst upon the scene in the 1960s. The Rolling Stones also made quite an arrival and had a significant impact internationally on music, fashion, and culture. The band formed in 1962 and included the following original band members: lead singer Mick Jagger, guitarists Keith Richards and Brian Jones, bassist Bill Wyman, drummer Charlie Watts, and pianist Ian Stewart. Playing their first show in 1962 and releasing their first single in 1963, the band quickly became successful in Britain. Competing with the more wholesome band the Beatles, the Rolling Stones' manager Andrew Loog Oldham shrewdly calculated that the band could easily be marketed as the anti-Beatles and draw on a completely different fan base. Paralleling the Beatles' appearance on the *Ed Sullivan Show*, the group's 1967 appearance was noteworthy when Jagger mumbled the lyric, "let's spend the night together" (also the title of the song). Although that line is tame by current standards, it was censor-worthy in 1967.

Mick Jagger was impressed by 1950s artists like Fats Domino and Chuck Berry. His father apparently referred to the music that Jagger was drawn to as "jungle music." It's hard to imagine that this comment was anything other than racist, but it only encouraged Jagger to continue listening to the artists and eventually emulating them to some degree.

As with Elvis Presley and other musical artists covered in this book, the Rolling Stones' music was significantly influenced by and borrowed from black musicians. In the early part of their career, the Stones recorded songs originally released by black artists, and many of the lyrics were steeped in coded sexual imagery and activity: "King Bee," "Little Red Rooster," and "Not Fade Away," for example. Because of censorship issues at the time and also because of continued physical and legislative threats against their community, black jazz artists were forced to be incredibly creative with language when describing sexual activities and even genitalia in song.

Unlike their counterparts the Beatles, the Stones concentrated almost exclusively on sexuality in their early music. Rather than focusing on what they may have considered the more maudlin aspects of intimate relationships, the band recorded songs that delved into the physical aspects of love and lovemaking. They offered their fans the same (or nearly the same) escape that jazz artists offered theirs: feelings of validation in their lives that contradicted what white authoritarianism communicated. Sex was something to be enjoyed and celebrated, not restricted or shamed.

One of the most commercially successful songs of the Stones' career, "Satisfaction," is rife with sexual innuendo. Although Jagger's singing style relies heavily on the slurring of many words, one can hardly miss the line in this about "trying to make some girl." Ironically, while this line was viewed by censors as racy, Jagger bragged in an interview to *Time* magazine years later than they completely missed another coded term in the song about a girl's "losing streak." This apparently refers to the girl missing her period and subsequently becoming fearful that she may be pregnant.

Drug usage was prevalent among the band members, and, as with the Beatles, drugs certainly had an impact on their creativity. A prescription drug, Valium, is the subject of the 1966 Stones' hit, "Mother's Little Helper." The song addresses the popularity of "calming" medications prescribed by doctors. The song specifically targets harried mothers and housewives who use the pill to help them get through exhausting and stressful days dealing with their children.

Although Jagger and Richards have discussed their extensive histories with drug usage (Jagger and Richards were arrested and jailed for a short period of time for drug possession in 1967, and Richards again in 1977 for heroin possession), both claim to have much healthier lifestyles currently and have even spoken out about the dangers of drug use. Richards gave up heroin 35 years ago, and although he has stated he still enjoys smoking pot, his days of hardcore drug usage seem to be behind him.

The longevity of the Rolling Stones is evidenced by the fact that they still tour and do public performances. Although they have now been together for 50 years, they have won only two Grammy Awards: Best Rock Album for *Voodoo Lounge* and Best Video Short for "Love Is Strong," both in 1995. They continue to attract their longtime fans who are aging along with them.

See also: 1950s: Presley, Elvis; 1960s: Beatles, The; Monkees, The; 1970s: Clash, The; Led Zeppelin; Queen; 1980s: Blondie; Duran Duran; 1990s: Green Day; 2000s: My Chemical Romance

Further Reading

Cohen, Rich. 2016. *The Sun and the Moon and the Rolling Stones*. New York: Spiegel and Grau.

Havers, Richard. 2017. *Rolling Stones on Air in the Sixties: TV and Radio History as It Happened*. New York: HarperCollins.

Mazurek, Brooke. 2017. "Keith Richards Recalls the Genesis of Three Classic Tunes." *Harper's Bazaar,* October 26. http://www.harpersbazaar.com/culture/art-books-music /a13090699/keith-richards-interview/.

McKinley Jr., James. 2012. "Like the Band They Follow, Stones Fans Are Grayer But Still Spry." *New York Times*, December 9. https://artsbeat.blogs.nytimes.com/2012/12/09 /rolling-stones-fans-older-and-wealthier-but-still-enthusiastic/.

Schladebeck, Jessica. 2016. "From Threatening to Stab Donald Trump to Getting Caught with Drugs, a Look at the Rolling Stones' Brushes with the Law." *New York Daily News,* May 10. http://www.nydailynews.com/entertainment/rolling-stones-brushes-law -article-1.2631588.

ROOM 222

Room 222 (1969–1974), a groundbreaking, 30-minute dramedy (drama-comedy), covered a group of teachers and students at a fictional Los Angeles school named Walt Whitman High School. At a time when black characters were still predominantly supporting players in both film and television, *Room 222* featured not one but two central black characters: history teacher Pete Dixon (Lloyd Haynes) and guidance counselor Liz McIntyre (Denise Nicholas). Other central characters included Jewish principal Seymour Kaufman (Michael Constantine) and eager new teacher Alice Johnson (Karen Valentine).

At a time when the majority of television shows were broad comedies and music-variety shows, *Room 222* burst onto the scene with a diverse cast and topical subjects that included racism, homophobia, antiwar sentiment, and the displacement of Native Americans. To understand how a show like this made it onto network television to start with, it's important to put it in context. The country was in a period of upheaval and unrest in 1969. Issues of gender inequality, minority rights, and the deep divisions triggered by the Vietnam War were in the consciousness of most Americans. Because television is a for-profit entity, producers felt that they could capitalize on the always desirable youth market by offering a show that catered to the issues of the day while remaining entertaining and not too "radical."

In order to cover these potentially explosive topics, it made sense to cover them within the safety of a classroom setting. Allowing viewers to watch students debate sociopolitical issues within the confines of a school afforded a comfort level to some viewers who might otherwise be uncomfortable. In a controlled environment that is designed for learning, there was little to any danger of any "ugly" confrontations. Students, after all, are encouraged to voice their opinions respectfully and offer educated reasoning rather than personal attacks and arguments.

During this period in education, there was also a demand for content to be relevant. In order to instigate valuable classroom discussions and participation, students wanted authenticity. One way the show addressed this was through having diverse characters in the actual classroom. In an episode centering on the plight of Native Americans, the teacher attempts to draw Native American student Billy into the discussion while other students answer questions from Mr. Dixon. Billy is hesitant to respond to questions, but Mr. Dixon several times attempts to draw him into the conversation. In another episode that dealt with Jewish Americans, the class is treated to a visit from an immigrant who supplements their textbook learning with real-life accounts that enhance the narrative.

Room 222 also did an admirable service to the institution of education by making teachers seem hip or cool. Prior to this era, most media representations of teaching constructed a very clear line of demarcation between teachers and students. This wasn't just in terms of authority and discipline but also in terms of personality and age. Teachers had traditionally been treated with reverence in many media portrayals; *Room 222* portrayed these individuals as human, accessible, and flawed. Perhaps more significantly, the show portrayed two black educators who were committed to their profession with an authentic sense of realism tempered with compassion. In *Room 222*, it is the black teacher who mentors and develops the white newbie, Alice Johnson. Although the administration and teachers face expected dilemmas such as supply shortages, truancy, and high dropout rates, they work collectively within the system to make it as effective and productive as possible.

Viewing the show through a modern-day lens might induce some groans or laughs due to some of the outdated "lingo" that is used, but this can be true for almost all media productions that strive to reflect language that is used by the audience being represented, especially when that audience consists of teenagers.

Although the ratings dipped significantly during the fourth and final season, *Room 222* is now recognized as a significant television series that tackled sensitive issues and portrayed a diverse range of races and ethnicities. The show won three Emmy Awards in 1970: one for "Best New Series" and two for acting: Karen Valentine for Best Supporting Actress and Michael Constantine for Best Supporting Actor.

Room 222 was honored in 2010 by the Paley Center for Media. People involved with the show noted how the network had originally wanted it to be more of a comedy, even going so far as to use a laugh track. Fortunately, the vision that the producers and writers had for the show largely prevailed. The concerted effort to include a rich and diverse cross-section of society was revolutionary at the time and is still noteworthy even by today's popular media standards.

See also: 1950s: *Blackboard Jungle*; *Invisible Man*; 1960s: *Explosive Generation, The*; *To Sir, with Love*; 1970s: *Cooley High*; 1980s: *Fast Times at Ridgemont High*; *Saved by the Bell*; *Sweet Valley High*; 2000s: *Friday Night Lights*; *Glee*; *High School Musical*

Further Reading

Bort, Ryan. 2012. "The 20 Best Teachers from Popular Culture." *Paste*, October 16. https://www.pastemagazine.com/blogs/lists/2012/10/the-20-best-teachers-from-popular-culture.html.

Braxton, Greg. 2010. "'Room 222' Could Teach 'Glee' and '90210' a Thing or Two." *Los Angeles Times*, June 16. http://articles.latimes.com/2010/jun/16/entertainment/la-et-room222-20100616.

LoBrutto, Vincent. 2018. *T.V. in the USA: A History of Icons, Idols, and Ideas*. Santa Barbara, CA: Greenwood Press.

SLAUGHTERHOUSE-FIVE

Slaughterhouse-Five, or, The Children's Crusade: A Duty-Dance with Death (1969) is one of Kurt Vonnegut's (1922–2007) best-known novels. The story centers on a World War II soldier and chaplain's assistant, Billy Pilgrim. The story isn't linear in structure; it involves both flashback and time travel events in Pilgrim's life. Billy hates war and refuses to fight. This, of course, is treated as cowardice by fellow soldiers. During the Battle of the Bulge, he is captured by the German army. Another solider named Roland Weary chides Billy and berates him for his weakness. After Weary contracts gangrene and is dying, he convinces another soldier, Paul Lazzaro, that his death should be attributed to Billy and that Lazarro should track him down and kill him.

Religion and Christianity in particular play an important role within the novel. As the story progresses and Billy is exposed to more and more atrocities and sees the darkest side of human nature, his initial unconditional acceptance of Christianity wavers. Once he begins reading the novel *The Gospel from Outer Space,* Billy becomes fascinated with the concept of a Christ that is human. Not divine. Human. The novel within a novel ponders why Christians can act so hatefully and in contrast with the teachings of Christ and the Gospel. The idea that Jesus Christ is literally "one of us" appeals to Billy in its implications. It is humanist in nature and requires that all humans treat one another with respect and as equals.

The story line has some bizarre twists and turns. After his capture, Billy is kept along with other prisoners of war in an empty slaughterhouse in Dresden (hence the title). Once the Allies defeat the Germans, he is honorably discharged and sent to the United States for treatment. He later marries and has two children with his wife, Valencia. On the night of his daughter Barbara's wedding, Billy is abducted and transported to a planet named Tralfamadore. The Tralfamadorians have supernatural senses and do not subscribe to physical death as the end of life. They believe that beings continue to live in another time and/or place. Their belief system echoes that of reincarnation.

To make more sense of the religious theme of the novel, it helps to know more about the author's background and beliefs. Kurt Vonnegut was also a soldier and was captured and imprisoned by enemy forces during the Battle of the Bulge. His experiences while interned influenced his feelings on war in general. When *Slaughterhouse-Five* was released, it was praised by many as an antiwar novel. This was at a time when strong public sentiment was turning against the ongoing war in Vietnam. Young readers especially connected with the antiwar sentiment.

Vonnegut was an atheist and strongly believed in separation of church and state. Although not affiliating with any official political party, he believed that extremes on either side of the political divide were corrosive to society. He was, however, deeply interested in religion and religious customs. In numerous speeches and writings, he referenced Jesus or God and often talked about the community aspect of being affiliated with churches. He was strong-willed and was named honorary president of the Humanist Association.

His friend and fellow author Dan Wakefield has written about Vonnegut's relationship with religion and spirituality. Wakefield himself became an atheist during college but later converted and became a member of the Unitarian Universalist denomination. Vonnegut was a mentor of sorts to Wakefield, and, after Wakefield announced his newfound religious path, Vonnegut left him a voicemail message that simply said, "I forgive you."

The parallels on religious views between Vonnegut and the fictional character Billy Pilgrim are striking. Just as the character in the novel became fascinated with the concept of a human Christ rather than an all-powerful and divine being, Vonnegut was intrigued with the Sermon on the Mount and the resulting Beatitudes. The author noted that many fundamentalist Christians venerated the Ten Commandments, but ignored or paid scant attention to the overlapping themes of mercy and forgiveness contained within the Beatitudes. This again supports the notion that, according to Vonnegut, of paramount importance is to treat our fellow human beings with compassion and love simply because it is the right thing to do and not out of fear of repercussions in the afterlife for failing to do so.

Teen readers gravitate toward content that questions or challenges formal religion. This reflects their curiosity and sometimes cynicism toward institutions of power and authority. It also echoes themes of rebellion and nonconformity.

Although Vonnegut wrote 14 novels, plays, short stories, and 5 works of nonfiction, he is best known for *Slaughterhouse-Five*. In addition to fast becoming a best seller, *Slaughterhouse-Five* launched him into the professional speech circuit where he was lauded for his dark humor and ability to discuss important societal issues within the realm of fiction. The success of the novel provided him with financial security and also enabled him to teach at both Harvard and City College of New York. His personal life, however, began to disintegrate when his wife became a Christian, driving a wedge between them due to their different belief systems. The two divorced but remained close until her death.

Since its publication, *Slaughterhouse-Five* has been the target of book bans multiple times. As recently as 2011, a school board in Republic, Missouri, unanimously voted to ban the book from school curricula because of its frequent use of profanity and adult themes. According to reports, only one member of the school board had actually read the novel. Books that are controversial and banned, of course, trigger intense interest, especially from the readers that the bans are intended to protect, children.

The novel won the Hugo Award for Best Novel, the Nebula Award for Best Novel, and the National Book Award for Fiction. It is also listed in *Time* magazine's "100 Greatest Novels of the 20th Century" issue. Kurt Vonnegut died in 2007 after brain injuries sustained during a fall at his New York home.

See also: 1960s: *Catch-22*; *Twilight Zone, The*; 1970s: *Six Million Dollar Man, The*; 2000s: *Divergent*; *Hunger Games, The*

Further Reading

Baggett, MaryBeth Davis. 2014. "Kurt Vonnegut: Unlikely Apologist." *Patheos*, February 5. http://www.patheos.com/blogs/christandpopculture/2014/02/kurt-vonnegut-unlikely-apologist/.

Vonnegut, Kurt. 1969. *Slaughterhouse-Five, or, the Children's Crusade: A Duty-Dance with Death*. London: Vintage.

Vonnegut, Kurt, and Dan Wakefield. 2014. *Kurt Vonnegut: Letters*. New York: Delacorte Press.

Wakefield, Dan. 2014. "Kurt Vonnegut, Christ-Loving Atheist." *Image,* Fall. https://imagejournal.org/article/kurt-vonnegut/.

TO KILL A MOCKINGBIRD

Published in 1960, *To Kill a Mockingbird* by Harper Lee received literary praise for its examination of race relations, and remains a staple in many high school literature courses still today. The book has autobiographical elements as Lee wove in some of the events and people from her childhood in rural Alabama. The protagonist and narrator of the story is six-year-old Jean Louise Finch, referred to as "Scout." Scout's father is lawyer Atticus Finch, who takes on the job of defending Tom Robinson on rape charges. The racial element of the story is critical due to the time and setting of the story. Tom is black and the rape victim, Mayella Ewell, is white.

The story takes place between 1933 and 1935, decades prior to the passage of civil rights legislation that was designed to afford equality to black Americans and other minorities. The novel is set in the Deep South, which at the time was rife with open racism and bigotry. Atticus's acceptance of Tom's case creates conflict in the small town where Scout lives with her father and older brother Jeremy ("Jem"). The children in the story are exposed to the worst of human nature when some of the townspeople arrive to lynch Tom. The crowd utters racial epithets and makes threats of violence, but ultimately they are shamed into leaving before any physical harm can be done.

Another story line in the book involves a mysterious neighbor named Arthur "Boo" Radley. Scout, Jem, and their friend Dill, who visits every summer to stay with his aunt, concoct all sorts of possible reasons why Boo is a recluse. They long to draw him out of his house so that they can see him, but he remains elusive for most of the story.

One overriding theme of the novel is the loss of innocence. It becomes evident fairly quickly that Tom is not guilty of the crime of rape. Rather, Mayella took sexual advantage of him and then lied about it when confronted by her father, who physically assaults her when he discovers what really happened. Despite these revelations, Tom is convicted by a jury and is later shot and killed while attempting to break out of prison. This story line obviously shows the ugliness of bigotry, but, perhaps more significantly, it causes young Scout to lose faith in the justice system. It also causes her, at some level, to lose faith in humanity.

Themes of racial inequality and the loss of innocence are timeless, but what Harper Lee did with this story was exceptional. By reading about the events through the lens of a child, readers are able to see how racist and unjust attitudes and actions do exponential harm. Besides the immediate damage they inflict on their victims, these beliefs and actions sow confusion and anger among those who look to adults as role models who enforce fairness. Atticus brings sanity and clarity to this when he tells his children that the key to understanding is empathy, something that the jurors in Tom's court case sorely lacked.

During classroom discussions in the novel, the children quiz their teacher about Hitler and Nazi Germany. The teacher quickly explains that one possible reason for the persecution of Jews is that Germans are not religious people. Scout's classmate Cecil alludes to the fact that both Germans and Jews are white, so he is confused as to why they would be treated differently. The teacher abruptly ends the discussion and moves on to another topic. Knowing that her lesson plan on democracy might take an awkward turn when issues of race surface, the educator avoids the discussion. At this point, Scout becomes angry and dismisses the relevance of education altogether. This is because no one provided her with a rational explanation as to why an innocent man was found guilty of a crime simply due to the color of his skin.

The title of the book comes from a line of dialogue from Atticus to Scout: "it's a sin to kill a mockingbird." During a discussion about different types of birds and their behaviors, Atticus warns that while other types of birds might be shot, mockingbirds are to be left alone. Scout is confused and seeks an explanation from a neighbor named Miss Maudie, who tells her that mockingbirds are pure creatures who live to make beautiful music and do no harm to anyone. This, of course, applies to Tom Robinson and ultimately to Boo Radley as well.

Walking home after a Halloween play, Scout and Jem are physically attacked by Mayella Ewell's father, Bob, who swore vengeance against Atticus after the trial ended. Boo Radley saves both children and delivers them safely back home. The sheriff arrives and talks with Atticus, informing him that Bob Ewell is dead. After some discussion, it's decided that no further investigation is needed and that Mr. Ewell died when he fell upon his own knife.

Harper Lee was repeatedly questioned about various elements of the book in the year after it was published. She seldom provided any substantive responses and shied away from publicity of any kind. Few authors in history have been as celebrated as Lee for one specific piece of work. In addition to winning the Pulitzer Prize in 1961, she received an honorary doctorate degree from the University of Notre Dame in 2006. She was also awarded the Presidential Medal of Freedom on November 5, 2007, by President George W. Bush.

To Kill a Mockingbird sold more than 30 million copies and was adapted into an Oscar-winning 1962 film directed by Robert Mulligan and starring Gregory Peck as Atticus Finch. Peck won an Academy Award for "Best Actor in a Leading Role" and Horton Foote won for "Best Adapted Screenplay." The film is as beloved as the novel and was selected for preservation in the United States National Film Registry by the Library of Congress in 1995.

Shortly before Lee's death, the novel *Go Set a Watchman* was published. Although it was touted as a sequel to her famous first novel, it was later revealed that it was instead a very rough draft of *To Kill a Mockingbird*. The publication of *Go Set a Watchman* created a buying frenzy, with many bookstores staying open past midnight on the publication date in order to meet demand. Amazon reported that it was the most preordered title since *Harry Potter and the Deathly Hallows* in 2007.

Harper Lee, born Nelle Harper Lee, died February 19, 2016.

See also: 1950s: *Invisible Man*; 1970s: *Little House on the Prairie*; 1990s: *Harry Potter*; 2000s: *Book Thief, The*

Further Reading

Johnson, Claudia Durst. 2018. *Reading Harper Lee: Understanding* To Kill a Mockingbird *and* Go Set a Watchman. Santa Barbara, CA: Greenwood Press.

Lee, Harper. 1960. *To Kill a Mockingbird, 50th Anniversary Edition*. New York: Harper Perennial.

Mahler, Jonathan. 2015. "The Invisible Hand behind Harper Lee's 'To Kill a Mockingbird.'" *New York Times*, July 12. https://www.nytimes.com/2015/07/13/books/the-invisible-hand-behind-harper-lees-to-kill-a-mockingbird.html.

Murphy, Mary McDonagh. 2010. *Scout, Atticus, and Boo: A Celebration of Fifty Years of* To Kill a Mockingbird. New York: Harper.

Selk, Avi. 2017. "The Ironic, Enduring Legacy of Banning of Banning 'To Kill a Mockingbird' for Racist Language." *Washington Post*, October 17. https://www.washingtonpost.com/news/retropolis/wp/2017/10/15/the-ironic-enduring-legacy-of-banning-to-kill-a-mockingbird-for-racist-language/.

Shields, Charles J. 2017. *Mockingbird: A Portrait of Harper Lee: Revised and Updated*. New York: Owl Books.

TO SIR, WITH LOVE

To Sir, with Love, a 1967 British drama, features Sidney Poitier (1927–) in the lead role as a teacher, who accepts a temporary job in a rough area of London. Adapted from the autobiographical 1959 novel by E. R. Braithwaite, the film received mixed reviews upon its release. However, it was also a modest box office hit that spawned a hit record of the same name sung by one of the film's stars, Lulu. Poitier's character, Mark Thackeray, is awaiting word on an engineering job that he has applied for, but he needs an income in the interim. He applies for and gets a job teaching at the North Quay Secondary School in London's East End. The students there have largely been rejected (expelled) from other schools, so Thackeray knows beforehand this will not be an easy task.

As Thackeray anticipated, the students are tough to deal with; they are rude, unruly, and at times unmanageable. The savvy moviegoer at this point should be able to predict what happens next: Thackeray begins treating the students as adults, taking them on various outings, and allowing them to generate ideas for topics and

Sidney Poitier and Judy Geeson dance in a scene from the movie *To Sir, with Love*. The popular film highlights the life-changing effects that a thoughtful school teacher has upon his students. (Michael Ochs Archives/Getty Images)

discussions in class. All appears to be going well until an incident between Potter (Chris Chittell), one of his male classmates, and the authoritarian gym teacher creates conflict in the classroom again. Thackeray asks Potter to apologize to the gym teacher, but Potter refuses and manages to turn the rest of the class against Thackeray once again. Eventually, Thackeray rebuilds trust and again commands respect from his students after beating Potter in a boxing match and encouraging Potter to continue training in the sport as he shows talent and promise. Thackeray is invited to the school dance where Barbara (Lulu) sings the title song, "To Sir, with Love," to him as his students look on with great affection. Thackeray realizes that teaching is his true calling, and, at the end of the film, he tears up the offer letter for the engineering position, a dramatic gesture signaling his commitment to education.

Countless films have been made about student-teacher relationships. They range from topical and jarring, like 1955's *The Blackboard Jungle*, to juvenile and overtly sexual, like 1983's *My Tutor*. This is because the role of the educator begets ample storytelling possibilities. The profession is viewed by many as valuable and even noble. Additionally, the conventional roles of teachers and students are prescribed culturally: teachers are largely seen as authoritarian, and students are malleable individuals who can be seriously impacted by their teachers. The effect can be positive, negative, or even both. Inherent in these predefined roles is struggle—struggles between authority and autonomy, and struggles with balancing the personal with the professional.

Perhaps the greatest conflict, and one that audiences seem to gravitate toward the most, is the internal struggle that teachers experience while finding their own authenticity in the confines of an educational system rife with limitations and restrictions. How involved should a teacher get with his students' personal lives? How does a teacher separate student's personal lives from their academic lives? What and where are the boundaries?

The impact of *To Sir, with Love* largely hinges on its setting and time period. Seeing a black schoolteacher in London in the 1960s was rare. Before the story even begins, viewers have preconceived ideas about the role of black men and women in society. To broaden and deepen this, the teacher in *To Sir, with Love* is male, and teachers tend to be female. Additionally, the film smartly avoids any romantic entanglements unlike many of its counterparts, but given the time frame in which it was produced, it can't be certain whether this was intentional, in order to avoid that clichéd plotline, or if hinting at potential romantic undertones was deemed too risky at the box office.

Another pitfall that the film largely sidesteps is that of the myth of the "superteacher." In many teacher-student Hollywood films, the role of the teacher is almost superhuman. Educators are able to solve even the most complicated issues with ease, and they have no qualms about getting involved in the personal lives of their students—all for altruistic reasons, of course.

The 1996 made-for-television sequel to this film, *To Sir, with Love II*, however, utilized the trope of the super teacher. In the movie, Mr. Thackeray (Sidney Poitier) gets embroiled in the family and personal lives of his students. He goes so far as to conceal evidence from police to help a student, even risking his own life in order to save another student from being shot. This plot more closely resembles other student-teacher films such as *Dangerous Minds*, which also features an educator who becomes intimately involved with her students, and places both her physical safety and career in jeopardy in order to save them.

See also: 1950s: *Blackboard Jungle*; 1960s: *Explosive Generation, The*; 1970s: *Cooley High*; *Welcome Back, Kotter*

Further Reading

Braithwaite, E. R. 1959. *To Sir with Love*. New York: Jove Books.
Crowther, Bosley. 1967. "Screen: Poitier Meets the Cockneys: He Plays Teacher Who Wins Pupils Over." *New York Times*, June 15. http://www.nytimes.com/movie/review?res =9E06E3DF103AE63ABC4D52DFB066838C679EDE.

Quinn, Eithne. 2011. "Sincere Fictions: The Production Cultures of Whiteness in Late 1960s Hollywood." *The Velvet Light Trap*, Spring, Vol 67.

Thomas, Susie. 2013. "E. R. Braithwaite: 'To Sir with Love'—1959." *London Fictions*, https://www.londonfictions.com/er-braithwaite-to-sir-with-love.html.

TWILIGHT ZONE, THE

The Twilight Zone (1959–1964), which had a significant impact on its coming-of-age viewers because of its surreal content, originated from the mind of Rod Serling. The show debuted in 1959, and was unlike anything else on television. At the time, Serling was a writer who had experienced some success with television scripts. He initially developed *The Twilight Zone* as a series of anthologies/stand-alone stories featuring both established Hollywood talent and rising stars from the industry. Each episode featured a fully developed story line that usually centered on either science fiction or supernatural events. Episodes often had a moral message designed to make viewers think about issues after the episode ended.

The most effective or powerful *Twilight Zone* episodes were entertaining while illuminating a more significant issue than the plot indicates on its surface. One such episode, "The Little People," focuses on two astronauts stranded on a planet after their spaceship crashes. During the course of repairing it, one of the spacemen (Craig) comes upon a race of people who are miniature. Triggered by his sadistic and narcissistic tendencies, Craig intimidates the tiny people into recognizing him as a Supreme Being and mandating that they must serve and worship him. His power trip, however, is short lived after he forces his partner to leave the planet once the ship is repaired. His plans to rule over the Little People ends abruptly when a new group of people arrive on the planet—they are giants who dwarf Craig. He is so miniscule now in comparison that he is accidentally crushed to death by one of them.

The episode questions what is worthy of worship in American culture. The misleadingly simple plot illuminates issues of the dangers of those who believe that "might makes right." Besides that fairly obvious message, that there is always someone or something that is bigger or stronger, the story highlights human foibles such as ego desires, and the human desire to dominate that which is weaker—or even perceived to be weaker—and ultimately issues of what determines who or what should be in positions of power.

Another popular and critically acclaimed episode is "The Monsters Are Due on Maple Street." Penned by Serling, this story line unfolds in a picturesque suburban American neighborhood. A power outage unleashes a flurry of fear, paranoia, and blind rage among a group of neighbors who are attempting to determine both the cause of the outage and the intentions of whatever caused it. This story serves as an effective allegory for any number of scenarios and situations. Although there is no evidence to suggest that malevolent forces have caused the outage, residents begin to concoct half-baked stories about aliens invading and all sorts of conspiracy theories. Given that the show aired in 1960, one very possible motivation for it

Groundbreaking and innovative, the TV series *The Twilight Zone* focused upon human relationships and behavior within science-fiction settings. The series was later adapted into a theatrical release that was met with mixed reactions from the media. (CBS Photo Archive/Archive Photos/Getty Images)

was a response to the McCarthyism that enveloped the country in the 1950s. The message about the danger of becoming monsters while in search of them is a timeless one.

Few other genres offers more opportunities to explore social issues than science fiction due in large part to its very nature of examining how technology and science dramatically alter the way that human beings function and interact; the genre allows its creators to present stories that provide significant insight into human nature and how human behavior can be impacted by these forces. Though not all episodes of *The Twilight Zone* focused on advancements in technology and science in a futuristic manner, many of the episodes did question some of these "advancements" and their correlation to human relationships.

The growth and popularity of science fiction programs—especially *The Twilight Zone*, which often incorporates other genres as well—owe a creative debt to the early days of horror and mystery thriller radio programs. Long before horror and science fiction shows aired on television, their predecessors were broadcast on radio shows during the 1930s. In these mystery radio shows, the term "mystery" was much broader and encompassed the supernatural as well. These stories combined all sorts of genres including horror, fantasy, and science fiction.

Today, many mystery shows are primarily rooted in the real world, and center upon crimes, usually murder, that have human perpetrators. These shows are fast-paced, and usually focus more on plot than character development or larger themes. The tales are similar to one another, centering on catching murderers or serial killers as the body count grows. The victims are usually attractive women who rely on police to protect them. Regardless of the subgenre of thriller, the formula is fairly predictable, and the viewer is comforted that law and order will vanquish evil in the end.

Given the very limited state of special effects during that period, the subjects of many of these stories could play out only on radio quite easily. Listeners were required to use their imaginations for visuals. For example, the radio show *The*

Demon Tree featured a tree that strangled its victims and then hid them beneath its branches. Were this to be filmed, it would have looked ridiculous, even laughable. But, in radio, horror was telegraphed by sound—music and sound effects—and, perhaps most effectively, the shrieks and screams from the actors who encountered the various monsters and terrors.

Before these types of stories were commonplace in films and books and TV shows, a different type of mystery thriller was born on radio. *Dark Fantasy*, a late night radio show featured on NBC's Red Network, offered stories that shocked and terrified listeners. Although the show only aired for less than a year, its impact is significant. What disturbed listeners and networks in much of the content on *Dark Fantasy* was that it didn't attempt to rationalize or explain away the supernatural elements of its stories. Earlier works that featured supernatural activities almost always presented a natural explanation of the events at the climax of the story; the resolution was grounded in reality.

Dark Fantasy stories examined external horrors that intruded on—even attacked—the routine lives of its protagonists. Content capitalized on the fear that not all was as safe and mundane as it appeared on the surface. This notion that evil and menace lurked beneath the comforts of middle-class existence was noteworthy in that it challenged its listeners to ponder the possibility that two alternate universes commingled with one another. Since the characters in the stories were basically substitutes for the audience members, this was especially jarring.

The success of *The Twilight Zone* TV series later spawned a big screen remake in 1983 that was produced by Steven Spielberg and directed by John Landis. It featured four vignettes, three of them remakes of popular episodes and one original. Baby boomers who were coming of age back in the 1960s still appreciate the show today, which can be found on various streaming platforms, as do more recent millennial viewers. Its impact on television remains significant as is evident by the popularity of shows like *Black Mirror*.

See also: 1950s: *Blob, The*; *I Was a Teenage Werewolf*; 1960s: *Addams Family, The*; *Slaughterhouse-Five*; 1970s: *Carrie*; *Six Million Dollar Man, The*; 1980s: *Back to the Future*; *It*; 1990s: *Buffy the Vampire Slayer*; *Charmed*; *Craft, The*; 2000s: *Divergent*; *Hunger Games, The*; *Twilight*; *Vampire Diaries, The*

Further Reading

Bianculli, David. 2017. "'The Twilight Zone' Is Still One of TV's Most Influential Series." *TV Insider*, September 30. https://www.tvinsider.com/439447/the-twilight-zone-most-influential-tv-series/.

Dawidziak, Mark. 2017. *Everything I Need to Know I Learned in The Twilight Zone: A Fifth Dimension Guide to Life*. New York: Thomas Dunne Books.

Grams Jr., Martin. 2008. *The Twilight Zone: Unlocking the Door to a Television Classic*. Maryland: OTR Publishing.

Killmeier, Matthew A. 2013. "More Than Monsters: Dark Fantasy, the Mystery-Thriller and Horror's Heterogeneous History." *Journal of Radio and Audio Media* 20 (1).

Rubin, Steven Jay. 2017. *The Twilight Zone Encyclopedia*. Chicago: Chicago Review Press.

WHERE THE BOYS ARE

Where the Boys Are, which was released in 1960, is noteworthy for its depiction of teenage sexuality at a time when that topic was still largely ignored by Hollywood. It is based on the book of the same name by Glendon Swarthout. The plot focuses on four female college students headed to Florida for spring break. Merritt Andrews (Dolores Hart) initiates a discussion with the other girls about the potential benefits of premarital sex. While Melanie Tolman (Yvette Mimieux) is the first of the group to follow through on the idea, Tuggle Carpenter (Paula Prentiss) is more focused on finding a husband that just a sex partner. And Angie (Connie Francis) is physically strong and athletic but woefully naive when it comes to interpersonal relationships.

Keep in mind that societal expectations at this time were that women would and should automatically select marriage, regardless of their career plans—if there even were any. In that context, the film is revolutionary in the way it depicts young women who approach sex and relationships very differently from their peers. But the film still presents stereotypes that were prevalent then (and still are to some degree today). For example, Angie is desperate for love and has low self-esteem. Because of her athletic prowess, she is portrayed as the one least likely to find physical love. The implication is that athletic girls are less feminine or appealing and less ladylike than their nonathletic friends. Athletes typically are competitive as well, which is not a trait that was usually afforded to women during this time period. Angie also makes references about the physical qualities of a potential suitor and remarks that he isn't considered handsome by conventional standards. Again, the implication is that it might be the best that she can do.

Merritt, although vocal about a young woman's right to consider premarital sex, discovers that she isn't ready for it after she meets the handsome and charming Ryder Smith, a preppy college boy.

Tuggle admits that she wants to become a "baby making machine." While this goal fits perfectly with social mores at the time, it would most likely be met with cynicism or incredulity in present day. However, the interesting thing about Tuggle's desire is that she doesn't prescribe it for others. She doesn't criticize the others for their choices or desires; she merely has different ones. That can be viewed as refreshing given that so many movie plots rely on infighting among female characters, many times centered on securing the attentions of an available male.

Melanie endures the worst treatment in the film. After having sex with the first boy who tells her that he loves her, she later goes to meet him at a hotel only to discover that he's no longer interested but has set her up with his friend Dill who is told that she is a "sure thing." Then, Melanie is raped. After the assault, she wanders out into traffic, apparently so traumatized that she is either unaware of her surroundings and actions or guilt-ridden over the sexual attack. The other girls find out about the setup and rush to try and help their friend. Upon their arrival, Melanie is struck by an automobile and taken to a hospital.

This is arguably the first depiction of "date rape" in a Hollywood movie. Though the term itself wasn't in existence at this time, it fits the criteria. The assault is reported to the police by one of the girls, and Melanie is kept in the hospital for treatment. Although none of the other girls explicitly blames Melanie for the attack, there are questions about the possible implications. Was Melanie being punished for her sexual activity? Is there an underlying message about the dangerous outcomes of casual sex? Was she simply a victim?

The timing of this film is important. Coming out in 1960, it might have been a response to the stifling sexual oppression of the previous decade. It was a precursor to the wave of "beach films" that would come after it, but none of them delved into issues of overt sexuality or sexual violence. It can be viewed as a possible reflection of the confusing and changing landscape of shifts in sexual mores of the time.

The film ends with Merritt and Ryder sitting on the beach and talking. He offers to drive her, Tuggle, and Angie back to school from Florida. There is talk of possible love, and Ryder indicates that he may be in love with her. The outcome for these three is clearly better than it is for Melanie. Is that because they refrained from having sex?

Where the Boys Are triggered an intense interest from college students in going to Florida for spring break. Prior to the release of the film, the state hadn't been a primary destination point for young people in college. The title song of the film became a huge hit and was sung by one of its stars, Connie Francis.

See also: 1960s: *Gidget*; *Group, The*; 1970s: Blume, Judy; *Harrad Experiment, The*; *National Lampoon's Animal House*; 2000s: *Sisterhood of the Traveling Pants, The*

Further Reading

Coffin, Lesley. 2015 "Re-View: Spring Break Begins with *Where The Boys Are* (1960)." *The Mary Sue*, April 10. https://www.themarysue.com/re-view-where-the-boys-are/.

Reid, Danny. 2015. "Beach Party Summer: Where the Boys Are." *The Retro Set*, June 10. http://theretroset.com/beach-party-summer-where-the-boys-are-1960-2/.

Swarthout, Glendon. 1960. *Where the Boys Are*. New York: Random House.

The 1970s

DECADE OVERVIEW

The 1970s were, in many ways, a continuation of the turbulent 1960s. Opposition to the ongoing Vietnam War increased and women and minorities continued to push for their civil rights. The overall tone of the country, however, was changing. A growing group of individuals, later called "The Silent Majority," rejected the socially and economically liberal policies of the previous decade and its leaders. Republican president Richard Nixon easily won the 1968 national election in a landslide. His victory was a repudiation of previously enacted liberal government policies. His second term would go unfinished, however. Following the fallout from the Watergate scandal, Richard Nixon resigned before being impeached. He was fully pardoned by his successor and former vice president, Gerald Ford, in 1974.

The shooting deaths of four student protesters by National Guardsmen at Ohio State University in 1970 set the tone that would consume the decade. A national culture clash would fuel many of the upcoming battles that would exacerbate deep divisions within the United States' citizenry.

In 1971, the Twenty-Sixth Amendment to the U.S. Constitution lowered the legal voting age from 21 years of age to 18. The argument driving this change was the unfairness of asking young men to serve their country in the military right out of high school but not allowing them to participate in the democratic process of choosing their own government representatives.

Within popular culture, the top-selling novel of 1970 was Erich Segal's *Love Story*. A story about a young couple who meet and fall in love in college, the tale turns tragic when the heroine is diagnosed with leukemia. Despite lukewarm reviews, the book stayed on top of the *New York Times* Best Seller list for more than 10 months. The novel had originated as a screenplay by Segal, but the movie studio asked him to adapt into book format prior to the film's release as a publicity effort.

The top-grossing films of 1970 were *Love Story*, *The French Connection*, and *Airport*. Top-rated television shows in 1970 included *Marcus Welby, M.D.*, *Here's Lucy*, *Ironside*, and *Gunsmoke*.

In a decade that would largely be dominated by rock bands, the most popular groups included the Beatles; Led Zeppelin; Crosby, Stills, Nash, and Young; and Santana. Stadium rock bands such as Aerosmith, Journey, and Styx enjoyed phenomenal success in the mid- to late 1970s. These groups played to massive crowds and employed special effects and pyrotechnics to enhance the audience experience. Though some of it was overhyped by the media, these groups typically lived more hedonistic lifestyles than their 1960s predecessors, with an emphasis on money and fame.

Middle-class families suffered serious financial setbacks during the 1970s. An oil/energy crisis coupled with rising unemployment caused turmoil in a lot of homes. Loan rates at banks increased as individuals and families struggled to pay bills and hold onto their houses and cars. This also served to nurture further divisions along racial and ethnic lines. A counterculture backlash began wherein many blue-collar workers—mainly white—viewed minorities as threats to their economic stability. Factory closings and layoffs fueled this animosity and created conflict and resentment.

Marijuana usage increased in the 1970s, especially among young adults. At the same time, there were concerted education and prevention efforts made to curb this behavior. With a "New Right" wielding political power in the country, President Richard Nixon said he was committed to a war on drugs. John Ehrlichman, who served as Nixon's domestic policy chief, revealed decades later that this was a veiled government effort to disrupt the lives and activities of inner-city blacks and antiwar protesters. Rather than singling them out by name, Nixon believed it would be effective to turn public sentiment against these groups by linking them to heroin and marijuana usage.

By the late 1970s, feminist icons like Gloria Steinem and Shirley Chisholm were at the forefront of the women's rights movement, challenging still present patriarchal domination in the boardrooms and beyond. Some of this was fueled by the failure of the Equal Rights Amendment to be ratified by its original 1979 deadline, preventing legislation that would have guaranteed equal rights to women in matters of divorce, property, and employment.

It is against this evolving backdrop that 1970s popular culture emerged. Some of the most significant media of the decade is covered in this section, which focuses on life in school, shifting sexual boundaries, women's increasing power and autonomy, and the rise of the rock star. All of these had major impacts on young people who came of age in the era of disco and cars.

Further Reading

Cooper, Gael Fashingbauer, and Brian Bellmont. 2011. *Whatever Happened to Pudding Pops? The Lost Toys, Tastes, and Trends of the 70s and 80s.* New York: Perigee.

Rymsza-Pawlowska, M. J. 2017. *History Comes Alive: Public History and Popular Culture in the 1970s.* Chapel Hill: University of North Carolina Press.

Sagert, Kelly Boyer. 2007. *The 1970s: American Popular Culture through History.* Westport, CT: Greenwood Press.

AMERICAN GRAFFITI

American Graffiti (1973) is one of the most iconic and profitable coming-of-age movies in film history. Directed and cowritten by George Lucas of *Star Wars* fame, the film chronicles the events of a group of teenagers living in California over the

The movie poster for George Lucas's *American Graffiti*. The film resonated with critics and audiences alike, due to its authentic portrayal of teens on the brink of adulthood. (Movie Poster Image Art/Getty Images)

course of one evening. Lucas was inspired by his own teenage years growing up in Modesto, California; he felt that many of his experiences were universal, and that these stories connect with a wide audience. However, Lucas faced serious challenges from studio executives over creative control of the finished product. This was due to his relative inexperience in filmmaking at the time, as well as the financial disappointment with his directorial debut, *THX 1138* (1971).

The film takes place in America in 1962, when the nation was culturally between the conservatism and authoritarianism of the 1950s and the counterculture movement of the mid- to late 1960s. The world that the characters inhabit is set before Vietnam War protests were commonplace, and the Civil Rights Act of 1964 had not yet been passed. For most middle-class white teenagers, they did not have major problems, and their lives revolved around hanging out with friends, first romantic encounters, and the fallout from breakups. This was true for the characters in *American Graffiti*, who spend much of their time at Mel's Drive-In. Additionally, the trials and travails of the characters in the film can be viewed to some degree as an analogy of the growing pains that America itself was experiencing simultaneously.

At the start of the film, Curt Henderson (Richard Dreyfuss) and Steve Bolander (Ron Howard) are enjoying their final night of summer vacation as high school seniors. The next morning, they will be heading off to college to start the next chapter of their lives. However, Curt is struggling with the impending move away from home. This theme resonates with teens and young adults who are preparing to leave home for the first time, thereby becoming more autonomous. The transition from high school to college is a common experience and touches on issues of independence, self-confidence, and learning how to navigate the world independently.

Throughout the film, Curt sees a physically attractive but elusive woman driving a Thunderbird (Suzanne Somers). He is intent on meeting her and even makes his way into a radio station where he convinces local deejay Wolfman Jack to broadcast a message to her asking that she call him at a provided phone number. In the original draft of the story, a scene of the woman in her car at a drive-in theater establishes that she is a figment of Curt's imagination. Within the context of the film, this phantom figure may represent Curt's reluctance to leave his hometown—he is looking for any reason to delay that move to college.

Steve informs his girlfriend Laurie (Cindy Williams) that they should date other people while he is away at college. She doesn't directly challenge this idea, but her displeasure is evident. Throughout the film, the two argue and then reconcile until Laurie ultimately leaves him and joins up with Bob (Harrison Ford), a thrill-seeker who loves to drag race.

Two other characters—The Toad (Terry) and John (Paul Le Mat) cruise the strip of Modesto in their automobiles looking for girls. The Toad is using Steve's car, which has been entrusted to him for care while Steve is away at school. Terry meets a girl named Debbie (Candy Clark). Though he is usually socially clumsy, she flirts with him and seems to be interested in possible romance. Bob, in the meantime, is in search of John, whom he wants to challenge in a car race.

The role of the automobile in teen culture has always been significant, but it was especially relevant in the 1950s and 1960s. In many small towns, teen boys would drive their cars in busy commercial areas, usually referred to as "strips," in search of potential female companions or love interests. These were the prime years of "hot rods," cars that were usually very fast and often painted colorfully, sometimes with racing stripes, decals, or even words painted on them to attract attention. The role of the automobile in teens' social lives has always been important because it allows them access to other places away from parent's home. It creates a sense of autonomy and even individuality depending on the automobile.

Near the end of the film, Bob and John have their race at Paradise Road. Laurie is in the car with Bob. Although in the lead, Bob loses control of his car when a tire blows out. The car crashes and then explodes shortly after he and Laurie escape. Steve is there and comforts Laurie, who pleads with him to stay in Modesto. He agrees that he will.

Despite making phone contact with the mysterious blonde woman in the Thunderbird, Curt opts not to meet up with her since he decides that college is the right step for him after all. At the end of the film as his plane takes off, Curt spies the Thunderbird making its way down a country road.

American Graffiti opened to largely positive reviews and decent box office in 1973. Many reviewers applauded both its realism and the performances of its young stars. It was nominated for an Academy Award for Best Picture. The film also received nominations for Best Original Screenplay (George Lucas, Willard Huyck, and Gloria Katz), Best Director (George Lucas), and Best Supporting Actress (Candy Clark). Due to its growing popularity, the movie was rereleased in 1978 when it reaped another $63 million, making it one of the most financially profitable films in history.

George Lucas created what many believe is an American masterpiece that spoke to a generation about teen rites of passage. It assigned real value to an important period of their lives that shaped their adult experiences.

See also: 1950s: *Catcher in the Rye, The*; 1960s: *Group, The*; *Where the Boys Are*; 1970s: *Breaking Away*; *Jaws*; 1980s: *Dirty Dancing*; *Fast Times at Ridgemont High*; *Say Anything . . .*; 1990s: *American Pie*; *Kids*

Further Reading

Abramson, Larry. 2011. "On Location: Cruising with 'American Graffiti.'" *NPR*, August 11. https://www.npr.org/2011/08/11/139280283/on-location-cruising-with-american -graffiti.

Saporito, Jeff. 2015. "What Makes 'American Graffiti' Such a Beloved Picture of Nostalgia for the 1950s?" *ScreenPrism*, November 20. http://screenprism.com/insights/article /what-makes-american-graffiti-such-a-beloved-picture-of-nostalgia-for-the-19.

Stein, Joshua David. 2015. "Review: How American Graffiti's Diner Forever Changed Film." *Eater*, January 29. https://www.eater.com/2015/1/29/7932901/review-how-american -graffiti-diner-forever-changed-film.

Wilkinson, Alissa. 2017. "American Graffiti, George Lucas's Last Film before Star Wars, Is the Perfect End of Summer Movie." *Vox*, September 2. https://www.vox.com /culture/2017/9/2/16219996/american-graffiti-labor-day-movie-of-week-george-lucas.

BEE GEES, THE

If Donna Summer was the Queen of Disco, then the Bee Gees were the Kings of Disco. The band consisted of three brothers: Barry, Robin, and Maurice Gibb. Although they formed as a pop band in the late 1950s, the group achieved huge commercial success in the 1970s, when disco was at its peak. But before that, in the late 1950s, they moved to Australia from England, where they experienced limited success during their early career. After that, in the mid- to late 1960s, the band headed back home to England to continue making music. Although they were initially known for their popular ballads "How Do You Mend a Broken Heart" and "To Love Somebody," they would achieve monumental success and international recognition when they embraced the disco trend. Additionally, songs like "How Deep Is Your Love" and "Night Fever" became coming-of-age anthems for teens discovering and exploring their sexual feelings and impulses.

Where musical artists like Donna Summer and Gloria Gaynor arguably catered to the gay demographic of disco fans, it can be argued that the Bee Gees mainstreamed disco more than any other artist at the time. Unlike the gay culture that was closely associated with disco, the Bee Gees consisted of three white brothers who presented as heterosexual. Additionally, their rise to fame cannot be separated from their inclusion on the soundtrack of seminal disco and coming-of-age film *Saturday Night Fever*. Because of that soundtrack, their image was linked to Tony Romero (John Travolta), the aggressively sexual main character of the film. Romero used his dance talents to seduce single women at dance clubs. By presenting a hypersexualized, heterosexual male as the protagonist, the filmmakers easily side-stepped any pitfalls that might have limited the widespread appeal of the film. Tony's friends are also portrayed as heterosexual, and are fixated on meeting and seducing women at dance clubs.

The Bee Gees' inclusion on the soundtrack connected them not only to the film but also to the disco mania that was sweeping the country. The group was propelled into enormous popularity and success, especially among teens and young adults. Arguably, they also made it more acceptable for young straight men to dance at disco clubs. And since they had recorded and released hit music prior to the *Saturday Night Fever* phenomenon, they already possessed credibility within the music industry.

Prior to being featured on the *Saturday Night Fever* soundtrack, the band had experimented with the disco sound, resulting in the hit singles "Jive Talkin'" and "Nights on Broadway." Both were Billboard Top 10 hits in the United States. The Bee Gees realized quickly that they had found a musical formula that worked for them both stylistically and commercially.

The Bee Gees were known for their very distinctive sound. That sound can be almost exclusively attributed to the falsetto voice of Barry Gibb, in particular. When men sing in the falsetto range of their voice, it produces a high-pitched, somewhat unnatural sound. Often it can obfuscate the gender of the singer, as well as provoke a sense of urgency in the listener. This was ideal for many disco songs that communicated raw emotions and overt sexuality.

However, not everyone appreciated the falsetto-fueled sounds of the Bee Gees' brand of disco. The use of the falsetto by the Bee Gees and other artists drew homophobic criticism from particularly vociferous opponents of disco. Notably, popular disco singer Sylvester also dealt with homophobic criticism. A San Francisco staple in the 1970s club scene, Sylvester James Jr. struck out on his own after leaving a drag ensemble called *The Cockettes*. Known for his garish attire and distinctive falsetto voice, Sylvester was unabashedly comfortable with his flamboyance and sexuality. Although he later attempted to put some distance between himself and his success in the disco genre, he is still primarily known for his dance hits "You Make Me Feel (Mighty Real)" and "Dance (Disco Heat)."

The Bee Gees were also criticized for another reason: cultural appropriation. Although the use of falsettos rose to mainstream popularity during the disco era, the practice has its roots in both gospel and rhythm and blues music. Some contend that they mimicked a vocal style with black American roots and parlayed that into a successful career. The criticism posits that they reinvented themselves and almost exclusively relied on their distinctive sound as a gimmick to sell records without any real connection to the history or origins of the style. But the Bee Gees are not the only artists to be called out for cultural appropriation. It's important to remember that this same criticism has been leveled at artists such as Elvis Presley and Jerry Lee Lewis from earlier decades.

The *Saturday Night Fever* soundtrack became a pop cultural phenomenon. The album remained on the Billboard charts for more than two years and won a Grammy Award for Best Album of the Year. Its success put the Bee Gees into the musical spotlight by reviving their career; it also rejuvenated the popularity of disco music and nightclubs all over the country. In addition to selling more than 200 million records, the Bee Gees have achieved notoriety as a musical group that largely defined an era. Though their last studio recording was more than 15 years ago, their name is still recognized today and is synonymous with the age of disco.

See also: 1970s: Summer, Donna

Further Reading

Bryon, Dennis. 2015. *You Should Be Dancing: My Life with the Bee Gees*. Toronto, Canada: ECW Press.

Kerr, Jack. 2014. "Stayin' Alive by Bee Gees—Embracing a Very Un-Australian Anthem." *The Guardian*. October 27. https://www.theguardian.com/music/australia-culture-blog/2014/oct/28/stayin-alive-by-bee-gees-embracing-a-very-un-australian-anthem.

Meyer, David. 2013. *The Bee Gees: The Biography*. Philadelphia: De Capo Press.

Spence, Simon. 2017. *Staying Alive: The Disco Inferno of the Bee Gees*. London: Jawbone Press.

BLUME, JUDY

Author Judy Blume (1938–) is synonymous with the literary genre now known as "young adult." Given the current popularity and success of numerous young adult novels, it's difficult for some younger readers to imagine a time before this market existed. These are books specifically written for and targeted toward teen readers (in some cases, even preteen). Decades before *The Hunger Games* trilogy and the *Divergent* series, Blume penned a number of novels that connected with young readers and became best sellers that shaped a new genre of fiction that has enjoyed significant success ever since.

Blume's second book dealt with the issue of race. *Iggie's House* (1970) examines what happens when the first African American family moves into an all-white neighborhood. Although the effort itself was well intentioned, Blume was largely dismissed by critics who felt the characters and the dialogue were weakly developed. Her second novel, *Are You There God, It's Me, Margaret* (1970) was met with a much more positive reception. The story's title character navigates adolescence and all of the trials and challenges that come along with it, including menstruation. Readers and critics alike embraced the novel for its forthright tone that masterfully balanced the serious with the comedic. What resonated with readers was Blume's uncanny ability to tap into the minds of adolescent girls and share their thoughts and fears and desires so realistically.

Margaret attends all sorts of worship services in all sorts of settings but becomes frustrated when she cannot seem to "find" God in any of them. She observes that she only feels connected to God when she is alone and speaking to him privately. Both sets of grandparents feel compelled to weigh in on the issue, further confusing and frustrating Margaret. By the end of the book, Margaret's dilemma is still unresolved, or perhaps it is when she chooses neither Christianity nor Judaism. This issue resonates with teens as they grapple with self-identity and relevant issues such as spirituality and religious identity. Blume's story provides comfort in showing that it's perfectly normal to question these big issues and not to automatically adopt whatever has been practiced by parents and other adults.

Margaret's parents' interfaith marriage and its effects on her had a significant impact on the novel. At a time when interfaith marriages between Jews and Christians were just gaining traction, Blume made a conscious effort to address this within Margaret's story. Though Margaret isn't being raised to practice a specific religion, her father is Jewish and her mother is Christian. She searches for meaning (religion/God) throughout the story and agonizes over whether she should attend the YMCA or a Jewish Youth Center.

Blume's many subsequent titles, such as *Tales of a Fourth Grade Nothing* (1972), *Blubber* (1974), and *Superfudge* (1980) also enjoyed critical and commercial popularity and tackled issues of burgeoning sexuality and the effects of divorce on preteens. She fast became the most popular author of young adult literature in the 1970s and beyond.

The author broke from this genre in 1975 with the publication of her novel, *Forever.* Unlike her previous books, this one dealt explicitly with teenage sexuality. The novel's two central characters, Katherine and Michael, meet and begin a sexual relationship that both believe will last forever. The novel received mixed reviews but was the target of a serious backlash from censors. Abstinence groups and other religious groups took aim at the book because of its depiction of teenage sexuality and its character's use of contraception.

Blume's 1981 novel, *Tiger Eyes,* is considered by many to be her best young adult novel. The story addresses the issue of loss of a parent. Davey Wexler experiences tremendous grief after the murder of her father; she then moves to Los Alamos with her mother and begins a new phase of her life with the help of an uncle and a boyfriend. Perhaps weary of earlier controversy and censorship efforts, Blume allegedly self-censored the novel by omitting an original passage where Davey masturbated while thinking about her new boyfriend. Blume's editor convinced her that the book would more likely reach more readers if this passage was removed.

Judy Blume's first novel written for and marketed toward adults was published in 1978. *Wifey* told the story of unsatisfied housewife Sandy Pressman and her search for fulfillment through an extramarital affair. In an era of open marriages and a sexual liberation movement for women, the timing of the book (along with the already established popularity of its author) was fortuitous. *Wifey* became a publishing sensation and sold more than four million copies.

Judy Blume is an icon within the publishing industry. Her books, especially the ones written for teens and preteens, are woven into popular culture. In addition to creating characters and voices that young readers could relate to, she is a fierce advocate for intellectual freedom and has battled censorship throughout her career. Blume continues to write adult novels today, her most recent being *In the Unlikely Event* published in 2015. Her books have sold more than 80 million copies, and she has won countless awards for her work. *Are You There, God, It's Me, Margaret* is listed on *Time* magazine's All-Time 100 Novels list.

See also: 1950s: *Catcher in the Rye, The*; *Summer Place, A*; 1960s: *Outsiders, The*; *Where the Boys Are*; 1970s: *Go Ask Alice*; 1980s: *Flowers in the Attic*; 1990s: *Harry Potter*; McDaniel, Lurlene; 2000s: *Divergent*; *Hunger Games, The*

Further Reading

Bristol, Margaret. 2012. "Most Controversial Judy Blume Books." Huffington Post, February 12. https://www.huffingtonpost.com/2012/02/12/judy-bloom-books_n_1269464 .html.

Dawson, James. 2015. "Judy Blume's 'Forever:' The First and Last Word on Teen Sex?" *The Guardian*, September 6. https://www.theguardian.com/childrens-books-site/2015 /sep/06/judy-blume-forever-teen-sex-james-dawson.

Dominus, Susan. 2015. "Judy Blume Knows All Your Secrets: After 17 Years, the Confidante for Legions of Young Readers Is about to Publish a New Novel for Adults." *New York Times*, May 18. https://www.nytimes.com/2015/05/24/magazine/judy-blume -knows-all-your-secrets.html.

BREAKING AWAY

Breaking Away, a 1979 coming-of-age story, focuses on a Midwestern teen who dreams of becoming a professional bicycle racer. Dave Stoller (Dennis Christopher) and his friends Mike (Dennis Quaid), Cyril (Daniel Stern), and Moocher (Jackie Earle Haley) have just graduated from high school and spend most of their time swimming in a local abandoned quarry. They are all sons of "cutters"—laborers who worked at the local limestone quarry and literally cut stone for a living. The term is used as an insult by local college students at Indiana University to identify lower-income residents of the town. Dave becomes fixated on bicycle racing and is especially intrigued with Italian racers. He soon becomes obsessed with Italian culture and language as well, much to the dismay of his father, Ray (Paul Dooley).

Dave's preoccupation with bicycling and Italian culture irritates his father, a former cutter who now runs his own used-car business. Dave's mother, Evelyn (Barbara Barrie), makes an effort to understand and be supportive by preparing Italian food dishes for the family and indulging Dave's interest. Dave soon finds himself attracted to a local university student, Katherine (Robynn Douglass), and pretends to be an Italian exchange student in order to get close to her.

The young cast of the sleeper hit *Breaking Away*. The film delighted audiences with its comedic take on one teen's obsession with professional cycling. Its examination of small town life
and its teen characters was refreshingly honest, even poignant. (John Springer Collection/
Corbis via Getty Images)

Many teen comedies go for the "easy laugh." Pandering to their target audiences,
they focus on sight gags, excessive profanity, casual drug usage, and an obsession
with sex. A wave of these types of films were produced and released in the 1980s,
starting with *Porky's* (1981) and continuing through the following decade with
American Pie (1999). However, *Breaking Away* is a "quiet" teen comedy that shows
respect for its characters and their plight. It earns its laughs primarily through
character development and interpersonal relationships.

The transition from high school to the next phase of life is often a challenging
experience for youths. Young adults are expected to know what they want to do
with the remainder of their lives, career-wise, and then go off and obtain a degree
in that field. Many times, this means leaving home for the first time, and potentially ending a romantic partnership because of the challenge of long-distance relationships; the desire for other intimate experiences can be tempting.

The issue of identity is critical to teenagers. We form our identities based on a
number of factors, not the least of which is our families and environments. Dave is
similar to many teens who may lack self-confidence and are keenly aware of socioeconomic differences between themselves and others. Regardless of this, or maybe
because of it, the bonds that are formed among the four boys are strong. After Cyril
helps Dave arrange a romantic gesture for Katherine, her boyfriend and some of his
fraternity brothers beat up Cyril, mistaking him for Dave. Mike wants retribution

and insists that they confront the attackers. The university president, in an effort to make amends, invites Dave and his friends to participate in the annual Indiana University Little 500 race.

As the story progresses, it becomes even more obvious how dedicated Dave is to his racing. In one scene, he is training for speed by riding his bike on the shoulder of the highway. A truck driver begins signaling him to communicate his speed—four fingers for 40 miles per hour, five fingers for 50 miles per hour, and so on. Most people don't typically associate the sport of bicycle racing with edge-of-the-seat suspense, but the director (who also helmed the action classic *Bullitt*) is able to do so, partly because the audience members are so invested in the protagonist by this point.

After taking an opportunity to cycle with a group of Italian racers who come to town, Dave is devastated to learn that they cheat in order to win. When he shares this and confesses his deception to Katherine, she is furious and ends their budding relationship. Dave and his friends form their own team to compete in the Little 500 annual bicycling race. Rather than shy away from their status, they celebrate it by naming their team "Cutters" and brandishing the word on their shirts.

Another thing that *Breaking Away* does much better than most teen comedies is the manner in which it depicts the parents. Dave and his mother are close, and there is a warmth there that seems very natural. Even though his father is depicted as gruff, a scene near the end of the film reveals him to be more sensitive and empathetic than Dave—and the audience—have been led to believe. Fleshing out these two characters and making them more than one-dimensional stooges enhances the story line and makes Dave appear more like a "normal" teenager than he otherwise would.

By demonstrating stellar teamwork and relying heavily on Dave's prowess in the race, the "Cutters" are victorious. Dave enrolls in college at the end of the film and immediately begins trying to impress a female French exchange student with his knowledge and love of the Tour de France biking competition.

Breaking Away received rave reviews from famed critic Roger Ebert and others. It won an Academy Award for Best Original Screenplay and also a Golden Globe for Best Motion Picture-Musical or Comedy. Dennis Christopher also snagged a few acting awards for his role in the film.

See also: 1950s: *On the Road*; 1970s: *American Graffiti*; 1990s: *American Pie*

Further Reading

Brooks, Xan. 2013. "Why I Love . . . the Quarry in Breaking Away." *The Guardian*, August 22. https://www.theguardian.com/film/2013/aug/22/why-i-love-breaking-away-quarry.

DiMare, Philip C., ed. 2011. *Movies in American History: An Encyclopedia*. Santa Barbara, CA: ABC-CLIO.

Leonard, Mike. 2014. "How True Was 'Breaking Away?'" *Bloom Magazine*, June 12. http://www.magbloom.com/wp-content/uploads/2014/06/16_breakingaway.pdf.

Vallely, Jean. 1980. "Breaking Away: A Real Life Fairy Tale with a Happy Ending." *Rolling Stone*, April 17. https://www.rollingstone.com/movies/features/breaking-away-19800417.

CARRIE

Stephen King (1947–) is one of the most prolific writers in modern American history. He has written more than 50 novels (several written under the pseudonym Richard Bachman) and sold more than 350 million copies. Although he had limited success with a few short stories that were published after he graduated from college, his first novel *Carrie* became a best-selling novel that catapulted him into commercial and critical success. *Carrie* is a supernatural coming-of-age story focusing on a socially awkward high school girl and her tormentors. Carrie White is a teenager with a dark secret. Her mother is a religious zealot who routinely ridicules and assaults her for perceived failings. Carrie is not allowed to wear current styles of clothing or to wear makeup due to her mother's rigid religious beliefs. She has no friends at school and suffers under a group of female bullies. Carrie also has telekinetic powers; she can move objects with the power of her mind. After a particularly vicious prank in the girl's locker room in which she is pelted with menstrual products, the bullies are punished by a sympathetic gym instructor. The leader of the group rebels and loses her prom privileges. She then vows revenge on Carrie and devises a plan to humiliate her at the school prom.

On a superficial level, the book may be viewed as a standard horror tale, but at its core it is a sympathetic tale of an outsider who's coming of age and wants only to fit in with her peers. Stripped of its horror element, the story is about alienation and psychological abuses perpetrated by parents upon children.

The film and book both contain unforgettable images of a prom that morphs into a gruesome bloodbath. King doesn't shy away from the level of carnage that the protagonist unleashes after she is humiliated in front of the entire school, which made the book so different from other horror novels at the time.

Because the prom is a universal rite of passage for teens, and the overall high school experience can be negative and challenging for so many, having the teen protagonist literally destroy the school and her tormentors at a prom connects with a young audience on a deep-rooted level. The book was written at a time before "teen bullying" was as widespread and vicious as it seems to be currently. It was also pre–social media and pre–school mass shootings.

Another unique element of the book is its form. Rather than using a standard first or third person narrative, King mixes several forms and devices together that include fictional newspaper articles and even fictional academic papers written by "students" in the book. It's interesting to note that, for an author not known for brevity in his novels (many of them being over 500 pages long), his first effort came in under 300 pages and is economical in word choice.

King was inspired to write the story after working one summer as a janitor in a high school. He noticed while cleaning the bathroom and shower areas of the girl's dressing area that the showers had plastic curtains unlike those in the boy's locker room. He imagined what might happen if a young girl was showering without this element of privacy and experienced her first menstrual period without having any idea what was happening to her. How would other girls react to this? An unrelated event—something he read about telekinesis—made its way into the origin of the story as well. This shower image became the opening scene of the film adaptation and conveyed the horror and casual cruelty of Carrie's high school experience. He based the character of Carrie White on a composite of young girls he'd attended school with as a boy. And even though Stephen King is a household name at this point, the initial idea and outline for *Carrie* was (literally) tossed in the garbage can by King before his wife Tabitha retrieved it and discussed its potential for success. King apparently felt unable to write from the perspective of a teenage girl and felt it was ultimately a futile effort to give an honest and authentic voice to the character.

Carrie resonates with readers—as do most of King's books—because they can relate to the realness of the character's situations. Most teens despise the caste system of high school with its self-appointed "insiders" and hierarchy of social status. Carrie White has everything going against her: mean-spirited peers, unsympathetic school administrators, and a rabidly oppressive mother. It's no wonder that readers identify with her even when she's setting her high school ablaze and killing her foes.

The film version of King's novel was released in 1976. It garnered largely favorable reviews and earned Oscar nominations for two of its stars: Sissy Spacek as Carrie White and veteran actress Piper Laurie as her mother, Margaret White. The film was remade in 2013 and starred Chloe Grace Moretz in the title role and Julianne Moore as Carrie's mother. The effort was largely panned as unnecessary, and the film didn't fare well at the box office.

See also: 1960s: *Twilight Zone, The*; 1970s: *Chocolate War, The*; 1990s: *Buffy the Vampire Slayer*; *Charmed*; *Craft, The*; *I Know What You Did Last Summer*; *Scream*; 2000s: *Mean Girls*; *Pretty Little Liars*; *Twilight*; *Vampire Diaries, The*

Further Reading

Cardin, Matt, ed. 2017. *Horror Literature through History: An Encyclopedia of the Stories That Speak to Our Deepest Fears.* Santa Barbara: ABC-CLIO.

Flood, Alison. 2014. "How Carrie Changed Stephen King's Life, and Began a Generation of Horror." *The Guardian*, April 4. https://www.theguardian.com/books/2014/apr/04/carrie-stephen-king-horror.

Gleiberman, Owen. 2013. "The Original 'Carrie' Is the Movie That Made Me Want to Be a Critic." *Entertainment Weekly,* October 18. http://ew.com/article/2013/10/18/carrie-made-me-want-to-be-a-critic/.

King, Stephen. 1974. *Carrie.* New York: Doubleday

CHARLIE'S ANGELS

Charlie's Angels (1976–1981), a popular 1970s television series, became a pop cultural phenomenon that propelled the careers of all three of its stars: Jaclyn Smith (1945–), who played Kelly Garrett, Kate Jackson (1948–), who played Sabrina Duncan, and Farrah Fawcett-Majors (1947–2009), who played Jill Munroe.

Produced by TV hit maker Aaron Spelling, this police drama featured three female detectives who routinely took on dangerous assignments for their boss, Charlie. The weekly opening of the show succinctly communicated the backstory of the "angels" and their foray into crime solving: "Once upon a time, there were three little girls who went to the police academy. And they were each assigned very hazardous duties but I took them away from all that and now they work for me. My name is Charlie." Charlie was the owner of the Charles Townsend Detective Agency. The "hazardous duties" referred to in the opening was tongue in cheek humor. All three angels were dissatisfied with the mundane daily duties assigned to them as novice cops, so they eagerly join the detective agency in order to further their professional careers.

The actresses taking on these roles varied in their acting experiences prior to the show. Kate Jackson was the most well-known and had already appeared regularly on several television shows including *The Rookies*. Jaclyn Smith had done smaller parts on various TV programs, and Farrah Fawcett-Majors was primarily known for being married to the star of the popular show *The Six Million Dollar Man*, starring Lee Majors.

The show was an immediate ratings hit, but the critics largely savaged it. The plots were unsophisticated and lacking in complexity and the acting was considered subpar. However, the show made no pretense about its ambitions. It featured three physically attractive women who regularly appeared in swimsuits and other revealing outfits. It can also be argued that it did empower women to take on roles usually reserved for men.

Teen boys enjoyed the show largely because of the sex appeal of the three young actresses. Teen girls, however, were exposed to three young women who were working as private detectives in occupations that historically had been occupied by men. Young girls could also identify more strongly with one angel over another based on their personalities. There was also the undeniable glamour of seeing the women go undercover and pretend to be other people and dressing for the part. The influence of their styles and overall appearance cannot be denied. One of the most popular hairstyles of the late 1970s was the one sported by Farrah Fawcett-Majors on the show.

The question of whether or not this show was feminist has been debated for decades. Some argue that the characters were comfortable with their abilities and their sexuality and placed themselves in dangerous situations in order to accomplish their work. Others contend that the emphasis on physical beauty and sexuality negated whatever positive messages might have come from these characters' professional successes.

Extending the argument against any feminist progression, critics noted that the show's leads presented a nonthreatening brand of feminism where it was always clear that, while they could do the same work as a man, they realized and exploited their sexuality to further their goals. In other words, they would never say or do anything that would be considered radical by men or even other (more conservative) women.

A counterpoint to this perspective notes that, even though the angels used their physical beauty to gain access to people and situations that would further their cases, their work always came first. When they posed as models or dance instructors, they did so with the sole intent of solving a crime—the job for which they had been hired. Many of these professions were appealing to young girls at the time because women hadn't yet made equitable inroads into male-dominated professions. These were the most widely available career paths at the time, especially for women with limited resources and access.

Keeping the discussion within context of the time period, this was a critical point in the history of the women's movement where equal rights activists were deeply concerned about equal pay and equal opportunities for women while more socially conservative individuals and groups felt that clear lines had already been established about women's roles in our culture. The fact that a primetime TV show even attempted to address this in any way is noteworthy. Its possible impact or influence on young girls is an important issue for historical discussion and analysis.

Farrah Fawcett-Majors was the breakout star of the first season but refused to come back for another season. She was sued by the network and agreed to do a number of guest appearances in subsequent seasons as part of the financial agreement that was reached. Her character was replaced by actress Cheryl Ladd, who played Jill's younger sister, Kris. Other cast changes followed with the addition of Shelly Hack and Tonya Roberts as "replacement" angels.

The show nosedived in popularity after season two but held on for several more seasons. Some of this was attributed to cast changes; some of it was due to the novelty of the premise wearing off. Fawcett-Majors moved on to make a series of box office disappointments while Smith and Jackson continued to do television movies and series. Eventually, Fawcett (who dropped "Majors" after a divorce) won critical acclaim for her performances in serious TV movies such as *The Burning Bed* and in a strongly regarded performance in the off-Broadway play *Extremities* (she also starred in the film version).

An updated version of the show entitled *Angels '88* suffered production delays and was never picked up. Theatrical adaptations of the series were released in 2000, *Charlie's Angels*, and in 2003, *Charlie's Angels—Full Throttle*. The films starred Drew Barrymore, Lucy Liu, and Cameron Diaz.

See also: 1970s: *Six Million Dollar Man, The*; *Starsky & Hutch*; 1990s: *Buffy the Vampire Slayer*

Further Reading

Metraux, Julia. 2016. "Flashback: Charlie's Angels." *McGill Tribune*, November 25. http://www.mcgilltribune.com/a-e/flashback-charlies-angels-657456/.

Poole, W. Scott. 2014. "'Jiggle TV?' Charlies Angels.'" *PopMatters*, February 18. https://www.popmatters.com/179217-charlies-angels-season-one-2495686463.html.

Zaslow, E. 2009. *Feminism Inc.: Coming of Age in Girl Power Media Culture*. New York: Palgrave Macmillan.

CHOCOLATE WAR, THE

Most people are familiar with the controversies and bans surrounding books such as *The Catcher in the Rye* and *1984*. Although it didn't receive as much attention as those two renowned works, Robert Cormier's (1925–2000) *The Chocolate War* (1974) has also been a target of criticism for its content and has been challenged by parents' groups and others as unsuitable material for school children. *The Chocolate War's* plot summary may at first seem benign: on a dare, an incoming high school freshman refuses to take part in an annual candy bar sales drive that profits the school. How that unfolds and the issues raised by the story, however, challenge notions of conformity, abuse of power, and inherent dangers of individualism within a group.

Jerry Renault, a new student at Trinity Catholic High School, is coping with both the aftermath of his mother's death and his grief-stricken father. The school houses a secret society of mean-spirited students known as "The Vigils." The leader of the group, Archie Costello, schemes to manipulate Jerry into a prank where Jerry will refuse to sell any candy for the yearly school fund-raiser. The catch is that he will only abstain for 10 days and then will join in with the other students. Jerry then decides that his refusal should be absolute rather than temporary. This attracts the attention and scorn of Trinity's vice principal, Brother Leon. Archie and Leon are colluding, but both become incensed when Jerry attempts to make a statement and not back down from his stance.

Viewed initially as heroic, the student body reveres Jerry; that changes quickly when Leon and Archie intimidate and coerce them into executing a series of pranks on Jerry that culminate in a physical attack from school bully, Emile Janza.

The Chocolate War examines issues of conformity and individuality, institutional abuse of power, bullying, and groupthink. While these topics have been explored in other novels, *The Chocolate War* is somewhat unique in its conclusion and bleakness. The typical young adult novel confronting these issues usually has a "feel good" ending where the rebel, while temporarily displaced or challenged, realizes that his efforts are worthwhile and he or she has done the right thing. The audience is assured that things will be okay and that justice and equality has prevailed.

The Chocolate War offers no such redemption. The finale of the book centers on a boxing match between Jerry and Emile. Although the fight is stopped short by a teacher, Brother Leon comes to the aid of Archie, who arranged it, and contends that he shouldn't be punished because of his outstanding contributions to the success of the candy sales fund-raiser. Jerry concedes defeat and confides in his best friend Goober that his efforts were ill-fated and futile.

Books like *Lord of the Flies* examine societal breakdowns among children when adults are not present to intervene or provide guidance on moral issues. In this book, however, the authority figure, Brother Leon, is corrupt himself. The other children at Trinity are psychologically manipulated into harassing their fellow student. Jerry has no one to advocate for him, at least no one in power who can have sway over events.

The takeaway from the novel is painful. It's also realistic. Standing up and speaking truth to power isn't easy, and many times the consequences are severe. Children and adolescents are powerless within an institution like Trinity. Their role is to do what they are told and not to question authority. To worsen matters, here they become part of the abuse as they are used by a central power figure at the school to commit mean-spirited and cruel acts.

The character of Brother Leon is especially disturbing as he is shown to be a consistent bully. In one passage of the book, he denigrates a bright student in front of the class and then manages to make himself look like the hero when he blames the rest of the class for not coming to the aid of the boy he is berating.

The Chocolate War was critically acclaimed for its intense writing and gritty portrayal of life inside a private high school. The novel won several prestigious awards including: ALA Best Books for Young Adults, School Library Journal Best Books of the Year, Kirkus Reviews Choice, and New York Times Outstanding Books of the Year. The books spawned a sequel, *Beyond the Chocolate Wars* (1985), which followed more mayhem and bullying at the hands of Archie Costello.

The Chocolate War was adapted into a theatrical film in 1988 that was well-received critically but a commercial failure. In the film adaptation, the ending has been changed to allow Jerry to win the boxing match at the end, and via a plot contrivance, Archie must step in for Emile. This altered conclusion negates or at least softens many of the themes explored within the novel.

See also: 1950s: *Catcher in the Rye, The*; *Lord of the Flies*; 1970s: *Carrie*; 2000s: *Mean Girls*

Further Reading

Cormier, Robert. 1974. *The Chocolate War*. New York: Ember.

Junko, Yoshida. 1998. "The Quest for Masculinity in *The Chocolate War*: Changing Conceptions of Masculinity in the 1970s." *Children's Literature 26*, 105–122. Project MUSE.

Robinson, Tasha. 2012. "Robert Cormier's The Chocolate War Is a Much-Banned, Malevolent Gem." *AV Club*, August 6. https://www.avclub.com/robert-cormier-s-the-chocolate -war-is-a-much-banned-ma-1798232684.

CLASH, THE

One of the most popular punk rock bands in history, the Clash formed in London in 1976 with members Joe Strummer (lead vocals, rhythm guitar), Mick Jones (lead guitar, lead vocals), Paul Simonon (bass guitar, vocals) and Nicky "Topper" Headon (drums, percussion). Although it wasn't until their third album, *London Calling*, was released in the United States that they gained international attention, they were popular in the United Kingdom almost immediately. Capitalizing and building on the existing popularity of fellow British punk band the Sex Pistols, the Clash began playing clubs, where they quickly gained fans. Strummer understood the appeal of punk rock and appreciated its contrary, even antagonistic relationship with its audiences. Bands that typically played in pubs strained to please their audiences and react to the "tone" of the room accordingly. Punk rock bands, however, played what they wanted when they wanted with no apologies.

Punk rock's origins can be found in the mid-1970s in both the United States and Great Britain, primarily in New York City and London. Stateside, the punk movement was an outgrowth of the work and influence of various artists including Andy Warhol. Popular punk groups like the Stooges and the New York Dolls flourished in this environment. There were countless other punk rock bands in New York City, but because of excessive drug usage and other unsafe behaviors, many of them had only short-term success. Other large cities, including San Francisco and Boston, soon developed their own punk rock communities. Regardless of the location, the driving force behind the Punk movement was anger—anger at the government, and anger at other institutional hierarchies of power. Although the punk attitude is often associated with liberal politics, fans cross the ideological spectrum. Punk rockers have varying beliefs and ideologies, but they all find inherent value in individualism and nonconformity.

In 1976, the Clash played with the Buzzcocks and the Sex Pistols at a large concert in the United Kingdom, solidifying their up-and-coming status within the punk rock movement. One year later, the band signed a record deal with CBS Records. The contract drew a lot of negative attention from press and fans. Given the roots of the punk movement and its fierce opposition to the idea of "selling out," many punks viewed this transaction with skepticism and disdain. Although their first album with CBS, *The Clash*, did well in Great Britain, record executives nixed giving it an American release as they felt the sound was too unpolished and "raw" for audiences in the United States.

Punk rock connected deeply with disaffected youths on both sides of the pond. The content and style of the music reflected teen angst and rebellion in a new and unique way. Young fans felt a deeply personal connection to songs that derided authority and control and that promoted autonomy and self-expression in their lyrics.

Fashion was also extremely important in the punk rock movement. Punk style thumbed its nose at mainstream trends and defied all manner of conventional fashion. Fans wore wild, often colorful, hairstyles, and sported edgy, DIY fashions. The typical haircut for male punk rockers was short and spiky, although mohawks were popular as well. Johnny Rotten and Sid Vicious of the Sex Pistols were early influencers, sporting ripped white T-shirts and safety pin embedded leather jackets. Tattoos and all manner of body piercings soon became standard as well.

Female punk rockers often sported the same short spiky hairstyles favored by men. They also gravitated toward black leather jackets and ripped T-shirts, defying traditional gender conventions. One reason that so many young women sported what would be considered typically men's clothing styles is that they wanted to make others uncomfortable in their assumptions. Causing strangers to take a "second look" to try and determine the gender of a punk rocker was a victory, because it challenged many stereotypes that extend beyond fashion. Female punk rockers got raucous at concerts and clubs, getting just as physically aggressive in mosh pits as their male counterparts. Some chose to wear nothing but bras and panties out in public, pushing the notion of what was considered ladylike attire.

The Clash's third studio album, *London Calling*, was a smash hit in the United States and brought the group intense popularity and notoriety. Released as a double album in Great Britain, *London Calling* was released in 1980 in America where it reached platinum sales status (one million copies sold). One song that was added at the last minute entitled "Train in Vain" became a hit single in America and propelled the band into superstardom. The band had a distinct political bent and were antimonarchy and antielitism, though maybe not to the conspicuous degree that the Sex Pistols had been.

A 1981 hit entitled "This Is Radio Clash" demonstrated that the band could mix musical genres successfully, featuring a hip-hop sound embedded within their trademark rock sound. Additional hits followed along with heavy video rotation on MTV, keeping the band in the forefront of the Western musical scene through the mid-1980s. Two hits from 1982 were immensely popular with high school and college students: "Should I Stay or Should I Go?" and "Rock the Casbah." They became staples at parties and dances.

As the group became more mainstream in terms of popularity, their punk label seemed to erode. It's difficult to maintain an outsider status while selling millions of records and having singles played on popular radio. The group disbanded in 1986 after a troubled production on their sixth and final studio album, *Cut the Crap*. Although their time in the musical spotlight was short compared to other iconic bands, their influence is significant. They inspired popular modern groups that include Green Day and No Doubt, both of whom were very popular with teenagers and coming-of-age youth.

Rolling Stone magazine puts The Clash at #28 on the list of the Top 100 Artists of All Time. In their list of the Top 500 Albums of All Time, *Rolling Stone* ranked *London Calling* at #8, a noteworthy achievement for a punk rock band.

See also: 1960s: Beatles, The; Monkees, The; Rolling Stones, The; 1970s: Devo; Led Zeppelin; Queen; 1980s: Blondie; Duran Duran; 1990s: Green Day; 2000s: My Chemical Romance

Further Reading

Clash, The. 2008. *The Clash*. New York: Grand Central.

Doane, Randall. 2014. *Stealing All Transmissions: A Secret History of The Clash*. Oakland, CA: PM Press.

Egan, Sean. 2017. *The Clash on The Clash: Interviews and Encounters*. Chicago: Chicago Review Press.

Gilbert, Pat. 2005. *Passion Is a Fashion: The Real Story of The Clash*. New York: De Capo Press.

Popoff, Martin. 2018. *The Clash: All the Albums, All the Songs*. Minneapolis, MN: Voyageur Press.

COOLEY HIGH

Cooley High, a 1975 comedy-drama, was one of the first teen-centric films that featured a black cast; it proved that quality films centered on minority groups could be profitable. Leroy "Preach" Jackson (Glynn Turman) and Richard "Cochise" Morris (Lawrence Hilton-Jacobs) are the protagonists of the film. After drinking all day and linking up with two peers, Stone (Sherman Smith) and Robert (Norman Gibson) who are bad influences on them, the four boys are arrested the next day at school after joyriding the night before. An intervening teacher convinces the police to release Preach and Cochise; the other two boys remain in custody. Sparked by anger, Stone and Robert seek out Preach and Cochise for vengeance. They find and beat Cochise to death. Preach finds the body and makes the decision that his fate might be sealed if he remains in the housing projects where he lives. After Cochise's funeral, Preach moves away in order to better his life.

Although *Cooley High* isn't mentioned alongside other influential films by black filmmakers such as *Boyz N the Hood* or *Do the Right Thing*, it should be viewed as a milestone movie in the way that it portrayed young black teens. Prior to this, black men largely were defined by Hollywood through gritty crime thrillers such as *Super Fly* and *Shaft*. These films featured black men who were physically strong and street smart and worked to further themselves within the confines of a white establishment. On the surface, the success of these films can be attributed to their aesthetics and fast-paced action. On closer analysis, though, these films were reflections of turmoil and frustration within the black community and reflected the need for mythic figures to represent their struggles on the big screen. In *Super Fly*, Youngblood Priest a.k.a. Super Fly (Ron O'Neal) is a drug dealer. He plans to coordinate one last big transaction before leaving the business. Much of the film depicts him as a black warrior doing battle with the white establishment. His actions are reflective of the survival of the black community and predictive of future advancements as well. This character rejects the materialism of the white community, but only in words. He has the same or similar goals for himself relative to wealth. Regardless of the contradiction here, the films were profitable.

Super Fly and other films like *Black Caesar* represented an alternate reality from poverty and blight for many urban minorities. Although Hollywood might have discounted or dismissed these films as blaxploitation, they nonetheless attracted and retained an audience and were profitable. There was also heavy criticism from within the community that these movies celebrated crime and drug use and perpetuated negative stereotypes. The NAACP went so far as to try to block the distribution of *Super Fly*.

Then *Cooley High* came along and offered a media portrayal of black teens that was deceptively simple. The characters in the film have the same priorities that most teens have regardless of race or ethnicity. The young protagonists of the film are not dealing drugs or committing violent crimes. They are living their lives and experiencing all the typical rituals of teenage life including sexual awakening and attractions and partying.

Viewing this film through a historical lens provides insight into its appeal and its importance at the time it was released. Unemployment among black Americans was very high in the 1970s, among both adults and teens, and the racial divide still existed even after the progress made in the 1960s. Inner-city housing projects were not well maintained, and drugs and violence permeated many of them on a daily basis. For black teens to see themselves portrayed on-screen as regular kids with regular lives was revolutionary for many of them.

Cooley High was loosely based on the real-life experiences of its writer, Eric Monte. Growing up in a similar environment as the central characters in the film, Monte had been involved with the TV sitcom, *Good Times*. He eventually was ostracized by that show's producers because he was very vocal about his dissatisfaction with the show's story line direction.

The surprise success of *Cooley High* opened up new storytelling opportunities for black Americans. Because the film was critically and commercially successful, it was now possible to tell more diverse narratives that contained positive or at least more complex stories. It even prompted an effort to translate it to the small screen. The pilot wasn't well-received by the ABC network, so it was completely retooled with new teen characters and eventually became the mildly successful sitcom, *What's Happening!!*

Cooley High didn't receive the level of notoriety that similar films like *American Graffiti* did, but its cultural impact is now recognized as having a significant effect on the evolution of black American filmmaking in the subsequent decades since its release. It was listed at #23 on *Entertainment Weekly*'s list of the "50 Best High School Movies."

See also: 1950s: *Blackboard Jungle*; *Invisible Man*; 1960s: *Explosive Generation, The*; *To Sir, with Love*; 1970s: *American Graffiti*; 1980s: *Fast Times at Ridgemont High*

Further Reading

Hoberman, J. 2015. "'Seventeen' and 'Cooley High': No Easy A's, but Powerful Lessons." *New York Times*, September 2. https://www.nytimes.com/2015/09/06/movies/homevideo/seventeen-and-cooley-high-no-easy-as-but-powerful-lessons.html.

John, Derek. 2015. "40 Years Later, the Cast of Cooley High Looks Back. *NPR*, June 26. https://www.npr.org/sections/codeswitch/2015/06/26/417185907/40-years-later-the-cast-of-cooley-high-looks-back.

Susman, Gary. 2015. "'Cooley High' Is the Most Influential Movie You've Never Seen." *Moviefone*, June 25. https://www.moviefone.com/2015/06/25/cooley-high-most-influential-movie/.

DEVO

American band Devo formed in 1973. In many ways the band defies easy genre categorization, but it is often labeled as "punk" or lumped into the more general "New Wave" musical genre that was popular in the late 1970s and throughout the 1980s. The original composition of the band was two sets of brothers, Mark

New Wave band Devo is best known for their crossover hit, "Whip It." The group attracted as much attention for their unconventional style of clothing as they did for their unique sound. (Ebet Roberts/Redferns/Getty Images)

and Bob Mothersbaugh and Gerald and Bob Casale, and Alan Myers. The name of the band originates from the word "devolution." This was a term used to describe regression within the human race opposed to evolution or growth. What started out as a joke soon developed into a musical act that entertained crowds at several arts festivals at Kent State University in Ohio.

In the early to mid-1970s, mainstream artists and bands that enjoyed commercial success varied in genre. Rock bands like Led Zeppelin, Black Sabbath, and Deep Purple attracted large concert crowds and sold lots of albums. Soft rock bands like Chicago and Fleetwood Mac were incredibly popular as well, and singer-songwriters Carole King and James Taylor also had large fan bases. Because of the deaths of 1960s icons like Jim Morrison, Jimi Hendrix, and Janis Joplin, psychedelic rock faded, and in its place, the popularity of heavy metal bands grew as did arena rock groups like Boston and Aerosmith.

Although the roots of punk rock music had been planted by 1973, the genre was still in its relative infancy. There is disagreement concerning exactly when the punk movement got its "legs" within the musical scene in the United States, but many agree it happened with the rise of groups that came to prominence in the Bowery section of New York City. Groups like Iggy and the Stooges, the Ramones, and the Velvet Underground all played an important role in what was later labeled as "punk rock" music. Some commonalities among these bands that would become clear identifiers of later punk rock bands, include: defiance of authoritarianism, nihilism, and hedonism. Although some argue that the origins of punk music are apolitical, it's very difficult to argue that anger and dissatisfaction with the status quo drove much of the movement.

Devo and other bands that went against standard conventions of rock and pop music were embraced by many who felt they existed in the margins. Teens who feel alienated or just different from their peers tend to gravitate toward artists who are also outsiders, feeling that they are being represented or validated to some degree. Devo's innovation and self-awareness resonated with fans who sought alternatives to Top 40 bands and artists that were easily identifiable and placed within a specific musical genre.

As an indicator of their growing popularity within the New York music scene, Devo secured a spot as the musical guest on *Saturday Night Live* in the fall of 1978. They appeared onstage dressed in yellow maintenance suits and 3-D glasses. Their wild and eye-catching outfits would become a staple of the band's optics and emblematic of both their unconventional music and their stage persona. Although many home viewers may have been alternately confused and entertained by the performance, music critics and industry insiders immediately recognized the novelty of the group and its potential for success. Tickets to their next few live performances were quickly purchased by many within the business so that they could see the band perform at length.

The song chosen by the band for their television debut seemed an odd one: a cover of the Rolling Stones' "Satisfaction." Given the persona of the Rolling Stones and the sexual swagger of its leader singer, Mick Jagger, it seemed a strange choice for a band that presented themselves as robotic in demeanor and action and lacking any real emotion in delivery of lyrics. As it turned out, it was a perfect match for the group. The song is about both sexual frustration and rejection of consumerism. In interviews early in their career, members of Devo observed how America was becoming a society devoted to mindless consumerism and obsessed with a work ethic that was fixated on the means to accumulate and retain material goods.

In some ways, Devo represented the white male and his discomfort with his own body. Punk and New Wave music attracted an almost exclusively white audience. Although some of the music may have focused on sexuality, it wasn't the same kind of liberated sexuality found in the work of many African American musical artists at the time. This discomfort stems from a long history of sexual repression and a religious and cultural emphasis on self-restraint and the denial of bodily pleasures. The music video for Devo's cover of "Satisfaction" focuses significantly on conflicting messages about sexual activity and desire, with adult figures intervening or intruding on a young couple's efforts to get physical with one another. This physical awkwardness struck a chord with teens who weren't athletically gifted or sexually confident with themselves or their bodies.

Devo found mainstream success with their smash hit single "Whip It" in 1980. The popularity of the single and the album that spawned it—*Freedom of*

Choice—opened up international success for the band as they toured France, Germany, Italy, and other countries that were receptive to their unique sound. "Whip It" was a favorite dance song with high school and college students and exposed the band to listeners who otherwise may have never heard of them.

The band continued making records under various formations into the 1990s and 2000s, but they never recaptured the level of success they had in the 1980s. Part of this was due to changing musical tastes and significant changes within the music industry itself relative to marketing and distribution and record labels' focus on younger artists and groups. Member Alan Myers passed away in 2013, and Bob Casale passed away in 2014.

See also: 1960s: Beatles, The; Monkees, The; Rolling Stones, The; 1970s: Clash, The; Led Zeppelin; Queen; 1980s: Blondie; Duran Duran; 1990s: Green Day; 2000s: My Chemical Romance

Further Reading

Nagie, Evie. 2015. *Devo's Freedom of Choice: 33 1/3*. New York: Bloomsbury.

Popoff, Martin. 2015. "Devo Bassist Celebrates Release of 'Miracle Witness Hour.'" *Goldmine*, February 20. http://www.goldminemag.com/features/devo-bassist-celebrates-release -miracle-witness-hour.

Reynolds, Simon. 2006. *Rip It Up and Start Again: Postpunk, 1978–1984*. London: Faber and Faber.

Savage, Jon. 2013. "Cleveland's Early Punk Pioneers: From Cultural Vacuum to Creative Explosion." *The Guardian*, November 14. https://www.theguardian.com/music/2013 /nov/14/clevelands-early-punk-pioneers-ohio.

GO ASK ALICE

Taken from the lyrics of a popular Jefferson Airplane song, "White Rabbit," *Go Ask Alice*, a fictitious teenage diary, was published at the height of the hallucinogenic drug craze that had enveloped young adults in the late 1960s and early 1970s. In the book, Alice is an average teenager whose family moves around quite a bit. In an effort to make new friends she attends a party where she is given soda that is laced with acid. She enjoys the experience and begins to experiment more with drugs and with her sexuality. She and her friend become involved with two boys who convince them to have sex for money so that they all can keep a steady supply of drugs coming in. Alice continues her drug spiral, and a post-script to the book tells readers that she died of a drug overdose shortly before its publication.

The book was marketed as the "real life" diary of a teenage girl named Alice whose experimentation with drugs served as a cautionary tale for others who might fall under the same influences. Although the book was praised more for its morality lessons than its literary merit, it was widely embraced by parents and educators who viewed it as an effective antidrug vehicle that teenagers would be receptive to since the main character was also a teen.

The authenticity of the book's author was in question. Sparks was originally listed as the "editor" of the book, but the level of her involvement in the writing was initially unclear. Some critics zeroed in on the style and content of the "diary entries," contending that they sounded nothing like the language of an average teen at that time. It also followed a now familiar formula where the protagonist is "tricked" into taking drugs for the first time and then falls mercilessly into the grip of its power, thereby increasing sympathy for the protagonist and his or her struggle. Given the focus of the book and the revelation that Alice had died of a drug overdose shortly before the book was published most likely quelled additional criticisms.

An interview with Sparks from more than three decades ago revealed that she had used "several diaries" from several young girls to create a composite for Alice; she also admitted that some elements of the story had been added or exaggerated for dramatic effect. It is now listed under the fiction category with the publisher and with bookstores, but some schools still categorize it as nonfiction and use it in antidrug workshops and outreach programs. Many teens gravitated toward the material because of its forbidden nature. Media vehicles that focus on behaviors considered illicit or unsavory are sometimes viewed as rebellious and appeal to a nonadult audience.

One way to effectively decipher a message is to analyze the messenger. Sparks was a Mormon child counselor. She claimed to possess a PhD, but that achievement was challenged by a reporter in the late 1970s who interviewed her for an article in *School Library Journal*. In addition to *Go Ask Alice*, Sparks also authored a series of "real life diary" books that included *Jay's Journal*. The family of Alden Barrett, a 16-year-old boy who had committed suicide, felt that Sparks was capable of doing justice to their son's story, so they contacted her and provided his journal for source material. *Jay's Journal* chronicled the story of a teen's obsession with a satanic cult and his absorption into the world of the occult. Alden's mother Marcella claimed that her son was never involved in any cult or in any type of occult activities, but Sparks claimed that the information came from Alden's peers. The family was outraged with the end result.

Spark penned other, similar books, almost all of them containing the word "Anonymous" in the author credit line. The stories cover topics including AIDS, gang violence, and eating disorders—all issues that are especially relevant to teens. Although none of them enjoyed the commercial success of *Go Ask Alice*, that book's reach clearly afforded Sparks the access and ability to get these other books published.

Go Ask Alice experienced its share of critics at the time it was published. Some adults felt that it glorified the subculture of drug users and glamorized teenage sex and promiscuity. Its use in some schools and its availability in public libraries was challenged.

Go Ask Alice sold more than 4 million copies. The book was adapted into a 1973 made-for-television movie starring William Shatner with Jamie Smith-Jackson in the title role. Regardless of the true authorship of *Go Ask Alice,* the book was a runaway best seller and sparked conversations and debate about drug usage among America's teens. The book is now largely regarded as an antidrug public service announcement with questionable literary credentials. This coupled with the suspicion and cynicism around the origins of the book and the author's credibility haven't helped it age well.

See also: 1960s: *Bell Jar, The*; *Outsiders, The*; 1970s: Blume, Judy; 1990s: *Kids*

Further Reading

Anonymous and Sparks, Beatrice. 2010. *Go Ask Alice/Jay's Journal*. New York: Simon and Schuster.

Godbersen, Anna. 2017. "In the 1970s, This Fake Diary Scared—and Tempted—Teenage Girls All Over America." *Timeline*, March 22. https://timeline.com/go-ask-alice-diary -55c538282b6f.

White, Caitlin. 2014. "'Go Ask Alice' Is Still Awash in Controversy, 43 Years after Publication." *Bustle*, July 3. https://www.bustle.com/articles/29829-go-ask-alice-is-still-awash -in-controversy-43-years-after-publication.

GREASE

Grease originated as a musical play in Chicago. Although most people are familiar with it from its long and successful run in New York City and the 1978 film adaptation, the original work was a much grittier piece than the versions that followed. Taking place at the fictional Rydell High School in the 1950s, the story focuses on a group of teenagers navigating their way through romantic dramas and peer conflicts. The main story line focuses on "greaser" Danny Zuko and girlfriend Sandy Dumbrowski. Danny is a stereotypical bad boy who spends his time fixing up cars and drag racing and dating as many girls as he can in an effort to prove his masculinity. He falls for Sandy, but, because they come from different backgrounds and have different ideas about love and romance, their relationship is challenged throughout the story. The original production dealt with issues of teen pregnancy, sexuality, and even gang violence. It even touched lightly on social class, though future versions of the work ignored this.

The show moved to Broadway and became a smash hit—nominated for multiple Tony Awards and ending its run in 1980 after more than 3,000 performances. When the popular Broadway musical was slated to be adapted to film, it came with multiple challenges. Although the story takes place in the 1950s, how would that era appeal to a 1970s audience? The film studio didn't want to limit the appeal to adults who may have been teens in the 1950s; it had to expand the target audience to teens without dramatically changing the story.

Key to its potential box office success was in the casting. They needed a current popular actor for the role of Danny who would attract a younger demographic. John Travolta, enjoying commercial and critical success for *Saturday Night Fever*, was selected for the part. Although *Saturday Night Fever* was an R-rated film with explicit language and sexuality, Travolta had wide appeal and the type of physical appearance that would allow the character of Danny to be sexually enticing but not too threatening or perceived as dangerous. Australian pop singer Olivia Newton-John was chosen for the role of Sandy. Despite a lack of acting experience, Newton-John was incredibly successful as a singer with multiple hit songs in the United States. She exuded the type of naïveté the producers wanted and she also had a fresh and wholesome appearance that fit the character.

Another effort to appeal to a modern audience was the creation and inclusion of the movie's theme song. The title song *Grease* by Frankie Valli sounded modern and not like something that would have existed in the 1950s. Split-screen optics were also employed to make the film appear more current, a cinematic device not available or used in the 1950s.

Perhaps most important, the setting and characters of *Grease* are universal—at least to a Western audience. High school is an experience that nearly all audience members can relate to in some way. Even though the Broadway version was set on the West Coast, the film version scrubbed all visuals that alluded to this and kept the story anchored in a generic setting with locations such as a malt shop, a garage, the interior of the some of the teens' homes, and, of course, the high school itself. Doing this makes the experience relatable on a personal level to all audience members regardless of geography.

In spite of the racial and social inequality that existed in the 1950s, the world presented in *Grease* is one of absolute Utopia. Its focus on teen activities and rites of passage such as dating, peer pressure, and high school dances and athletics kept it anchored in the easily digestible category. Nothing too edgy or offensive was given screen time or serious examination. Issues of race or class distinctions or liberated roles of women are completely ignored.

In the movie, the female character Betty Rizzo (Stockard Channing) is presented as sexually promiscuous. Her on again/off again boyfriend Kenickie Murdoch (Jeff Conaway) is another bad boy. Only after a pregnancy scare does the couple make amends and reconcile. Rizzo is redeemable only if she has the chance to marry her boyfriend and (presumably) commit to a monogamous and committed relationship. Sandy is presented as the "good girl" who is only able to win Danny's love by dramatically altering her appearance and persona at the conclusion of the story. Rather than expecting him to make behavior modifications, she dresses more provocatively and morphs into an overtly sexual creature to please him. Any and all strains in the relationship are forgotten as the two literally drive off into the sunset in the film's closing sequence.

Confining the world of *Grease* and its characters to an insular environment, societal issues and problems are easily ignored. Even though much angst and turmoil existed during the 1950s, one would never know it from viewing this production. No mention of the outside world is included. Parents are absent and authority figures like teachers are depicted as inept—sometimes even bumbling—individuals.

The goal of marketing the film to the widest possible audience worked. It is the third highest grossing musical film in history. Its soundtrack sold millions of copies and produced several hit singles. The film was nominated for several Golden Globe

Awards—with one win for Stockard Channing as Best Supporting Actress. The stage version has enjoyed several revivals, an American one as recently as 2011. A filmed musical version of the play was broadcast on network TV in 2016. The sequel to the film, *Grease 2,* was released in 1982 and was a critical and commercial failure, even though it has developed a cult following in the ensuing decades since its theatrical release.

See also: 1950s: *American Bandstand*; 1960s: *Outsiders, The*; 1970s: *Happy Days*; 2000s: *Glee*; *High School Musical*

Further Reading

Callahan, Michael. 2016. "How Grease Beat the Odds and Became the Biggest Movie Musical of the 20th Century." *Vanity Fair,* January 26. https://www.vanityfair.com/hollywood/2016/01/grease-movie-musical-john-travolta-olivia-newton-john.

Hischak, Thomas S. 2016. *Musicals in Film: A Guide to the Genre.* Santa Barbara, CA: ABC-CLIO.

Miller, Scott. 2011. *Sex, Drugs, Rock and Roll, and Musicals.* Boston, MA: Northeastern University Press.

Robinson, Mark A. 2014. *The World of Musicals: An Encyclopedia of Stage, Screen, and Song.* Santa Barbara, CA: ABC-CLIO.

HAPPY DAYS

Happy Days (1974–1984) is one of the most popular and longest-running sitcoms in television history. The show featured an "all-American" family in the Midwest: The Cunninghams. The family was composed of parents Howard (Tom Bosley) and Marion (Marion Ross) and their children Richie (Ron Howard) and Joanie (Erin Moran). Although Richie was the main character of the show (at least initially), his family and friends "Potsie" Weber (Anson Williams) and Ralph Malph (Don Most) also featured prominently in many of the plots and subplots. Initially intended as a minor character, Arthur "Fonzie" Fonzarelli (Henry Winkler) became a hugely popular character and became a more prominent figure in the show as seasons progressed. Much of the action in the show revolved around home life and teen life at Arnold's food drive-in. Most of the story lines focused more on the teen characters than the adult ones.

One interesting approach to analyzing a show like *Happy Days* is to view it from a domestic cultural lens. Culturally, it showed the tradition and importance of the family unit. Given the era in which it took place, this was, of course, a narrow view of what a family is: husband, wife, and their biological children. Gender roles as represented on the show supported a male-dominated society. Men worked outside of the home to provide for their families. They made the money and the decisions and did the bulk of the disciplining of their children. Women were housewives and mothers whose primary role was to care for their husbands and children. Young women were mainly passive and adhered to strict societal expectations with regard to dating and sexuality. Young men were expected to aggressively pursue young women; their other interests were expected to be in the areas of sports, cars, and other prescribed activities associated with typical men during the time period. Many of the plots on the show involved Richie and his friends trying to find girlfriends. They fixated on the opposite sex and the allure of having a physically appealing romantic partner.

Fonzie is an especially interesting character in that he is portrayed as an extreme alpha male. He is not overly verbal and relies many times on his ability to coerce or intimidate people into doing what he wants them to do. This toughness is expressed not only in his behavior but also in his mode of dress. Where Richie, Ralph, and Potsie are clean cut and dress in a conservative/preppy style, Fonzie wears white T-shirts, jeans, and a black leather jacket. He is also easily able to make contact with attractive girls on a regular basis; they literally come to his attention when he snaps his fingers. He appealed to teen boys whose notions of male behavior and appearance were represented through the "macho" character of Fonzie.

Although the show was produced in the 1970s and 1980s, it was set in the 1950s and 1960s. Setting the show during that era allowed its producers and writers to depict gender stereotypes prevalent at that time. Much of what would be considered questionable or offensive behavior by today's standards is intended to seem "quaint" by the standards of an earlier time. Additionally, as with many media productions, a relatively easy method for determining the intended purpose of the show is to analyze what was happening culturally at the time that it's produced. The 1970s were in many ways an extension of the 1960s. Women were still fighting for equal rights, and minority groups such as African Americans and gays and lesbians were making their own demands with respect to equality as well. These cultural issues along with still lingering resentment and resistance to the Vietnam War created a desire for nostalgia among many Americans. Going back to the era of the 1950s seemed like an obvious choice. Although many younger Americans may have been involved in peaceful protests and marches, a lot of older Americans longed for a time where things seemed simpler and less conflicted.

History shows that the generational and cultural wars of the 1960s and 1970s were sown from racial, gender, and sexual orientation disparities that began much earlier. Although white, middle-class Americans may have been content overall in the preceding decades, institutional racism, sexism, and homophobia created an unwelcome and at times hostile environment for others. After the upheaval of the 1960s, a conservative movement grew that was called the Silent Majority. This defined a large group of Americans who longed for a return to what they referred to as "traditional values." This movement was in direct response and contrast to the counterculture that they believed was unpatriotic and in some respects immoral.

Happy Days spun off several other popular 1970s series including *Laverne and Shirley* and *Mork and Mindy*. Although the show was nominated for several Emmy Awards over the years in major and supporting acting categories, it only scored a win for Best Film Editing for a Comedy. The show won several Golden Globe Awards and a People's Choice Award in 1977 for Favorite TV Comedy Program. Ron Howard went on to become a successful film director, helming movies that include *Cocoon, A Beautiful Mind,* and *Apollo 13.* Although other 1970s sitcoms like *Maude* and *All in the Family* took aim at topical issues within our culture at that time, *Happy Days* worked as escapist entertainment that presented a simplistic and nonthreatening view of the 1950s.

See also: 1950s: *Adventures of Ozzie and Harriet, The; Father Knows Best; I Love Lucy; Leave It to Beaver;* 1960s: *Patty Duke Show, The;* 1970s: *Grease;* 1980s: *Cosby Show, The; Family Ties; Full House; Wonder Years, The;* 1990s: *Boy Meets World; Clarissa Explains It All; 7th Heaven; That '70s Show;* 2000s: *Friday Night Lights*

Further Reading

Caldara, Abby. 2016. "The 'Happy' Days." *Odyssey,* May 2. https://www.theodysseyonline .com/happy-days.
Journey, Anna. 2014. "Arthur Fonzarelli, Spirit Guide." *Antioch Review* 72 (2): 365–370.
Terrace, Vincent. 2017. *Television Series of the 1970s: Essential Facts and Quirky Details.* Lanham: Rowman and Littlefield.

HARRAD EXPERIMENT, THE

This controversial film was based on a 1966 novel written by Robert Rimmer. *The Harrad Experiment* (1973) takes place at a fictional college where the married couple who run the institution use selected college students as guinea pigs in a social experiment. The experiment is designed to promote an alternative to monogamous relationships between men and women. A computer "matches" couples, who will then cohabitate with one another for the duration of their four years at school. The preferred outcome of the experiment is that these young men and women will learn to resist emotions such as jealousy and possessiveness and gravitate toward a less conventional lifestyle.

In the book, the president of the college gives a welcome speech in which he explains that sexual activity with strangers will not provide satisfaction. He instead encourages the six couples who have been chosen for the experiment to approach it with an open mind and allow themselves to become emotionally attracted to their co-ed roommate before the sexual activity takes place. He also promises access to birth control to avoid any unwanted pregnancies.

The Harrad Experiment was released at the perfect time in terms of capitalizing on a taboo topic. In 1962, the notion that men and women could have premarital sex wasn't necessarily revolutionary. However, the idea that they could have multiple sex partners without guilt or shame certainly was, especially within the context of a marriage—which is ultimately what the novel presents since all six couples are "group married" at the conclusion of the story.

The author of the novel drew his inspiration from an actual academic paper written by a married couple that advocated for a non-monogamous alternative to a traditional marriage, which, in this sense, is defined as a man and woman who are committed to one another romantically and sexually and do not have sexual relationships outside of the marriage. Although this was shocking in the 1960s, it was also the beginning of the free love movement that was partially a reaction to the socially conservative decade that preceded it. "Free love" as defined within the context of the 1960s referred primarily to consensual sex between partners without an obligatory commitment to each other. On a broad scale, the movement sought to keep government interference out of relationships; on a narrower scale, it advocated sexual liberation and the rejection of societal conventions with respect to intimate relationships. It was associated with the rise of hippie culture, but the two aren't necessarily symbiotic.

But the idea of free love wasn't invented in the 1960s. Multiple influences, both domestic and international, were instrumental in moving the culture forward with respect to marriage and sexuality for more than 100 years prior. Several specific issues closer to this time frame, however, propelled it into the social conscience of the country.

Hugh Hefner and his *Playboy* empire triggered dialogue on this concept. Hefner was the embodiment of the perennial bachelor who surrounded himself in his lavish mansion with multiple women with whom he apparently had sexual relationships. While this was happening, women were also fighting for equality, and part of that equality was sexual freedom. So even though many abhorred the perceived lecherous antics of someone like Hefner, women like Gloria Steinem were vocalizing about the oppression that traditional marriage typically imposed on women. She contended that the very institution of marriage was designed to make women "less than," and place societal constraints upon them. In addition, birth control was widely available, and the research team of William H. Masters and Victoria E Johnson conducted extensive studies on human sexuality at that time. They published their initial findings in 1966, the same year that *The Harrad Experiment* was published.

Young people that rejected war, capitalism, and institutional power systems were open to this new way of defining sexual activity and relationships, and discarding the mandate of monogamy. Additionally, Beat authors such as Allen Ginsberg and William S. Burroughs advocated for this practice among gay men. Although many attribute the political counterculture and access to birth control as driving forces for the advance of the movement in the 1960s, others point to the medical advances for treating sexually transmitted diseases to its popularity.

Although some may have laughed off the idea of free love as a contrived by-product of hippies, it gained some traction within Middle America in the form of "swinging." This practice involved married couples who had sex with other couples or individuals. Unlike proponents of the free love movement, swingers were typically more socially conservative or apolitical. The majority of the married men in these scenarios were white-collar professionals, and many of the women were housewives. Access was offered via personal ads in magazines; larger cities like New York City also had bars that catered to this clientele. Swinger functions were mostly drug-free and not overly inclusive with respect to minority groups.

Hollywood covered this terrain in the 1969 sex comedy, *Bob & Carol & Ted & Alice*, in which two married couples decide to sexually share spouses with each other. A more serious examination of the topic was done in the 1997 film, *The Ice Storm.*

By the mid-1970s, the practice of swinging was in decline. Married couples were discovering that, contrary to what they had hoped would happen, their marriages were not reinvigorated. Even authors who had previously advocated this practice began to retreat and suggest other avenues for relationship enhancement to married couples.

The film version of *The Harrad Experiment* wasn't released until seven years after the novel was published. The novelty by that time had largely worn off. The film was lacerated by critics and dismissed as gimmicky and poorly done. Despite this, a sequel was released one year later entitled *The Harrad Summer.* The film followed the same characters from the original film as they attempted to integrate back into society after graduating from college.

See also: 1960s: *Where the Boys Are*

Further Reading

Allyn, David. 2001. *Make Love, Not War: The Sexual Revolution—An Unfettered History*. New York: Routledge.

Rimmer, Robert. 1966. *The Harrad Experiment*. Los Angeles: Sherborne Press.

Samuel, Lawrence R. 2013. "The American Way of Swinging." *Psychology Today*, August 11. https://www.psychologytoday.com/blog/psychology-yesterday/201308/the-american -way-swinging.

Shute, Nancy. 2013. "Did Penicillin, Rather Than the Pill, Usher in Age of Love?" *NPR*, January 30. https://www.npr.org/sections/health-shots/2013/01/28/170491287/did -penicillin-rather-than-the-pill-usher-in-age-of-love.

JAWS

The 1975 thriller *Jaws* is one of the most commercially and critically successful films in movie history. Based on the best-selling 1974 novel by Peter Benchley, the story takes place in a fictional New England resort community where a killer great white shark wreaks havoc during a terrifying summer. The film begins with an evening swim in the ocean. Chrissie Watkins (Susan Backlinie) goes skinny-dipping by herself, and within a few minutes of being in the water, she is violently pulled under and attacked by an unseen predator. The following day, her remains wash ashore, and the Amity Island sheriff, Martin Brody (Roy Scheider), decides to close the beaches after he suspects that the young woman was killed by a shark. Mayor Larry Vaughn (Murray Hamilton) intervenes, concerned about the monetary impact to the island with lost tourist revenues, and convinces the coroner to change the cause of death to a boating accident. After the killing of a tiger shark in the waters of Amity, everyone believes that the menace has been eliminated. Brody is unconvinced, and with the help of professional shark hunter Quint (Robert Shaw) and oceanographer Matt Hooper (Richard Dreyfuss), the three set out to destroy the killer white shark on their own.

Although *Jaws* played to a wide audience, teens especially gravitated toward it for several reasons. Although it was fairly gory for the times, it was only rated PG (Parental Guidance). There was no PG-13 (Parental Guidance for children under the age of 13) at the time the film was released. Therefore, kids didn't need to "sneak in" to see it at theaters—they could go by themselves, or even go with their parents as many did. It was exciting and action-packed, offering special appeal to teen boys with its trio of male heroes fighting a deadly force of nature. The story was simple, but the novelty of it attracted mass audiences. In a pre-Internet and pre–social media world, this film created "buzz" that was unparalleled. Anyone who saw the film while they were coming of age can also attest to the fear of sharks many young viewers developed.

Another reason for its youth appeal is that it features a few supporting characters that are teenagers. Brody's sons Michael and Sean appear in several scenes, and in one pivotal sequence, several young boys prank swimmers into thinking that they are the killer shark. Older son Michael is almost killed by the real shark and goes into shock.

The production of *Jaws* was fraught with issues. Just getting the screenplay written proved to be a challenging feat. The source material by Benchley contained several subplots that director Steven Spielberg felt were not necessary to the story and might even detract from the main theme of "man versus beast." For example, the novel included an adulterous affair between Brody's wife and another male character who ends up working with Brody to try and kill the shark. Spielberg felt that dynamic would dampen the camaraderie between the two male characters once they joined forces to defeat the shark. The screenplay went through several writers—including novelist Benchley—before a final draft was created.

Three fake sharks were used for the filming of the movie. There were multiple mechanical failures in addition to challenging natural elements such as sea salt and water. These caused countless production challenges, destroying cameras and props, and putting the film significantly overbudget for its production time frame. One of the pneumatically powered prop sharks actually sank to the bottom the first time it was used. Because of all of these unanticipated incidents, the story was changed to show only glimpses of the shark. With the exception of a few key scenes toward the end of the movie, the shark is mainly shrouded from the audience. Ironically, this forced change made for a more suspenseful end product; audiences literally were jumping out of their theater seats during scenes where the shark was visible, as they were infrequent.

Jaws is attributed as the original "blockbuster" film that would spawn countless high-budget and high-concept Hollywood movies from the time of its release through current day. It broke box office records and was the highest-grossing film ever until bested by *Star Wars* (1977) two years later. Unlike most films released today that typically open in wide release immediately (to try and generate as much box office revenue as possible), *Jaws* opened in June 1975 on 464 screens across the country. By the end of July, it had doubled that number due to glowing critic's reviews and word of mouth.

The film spawned several sequels, though the only one that received any significant attention was *Jaws 2*. That film focuses primarily on teenagers in Amity who are under attack by another killer white shark. Brody's son Mike once again finds himself in trouble when he and a group of friends sneak off to go sailing. His younger brother Sean convinces him to let him come along as well. After the shark attacks them and creates chaos, the group of teens ultimately find themselves near Cable Island, where they attempt to make it onshore from their battered boats. Just as in the original film, Sheriff Brody kills the shark. The teens are rescued and order is restored to the island. The film received mixed reviews but was a box office success.

Jaws won three Academy Awards for Best Film Editing, Best Original Dramatic Score, and Best Sound. It won the People's Choice Award for Best Movie. A plethora of merchandise sprang up after its release including posters, T-shirts, and beach towels. *Jaws 3-D* (1983) and *Jaws: The Revenge* (1987) were both universally panned by critics and failed to connect with audiences.

Jaws is an iconic American thriller that continues to entertain audiences today and is considered by many to be one of the best films ever made. In 2001, it was selected by the Library of Congress for preservation in the United States National Film Registry.

See also: 1970s: *American Graffiti*; 1980s: *It*

Further Reading

Benchley, Peter. 1975. *Jaws*. New York: Bantam Books.

Choi, Charles Q. 2010. "How 'Jaws' Forever Changed Our View of Great White Sharks." *Live Science*, June 20. https://www.livescience.com/8309-jaws-changed-view-great -white-sharks.html.

Gambino, Megan. 2012. "The Shark Attacks That Were the Inspiration for Jaws." *Smithsonian*, August 6. https://www.smithsonianmag.com/history/the-shark-attacks-that-were -the-inspiration-for-jaws-15220260/.

Jackson, Kathi. 2007. *Steven Spielberg: A Biography*. Westport, CT: Greenwood Press.

Kermode, Mark. 2015. "Jaws, 40 Years On: One of the Truly Great and Lasting Classics of American Cinema." *The Guardian*, May 31. https://www.theguardian.com/film/2015 /may/31/jaws-40-years-on-truly-great-lasting-classics-of-america-cinema.

Taylor, Matt. 2012. *Jaws: Memories from Martha's Vineyard: A Definitive Behind-the-Scenes Look at the Greatest Suspense Thriller of All Time*. London: Titan Books.

LED ZEPPELIN

Led Zeppelin, a four-person rock band, formed in London, England, in 1968. The band, consisting of guitarist Jimmy Page, singer Robert Plant, bassist and keyboardist John Paul Jones, and drummer John Bonham, became known for their elaborate stage shows that incorporated music with flashy visuals to engage audiences. Their epic hit single, "Stairway to Heaven" is one of the most requested and played songs on FM radio stations. They enjoyed both domestic and international success as they toured the globe in support of the album *Led Zeppelin IV*. Part of the reason for their hugely successful album sales was rooted in their practice of not releasing singles from albums as they felt all of the music was interconnected and part of a tapestry of their work.

The band is most associated with the 1970s, the decade that ushered in hard rock music to the masses and took excess to an unprecedented level. They released six studio albums during the decade, including *Led Zeppelin III* and *IV*, *Houses of the Holy*, and *Physical Graffiti*, and are considered one of the most influential bands of that time. Fusing diverse genres including blues, folks, and psychedelic, the band created a unique sound that attracted hordes of fans and sold millions of records. Additionally, teen fans appreciated the J. R. R. Tolkien references and themes that Plant mentions in several *Zeppelin* songs, including "The Battle of Evermore" and "Ramble On." In the second title, specific references are made to the character of Gollum from the popular *Lord of the Rings* trilogy and to Mordor, a specific region of the fictional Middle Earth in the novels. In the first song, more general references are made that readers of the fantasy series of books recognize.

When the 1960s was winding down, a new generation of music fans was coming of age in the United States. Younger siblings of those who had experienced the counterculture of the 1960s were seeking new sounds and bands to claim as their own. Many of these individuals were not necessarily motivated by social or political causes but rather intrigued by the celebrity culture of rock and roll. Additionally, a change was also taking place within the music business. Promoters and band managers were realizing the potential monetary rewards to be reaped from bands that played larger venues and took a bigger "cut" of the profits than those who had come before them.

Artists and bands that rose to prominence in the 1960s had a close relationship with their fans. Many of them believed in the same social and political causes that their young listeners did. Their material reflected this lyrically, and many of them marched and protested alongside regular citizens in a fight for equality and social justice. With a few notable exceptions including Woodstock, these artists gravitated toward smaller and more intimate venues that allowed less physical distance between singers and fans. There was a perception that many of these bands and singers were activists who just happened to be musically talented.

At the start of the 1970s, a new generation of rock stars and rock bands emerged, and Led Zeppelin along with a few others embodied its spirit. Author Michael Walker contends that 1973 was the year when everything changed within the world of rock music. He attributes this to the pinnacle of not just Led Zeppelin's meteoric rise, but also to the peak of Alice Cooper and the Who. All three acts had significant success at this time and created a blueprint for future bands in terms of style and excess. Suddenly, there was a significant distance between artist and fan; this was embodied by the now clichéd perk of a backstage pass. Some of this newly created barrier he attributes to the untapped financial possibilities of moving shows from clubs to huge arenas and stadiums that could accommodate tens of thousands of fans. More seats equal more money. Personal excess played a part as well. Gone were the days of humble artists who presented themselves as enjoying modest lifestyles. Suddenly, it became the norm for rock bands to flaunt their material wealth via private jets, limos, and conspicuous consumption.

Young, adoring fans would go to great lengths to meet or even just get a peek at band members after a show. This applied especially to fans in their teens who idolized rock stars. Teenage girls especially were attracted to the possibility of meeting their favorite singers or musicians. Teenage boys gravitated toward the macho appeal of the hedonistic lifestyle that Led Zeppelin and other bands enjoyed. Although male pop idols still existed within this period, rock music rode a wave of immense popularity, and rock stars became the ultimate celebrities within the music world. Everything was about being bigger and better and louder. This, of course, extended into the band member's personal lives where legendary tales of decadence and debauchery fueled media reports about trashed hotel rooms, underage girls having sex with band members, and copious amounts of illegal drugs being consumed.

The release of *Physical Graffiti,* their double album, marked the end of their collaborative efforts with respect to new material. It was a significant commercial and critical success and also reignited interest and sales in their earlier albums. There were plans for the group to tour in 1980, but after the death of drummer John Bonham, everything was canceled. Several reunions of the remaining members of the band have taken place over the decades since then.

Led Zeppelin influenced numerous bands in both sound and style. The "hair bands" of the 1980s are especially indebted to them, but their impact extends to other artists ranging from the Ramones to the Smashing Pumpkins. The band was inducted into the Rock and Roll Hall of Fame in 1995 and the U.K. Music Hall of Fame in 2006. They've sold somewhere between 200 and 300 million albums worldwide.

See also: 1960s: Beatles, The; Monkees, The; Rolling Stones, The; 1970s: Clash, The; Devo; Queen; 1980s: Blondie; Duran Duran; 1990s: Green Day; Nirvana; Smashing Pumpkins, The; 2000s: My Chemical Romance

Further Reading

Davis, Stephen. 2008. *Hammer of the Gods: The Led Zeppelin Saga*. New York: It Books.
Robinson, Lisa. 2014. "Stairway to Excess." *Vanity Fair*, February 18. https://www.vanityfair.com/culture/2003/11/led-zeppelin-1970s-lisa-robinson.
Walker, Michael. 2013. *What You Want Is in the Limo*. New York: Random House.
Wall, Mick. 2008. *When Giants Walked the Earth: A Biography of Led Zeppelin*. New York: St. Martin's.

LITTLE HOUSE ON THE PRAIRIE

Little House on the Prairie ran on NBC for nine seasons (1974–1983). It was incredibly popular with viewers and garnered solid TV ratings. The show focused primarily on the Ingalls family: mother and father Charles and Caroline (Michael

Landon and Karen Grassle) and their four daughters Mary (Melissa Sue Anderson), Laura (Melissa Gilbert), Carrie (Lindsay and Sidney Greenbush), and Grace (Brenda Turnbaugh). Additional Ingalls characters were added in later seasons via adoption: son Albert (Matthew Laborteaux) and Cassandra and James (Missy Francis and Jason Bateman).

The show takes place in the 1870s and 1880s and depicts the struggles and successes of a Midwestern frontier family. Many of the episodes deal with the daily lives of the characters, especially younger daughter Laura. Another family that plays a pivotal role in the series is that of the Olesons. Married couple Nels (Richard Bull) and Harriet (Scottie MacGregor) and their children Nellie (Alison Arngrim) and Willie (Jonathan Gilbert). The two families represent two different lifestyles

Hugely popular family TV series *Little House on the Prairie*. The show focused on the lives of the Ingalls family, a Midwestern frontier clan facing an assortment of challenges in the late 1800s. Sisters Laura and Mary played central roles in the storylines, which held wide appeal for both children and adults. (Silver Screen Collection/Getty Images)

and socioeconomic experiences. The Ingalls live on a farm and struggle financially. The Olesons live in town and run a general store, Oleson's Mercantile. Nels is a mild-mannered man who is generally amiable while his wife Harriet is a combative and mean-spirited gossip. Daughter Nellie is also an instigator and serves as the chief tormentor among the town's children.

The source material for the show is a series of books by author Laura Ingalls Wilder. There are nine books in this series and they are referred to as the *Little House* series. Published throughout the 1930s and 1940s, the books are largely autobiographical but are categorized as fiction. This is largely due to that fact that the stories heavily rely on the memory of the author, so creative license is applied with respect to the storytelling. Wilder's daughter, Rose Wilder Lane, assisted with the editing of the books, which have been wildly popular among young readers. According to *School Library Journal*, the first book in the series, *Little House in the Big Woods*, ranks as number 19 among all-time best children's novels. Five of the eight books were Newbery Medal runners-up. They are considered classic children's literature and are beloved by millions.

One cannot read these novels now or watch the TV series without examining them through a different lens with regard to ethnicity and all of the implications that it brings. In the books, Caroline ("Ma") is very explicit about her disdain for Indians. She frequently makes derogatory or dismissive comments about "brown skinned" people and cannot understand Laura's interest in seeing a papoose in one of the *Little House* stories. Given the history and plight of Native Americans in the United States, Caroline's worldview regarding them was fairly prevalent at the time. Author Laura Ingalls Wilder moved to Kansas with her family as a child and was exposed to the strife and despair within the population that had been displaced, and in some instances relocated, by the American government.

Within the context of the stories, young Laura had been sheltered from other populations and cultures until the time that the family uprooted (which they did frequently within the books) and moved to another locale. Without any frame of reference and little to no context from her parents, Laura learns about Indian culture from her father. This includes education about different foods and cooking outside over an open flame. Charles ("Pa") teaches his daughters about the behavior and customs of the Native Americans, but an honest depiction of their treatment and history isn't necessarily part of that narrative.

Female teen viewers enjoyed the story lines that focused on the Ingalls sisters and their adventures. The ongoing battles with bratty and malicious Nellie provided entertainment but also showed a clear contrast between the values of the Ingalls' and how they raised their children as opposed to the upbringing of their nemesis by the Olesons. The warmth and unity of the Ingalls family and close relationship between the sisters was also a draw for teen viewers, particularly young girls.

The acculturation that occurs within the books, while well intentioned, romanticizes events; it fails to convey the inhumane treatment of Native Americans at the hands of both the U.S. government and its settlers. Some have adopted the themes and values communicated within the *Little House* series as examples of successful conservative ideologies. Among these is the adherence to stereotypical gender roles for women. Given the period in which it takes place, it is understandable that the primary role shown for adult women was that of caregiver and homemaker. Implying that this still holds true today ignores the advancement of women socioeconomically and reinforces a patriarchal worldview. At the same time, Charles Ingalls is portrayed on the show as a very involved parent—one not necessarily defined and limited by expected gender roles. In fact, Caroline is often portrayed as more harsh in her interactions with the children than their father, who is often depicted as nurturing and thoughtful.

The television show largely sidestepped problematic historic and cultural issues by focusing more on the family unit and universal issues of loyalty and honesty and the rewards of a strong work ethic. It did, however, address issues of alcoholism, child abuse, and even rape. The show also depicted the physical hardships of life at that time that included natural threats such as blizzards and medical scares including typhoid fever. It also had its comic moments, many of them centering on the rivalry between Nellie Oleson and Laura Ingalls. The rewarding and frequent comeuppance of Harriet Oleson was also a delight for the show's fans.

Little House on the Prairie aired for eight seasons. It was renamed and retooled for its ninth and final season and ran under the name *Little House: A New Beginning.* The show's enduring legacy was evident in three made-for-television movies that were made after the show's run ended: *Little House on the Prairie: A Look Back to Yesterday* (1983), *Little House: The Last Farewell* (1984), and *Little House: Bless All the Dear Children* (1984).

See also: 1960s: *To Kill a Mockingbird*

Further Reading

Flood, Alison. 2014. "Laura Ingalls Wilder Memoir Reveals Truth behind Little House on the Prairie." *The Guardian,* August 25. https://www.theguardian.com/books/2014/aug /25/laura-ingalls-wilder-memoir-little-house-prairie.

Ingalls Wilder, Laura. 1994. *The Little House* (9-Volume Set). New York: Harper Trophy.

Lifson, Amy. 2014. "Reading Laura Ingalls Wilder Is Not the Same When You're a Parent." *Humanities,* July/August. https://www.neh.gov/humanities/2014/julyaugust/feature /reading-laura-ingalls-wilder-not-the-same-when-youre-parent.

Limerick, Patricia Nelson. 2017. "'Little House on the Prairie' and the Truth about the American West." *New York Times,* November 20. https://www.nytimes.com/2017/11/20 /books/review/prairie-fires-laura-ingalls-wilder-biography-caroline-fraser.html.

NATIONAL LAMPOON'S ANIMAL HOUSE

National Lampoon's Animal House (1978) is one of the most successful comedies in film history. It was directed by John Landis, and starred John Belushi in the iconic role of John "Bluto" Blutarsky. Taking place at the fictional Faber College, the movie chronicles the exploits of a gang of fraternity brothers from the raucous Delta Tau Chi fraternity and their feud with the upscale (snobbish) rival fraternity, Omega Theta Pi. The dean of the college loathes the lowbrow behavior and academic failures of the "Deltas" and concocts a plan to get them ejected from the university. With the aid of an "Omega," traps are set for the Deltas, and they, of course, fall right into them, resulting in their inevitable expulsion from the college.

Animal House famously features a toga party scene that has become iconic and most likely helped this traditional fraternity event remain popular through the late 1970s and well into the 1980s at college campuses nationwide. Dean Wormer (John Vernon) discovers that his wife, Marion (Verna Bloom), has attended the toga party and had sex with the suave and handsome Eric "Otter" Stratton (Tim Matheson). In addition to this being a plot development to push the story forward, it reinforces the theme of rebellion and disrespect for authority figures and institutions. It's ultimately what pushes the dean to revoke the Delta Tau Chi's charter. The film's plotline also includes academic dishonesty when Bluto and Daniel Simpson "D-Day" Day (Bruce McGill) discover a discarded set of test answers, not realizing it's a fake planted by their rivals at Omega Theta Pi. They, of course, all fail the test, causing collective grade point averages among the members to plummet.

In keeping with the tone and theme of the movie, The Deltas concoct an elaborate scheme to disrupt the college's homecoming parade in response to the dean's actions. They use Flounder's (Stephen Furst) damaged car to wreak havoc during the event. While chaos is unfolding, a series of freeze-frames are used to communicate the future fates of most of the main characters. Not surprisingly, the Deltas mostly go on to become successful professionals whereas the fate of their enemies is negative and even grim.

The film is largely credited with originating what is now referred to in the movie industry as the "gross out" genre. *Animal House* includes heavy profanity, nudity, and an arguably undue emphasis on the joys of college drinking. The Deltas excelled at partying but not much else. They disregarded their studies and focused their energies on getting intoxicated and seeking casual sex. While those themes have become commonplace in modern teen movies, the casual depravity included in the film shocked some at the time of its release.

College and alcohol consumption have long been paired together in popular media. Since the time of *Animal House*, most college-based comedies include heavy drinking references. Since going away to college is associated with freedom for many young adults, it makes sense that part of this milestone is linked to activities and behaviors that most parents would not approve of. This is portrayed in many books and films as a time of experimentation, both socially and sexually. Examining the film through today's lens—even when keeping in mind that it's a comedy—is jarring. Alcohol abuse, especially binge drinking, is a serious issue on many college campuses. According to the National Institute of Alcohol Abuse and Alcoholism, heavy drinking among college students directly correlates with increases in sexual assault, nonsexual assault, and even death.

One element of the film that may explain part of its mainstream appeal is its celebration of the underdog. The Deltas are clearly the group that audience members are rooting for. Their excesses aside, they are more representative and inclusive than their counterparts in the Omegas. The Omegas are referred to in the film as "Hitler youth," and while that assertion is hyperbolic, they do exclude minorities including blacks and Jews. Through group association, many viewers may tend to identify more with the Deltas than the Omegas due in part to their rejection of authority and the status quo.

Animal House triggered a rash of imitations within the film industry; countless teen comedies since then have highlighted the drinking rituals of the college student. These range from *Old School* to *Road Trip* to *Neighbors*. The story line always features irresponsible drinking and the ramifications are seldom serious. Debate continues on the impact of how drinking is portrayed in these types of productions and its effect on younger audience members. One thing that does not seem to be in question, however, is that it remains a popular story formula even today.

The film was a box office smash, eventually netting more than $140 million in revenue on an estimated production budget of less than $4 million. It helped launch the careers of then young actors Kevin Bacon and Tom Hulce. *Saturday Night Live* cast member John Belushi was the most recognizable star in the film. It has been preserved through the National Film Registry as culturally significant and it also appears on the American Film Institute's list of the Top 100 Comedies of all time.

See also: 1980s: *Fast Times at Ridgemont High*; *Revenge of the Nerds*; 1990s: *American Pie*

Further Reading

Fetters, Ashley. 2014. "Pop Culture's War on Fraternities." *The Atlantic*, February 28. https://www.theatlantic.com/entertainment/archive/2014/02/pop-cultures-war-on -fraternities/284126/.

Hevel, Michael S. 2014. "Setting the Stage for Animal House: Student Drinking in College Novels, 1865–1933." *Journal of Higher Education* 85 (3): 370–401.

McCurdy, Christen. 2012. "Lady Liquor: Fraternities as 'Underdogs' in Animal House, Revenge of the Nerds, and History." *Bitch Media*, November 28. https://www.bitchmedia .org/post/lady-liquor-fraternities-as-underdogs-in-animal-house-revenge-of-the-nerds -and-history.

Miller, Chris. 2007. *The Real Animal House: The Awesomely Depraved Saga of the Fraternity That Inspired the Movie*. New York: Little, Brown.

Simmons, Matty. 2014. *Fat, Drunk, and Stupid: The Inside Story behind the Making of Animal House*. New York: St. Martin's Press.

OSMONDS, THE

Though this boy band composed of brothers from Utah begin singing and performing as children, the Osmonds reached the pinnacle of their success as young men in the 1970s. Brothers Alan, Wayne, Merrill, and Jay Osmond showed an interest in music at a young age; one of their first professional gigs was a spot on the "Disneyland after Dark" special in 1962. Famed entertainer Andy Williams took notice of the group and booked them for numerous performances on his television show between 1962 and 1969. The Osmonds were known for their polish and professionalism—impressive for a group of young boys without professional training or management in their early years.

Record producer Mike Curb saw promise in the group and managed to get them a recording contract with MGM. A song entitled "One Bad Apple" that had originally been written for the Jackson Five—another hugely popular boy band— ended up being the Osmonds' debut release for MGM and a subsequent number one hit single. Then younger brother Donny joined the group and began singing the chorus on most of their songs. Other hits followed including "Double Lovin'" and "Yo-Yo," both of which landed in the top 20 spots on Billboard. Youngest sibling Jimmy Osmond was also musically added to the roster and became the youngest singer ever to have a gold record (sales of 500,000 units) in Great Britain with the hit, "Long Haired Lover from Liverpool."

As with many groups, a breakout or fan favorite often emerges, and with the Osmonds, it was Donny. He sang lead vocals on four hit singles that all made it into the Billboard Top 10 in 1971: "Sweet and Innocent," "Go Away Little Girl," "I Knew You When," and "Puppy Love." Eventually, the band began writing and performing their own music, gravitating away from the pop and soft R&B sound they'd become known for and toward rock and roll.

The Osmonds, along with the Jackson Five and the fictional family band the Partridge Family all rocketed to success and became staples of what was termed "bubblegum" music within the industry. This type of music was safe and non-threatening both in sound and content. A sharp departure from the raucous and social issues–driven bands of the 1960s, the Osmonds and their counterparts stuck strictly to love songs that would not offend anyone's sensibilities. Even the parents of fans approved of the wholesome image and entertainment value of these bands.

Image is critically important with these types of bands, and, in addition to their benign material, these groups typically adhere to style "norms," avoiding making any type of statements with their clothing or hairstyle choices. It's noteworthy that the fan favorite (Donny) had a "fresh scrubbed" look that was almost androgynous, similar to many boy band favorites in modern times.

At the same time that Donny was churning out his hit singles, the group also scored with top five smashes like "Down by the Lazy River." It was during this phase of their career that the group enjoyed an almost cultlike following, packing venues for concerts and playing to massive crowds primarily composed of screaming young girls. The 1972 album *Crazy Horses* kept the band toward the top of the music charts and maintained their popularity with adoring fans. Their appeal was international as they also scored Top 10 hits in the United Kingdom and other European countries as well.

A sure sign of reaching iconic status among the female youth demographic at the time, Donny began appearing in teen publications *Teen Beat* and *Tiger Beat*. The cover of the April 1972 edition of *Tiger Beat* was a "Super Donny Issue!" Merchandising included Osmond Brothers lunch boxes, posters, and socks. There was even a Saturday morning cartoon show called *The Osmonds* that aired for one season on ABC in 1972.

Several events happened at roughly the same time that dethroned the group from their superstar status in the music world. Their 11th studio album entitled *The Plan* relied heavily on their Mormon upbringing. Although the album scored a few minor hits that got into the Billboard 100, the work overall was a misfire and confused fans with its mish-mash of styles and religious influences. Donny's voice was also changing, so the group could no longer rely on that trademark vocal to generate interest and hit records.

Although the group's popularity waned, Donny's increased. Soon, he and his sister Marie Osmond were enjoying success as a duo. Marie recorded a number one country hit, "Paper Roses," in 1973. While airplay and record sales for the Osmond Brothers albums were on the decline, they decided to put their collective efforts into producing a new TV variety show: *The Donny and Marie Show*. Broadcast on

ABC from 1976–1979, the series featured the brother and sister pair performing in skits and popular songs. Their gimmick each week was the song, "I'm a Little Bit Country, I'm a Little Bit Rock and Roll," which allowed each of them to shine in their respective musical genres.

Once the show was canceled, the Osmond brothers found themselves out of work and in significant financial debt, primarily due to a state-of-the-art studio they'd had built in Utah for the TV show. The brothers, minus Donny, forayed into country music just like sister Marie and enjoyed moderate success. They relocated to Branson, Missouri, where they were well received and continue to perform.

Donny Osmond enjoyed a resurgence of sorts in 1989 with the hit single, "Soldier of Love." He also made a splash in the national theater scene in a touring company of *Joseph and the Amazing Technicolor Dreamcoat*. Marie Osmond continues to do TV appearances and record music, with her most recent album being released in 2016. The Osmonds' popularity as an early boy band was relatively short lived, but their staying power as an entertainment family is impressive.

See also: 1950s: Avalon, Frankie; Boone, Pat; Darin, Bobby; 1960s: Beach Boys, The; Beatles, The; 1980s: Gibson, Debbie; Lauper, Cyndi; Madonna; 1990s: Backstreet Boys; Spice Girls; 2000s: Cyrus, Miley; Spears, Britney; Swift, Taylor

Further Reading

Argetsinger, Amy. 2014. "A Brief Musical History of the Osmonds in 13 Songs." *Washington Post*, November 30. https://www.washingtonpost.com/news/arts-and-entertainment/wp/2014/11/30/a-brief-musical-history-of-the-osmonds-in-13-songs/?utm_term=.c318de50df06.

Osmond, Donny. 1999. *Life Is Just What You Make It: My Story So Far*. New York: Hyperion.

Osmond, Marie, and Marcia Wilkie. 2009. *Might as Well Laugh about It Now*. New York: New American Library.

Simpson, Dave. 2017. "The Osmonds: How We Made Crazy Horses." *The Guardian*, January 23. https://www.theguardian.com/culture/2017/jan/23/how-we-made-crazy-horses-the-osmonds.

QUEEN

The popular British rock band Queen made an indelible impression on the music world with their often over the top but wildly entertaining live performances and a string of memorable hit singles that propelled them into superstardom in the 1970s and early to mid-1980s. The original band members were: Freddie Mercury (lead vocals, piano), Brian May (lead guitar, vocals), Roger Taylor (drums, vocals), and John Deacon (bass guitar). Mercury joined May and Taylor in their earlier band, Smile. Mercury came up with the name "Queen" and also changed his name from Farrokh Bulsara to Freddie Mercury.

Although the group's first two self-titled albums were successful in the United Kingdom, it wasn't until the release of their third, *Sheer Heart Attack*, that they made inroads within the United States. The single "Killer Queen" landed in the

Billboard chart and peaked at number 12. The album appears on numerous music lists in the United Kingdom including "The 100 Greatest Rock Albums Ever" and "The 100 Records That Changed the World."

Queen's fourth studio album, *A Night at the Opera*, however, propelled them into what would become iconic status within the rock world. The album's sales were largely buoyed by the hit single, "Bohemian Rhapsody." The song is noteworthy even today for several reasons. When the song was released, the novelty of the format and structure gained a lot of attention. It mixes elements of opera, rock, and ballads together. The length of the song was also unusual, clocking in at just less than six minutes. The single plays an important role in the 1992 comedy film *Wayne's World*, a film that centers on the exploits of two rock-and-roll obsessed friends.

Hard rock music has historically been the terrain of hypermasculine men. Even with long hair and tight spandex outfits on, the typical rock star is depicted as raw, charismatic, and fixated on sex. Male teens during this time frame gravitated toward hard rock and heavy metal bands. During the 1970s and much of the 1980s, rock music was geared primarily toward teens and twentysomethings. Although some female teenagers may have actively enjoyed the music, the demographic most associated with the genre is boys and men.

After Mercury's death from an AIDS-related illness in 1991, the long-guarded secret of his sexuality began to come out in the media. Given his flair for the dramatic and flamboyant persona, it seems odd that so many in the public sphere were shocked to discover that he was gay. Keep in mind, however, that the rise of Queen occurred in a pre-Internet era. There were no swarms of paparazzi, no social media platforms or blogs, and no cell phones with cameras. Had any of these elements been present, the nature of Mercury's sexual orientation would have been much more difficult to hide from the public. This was also shortly before the fear and widespread paranoia brought about by the AIDS epidemic in the 1980s. The coming out process can be very difficult for anyone. Compounding that issue with elements of celebrity and potential negative effects on careers, it's understandable why someone would stay silent on the topic. Today, Mercury is lauded as a gay idol, and helped to pave the road to equality for LGBT youths and adults.

In 1976, Queen released their fifth studio album, *A Day at the Races*. The album reached the number five spot on Billboard and produced two hit singles: "Somebody to Love" and "Tie Your Mother Down." That same year, Queen played a free concert in Hyde Park in London that attracted a record number of attendees. The momentum continued into 1977 when the sixth studio album, *News of the World*, was released. That record produced two of the most well-known songs in modern popular history: "We Are the Champions" and "We Will Rock You." The songs would probably have been hits regardless, but the title and lyrics lent themselves to wide use at sporting events at every possible level, including high school and college athletics. "We Are the Champions" became a standard song played in sports stadiums all over the globe. It also reached number four on the American music charts. Due to the popularity of high school sports, many teenage athletes and cheerleaders connected with these hits as the lyrics and music showcased their competitive spirit.

The band heralded in the 1980s with the release of *The Game*. Their eighth studio album featured two more hit singles: "Crazy Little Thing Called Love" and "Another One Bites the Dust." Both songs hit the number one position on Billboard. And again, one of the songs became a mantra at competitive sporting events, "Another One Bites the Dust."

The rest of the 1980s brought varying levels of success, but the previous musical highs were getting more difficult to recapture. The band toured with Freddie Mercury as front man for the final time in 1986. The live double album, *Queen at Wembley*, recorded at that stop on the concert tour, was released on CD and video. Sales for the album achieved the status of five times platinum (5 million units).

A biographical film is in the works to highlight the career of Freddie Mercury and Queen. It has gone through some preproduction issues including a recasting of the actor who will portray Mercury. Some insiders allege that the producers will excise or seriously downplay Mercury's sexuality in the film. Members of the band who have been involved with the film deny this.

See also: 1960s: Beatles, The; Monkees, The; Rolling Stones, The; 1970s: Clash, The; Devo; Led Zeppelin; 1980s: Blondie; Boy George; Duran Duran; 1990s: Green Day; Smashing Pumpkins, The; 2000s: My Chemical Romance

Further Reading

Freestone, Peter. 2001. *Freddie Mercury*. London Omnibus Press.

Hince, Peter. 2011. *Queen Unseen: My Life with the Greatest Rock Band of the 20th Century*. London: John Blake Publishing.

Jones, Leslie-Ann. 2012. *Mercury: An Intimate Biography of Freddie Mercury*. New York: Touchstone.

McCormick, Neil. 2015. "Adam Lambert and Queen: 'Freddie Is Like a Myth, How Do You Live Up to That?'" *The Telegraph*, January 13. http://www.telegraph.co.uk/culture /music/rockandpopmusic/11343761/Adam-Lambert-and-Queen-Freddie-is-like-a -myth-how-do-you-live-up-to-that.html.

Teeman, Tim. 2017. "Keep Sex, AIDS, and the Closet in Freddie Mercury's Biopic." *Daily Beast*, July 26. https://www.thedailybeast.com/keep-sex-aids-and-the-closet-in-freddie -mercurys-biopic.

SIX MILLION DOLLAR MAN, THE

Popular action drama *The Six Million Dollar Man* ran on ABC from 1974–1978. It was a television adaptation of three made-for-television movies that aired in 1973 that were based on a novel entitled *Cyborg* by Martin Caidin. The central character is Steve Austin (Lee Majors), a former astronaut. The movies depicted him as a civilian, but the television series portrayed him as an Air Force Colonel, which was faithful to the source material. Austin is seriously harmed in an accident that occurs while testing a lifting body aircraft. Nearing death, Oscar Goldman (Richard

Anderson), the director of a fictional governmental agency named OSI (Office of Scientific Intelligence), pleads to save him, telling others that Austin can be rebuilt with available technology and made to be stronger and faster than he was previously. The surgery is successful and Austin is transformed into a government agent with superhuman skills. Both of Austin's legs, his right arm, and his left eye are replaced with bionic parts. This, of course, allows him to become a valuable government asset as he takes on various assignments. The legs allow him to run up to speeds of over 60 miles per hour, and the arm endows him with the strength of a construction vehicle akin to a bulldozer. The eye has night vision capabilities and can also detect infrared heat.

Although the term "bionics" was penned in the 1950s, Caidin's novel and *The Six Million Dollar Man* (and its spin-off, *The Bionic Woman*) made it a popular concept in the 1970s. The concept of fusing biology and electronics together to create something unique appealed to both the scientific community and the general public. Although nothing exists even today that resembles the technology used in these fictional TV shows, there are cochlear implants for deaf people and a fully developed artificial heart.

The Six Million Dollar Man was hugely successful with coming-of-age youth, teenage boys especially. Several elements propelled its appeal with this demographic. First, changing Steve Austin's affiliation back to the military gave the show a patriotic flavor as the hero was fighting for his government and country. Second, the science fiction genre has always been popular with young boys. Third, the action sequences, though rudimentary and even laughable by today's more high-tech standards, were popular with male teens who enjoyed fast-paced stories with a focus on movement rather than character development.

As with most media productions, the show reflected issues or concerns that were relevant at the time. While it may have not done this conspicuously, it certainly addressed them nonetheless. The 1970s were turbulent for many people, but especially for blue-collar workers. Rising energy prices, along with new forays into the workforce from women and minorities, created an atmosphere of uncertainty and even fear for status quo workers with respect to job security. This was felt most strongly among white men, especially among those who worked in factories. Racism and bigotry were an outgrowth of this as the majority felt threatened by a growing and vocal minority population. To add to this, political division from the Vietnam War and escalating Soviet tensions helped create and nurture and "us versus them" mentality that would eventually culminate in the election of Ronald Reagan as president of the United States in a significant victory for American conservatives.

Steve Austin became an emblem of American strength and resilience. Though younger fans may not have been aware of the sociopolitical implications, Austin represented white middle-class America. In the TV films that spawned the series, Austin is isolated and alone. When the material transitioned to television, and he was part of the military-industrial complex, he was no longer a victim. Austin's story of beating death and rising up from the proverbial ashes as an even stronger and faster fighter could easily be a surrogate for any number of hard-working

Americans threatened by layoffs, inflation, and a changing cultural landscape that threatened them on several levels.

Teens could view this positively without all of the political baggage. They enjoyed the mix of science fiction and comic book aspects along with adventure, and viewed Austin as an action hero. For adults grappling with real-life financial struggles and issues of autonomy and worth, the story line offered them a fantastical solution to a real problem. Perhaps this resonated with their need for an outside force to magically fix everything and move them forward as well.

The Six Million Dollar Man and its spin-off *The Bionic Woman* were Nielsen ratings hits. Originally intended as only a two-episode arc for the series, the character of Jaime Sommers (Lindsay Wagner) as Austin's love interest proved wildly popular with fans. Writers killed her character off in a parachuting accident initially, but later brought her back as *The Bionic Woman* after a similar procedure was done to repair her. That show ran for three seasons on network television. As imagined, it was especially popular with young girls who viewed Sommers as a strong female action hero. While neither may have been popular with TV critics, audiences loved them both. A wide variety of children's merchandise from the shows was also popular, such as lunch boxes, action figures, posters, and more. Development is under way for a big-screen adaptation of *The Six Million Dollar Man*. Slated for a 2019 release, the film will star Mark Wahlberg in the title role.

See also: 1960s: *Catch-22*; *Slaughterhouse-Five*; *Twilight Zone, The*; 1970s: *Charlie's Angels*

Further Reading

Jenkins, Tricia. 2011. "Nationalism and Gender: The 1970s, *The Six Million Dollar Man*, and *The Bionic Woman*." *Journal of Popular Culture* 44, no. 1 (February): 93–113.

Orpana, Simon. 2016. "We Can Rebuild Him and Her: Bionic Irony, Hysteria, and Post-Fordism's Technological Fix in *The Six Million Dollar Man*." *English Studies in Canada* 42 (1–2): 89–114. Project MUSE. https://muse.jhu.edu/article/648693.

Pilato, Herbie J. 2007. *The Bionic Book: The Six Million Dollar Man and The Bionic Woman Reconstructed*. Albany, GA: BearManor Media.

STARSKY & HUTCH

Running for four seasons on the ABC network, *Starsky & Hutch* was a popular police action series that both perpetuated aspects of earlier crime shows and redefined them with some updated twists. Detectives David Starsky (Paul Michael Glaser) and Richard "Hutch" Hutchison (David Soul) are crime fighters in the fictional burg of Bay City, California. As with most "buddy cop" media representations, each character has a unique personality that most times is oppositional to that of his or her partner's. Here, Starsky is an East Coast transplant with a rough exterior. He is ex-military, and often displays his anger and emotions openly. Hutch, on the other hand, is a Midwestern native who has a cool exterior and tends to employ logic more than emotion when handling conflicts.

The age of the actors/characters drew a younger demographic than earlier cop shows. *Starsky & Hutch* were "hipper" cops than those of previous decades. They worked with a black informant named Huggy Bear (Antonio Fargas), who owned and ran his own bar. Though seriously dated when examined through today's lens, this character at the time was very modern and cool and added to the youth appeal of the show. The duo's supervisor was the no-nonsense Captain Harold C. Dobey (Bernie Hamilton), who was also black. This use of minority characters and actors in recurring roles was also of significance at the time.

Another element of the show that attracted a male teen audience to the show was Starsky's iconic car. An apple red Gran Torino referred to as the "Striped Tomato," the conspicuous vehicle had white vector stripes down both sides. Apparently unable to obtain the original car that they wanted for the show, the producers selected this vehicle instead. Glaser allegedly despised it for several reasons, including his opinion that it would draw unwanted attention from suspects and criminals, as well as deter from the realism that the show strived for. The appearance and performance of the car, however, appealed to teenage boys and fed into gender stereotypes about boys and fast cars.

The first two seasons of the show contained a heavy amount of violence. This appealed to young male viewers, but, by the third season, Glaser expressed serious concern about it because overall violent crime within the country was also rising. Producers and writers agreed to tone down the violence, shifting the focus of the show to more personal story lines that focused on the lead characters' personal lives. Glaser also threatened to quit the show several times and was able to negotiate a more lucrative contract for his work. Additionally, he took on additional responsibilities such as directing some of the episodes. Producers began making alternate arrangements to insert a new character in place of Starsky should Glaser's demands become too egregious.

The show's popularity began to fade by the end of its third season. In the fourth and final season, a new character was introduced—Starsky's younger brother Nick (John Herzfeld). The idea was to have him step in and essentially take over Glaser's role, hopefully retaining the younger demographic for the show, but it was decided to end the show after the fourth season. In the final episode, Starsky is shot and seriously wounded. Rather than kill off the character, the writers allowed him to live, primarily as a method to potentially reboot the program in the future if it seemed profitable.

Police procedurals and cop action dramas like *Starsky & Hutch* have been around for decades. Some media analysts have segmented this genre into three categories based on timeline: The Golden Age (1967–1975), the Gilded Age (1976–1992), and the Dark Age (1993–present). Each of these segmentations attempts to define shifts in both technology and ideology relative to crime solving, as well as the relationship between law enforcement and the general public.

Prior to the categorization and analysis of this media subgenre, the TV series that provided a template to all that proceeded it was *Dragnet*. Starting as a radio show in 1949, *Dragnet* chronicled the efforts of Sergeant Joe Friday (Jack Webb) of the Los Angeles Police Department and his efforts to solve various crimes. The radio show was successful enough that is spawned a TV series featuring the same character. *Dragnet* depicted a very somber and professional police department. The role of law enforcement in this media representation was clear and inarguable: gather facts via victim statements, witness interviews, and basic investigative skills, and then pursue apprehension and arrest of the perpetrator. Friday and his cohorts were depicted as bland government officials who relied heavily on rigid methods (primarily paperwork forms) of detection to do their jobs. They were not known for their friendliness or finesse when interacting with civilians.

Although *Dragnet* accurately reflected conservative American culture at the time (it initially ran on network television from 1951–1959), police shows like *Starsky & Hutch* reflected the shifting cultural and societal changes taking place in the 1970s. In prior police procedurals and cop action dramas, the detectives were always men, and they were rarely if ever personal with one another. The relationship was strictly professional. In *Starsky & Hutch*, the two leads were friends. They had genuine affection for one another, so much so that the show is now jokingly referred to as the first "bromance" between partner cops on TV. This is noteworthy because open displays of affection between men were rare, especially within a profession like law enforcement.

David Soul went on to star in the television movie *Salem's Lot* based on the best-selling horror novel by Stephen King. He also sang several hit records including "Don't Give Up on Us" (1977), which reached No. 1 in the United States and the United Kingdom. Paul Michael Glaser has directed multiple episodes of various TV shows including *Miami Vice* and *Judging Amy*. He also continues to appear in film and television roles. A 2004 theatrical version of the series was released and starred Ben Stiller as Starsky and Owen Wilson as Hutch. The movie was more comedic in tone than the show and received generally positive reviews. Both Glaser and Soul had cameos in the film.

See also: 1970s: *Charlie's Angels*; 1980s: *21 Jump Street*

Further Reading

Craig, Steve, ed. 1992. *Men, Masculinity, and the Media*. Thousand Oaks, CA: Sage.

Nussbaum, Emily. 2004. "Television: Reruns; The Show That Made Police Brutality Stylish." *New York Times*, February 29. http://www.nytimes.com/2004/02/29/movies/television-reruns-the-show-that-made-police-brutality-stylish.html.

Snauffer, Douglas. 2006. *Crime Television*. Westport, CT: Praeger.

SUMMER, DONNA

Born LaDonna Adrian Gaines, Donna Summer (1948–2012) is considered the Queen of Disco. She became one of the most successful recording artists in history by capitalizing on the disco trend, which captured both late 1970s and early 1980s popular culture. Although she started out as the lead singer of a rock band named *Crow*, she left New York and moved to Europe to pursue acting and singing.

Early on, Summer joined forces with Pete Bellotte and Giorgio Moroder to produce a single entitled "Love to Love You Baby." Although the song would become a smash hit, Summer allegedly was uncomfortable with its reach as she originally intended it to be a "demo," only to be heard by future record producers. One of the reasons for the song's popularity and success was its novelty. Summer's throaty voice was overtly sexual in nature, and her vocals mimicked the female orgasm. Moreover, this type of song got a lot of airplay in discos and nightclubs, where extended versions of songs are commonplace. The sensuality and sexuality of the song promoted sensual slow dancing among young clubgoers.

Donna Summer, along with groups like the Bee Gees and Chic, became the face and voice of disco. After the wild success of "Love to Love You Baby," she continued to make a series of dance hits that dominated the charts: "On the Radio," "No More Tears (Enough Is Enough)," "Bad Girls," "She Works Hard for the Money," and many others. Summer's songs connected with young female listeners especially because she was a voice for those who had been disenfranchised, including youths. "Bad Girls" tackled prostitution, and "She Works Hard for the Money" celebrated working women. The song elevated their plight; she sang about all the work women do, and how they struggle to stay afloat financially in a male-dominated culture. Summer demanded that people "treat her right."

Disco significantly affected how teenagers dressed and what music they listened to. The fast and upbeat tempo attracted young girls who loved to dance at parties and clubs. Young men visited dance clubs because that was where they could meet single girls. Clothes that became popular during the disco era included skirts and dresses that were made of synthetic materials such as polyester and rayon. Many of the styles were derived from professional dancewear and showcased sparkly embellishments.

Disco evolved from an outgrowth of musical influences from Europe, but it was also shaped by nightclub circuits in large metropolitan cities. It differed dramatically from rock music not just in its sound but in its aesthetics as well. Club revelers tended to behave, dance, and even dress provocatively. Gay dance clubs in New York City, Chicago, and other cities across the country also played the music, and it became inextricably linked with gay culture and imagery.

Although disco music was a musical fad that enjoyed some mainstream popularity, it was also the object of a cultural backlash in the late 1970s and early 1980s. The backlash to disco was twofold: people objected to both its content and its symbolism. Additionally, the extent to which it was met with antagonism and vitriol was glaringly conspicuous. Many equated disco with a gay lifestyle, which they viewed with outright disdain, and condemned it as immoral and unhealthy. This resulted in what is known as "gay panic," a theory devised by Eve Kosofsky Sedgwick. Men were expected to be physically and emotionally strong and to adhere to heterosexual norms. The fact that people were openly deviating from this norm invoked fear and anxiety among more conservative individuals. In short, even the appearance of an LGBT relationship was cause enough for people to become antagonized and even violent.

Donna Summer's music was the backdrop to countless nights of debauchery at the infamous Club 54 disco in New York City. Young people danced into the late hours, many times under the influence on alcohol and recreational drugs, moving along with Summer's up-tempo songs. She won multiple Grammy Awards and had 32 hit songs over the course of her career. Although her last hit single came out in 1989, she remained popular with fans and in dance clubs for many years afterward.

Summer experienced controversy in the mid-1980s. She was quoted as making disparaging statements about AIDS patients, her remarks allegedly tied to her religious beliefs. Though she later vehemently denied making the comments, it nonetheless damaged her status with a loyal fan base. She also distanced herself from the hit song "Love to Love You Baby" that catapulted her to fame within the music industry. The artist died in 2012 and was posthumously inducted into the Rock and Roll Hall of Fame the following year.

See also: 1960s: Joplin, Janis; Mitchell, Joni; 1970s: Bee Gees, The

Further Reading

Bernstein, Jacob. 2012. "Memories of Donna's Disco Nights." *New York Times,* May 18. http://www.nytimes.com/2012/05/20/fashion/memories-of-donna-summer-from-her-disco-days.html.

Needham, Alex. 2012. "Donna Summer's Disco Was as Radical as Punk." *The Guardian*, May 1. https://www.theguardian.com/music/2012/may/17/donna-summer-disco-pop.

Summer, Donna, and Marc Eliot. 2003. *Ordinary Girl: The Journey*. New York: Villard.

UPDIKE, JOHN

The undisputed master of the short story genre is American author John Updike (1932–2009), although he has also written more than 20 novels. In his fiction, Updike wrote mostly about the middle class. His topics included activities and events often associated with married couples and families: extramarital affairs, the deaths of parents, career failures and struggles, and other issues that resonate with this demographic. In addition to these topics, Updike addressed coming-of-age sexuality in the short story, "A&P." In the story, the protagonist, Sammy, is a 19-year-old who works at an A&P grocery store. There he muses about the beautiful women who come into his store in their beach attire. In what he perceives to be a move of solidarity, he later quits his job when his boss tells the women to cover up next time; he finds this rude. However, the women are gone by the time he tenders his resignation, and they never see his gesture.

A Harvard graduate, Updike showed a propensity for writing even as a young boy. He consumed popular fiction as he came of age, and eventually got a job after high school as a "copy boy" for a newspaper. After graduating from college and marrying a fellow classmate Mary E. Pennington, Updike eventually took on a position at the *New Yorker* as a contributing writer. He continued writing poems and short stories while working there and had his first book of poetry published in 1958.

Updike's writing is largely autobiographical. Born in Pennsylvania, most of his short stories and novels take place on the East Coast. The fictional towns of Brewer and Olinger are substitutes for towns Reading and Shillington where he lived. The author drew on childhood, teenage, and adult experiences as material for his writing.

Another topic Updike addresses in his writing is death. Death is on the minds of many of his characters, to a point of obsession. They dwell on the inevitability of their passing and the finite nature of life. Linked to this is the view that time is a negative force, inching people toward their demise. In several interviews and writings, Updike discussed his view of death and how it looms over almost every event in life.

Another constant in much of Updike's writing is marital infidelity. His writing is so closely associated with this issue that it landed him on the cover of *Time* magazine in 1968 with the headline, "The Adulterous Society." Updike wrote extensively about navigating the landmines of marriage and extramarital affairs in the modern age. He contrasted the security of monogamy in marriage with sexual desires that extended beyond the partnership. Many critics believed that he placed a spotlight on the conflicting ambitions of marriage and freedom. He makes the argument that marriage and its parameters restrict freedom and prevent self-determination.

Updike's 1976 novel *Marry Me* explores these issues from the point of view of two different married couples. Well received critically, the novel was lauded for is simplicity not just in style but also in context. Updike was often criticized for his portrayal of women in his writing, and *Marry Me* was mostly recognized as a gentler work that showed empathy for its characters and their situations.

Updike also wrote about his experiences as a teenage boy and young man in the popular *Olinger Stories*. This collection of 11 short stories written while the author worked at *The New Yorker* showed a more nostalgic side of the author and tackled universal themes of youth. The stories are arranged chronologically and follow the same young protagonist from the age of 10 through early adulthood. "Friends from Philadelphia" examines young lust—a topic, of course, that he would revisit in his books written for adults—and "Pigeon Feathers" tackles religion. In it, a young man struggles with the meaning of death and goes to his parents for guidance. Ultimately, he comes to his own conclusion when carefully examining a dead bird and its intricate construction.

The most recognized and lauded writing in Updike's oeuvre is arguably the *Rabbit* series. This quartet of novels focuses on the complex character of Harry "Rabbit" Angstrom. An enduring character in American literature, the *Rabbit* series chronicles the life of its protagonist from young adulthood through death. The original book in the series, *Rabbit, Run*, examines Harry's dissatisfaction and sense of disillusionment with his life. A former high school basketball star, Harry is muddling through life and unable to reconcile its ordinariness with his former glory days as a celebrated jock. He cheats on his wife, Janice, with another woman and continuously seeks to fill the void in his life. After his wife accidentally drowns their newborn daughter in a bathtub after a bout of heavy drinking, Harry proclaims his innocence in the baby's death at the funeral. Guilt and the role of Christianity relative to sin and redemption are central themes in the book as they are in much of Updike's work.

Rabbit, Redux focuses on Harry's middle-aged angst. Divorced and working at a mundane job, he and his son forge new relationships that create additional drama. At the book's end, he is reunited with his ex-wife. 1981's *Rabbit Is Rich* finds Harry enjoying material success as the owner of an inherited Toyota car dealership. Harry may have money, but he is still burdened with an overactive libido and a family that he cannot control. *Rabbit at Rest,* the final book in the series, finds Harry and his wife Janice retired and living in Florida. Harry's health is bad, and he has a strained relationship with his son, Nelson, who steals money from him and uses illegal drugs. Harry slips back into his old ways and has a brief sexual encounter with his daughter-in-law. Janice forgives Harry before his death.

The *Rabbit* novels were commercial and critical successes. They catapulted Updike into the realm of prestigious American literary fiction. He is only one of three authors to ever win more than one Pulitzer Prize. Updike won two Pulitzers: one for *Rabbit Is Rich* and the other for *Rabbit at Rest.*

Updike tapped into deep-seated angst and fears among a certain segment of society. His examination of life's disappointments and struggles resonated with readers and critics alike. He wove together issues centered upon marriage, sexuality, and Western religion and gave voice to them through complex characters and stories that many times featured unlikeable protagonists. Although much of his writing focused on the adult experience, he still appealed to coming-of-age readers who looked to their marital and professional futures with anxiety.

Updike is also the author of *Witches of Eastwick*, a 1984 novel that was adapted into a 1987 box office hit film starring Jack Nicholson, Cher, Susan Sarandon, and Michelle Pfeiffer. He wrote the book in part as a response to critics who claimed that he failed to write about empowered female characters. The novel received largely positive reviews, though some felt it merely reinforced existing negative stereotypes of women.

In addition to his novels and short stories, Updike wrote multiple essays and works of poetry. He garnered two National Books Awards, three National Book Critics Circle Awards, and a National Medal of Arts and National Humanities Medal.

See also: 1950s: *Catcher in the Rye, The*

Further Reading

Batchelor, Bob. 2013. *John Updike: A Critical Biography*. Santa Barbara, CA: Praeger.

Begley, Adam. 2014. *Updike*. New York: Harper.

Menand, Louis. 2014. "Imitation of Life." *New Yorker*, April 28. https://www.newyorker .com/magazine/2014/04/28/imitation-of-life.

Power, Chris. 2015. "A Brief Survey of the Short Story: John Updike." *The Guardian*, April 14. https://www.theguardian.com/books/series/abriefsurveyoftheshortstory.

Updike, John. 2012. *Self-Consciousness: Memoirs*. New York: Random House.

WELCOME BACK, KOTTER

Welcome Back, Kotter (1975–1979), a network sitcom, featured stand-up comic Gabe Kaplan in the title role as a humorous teacher dealing with an eclectic group of high school misfits known collectively as the "Sweathogs." The premise of the series involves Gabe Kotter's return to his own high school to teach a group of remedial students who are challenging to handle. One way that he attempts to "get through" to them is to incorporate humor into his daily lesson plans and class-room interactions. Since his relationship with his students is positive overall, the antagonist of the show is inflexible assistant vice principal, John Woodman (John Sylvester White). He exhibits no tolerance for the Sweathogs and is depicted as a petty individual more consumed with administrative policies than education.

Although teachers have historically been portrayed in a largely positive light, the same cannot be said about school administrators. Films and television both have typically presented these characters as incompetent or ineffectual at best and preposterous or even malicious at worst. One need only refer to the administrators in films like *Animal House* (Dean Wormer) or *Ferris Bueller's Day Off* (Principal Rooney) to visualize the image of the petty bureaucrat who is meant to be the object of scorn by both the other characters in the film and, by transference, the audience.

On *Welcome Back, Kotter,* the role of the teacher is presented as multilayered. Although the primary purpose, of course, is to educate, another role—and one just as important as the primary one—is to bond with students on a personal level. One function of presenting positive media role models is that of inspiration. Within Western culture, teachers are well respected but aren't necessarily well compensated for their efforts compared to many other jobs and professions. Many choose the profession because they are passionate about teaching and about the possibility of shaping students' lives.

Within films and on television, teachers are often portrayed as mentors. Because of their important role within the educational system and their daily proximity and dealings with students, it makes sense that they are viewed as having significant influence on their wards. Their reach extends beyond the classroom. Teachers who have positive relationships with their students can assist them in viewing the world differently than they might otherwise.

The Sweathogs on *Welcome Back, Kotter* are all from disadvantaged socioeco-nomic backgrounds. The fictional setting of James Buchanan High closely resembles the school that Gabe Kaplan attended as a teen. Many of the characters he created for the show were inspired by actual students he knew while he was a student there. The students on the series included dimwitted lady's man Vinnie Barbarino (John Travolta), class clown and oddball Arnold Horshack (Ron Palillo), smooth and hip Freddie Percy "Boom Boom" Washington (Lawrence Hilton-Jacobs), and chronically tardy student Juan Epstein (Robert Hegyes).

A recurring theme of the show is the crossing of boundaries between the personal and the professional. Kotter and his wife, Julie (Marcia Strassman), live in a tiny and cramped apartment in Bensonhurst. His students routinely make unannounced visits there to seek his advice and counsel. His wife frequently expresses frustration at these intrusions into their home and personal lives. She and Gabe argue a bit about it, but the situation remains unchanged.

This is another example of that extension of roles that teachers are many times portrayed as having with some students. Given that many teens have serious challenges at home and may not receive the support and nurturing they need to evolve, the role of the teacher to also be a parent figure can seem like a natural outgrowth. Some teen viewers might have gravitated toward the show because of the nature of the relationship between Kotter and his pupils. He was a surrogate parent of sorts, but one who was more approachable and perhaps less judgmental.

The potential danger in portraying teachers universally or even frequently as flawless problem-solvers and gurus of life's journey is that they can be perceived as infallible. This archetype of the wise and trusted teacher can set unrealistic expectations with students and the general population. Although the intention of depicting these educators as hip and witty and empathetic to a fault is a positive one, it can ultimately set the stage for disappointment when young students realize they have the same issues and struggles as the rest of us.

Although the first two seasons of the show were impressive, ratings began to slide in season three. By that time, the characters in the show had established their own identities with the audience and relied heavily on catchphrases to garner laughs. While the majority of the actors who played the Sweathogs didn't rise to fame after the show was canceled, it was a launching pad for the very successful career of John Travolta. Clearly the breakout star of the series, he was lured into movies and starred in several box office hits including *Grease* and *Saturday Night Fever.*

The show was retooled significantly in the fourth and final season, but ratings continued to stagnate and it wasn't renewed for a fifth season. Its popularity, however, spawned merchandise including lunch boxes and even a board game. *Welcome Back, Kotter* was nominated for one major Emmy Award for Best Comedy after its first season but lost to the *Mary Tyler Moore Show.*

See also: 1950s: *Blackboard Jungle*; 1960s: *Explosive Generation, The*; *Room 222*; *To Sir, with Love*; 1970s: *Cooley High*; *Grease*; *National Lampoon's Animal House*; 1980s: *Facts of Life, The*; *Saved by the Bell*; 1990s: *Boy Meets World*

Further Reading

Murray, Noel. 2014. "10 Episodes That Show How *Welcome Back, Kotter* Was Like a Class in Comedy History." *AV/TV Club*, November 6. https://tv.avclub.com/10-episodes-that -show-how-welcome-back-kotter-was-like-1798273861.

Zurawik, David. 2012. "Honoring 'Welcome Back, Kotter's' Robert Hegyes for Being One of TV's First 'Tough Jews.'" *The Baltimore Sun*, January 27. http://www.baltimoresun.com /entertainment/tv/z-on-tv-blog/bal-honoring-robert-hegyes-for-being-one-of-tvs-first -tough-jews-20120127-story.html.

The 1980s

DECADE OVERVIEW

The election of Republican president Ronald Reagan in 1980 telegraphed the socially and politically conservative decade that was ahead. Reagan was one of the most popular presidents ever, and he had a friendly relationship with the media. In a pre–cable news and social media world, his unscripted moments with the press were rare. Reagan quickly set out to undo much of the socioeconomic legislation designed to benefit the poor ostensibly to help people become more independent and less reliant on the government for assistance.

Not surprisingly, the 1980s is most often defined as the era of wealth and conspicuous consumption for those who were doing well financially. The decade saw the rise of "yuppies"—young, urban professionals who worked mainly for large corporations and sought a fast track to financial wealth. They were largely defined by their lifestyles and material goods.

With a hyper-focus on physical appearance and wealth, teens became more aware of designer names and spent more money on clothing and accessories than ever before. Designer name fashions such as Ralph Lauren (Polo), Calvin Klein, and Halston were just some of the designers popular at this time. Fashion in the 1980s featured a mixture of neon-colored garments, boxy jackets and blouses, dresses with shoulder pads, and over-the-top gowns with large bows and puffy sleeves. Teen girls favored large earrings and hair bows along with "big hair" that was usually blown dry and heavily hair sprayed. Teen boys gravitated toward safe choices like blue jeans and khakis, but more adventurous young men sported parachute pants and leather jackets with multiple zippers. One "must have" accessory from the decade was a pair of Ray-Ban Wayfarers, sunglasses largely popularized by Tom Cruise's character in the film *Risky Business* (1983).

Working-class families continued struggling during the 1980s and this was reflected in popular TV shows like *Roseanne* and *Kate & Allie,* a show that depicted two divorced mothers raising their children in New York City. The top-rated TV show in 1980 was CBS's *Dallas* and the highest-grossing film of the year was *The Empire Strikes Back.* Comedies like *9 to 5* (1980), *Caddyshack* (1980), and *Airplane* (1980) were incredibly successful at the box office as well. Additionally, television shows that mirrored the obsession with glamour and wealth included ABC's *Dynasty* and *Falcon Crest.* TV shows popular with teens included *The Facts of Life, A Different World,* and *Head of the Class.*

The decade also featured some of the top blockbuster films of all time, many of them appealing to teenage audiences: *Raiders of the Lost Ark* (1981), *E.T.* (1982), *Ghostbusters* (1984), *Top Gun* (1986), and *Batman* (1989).

MTV, a cable music channel that would become a defining influence on music, fashion, and film throughout the 1980s and 1990s, launched in the summer of 1981. The channel was revolutionary, changing the way that groups and artists were marketed, with a new emphasis placed on visual storytelling that was just as important—if not more, in some cases—than the song itself.

John Lennon of the Beatles was assassinated in 1980, and millions of fans around the world mourned his death. One year later, John Warnock Hinckley Jr. attempted to assassinate President Ronald Reagan. Several others were wounded in the shooting, including Reagan's press secretary, James Brady.

Technological advances were made in this decade that included the first personal computer from Apple and the wide availability and use of the VCR (Videocassette Recorder), which allowed people to record their favorite television programs while they were gone and watch them later at their convenience.

Although the drugs of the 1960s and 1970s were now viewed largely with disapproval, new drugs such as crack cocaine infested many poverty-stricken communities in the 1980s. Public service announcements and other efforts created to curb widespread drug usage largely failed, indicating once again that the issue is complex and multilayered.

The HIV/AIDS epidemic that swept through the country in the 1980s devastated the gay male community in particular. Initially, doctors were not exactly sure what the disease was or how it was transmitted. Doctors and scientists conducted research, and learned that the disease could be potentially contracted by anyone who practiced unsafe sex with someone who was infected, received a blood transfusion that had the virus, or shared needles for drug usage with an infected person. Many in the LGBT community believed that the government dragged its feet on research and development of potential cures initially because it was labeled as a "gay disease."

Internationally, the end of the decade signaled change with the start of the removal of the Berlin Wall in 1989. The structure was built to divide West Berlin from its surrounding East Germany. In a rousing speech made by President Reagan in 1987, he implored Soviet Union leader, Mikhail Gorbachev, to "tear down this wall!" Though the physical destruction of the wall didn't begin until 1990, this event will forever be associated with Reagan and the 1980s.

The 25 entries in this section cover not only media popular with coming-of-age youth but also television shows, music, movies, and books that, while aimed at adult audiences, told stories about growing during the era of trickle-down economics and crimped hair. Depictions of families were evolving and changing, artists bucked gender norms, and overt sexuality ceased to be taboo. These hallmarks of the 1980s are impossible to miss in the entries that follow.

Further Reading

Batchelor, Bob, and Scott Stoddard. 2006. *The 1980s: American Popular Culture through History*. Westport, CT: Greenwood Press.
Harrison, Thomas. 2017. *Pop Goes the Decade: The Eighties*. Santa Barbara, CA: Greenwood Press.

Sirota, David. 2011. *Back to Our Future: How the 1980s Explain the World We Live in Now—Our Culture, Our Politics, Our Everything*. New York: Ballantine Books.
Smokler, Kevin. 2016. *Brat Pack America: A Love Letter to '80s Teen Movies*. Los Angeles, CA: Rare Bird Books.

BACK TO THE FUTURE

Back to the Future, a 1985 time travel comedy, was one of the biggest commercial hits of the decade and helped to solidify Michael J. Fox's status as a bona fide movie star. The film is a science fiction adventure comedy focused on the efforts of teenager Marty McFly (Michael J. Fox) and his quest to change the present by traveling to the past and altering events within the lives of his parents. At the beginning of the film, Marty is deeply disappointed in the state of his parents' marriage. His father George (Crispin Glover) is meek and allows himself to be bullied at work by his abusive supervisor, Biff (Thomas F. Wilson). His mother Lorraine (Lea Thompson) is depressed and in a perpetual state of despondency over the state of her life. During a family dinner, Marty learns the story of how his parents met and realizes that the origins of their relationship are significant to his mother. He understands that they were once very much in love but that their marriage has become stagnant, and they're unfulfilled in their daily lives.

Marty encounters his friend, scientist Dr. Emmett Brown (Christopher Lloyd), in a parking lot late one night. Doc Brown has been working on a time travel machine in the form of an automobile fueled by confiscated plutonium. Before they can finish, the Libyans (from whom Doc Brown stole the plutonium) arrive and shoot Doc Brown, but Marty escapes in the modified DeLorean. He unwittingly triggers the time travel component and ends up back in 1955. After discovering that there is an insufficient amount of plutonium to return, he realizes that he is stuck in the past.

Marty quickly finds himself in the company of his mother and father as teenagers. Originally, his parents met when George was accidentally hit by Lorraine's father in his car. Marty saves George from the accident, but, in doing so, he alters events. Marty's mother Lorraine instead develops a crush on Marty, adding another obstacle to the mix. Marty locates the teenaged Doc and explains what has happened. Doc instructs him that he must devise a plan to get his teenaged parents together or else the future will be permanently changed and he won't even exist.

Although *Back to the Future* is viewed primarily as a "popcorn" movie with little critical depth, it provides a clever presentation of gender roles and stereotypes in 1950s America. It is also a comedy that offers a more complex picture of teenagers than many Hollywood vehicles that aim for either raunchiness or depictions of teens as self-obsessed and insensitive.

Women had one primary goal in the 1950s: to attract and marry a man, and thereafter to keep the home. Although women had entered the workforce during World War II while many young men were off fighting in the military, they were largely expected to transition back into roles of mothers and wives once the men returned to civilian life. Lorraine is a typical 1950s teen in that she is consumed with romantic notions and, while not explicitly stated, realizes that her safest bet in life is to find a man that can marry her and take care of her while she tends to the home and the children.

George is, of course, a nerd. The archetype of the nerd has been around for decades, and 1950s media firmly entrenched it into popular culture. Nerds were seen as less masculine than their male counterparts. The fact that they actively enjoyed the disciplines of math and science flagged them as social misfits. This played right into prevalent cultural stereotypes of the expected roles of men and women at this time. In short, "successful" men were interested and/or active in sports and typically worked in the business world whereas academic types were often portrayed as "losers" who struggled to interact in socially acceptable ways. The nerd archetype resonates with teens, especially ones who might feel as though they are outsiders.

Back to the Future stands out from other teen-driven films of the 1980s in one very conspicuous way: the parents and not the teens are the focus of the story. Marty's mission or quest in the film is to ensure that his parents meet and fall in love. Although he has a love interest in the film, that is not the central story line. Marty is able to see and interact with his parents as they were when they were his age. The social divide between teens and parents is lessened if not erased by this element of the film.

Most teen comedies even today rely on the notion that parents are out of touch and cannot relate to the experiences of their teenaged children. In *Back to the Future*, Marty is able to views his parents as peers rather than authority figures. More importantly, he is able to connect with their plights and empathize with them. This is an unconventional alternative to the standard teen story line where parents are either absent or clueless, and their children are the clever and cynical ones. Teens savored the movie because it allowed them to relate more to their parents, giving them a window into their experiences and seeing that many teen struggles are timeless.

Back to the Future's premise grew from an idea of one of its producers: if I'd met my father in high school, would I have liked him? The creators were able to take that kernel of an idea and expand it into a film that connected with moviegoers and critics. It's also a film that may have turned out very differently had the original star, Eric Stoltz, retained the part of Marty McFly. After filming began, director Robert Zemeckis realized that he had miscast the lead. Stoltz was known more for dramatic roles whereas Fox had been doing a successful sitcom for several years and had proven his comedic acting skills.

The film remained in the number one box office position for more than two months and grossed more than $200 million in North America. It went on to become the highest-grossing film of 1985 and spawned two successful sequels: *Back to the Future Part II* and *Back to the Future Part III*. It has appeared on numerous "best of" lists including *Entertainment Weekly*'s list of the "50 Best High School

Movies" and the "10th Best Film in the Science Fiction Genre" created by a poll done by the American Film Institute.

See also: 1960s: *Twilight Zone, The*; 1980s: *Family Ties*

Further Reading

Freeman, Hadley. 2015. "Back to the Future's Parents Were Way Ahead of Their Time." *The Guardian*, October 1. https://www.theguardian.com/film/2015/oct/01/back-to-the -future-teenagers-parents.
Smith, Jamil. 2015. "How 'Back to the Future' Helped Make Me a Feminist." *New Republic*, July 6. https://newrepublic.com/article/122243/how-back-future-helped-make-me-feminist.

BLONDIE

Blondie, a New Wave band featuring lead singer Debbie Harry (1945–) made a significant impression on the American music scene in the late 1970s and early 1980s before their initial breakup in 1982. The band was formed by Harry and guitarist Chris Stein in New York City, and became an integral part of the burgeoning music scene that would blend elements of rock and pop together, creating a distinctive new sound. That sound was New Wave. Popular especially among teens and young adults, it dominated the airwaves throughout the decade. The rest of the band was fleshed out by bassists Fred Smith and Nigel Harrison, drummer Billy O'Connor, keyboardist and pianist Jimmy Destri, and guitarists Gary Valentine and Frank Infante. Blondie was already an established hit in Australia before enjoying success in its home country. The single "Denis" on their second studio album (*Plastic Letters*) was a hit in the United Kingdom as was the album itself.

Blondie's third studio release *Parallel Lines* (1978) was their breakout album. It reached the number one sales spot in Great Britain and peaked in the United States at number six on the Billboard charts. The biggest hit single from the album was "Heart of Glass," a newer sound for the band since it relied heavily on disco influences that were popular at the time. The band and Harry started receiving media attention for their sound and for Harry's alluring sexual persona. Harry was even featured on the cover of *Rolling Stone* magazine the following year.

Blondie's appeal to teenagers was rooted in both sound and optics. Their music was dance oriented, which is generally popular with teen girls. A pop group fronted by a young woman was still a rarity at the time, and this also had significant allure for young girls who were used to seeing only men as lead singers in musical groups. The mere existence of a popular group with a female front and center was significant to young women in terms of musical career options. Many teen boys were intrigued by this as well, though perhaps more for reasons of physical attraction and sexual appeal.

The next hit from the album was the rock-oriented "One Way or Another." The song is about obsession and stalking with multiple references to the singer driving past her target's home and then following his bus and trying to determine who he's calling on the phone. As with most pop songs that have dark motives, the average listener doesn't always zero in on the content or even the subtext as much as the beat or rhythm of the tune. Teens could relate to the song as many of them were experiencing their first romantic relationships and some of the jealousies and possessiveness that can accompany them.

Eat to the Beat, studio album number four, again hit the top spot overseas in Great Britain but only peaked in the 17th spot in the United States. The only hit single from the album in America was "Dreaming," which reached number 27 on the Billboard charts. Blondie's international smash hit "Call Me" from the *American Gigolo* soundtrack cemented their place in music history

Blondie's fifth studio album, *Autoamerican,* generated two hit singles—"The Tide Is High" and "Rapture." The second of those is noteworthy for being the first number one single in America to feature rapping. Once again, the group blended different styles and sounds to come up with something unique that appealed to a wide audience.

Although female recording artists were hardly a novelty in the 1970s, the genre of rock and roll especially has typically been a haven for heterosexual men. There were exceptions, like Freddie Mercury from Queen, but he wasn't open about his bisexuality when he was alive. Harry, however, made significant inroads for women in popular music by fronting a successful group at a time when this was the exception. Without her, the ability of someone like Madonna to gain access and acceptability in the early 1980s to a system still dominated by men would be called into question.

The band broke up in 1982 due to a perfect storm of negative impacts that included lagging concert ticket sales, financial mismanagement, and drug use among band members. Harry and Chris Stein at this point were romantically involved, and she cared for him when he was diagnosed with a serious illness around the same time that the group split. They soon parted ways as a couple but remained close and even worked together on several music projects.

> Harry now concedes that her sexual magnetism and physical appearance were a significant part of the formula that brought fame and success to Blondie initially, but they also may have limited her in terms of being viewed more seriously as an artist. She understands that the music business has changed dramatically since her early years with Blondie and even as a solo artist. While she notes that there are pluses and minuses with this, she commends current artists for taking more creative control of their images and also for being more financially savvy about their share in the profits of their labor. (Garratt 2015)

Harry also branched out into film and has appeared in numerous movies, including *Hairspray* and *New York Stories*, both released in 1988. Blondie has sold close to 40 million records internationally and was inducted into the Rock and Roll Hall of Fame in 2006. They continue making music today, and their most recent studio album, *Pollinator,* was released in 2017.

See also: 1960s: Doors, The; Joplin, Janis; Rolling Stones, The; 1970s: Devo; Led Zeppelin; Queen; 1980s: Duran Duran; Gibson, Debbie; Lauper, Cyndi; Madonna; 1990s: Green Day; Morissette, Alanis; 2000s: Cyrus, Miley; Rihanna; Spears, Britney; Swift, Taylor

Further Reading

Che, Cathay. 2014. *Deborah Harry: A Biography*. London: Andre Deutsch.
Garratt, Sheryl. 2015. "Debbie Harry on Punk, Refusing to Retire and Sex at 69." www .telegraph.co.uk/Sheryl Garratt. March 1.
Mcleod, Kembrew. 2017. "Blondie's 'Heart of Glass' and the punk rock myth of 'Death to Disco.'" Salon, July 8. https://www.salon.com/2017/07/08/heart-of-glass-excerpt/.

BOY GEORGE

Boy George (1961–) (born George Alan O'Dowd) formed the band Culture Club, which consisted of lead singer Boy George, bassist Mikey Craig, drummer Jon Moss, and guitarist Roy Hay. The name "Culture Club" represented the diversity among the group's origins ranging from Irish to British to Jewish. What garnered the most media attention, however, was Boy George's physical appearance and style.

Boy George personified androgyny. He routinely wore makeup that included bright red lipstick, eye shadow, and blush. His hair was long and often in braids that were adorned with brightly colored pieces of cloth. The clothes were often loose fitting and consisted of brightly colored tunics and coats and sometimes colorful hats. In the early days, he favored ballet flats for shoe wear. This sort of individual expression resonates with teens who often experiment with different looks, hairstyles (and hair colors) and fashions as they become more aware of their identities. Appearance is critically important to many teens as their clothing and hairstyles are most times a reflection of their personalities and can either set them apart from peers or show alignment with them.

Androgyny was nothing new within popular culture as musical artist David Bowie had evidenced many years before this. Bowie actively played with gender roles throughout his career. Although coy and later contradictory about his sexual orientation, Bowie defied convention by sometimes wearing women's clothes as he did on the cover of his 1970 album, *The Man Who Sold the World*. This was at a time when predefined gender roles were still fairly strict. Bowie frequently dressed and behaved on stage in a manner that failed to conform to a gender binary. By today's standards, this isn't shocking or provocative, but during the 1970s, it was revolutionary within mainstream culture. Young fans, especially teens, were intrigued by his playfulness with gender representations.

While androgyny and public awareness of transgender teens is more common nowadays, icons like Boy George paved the way for young people to express themselves and break down gender barriers. This comfort with individual expression resonated with teenagers who want to make a statement about their own gender identities and expressions. It's a nonconforming response to the traditional expectations of how "boys and girls" should express themselves.

When Boy George and Culture Club burst onto the American music scene in the early 1980s, his look was the primary point of discussion for many, sparking numerous questions about his sexuality and also about his "manhood." Even though he grew up in a middle-class household where his father taught boxing, he still dyed his hair orange while in high school and made it clear from an early age that he wasn't going to conform to gender norms and expectations. This defiance of gender and cultural expectations as a teenager carried into his adult life.

Although the novelty of Boy George's appearance might have attracted attention, the music was well-received internationally. Culture Club released their debut album, *Kissing to Be Clever*, in 1982. The record spawned three singles: "Time (Clock of the Heart)," "I'll Tumble 4 Ya," and the smash hit "Do You Really Want to Hurt Me?" The album stayed on the Billboard charts for 88 weeks and sold close to 5 million copies worldwide.

Demonstrating that they were not a one-hit wonder or novelty act with a limited shelf life, the sophomore album from the band, *Colour by Numbers,* was an even bigger hit and scored four top 10 hits in the United States. The biggest breakout single from the album was "Karma Chameleon." It reached the number one Billboard spot in both the United Kingdom and the United States and became the best-selling single of 1983.

The group's third album, *Waking Up with the House on Fire,* sold more than 2.5 million copies, but the reviews of it were lukewarm. It failed to produce a top 10 hit within the United States. Conflict within the band was also taking a toll on cohesion and creativity. George and drummer Jon Moss were involved with each other romantically but were keeping it a secret. George was also using drugs on a regular basis.

By the time the fourth album, *From Luxury to Heartache*, was released, things had soured dramatically between George and Moss. Media accounts of Boy George's drug use were prominently being featured in gossip columns by this time as well. The band officially broke up in 1986, but Boy George continued to do solo work. While Culture Club's catchy and clever pop songs attracted a young audience, Boy George's authenticity and fashion rebellion connected with teenagers at a deeper level. It validated their desire and need to express themselves and be accepted by others.

In late 2003, the musical *Taboo* opened on Broadway in New York City. It was set in a London club and re-created events and characters from the New Romantic scene that began in the United Kingdom. Boy George played the role of Leigh Bowery, the club's creator, and he also cowrote the lyrics for the songs. The show, which was financed by comedienne Rosie O'Donnell, was a critical and commercial failure and closed after 100 performances.

See also: 1960s: Beatles, The; Monkees, The; Rolling Stones, The; 1970s: Clash, The; Devo; Led Zeppelin; Queen; 1980s: Blondie; Duran Duran; Lauper, Cyndi; 1990s: Green Day; Smashing Pumpkins, The; 2000s: My Chemical Romance

Further Reading

Bright, Spencer, and George O'Dowd. 1995. *Take It Like a Man: The Autobiography of Boy George*. New York: HarperCollins.

Helligar, Jeremy. 2014. "Pop Music Could Use Another Decade as 'Gay' as the '80s." *Huffington Post*, April 9. https://www.huffingtonpost.com/jeremy-helligar/pop-music -could-use-anoth_b_5101352.html com.

COSBY SHOW, THE

Few sitcoms are considered to be transformational in terms of their effect on culture, but *The Cosby Show* (1984–1992) arguably changed the face of network television with its portrayal of an upper-middle-class black American family. Although earlier 1970s sitcoms such as *Good Times* and *What's Happening!!* also featured black families, *The Cosby Show* was one of the first TV sitcoms to focus on one that wasn't socioeconomically disadvantaged. Although characters on the aforementioned shows regularly struggled with money problems and other issues associated with the lower or middle class, the family members of *The Cosby Show* seldom encountered these harsh challenges.

The parents, Cliff and Clair Huxtable (Bill Cosby and Phylicia Rashad), a pediatrician and an attorney, respectively, lived in an urban townhouse with their children: Sondra (Sabrina La Beauf), Denise (Lisa Bonet), Theo (Malcolm-Jamal Warner), Vanessa (Tempestt Bledsoe), and Rudy (Keshia Knight Pulliam). Although the face of the show was somewhat revolutionary, the themes and ideas explored within the episodes were familiar and traditional. As the patriarch of the family, Cliff was often the individual who taught life lessons to his children; as with most sitcoms about a nuclear family, the father figure was the central character in the show. Although Clair also had a successful job, she often inhabited a traditional gender role at home. While Cliff claims to be a decent cook, for example, it is Clair that is almost always seen preparing meals in the kitchen.

Another carryover from decades' earlier sitcoms like *Father Knows Best* was that of the nagging wife. Even though the relationship between Cliff and Clair is a loving and mutually respectful one, the show still relies on the stereotype of the female as overly persistent in her demands and critical of her husband. This element of comedy dates back to the days of vaudeville, so it is more a criticism of our culture's familiarity with and acceptance of it than it is specifically of the show itself.

Those elements aside, the show depicted a positive image of a black family that resonated with viewers and many critics. During an era of unfettered capitalism and criticism of affirmative action legislation, TV offered viewers an upwardly mobile family of color. The parents were financially successful and the older children college bound. This was a powerful visual, and it was perhaps even more powerful due to the show largely avoiding issues of race and class—i.e., for the first time on television, the lives of upper-middle-class blacks seemed to be parallel to their white counterparts. Some in the community felt that this did a disservice to the very real issues of poverty within the black community.

Adolescent and teen viewers enjoyed the positive family dynamic of the show. Some of the relevant topics and situations that the show addressed included the following: Vanessa trying to prevent her parents from finding out about a poor grade she got in a class, Theo being accused of doing drugs when Cliff and Clair find a joint hidden in one of his books, Denise getting her driver's license and wanting to exhaust her savings to buy a car, and youngest sibling Rudy getting hurt when "horsing around" with Theo as they pretend to be circus performers.

For white teens watching the show, the story lines involving Theo, Denise, Vanessa, and Sondra were not much different than what they'd seen on other family sitcoms. For black teens, however, this representation of a black family on television was in many ways affirming and rewarding. They saw kids their own age living in comfortable surroundings and being raised by parents who had professional jobs, and who afforded their family access to a solid education and opportunities. The impact of this depiction on black teen viewers was immense and indisputable.

Some argued that there was a downside to this, though. In the world of the Huxtables, racism doesn't exist. Cliff and Clair embody the Horatio Alger myth: anyone can become rich in America if they just work hard enough, and their children will inherit their legacy. This presentation conveniently ignores those who were devastated during economic recession in the 1980s. As with most wide-scale financial failures, many at the bottom of the socioeconomic ladder are harmed the most. Viewing this show through the lens of political conservatism, it reinforces the notion that a black family has just as much potential to do well financially as their white counterparts. It conveniently ignores institutional racism, a public-school system that many times fails the poor and disenfranchised, and past governmental policies that prevented the advancement of minorities.

It isn't necessary for a sitcom to take on weighty topics. However, a few acknowledgments of race relations in America during the time frame of the show may have helped it achieve some authenticity or cultural awareness outside the walls of the Huxtables' comfortable brownstone. These criticisms aside, the series can be credited with changing race relations in America.

The Cosby Show was a phenomenal success for NBC and is largely credited for reviving the modern sitcom. The show was a Top 10 in the Nielsen ratings and won a plethora of awards including six Emmys, two Golden Globes, three NAACP Image Awards, and multiple People's Choice trophies. It also spurred the spin-off show, *A Different World*, which focused on the college adventures of daughter Denise (Lisa Bonet) and her group of friends.

The legacy of the show is now in potential jeopardy as numerous allegations of sexual abuse and rape have been levied against Bill Cosby from a large number of women. At the time of this writing, 46 women have accused the star of sexual assault. The media firestorm surrounding the allegations has damaged the aging celebrity's once-stellar career: several shows on his most recent tour were canceled due to the backlash, the TV Land network pulled reruns of the show from its schedule, and the topic has been daily fodder for TV talk shows and comedians.

See also: 1950s: *Adventures of Ozzie and Harriet, The*; *Father Knows Best*; *I Love Lucy*; *Leave It to Beaver*; 1960s: *Patty Duke Show, The*; 1970s: *Happy Days*; 1980s: *Facts of Life, The*; *Family Ties*; *Full House*; *Wonder Years, The*; 1990s: *Boy Meets World*; *Clarissa Explains It All*; *7th Heaven*; 2000s: *Friday Night Lights*

Further Reading

Devega, Chauncey. 2015. "How 'The Cosby Show' Duped America: The Sitcom That Enabled Our Ugliest Reagan-Era Fantasies." Salon, July 12. https://www.salon.com /2015/07/12/how_the_cosby_show_duped_america_the_sitcom_that_enabled _our_ugliest_reagan_era_fantasies/.

Kim, Kyle, et al. 2017. "Bill Cosby: A 50-Year Chronicle of Accusations and Accomplishments." *Los Angeles Times*, June 17. http://www.latimes.com/entertainment/la-et-bill -cosby-timeline-htmlstory.html.

Williams, Vanessa. 2014. "'The Cosby Show' and the Black American Dream." *Washington Post*, October 12. https://www.washingtonpost.com/blogs/she-the-people/wp/2014/10/12 /the-cosby-show-and-the-black-american-dream/?utm_term=.338b57e95b6a.

DIRTY DANCING

Released in 1987, *Dirty Dancing* received mixed reviews from critics but was a smash box office hit. The film has remained immensely popular since its release, more than 25 years ago. Marketed as a teen romance and dance film, *Dirty Dancing* resonated with young audiences and had universal appeal. Today, it is widely considered to be a significant rite of passage film for teenage girls. The story focuses on Frances "Baby" Houseman (Jennifer Grey), a young woman from an affluent family who plans on joining the Peace Corps after she graduates from college. The teen and her family spend their summer vacation at an upscale resort in the Catskills region of New York. Frances encounters the handsome dance instructor, Johnny Castle (Patrick Swayze), and convinces him to give her dance lessons. Things become complicated when Johnny's regular dance partner, Penny, becomes pregnant by a womanizing waiter at the resort.

The surface aspects of the plot that involve the formulaic romance between the "rich girl" and the "bad boy" and the inevitable romantic conclusion aren't what make the film particularly unique or even interesting. Considering that the film takes place in 1963, some of the issues and themes underlying the romance would have been considered quite revolutionary during that period. Frances is presented as a very bright and confident young woman who doesn't follow the path that her parents—particularly her physician father—assume she will follow. This is especially true when Penny becomes pregnant and decides to have an abortion.

Hollywood films and television shows consistently create plotlines that link abortion to the death of the woman having the procedure done. In fictional stories involving abortion, 9 percent of the women die directly as a result of the procedure; in reality, the statistical percentage of women dying from legal abortions is zero. More telling, however, is the percentage of fictional female characters who die indirectly after having an abortion: 14 percent. Of these fictional deaths that were analyzed, all but one was the result of murder. Although one can attribute this to the storyteller and not necessarily the larger Hollywood film system, it's hard to argue that this doesn't have a cumulative effect with messaging.

In the film, Penny does have complications after the abortion and ultimately has to be saved by Doctor Houseman (Jerry Orbach). However, when it's discovered that Penny is going to have an abortion, her friends and coworkers rally around her and offer unanimous support. Frances even obtains the money from her father, though she doesn't tell him what the money is needed for, and gives it to Penny for the procedure.

Penny doesn't die in the film, and there is no judgment about her actions from the other characters, and this straightforward method of dealing with teenage sexuality and possible ramifications of it connected with teen audiences. The film isn't overly didactic in its messaging. Unlike some teen-centered books and films that are clearly aimed at reinforcing negative consequences of premarital sex, *Dirty Dancing* recognizes that sexual activity isn't uncommon for many teens and doesn't always end in tragedy.

Another surprising element of the story involves Frances and Johnny's sexual encounter. At a time in Hollywood films where single women having sex was usually met with their demise (particularly in "slasher" films), or at least serious negative repercussions, Frances decides to have consensual sex with Johnny and doesn't regret it. There is no moral judgment placed on her or her decision within the film. This element of the story can be seen as empowering for young women.

The relationship between Frances and Johnny touches on issues of socioeconomic differences that create conflict for the young couple and heighten the emotional stakes. Additionally, Frances's coming-of-age story appeals especially to teen girls who might be experiencing their first romantic relationships, or at least preparing for the possibility of them. The setting and timeline of the film (a high-end resort over the summer) contribute to its youthful appeal as well, as does the sexual tension between Frances and Johnny.

Dirty Dancing, a low-budget film from a new studio with no big name stars, went on to gross $214 million. It also shattered sales records when it was later released on video, becoming the first video film to sell more than 1 million copies. The legacy of *Dirty Dancing* and its immense popularity continues today, more than 30 years after its theatrical release. It was rebooted as a made-for-television movie in 2017 that starred Abigail Breslin in the role made famous by Jennifer Grey. Most media critics panned the film and deemed it unnecessary.

See also: 1950s: *Blue Denim*; 1960s: *Group, The*; 1970s: *American Graffiti*; 1990s: *She's All That*; 2000s: *Juno*

Further Reading

Carmon, Irin. 2010. "*Dirty Dancing* Is the Greatest Movie of All Time." Jezebel, April 29. https://jezebel.com/5527079/dirty-dancing-is-the-greatest-movie-of-all-time.

Killen, Gemma. 2016. "Class, Gender and Sexuality in Dirty Dancing." Feminartsy, November 15. http://feminartsy.com/class-gender-and-sexuality-in-dirty-dancing/.

McEwan, Melissa. 2009. "Dirty Dancing, Feminist Masterpiece." *The Guardian*, September 16. https://www.theguardian.com/commentisfree/cifamerica/2009/sep/16/patrick -swayze-dirty-dancing-feminism.

Naish, Stephen Lee. 2017. *Deconstructing Dirty Dancing*. Alresford, UK: Zero Books.

DURAN DURAN

The early 1980s ushered in a new sound for American audiences. Referred to by several different terms, New Wave music (also called "synth-pop") gained incredible appeal and success in the United States. The period was so popular and influential that it is referred to as the Second British Invasion. There were a plethora of popular British bands in the 1980s, but few achieved the commercial success and relative longevity that Duran Duran has enjoyed. Original band members included: keyboardist Nick Rhodes, bass guitarist John Taylor, drummer Roger Taylor, guitarist Andy Taylor, and lead singer Simon Le Bon. Like many groups at the time, they relied heavily on the use of synthesizers in their music. The New Wave sound differed significantly in several ways from its predecessor—punk rock. Where punk rock's sound and style was dark and pessimistic, New Wave focused on both sound and lyrics that were largely optimistic and dance-oriented.

Duran Duran began as part of the New Romantic era in popular music along with contemporaries such as ABC and Spandau Ballet. The angst and anger of punk rock was replaced with a sound that was more melodic and lyrics that emphasized love and longing and the pain of romantic relationships. Using MTV as an international platform, Duran Duran produced heavily stylized videos to accompany their music. Sexuality permeated their videos for hit songs such as "Hungry Like the Wolf" and "Girls on Film." The latter video was originally intended to be shown in dance clubs, and included images of topless women in wrestling matches. But a heavily edited version was shown on MTV and became wildly popular. They also used large screens at their concerts to create a symbiotic connection between the music and their unique style and to give their fans a more sensory experience.

Teen fans gravitated to Duran Duran for all of the reasons stated above: the dance-oriented music, the fresh fashions, and the physical appeal of the young band members. The simmering sexuality and passion in the song lyrics were also captivating and spoke to teens' sexual awakening and interest in romantic relationships.

Their second album, *Rio*, had initial disappointing sales in the United States. The record company didn't have a clear marketing plan for the group, and cultural differences between the United States and Britain forced executives to get creative. The album was remixed and rereleased in the states after several songs were heavily promoted in dance clubs. Thanks to heavy rotations of several music videos on MTV and appearances on television dance shows, the album skyrocketed in popularity. Rio enjoyed several hit singles and stayed on the Billboard Top 100 for more than one year.

The business savvy of marketing the group is partly evidenced by the fact that they hired a fashion designer to help them create and maintain a consistent image. Their eye-catching videos were shot with 35-millimeter film—a standard in Hollywood at that time but not within the music video arena.

As the Romantic sound faded and newer artists reverted back to some of the political statements of the earlier punk movement, Duran Duran remained unwavering in their dedication to hedonism via flashy videos featuring beautiful women, parties, and lavish lifestyles. Their music and image embodied everything about 1980s popular culture: bold, flashy, decadent. Young fans especially embraced this focus on the riches of the wealthy and popular. It reinforced notions about capitalism and consumerism that were rampant in this decade and reinforced by society. Since Duran Duran avoided political statements in this music, their appeal among teens was wider as the emphasis was almost always on more universal themes of romance and sex.

Whether it was style over substance or simply a commitment to offering a fully realized sensory experience to their fans, Duran Duran excelled at eye-catching optics designed to entice listeners and viewers. Fashion played as big a part in their image as their music did—teased hair, leather and military gear, lots of denim, skinny ties, and colorful scarves were all on display. Teens are usually attuned to fashion, especially when it's considered edgy or distinct from conventional styles.

The band has released several albums since their heyday back in the 1980s. The remaining members—all in their 50s now—strive to remain relevant in an overcrowded pop music industry where the focus is often on youth. When faced with criticism that the band has never been more than a musical confection that puts style over substance, lead singer Simon Le Bon is quick to note that they have always worked very hard at what they do and that they have always been dismissed by many in the industry, particularly British music critics. Their influence has been undoubtedly significant, and while many of their counterparts have faded from the public eye, they continue to make music, tour, and experiment with new sounds and collaborations with other artists and producers.

Duran Duran has released 14 studio albums—the most recent being 2015's *Paper Gods*—and sold more than 100 million copies of their cumulative releases including compilations. They have won MTV Music Awards, Grammys, and two Brit Awards.

See also: 1960s: Doors, The; Rolling Stones, The; 1970s: Devo; Led Zeppelin; Queen; 1980s: Boy George; Madonna; 1990s: Green Day

Further Reading

Malins, Steve. 2013. *Duran Duran: Wild Boys*. Andre Deutsch.
Taylor, John. 2012. *In the Pleasure Groove: Love, Death, and Duran Duran*. New York: Dutton.

FACTS OF LIFE, THE

The Facts of Life (1979–1988), a popular 1980s sitcom, premiered in the summer of 1979 and ran through May 1988. The premise of the show was simple: a group of high school age girls live together in a boarding house at the Eastland School under the supervision of a strict but compassionate house mother, Mrs. Garrett (Charlotte Rae). The show was a spin-off from the very successful sitcom, *Different Strokes*. Like most shows of this type, each 30-minute episode was a morality play created to teach lessons to the characters and, by default, the audience. Plots of the show covered mostly familiar adolescent terrain: substance abuse, conflicts with parents and other authority figures, teen peer pressure, and so on. The main characters on the show featured stereotypes that included the rich, popular girl (Blair), the insatiable gossip (Tootie), and the easily influenced follower (Natalie).

Like many sitcoms, the show originally did not do well in the ratings. It was retooled significantly by writing out several of the secondary characters (notably "Molly" played by then teen actress Molly Ringwald) and adding a new character, Jo, who was a "tough girl" from the Bronx. Feuds between the gritty Jo and the spoiled Blair would become a signature element of the show as seasons progressed.

The ongoing conflict was popular with teen viewers as these types of fictional relationships can resemble everyday battles that occur in most high schools between both individuals and groups. Young female viewers typically identify more strongly with one character than the others, and this engages them as they can relate what happens to the character to issues within their own lives.

The show and its characters managed to wrap up all of their issues within the span of a single episode. Even though some serious issues were tackled, this show—as with many sitcoms—was bogged down with an overall sappy tone that oversimplified real-life challenges faced by teenagers.

The show was groundbreaking in that it featured a recurring character, Geri (Geri Jewell),

Popular sitcom *The Facts of Life* was a hit show for NBC and focused on the lives of a diverse group of female high school students living in a boarding house run by the motherly Mrs. Garrett (Charlotte Rae). (NBC Television/Getty Images)

with cerebral palsy. The comedy also received a lot of media attention for the weight of the young actresses. Mindy Cohn (Natalie) shared that producers were concerned with her weight loss due to her character being overweight. Rather than not diet, a compromise was reached that her character would wear baggy clothes in order to give the illusion that she still struggled with weight. Lisa Whelchel (Blair) has the opposite issue—due to the long workdays on the set and the ample quantities of food made available to cast and crew, she struggled to keep weight off. Both of these situations show the struggle that young actresses have to deal with in Hollywood regarding body standards, an issue that still plagues the industry today.

In terms of relatability, the show covers noncomplicated issues that are easily resolved. Considering what was occurring in the early 1980s—economic recession, the savings and loans failures, and the very real effects this had on millions of American families—*Facts of Life* avoided these topics. One can argue that this is the role of escapist entertainment; it's designed to help viewers forget about their own problems and be transported to a fictional realm where no significant threats exist. Others may argue that by "watering down" content, opportunities to educate while entertaining might be missed.

The setting of this show is important in terms of historical relevance as there is a long tradition of films set in boarding schools. Among these are *The Belles of St. Trinian's* (1951), *The Trouble with Angels* (1966), and *The Beguiled* (1971 and 2017). These films are exclusive to girls' boarding schools; many other films set in boarding schools for boys include *Goodbye, Mr. Chips* (1969) and *Dead Poet's Society* (1989). The issues and themes in these films vary and the tone verges from the comical to the sentimental to the terrifying, but they all have in common the hierarchy of teacher and student relationships. Regardless of the plot or outcome of the media presentation, there is a common theme of authoritarianism. Students are presented as individuals in need of direction and supervision, and the adult figures, be they teachers or administrators, are relied upon to provide it.

Facts of Life is no different in this universal aspect of these representations. Regardless of the conflict, Mrs. Garrett can be relied on to bring order to the situation. While she encourages the girls to learn and grow through their experiences, they know (and we do as well) that she will be there to tidy up any unresolved conflicts. The show reinforces preestablished and expected roles between adolescents and adults within society.

Though not an award winner, the series was successful and popular enough to spawn three made-for-television movies, *The Facts of Life Goes to Paris*, *The Facts of Life Down Under*, and *The Facts of Life Reunion*. The show enjoyed new life through syndication and VHS and DVD releases, enabling a new generation of viewers to watch the series.

Facts of Life was a significant hit for NBC, and although the show wasn't necessarily the critics' favorite, at the time it was the highest-rated sitcom in NBC history. In 1988, a survey polling teens in *USA Today* named it one of the top 10 shows on TV.

See also: 1960s: *Patty Duke Show, The*; 1970s: *Welcome Back, Kotter*; 1980s: *Cosby Show, The*; *Family Ties*; *Saved by the Bell*; 1990s: *Boy Meets World*; *Clarissa Explains It All*; 2000s: *Sisterhood of the Traveling Pants, The*

Further Reading

Harris, Will. 2015. "You Take the Good, You Take the Bad: An Oral History of *The Facts of Life*." *Entertainment Weekly*. https://web.archive.org/web/20170606114232/http://microsites.ew.com/microsite/longform/facts/.

Khan, Imran. 2015. "'The Facts of Life' Is the Ultimate '80s Comfort Food Sitcom." Pop Matters, January 24. https://www.popmatters.com/189575-the-facts-of-life-the-complete-series-2495572058.html.

FAMILY TIES

Family Ties (1982–1989), a popular NBC sitcom, capitalized on a new era of social conservatism that swept the country and coincided with the national election of Ronald Reagan as president of the United States. On the heels of a socially liberal culture that dominated much of the late 1960s and early to mid-1970s, a new wave of political conservatism flourished in the 1980s. Much of this was attributed to growing dissatisfaction with governmental social policies that were viewed as ineffective and wasteful and a strong desire on the part of many Americans for lower taxes and less government intrusion of the free market.

Family Ties had a very simple premise: "square kids, hippie parents." The show originally was conceived as a family sitcom mainly focused on the parents, Steven and Elyse Keaton (Michael Gross and Meredith Baxter). Their children consisted of teenage son Alex (Michael J. Fox), and daughters Mallory (Justine Bateman) and Jennifer (Tina Yothers). Early in the first season, producers took notice of the rising popularity of Fox's character and began developing more story lines around Alex. This refocus also allowed the show to attract a younger audience; with a teenager as the main character, a more commercially attractive demographic now tuned in to the show.

Alex P. Keaton was the quintessential young Republican and symbol of the evolving "yuppie" archetype that gained attention throughout the 1980s. He was obsessed with the idea of making money and viewed the government largely as a source of obstruction and interference. He represented the cultural response to the previous decades of socially and economically liberal policies that were largely rejected in the 1980 presidential election of Republican president, Ronald Reagan. As evidence of how strong this backlash was against liberalism, a severe economic recession in 1982 and stock market meltdown in 1987 failed to dampen broad and deep enthusiasm for Reagan and his economic policies, which purported the success of "trickle-down economics."

The ability to maintain a comedic tone while discussing ideology and beliefs isn't always an easy path for artists. Much of the success of the series was in large part due to the likeability of actor Michael J. Fox and his ability to bring nuances to

Alex rather than playing him as a one-dimensional character. Unlike earlier sitcom characters such as Archie Bunker from *All in the Family,* Alex was never portrayed as bigoted or mean-spirited; his conservatism was usually confined to economic matters. Also, many of his challenges involved universal issues such as relationship breakups and sibling rivalries that almost all teens experience during this life stage, so his relatability in general was positive despite potential political conflicts with some viewers.

Shows like *Family Ties* and *The Cosby Show* portrayed evolving roles of women within the family and society in the 1980s. This was important for young female fans to see normalized images of working mothers and women who weren't secondary to their husband's careers and ambitions. One episode that dealt with gender stereotypes head on had Elyse and Alex attempting to learn more about car maintenance after one of their automobiles breaks down. Alex is stunned that his mother thinks she can learn how to identify and diagnose mechanical problems. Predictably, Elyse demonstrates mastery while Alex struggles to make even rudimentary progress in the class they attend together. By the episode's conclusion, Alex reluctantly admits what everyone else already seems to know about making assumptions based solely on gender.

Mallory, while not overtly political, is an embodiment of the crass commercialism and consumerism of the decade. She is obsessed with materialism and spends much of her time pining over boys, especially boyfriend Nick Moore (Scott Valentine). These romance-based subplots appealed primarily to teen girls. Nick functioned as both a love interest for Mallory and as a comedic foil for Alex. Gentle but not intellectually gifted, Nick worked well in scenes as Alex's opposite. Alex poked fun at Nick's lack of sophistication and knowledge while Nick identified and played upon Alex's uptight nature. Youngest daughter Jennifer was a tomboy and seemed to identify more with her parents than either of her siblings. The differences between the three siblings both in age and personalities widened the appeal of the show to younger viewers. Teens could see parallels between issues within their own lives and ones being played out on the series, especially plots surrounding dating and romance.

The Keaton family expanded in season five when Andrew "Andy" Keaton (Brian Bonsall) was born and became the youngest sibling. Alex, of course, takes this as an opportunity to try and mold his little brother into a carbon copy of himself.

Family Ties was successful in depicting the unconditional love among family members even when politics and conflicting ideologies exist within a household. The show was nominated for multiple Emmy Awards, and Michael J. Fox won three of them consecutively for Outstanding Lead Actor in a Comedy Series in 1986, 1987, and 1988. He also won a Golden Globe Award in 1989 for Best Performance by an Actor in a TV-Series.

The show has remained popular in syndication and also through streaming services such as Netflix. Given the recent reboot of shows like *Full House (Fuller House),* there is speculation that a *Family Ties* reboot may be a reality in the near future, but no specific plans have yet been announced.

See also: 1950s: *Adventures of Ozzie and Harriet, The*; *Father Knows Best*; *I Love Lucy*; *Leave It to Beaver*; 1960s: *Patty Duke Show, The*; 1970s: *Happy Days*; 1980s: *Back to the Future*; *Cosby Show, The*; *Facts of Life, The*; *Full House*; *Wonder Years, The*; 1990s: *Boy Meets World*; *Clarissa Explains It All*; *7th Heaven*; 2000s: *Friday Night Lights*

Further Reading

Wallace, Kelly. 2017. "Sitcoms That Influenced Us and Our Parenting." CNN, February 22. http://www.cnn.com/2017/02/21/health/sitcoms-parenting-lessons-history-of-comedy/index.html.

Wright, Chris. 2013. "The Patriotic Genius of Family Ties." *Esquire*, June 25. http://www.esquire.com/entertainment/tv/a23225/family-ties-america/.

FAST TIMES AT RIDGEMONT HIGH

Fast Times at Ridgemont High (1982) was a sleeper hit at the box office and with critics, but it has since gained iconic status within the subgenre of teen-centered comedies. The film focuses on sophomores Stacy Hamilton (Jennifer Jason Leigh) and Mark Ratner (Brian Backer), and their interactions with older friends Linda Barrett (Phoebe Cates) and Mike Damone (Robert Romanus). Linda and Mike believe themselves to be well versed in romance and able to offer advice to their younger peers. Other characters include Jeff Spicoli (Sean Penn), a surfer dude who always seems to be high, battling rigid history teacher Mr. Hand (Ray Walston). Stacy's older brother, Brad (Judge Reinhold), is a senior who is consumed with working at his fast food job in order to pay off his car. He's also considering splitting with his girlfriend, Lisa (Amanda Wyss).

Stacy is sexually curious and is anxious to have her first sexual encounter. With some simulated practice engineered by her friend Linda, she feels as if she is ready to move forward. Her sexual initiation happens in a baseball dugout with an older man in his 20s. She realizes shortly afterward that it was a mistake but decides to give it another try. Unfortunately, her next partner doesn't fare much better. Mike Damone, a sleazy ticket scalper, exploits Stacy's vulnerability after his friend Mark doesn't respond to her sexual advances due to shyness. Stacy feels rejected and ends up with Mike. This type of story line resonates with teens because it taps into natural curiosities about sexuality and sexual initiation. Young girls see characters on the screen experiencing the same or similar struggles they may be enduring in real life. The relatability to the characters' plights creates a more vested interest in the fictional outcome on the part of the viewer.

Stacy becomes pregnant and ends up getting an abortion. The day of the procedure, Mike fails to show up to cover half of the expense. Stacy's brother Brad (Judge Reinhold) discovers what has happened and Stacy pleads with him to keep it private. When Mark finds out about it, he and Mike get into a heated altercation that is interrupted by a school teacher. Fear of sex is also an issue for many teens, especially for girls due to the risk of unwanted pregnancy.

Fast Times at Ridgemont High doesn't belong in the same category as broad teen sex comedies like *Porky's*. While sexual awakening and desire are part of the story line, it's not hypersexualized. The film portrays the teens as fairly ordinary and simply going through the same rites of passage that we all go through at this stage. Part of this may have to do with the source material. The screenplay writer, Cameron Crowe, is also the author of the source material: a book entitled *Fast Times at Ridgemont High: A True Story.* Crowe pitched the idea as an insider's guide to all of the teen drama unfolding at Clairemont High School in California. He enrolled there as a student after impressing the principal with an exaggerated resume of accomplishments.

Stacy's story arc and character development is central to the film. A preferred reading of the text is that she is empowered sexually to determine what type of relationship she wants by the end of the film when she ends up with Mark. She shares with Linda that she is no longer seeking sex but something more meaningful and potentially long lasting. She and Mark are waiting to have sex until they feel it's the right time.

An oppositional reading to this is that Stacy should have put off her sexual activity to begin with and suppressed her sexual desires. Sometimes within films when a female character has an abortion, it can be viewed as punishment for her sexuality. A socially conservative view of Stacy's story line is that she was "redeemed" by the end of the film, realized the error of her ways, and made a choice for celibacy— at least in the short term. Teens interpret it largely based on a combination of other factors including their own personal experiences and influences from parents, religion, and other societal factors.

Fast Times at Ridgemont High is notorious for a sexually charged dream sequence involving Brad and Linda. By today's standards, it seems fairly tame, but at the time it was considered risqué. The film is also noteworthy for the breakout performance of Sean Penn in the role of Jeff Spicoli. The running gag of that subplot involves the student ordering pizza deliveries to the classroom, which, of course, upsets the uptight instructor. Teen audiences enjoy story lines where authority figures are often undermined, outsmarted, or just aggravated as it is seen as rebellious.

The film received mixed reviews, though many critics praised the performances of its young stars. Crowe was nominated for a Writers Guild of America (WGA) award, and it appears in the number two position on *Entertainment Weekly's* list of the "50 Best High School Movies." The soundtrack to the film peaked at #54 on the Billboard charts. An ill-fated sitcom was developed in 1986 based on the film. *Fast Times* featured only a few of the same actors from the movie and was quickly canceled.

See also: 1970s: *National Lampoon's Animal House*; 1980s: Hughes, John, Films of; *Revenge of the Nerds*; *Risky Business*; *Say Anything . . .*; 1990s: *American Pie*; *Clueless*; *Dazed and Confused*; *She's All That*; 2000s: *Bring It On*; *Mean Girls*; *Napoleon Dynamite*

Further Reading

Bastanmeh, Rod. 2017. "'Fast Times at Ridgemont High' Was the Perfect Blend of Teen Sex Comedy and Stoner Classic." Merry Jane, September 8. https://merryjane.com /culture/fast-times-at-ridgemont-high-was-the-perfect-blend-of-teen-sex-comedy-and -stoner-classic.

Smith, Kyle. 2017. "Fast Times at Ridgemont High: A Conservative Sex Comedy." *National Review*, July 25. http://www.nationalreview.com/article/449793/fast-times -ridgemont-high-35th-anniversary-conservative-sex-comedy.

FLOWERS IN THE ATTIC

Although *Flowers in the Attic*, a popular novel by V. C. Andrews (1923–1986), was published in 1979, it became a runaway best seller in the 1980s. The book was initially written and pitched as adult fiction, but it gained traction and loyal readership from a teenage audience. The book—the first in a series of five—focuses on the Dollanganger children and their imprisonment and abuse at the hands of their mother and grandmother. The melodramatic plot of the story begins when Corrine Dollanganger attempts to keep her family financially afloat after the death of her husband, Christopher, in a car accident. Corrine takes her children—Cathy, Chris, and four-year-old twins Carrie and Cory—to her parents' home for monetary help. Shortly after their arrival, the grandmother (Olivia) of the children mandates that they be hidden from their grandfather (Malcolm) in a bedroom in the upstairs attic. Olivia physically assaults Corrine, who explains to the children that they must remain at their grandparents' home while she goes away to figure out a way to win back her father's approval and then introduce her children to him.

The story line then focuses on the children's daily lives as they are confined to the attic and only learn about life outside of the home through selected information provided by Olivia, who continues to verbally and physically attack the children on a regular basis. The older siblings, Cathy and Chris, end up having a sexual relationship largely due to the absence of contact with others their own age and no opportunities for routine teenage rites of passage. By the end of the story, the children discover that their mother had no intention of ever rescuing them or freeing them from their imprisonment; she needed to be rid of them because her new partner didn't like children, and she claimed to have none.

In the book, Andrews highlights and analyzes the psychological issues associated with children being abandoned by their mothers; the development of beliefs, ideas, and values in children is impacted significantly by the love and attention (or lack thereof) provided to them by their parents. Additionally, Andrews examines the "good mother/bad mother" schema that drives many works of popular fiction. A "good mother" schema in literature is one that depicts the woman as focused on caring for her children and adhering to the rules of society and the implicit rules of motherhood. But *Flowers in the Attic* strays from the traditional "good mother/bad mother schema" in that order is not restored at the conclusion of the story. Rather than Corrine realizing the error of her ways and making amends to her family, she leaves them in an unsafe, violent environment to fend for themselves. This disruption to the schema is deeply unsettling, and challenges children's perceptions of maternal love and security.

Flowers in the Attic resonated among teenage readers as it tapped into their sense of frustration, anger, and sometimes even rage at their parents, particularly their mothers. At a life stage when many teenagers are beginning to develop a very strong sense of self, the influence and control of parents can be seen an intrusive and even suffocating at a time when young people want autonomy. Although the events in the novel are horrific and violent, any teen reader can still relate to the overarching theme of control and domination by parental figures. The book also taps into a primal fear that parents can do real harm to readers as children, who are powerless to stop them since they are the authority figures.

Largely panned by critics, the novel has sold over 40 million copies. It has been adapted to film twice. The 1987 version sanitized the incestuous relationship between Cathy and Chris, a decision that was not met with approval from the legions of book fans. The Lifetime cable channel aired a remake of the film in 2014. Given the themes and plot of the novel, this was a strategic choice for the network given their target audience; Lifetime focuses exclusively on content designed to appeal to a female demographic. The melodramatic nature of *Flowers in the Attic* is similar to many of their made-for-television films that typically feature women in peril. The reviews were largely negative, with several critics noting how uninvolving the production was. The ratings, however, were solid enough to move forward with a sequel, *Petals on the Wind*.

The Dollanganger series of books falls under the Gothic genre. This style of writing dates back to the late 1700s and includes novels such as *Dracula* and *Frankenstein*. Gothic stories combine the elements of horror, romance, and death. It delves into primal issues of parental loss and fear of abandonment. Taking those themes and psychological issues and framing them within what is essentially a soap opera format holds strong appeal for a teenage audience. V. C. Andrews (born Cleo Virginia Andrews) wrote four of the five novels in the series. Ghostwriter Andrew Neiderman wrote the fifth after Andrews died. He also wrote a stage play of the original novel and released it as an electronic book (e-book).

See also: 1970s: Blume, Judy

Further Reading

Nussbaum, Emily. 2014. "Reading in the Attic." *New Yorker*, January 17. https://www.newyorker.com/books/page-turner/reading-in-the-attic.

Palkovich, Elinat. 2015. "The 'Mother' of All Schemas: Creating Cognitive Dissonance in Children's Fantasy Literature Using the Mother Figure." *Children's Literature in Education* 46: 175–189.

FULL HOUSE

ABC sitcom *Full House* (1987–1995) revolved around a San Francisco–based household that was fairly unconventional by 1980s standards. The premise of the show was that TV news anchor Danny Tanner (Bob Saget) was forced to care for his three young daughters—D. J. Tanner (Candace Cameron), Stephanie Tanner (Jodie Sweetin), and Michelle Tanner (Mary-Kate and Ashley Olsen)—after his wife is killed in a car accident. Typically, this would open the door for a sitcom to follow a safe and predictable route of having the central character search for a new wife and mother for his children. Instead, perhaps reflective of the broadening definitions of nuclear family, Danny recruits his brother-in-law Jesse Katsopolis (John Stamos) and best friend Joey Gladstone (Dave Coulier) to support him and his family. Although single mothers had been represented in TV sitcoms like *One Day at a Time* (1975–1984) and *Alice* (1976–1985) and single fathers were portrayed on shows going as far back as *The Andy Griffith Show* (1960–1968), it was not traditional to feature a family consisting of three adult males who all served various roles in the child rearing process.

As opposed to a conventional, biological family that one is born into, to some degree, this show illustrated that there are all sorts of compositions that can create a family. All three men have jobs or careers, but they also devote much time and energy to raising the Tanner girls. This allowed certain preestablished stereotypes to be challenged. For example, Jesse is the primary cook among the adults and becomes well known for his delicious food. In the past, cooking was usually deemed "women's work," along with housecleaning and the day-to-day activities of raising children. However, his cooking isn't a source of mockery on the show or indictment of his masculinity. Additionally, Danny Tanner was portrayed as a fastidious housekeeper in a manner that did not emasculate him, either. Joey Gladstone is the lovable "goof" who was always able to make everyone laugh and see things through a humorous lens. He was kind-hearted and supportive, and a positive male role model for the Tanner girls.

According to critical reception theory, people have different reactions and responses to media productions; based on their own experiences and beliefs, they assign meaning to the culture they consume. What *Full House* did for some viewers—especially single fathers and young children of single fathers—was establish the normalcy of that arrangement. Showing three adult men functioning in coparental roles for three young girls challenged both gender stereotypes and familial roles. Men could perform basic functions and tasks typically associated with women without drawing criticism from audiences. More importantly, they could express emotions often deemed feminine and be nurturing, thoughtful, and empathetic.

Teenagers, especially teen girls were drawn to the show for several reasons. As with most sitcoms featuring children, universal issues such as sibling rivalry, peer pressure, and struggles to become popular don't change much from generation to generation, so these story lines have built-in appeal. More importantly, though, the dynamic that existed between the three adult male caregivers and the girls was unique and positive. Teen girls got a window into a family unit that did not contain a mother or even a maternal figure. This could initially have been a draw as a novelty, but the affection and supportive nature of the Tanner family provided young girls with an alternate model of a family, and given inherent conflicts in the typical mother–daughter relationship, this may have been seen as a potentially desirable option.

Gender stereotypes remain deeply embedded within our culture, and they go far beyond clothing and toys that are categorized as either male or female in nature.

These stereotypes can have a negative impact on development for young people. If, for example, young girls are conditioned to play with toys gendered to be feminine, such as dolls, what message does that send about self-worth and even later career goals? Are girls then limited in what they can do or what they can dream of doing? What does it mean if a young boy would rather play with a doll than a truck? What messages are communicated and reinforced when children are taught at a very young age that they must conform to societal expectations with respect to gender roles? *Full House*—to some degree—challenged some of these perceptions at a time when doing so was considered edgy or even controversial. It demonstrated to younger viewers that these predefined roles weren't necessarily accurate or preordained.

Full House was never a critical success, but it was a TV ratings hit throughout its network run. An update of the show—*Fuller House*—debuted in 2016 on Netflix. The show is set in the same house as the original show and features most of the original cast with the notable exception of Michelle Tanner (Mary-Kate and Ashley Olsen).

See also: 1950s: *Adventures of Ozzie and Harriet, The*; *Father Knows Best*; *I Love Lucy*; *Leave It to Beaver*; 1960s: *Patty Duke Show, The*; 1970s: *Happy Days*; 1980s: *Cosby Show, The*; *Facts of Life, The*; *Family Ties*; *Wonder Years, The*; 1990s: *Boy Meets World*; *Clarissa Explains It All*; *7th Heaven*; 2000s: *Friday Night Lights*

Further Reading

Gloudeman, Nikki. 2014. "Throwback Thursday: How Full House Changed TV for the Better." Ravishly, July 31. https://ravishly.com/2014/07/31/throwback-thursday-how-full-house-changed-tv-better.

Leigh, Megan. 2016. "Masculinity According to Full House." Pop Verse, April 27. http://pop-verse.com/2016/04/27/masculinity-according-to-full-house/.

GIBSON, DEBBIE

More than halfway through the 1980s, a new teen superstar was on the rise within the world of popular music. Debbie Gibson (1970–) was a throwback to the squeaky-clean image of teen pop stars from decades past. Her trademark look was as well-known and recognized as her music. While an artist like Madonna pushed boundaries in her music, videos, and persona, Gibson delivered a wholesome package to teens and their parents. While in her late teens, she wrote and produced her own music and toured clubs along with her mother, Diane. She and her mother worked hard to get her music demos into the hands of influential people within the music business with hopes of launching her career as a performer. The success of her first promotional single, "Only in My Dreams" landed in the Billboard Top 100 and sealed a record deal for Gibson. Her debut album, *Out of the Blue*, sold approximately 3 million copies in the United States and produced two additional hit singles, "Shake Your Love" and "Foolish Beat."

Gibson's personal style was quintessential 1980s: bedazzled denim jackets, jeans that were tightly cuffed and then rolled, and her signature hat, usually a black bowler. She also toyed with a few accessories that were clearly a result of Madonna's influence—hoop earrings and scarves used to tie her hair back. It was a safe look for teens who steered clear of the revealing clothing and heavy makeup sported by some of her older colleagues.

Gibson was inarguably a teen idol. She was marketed specifically to appeal to a teen demographic. Image is critically important when promoting these types of performers. Painstaking detail goes into how they dress and behave and are perceived by their fans and by their fans' parents. Gibson's songs primarily focus on the joys and pains of first love and breakups and the exaggerated emotions that typically accompany these rites of passage. Her music videos showcased teen fashion and dance moves that her fans could emulate.

It's difficult to discuss Debbie Gibson without acknowledging her contemporary and alleged rival, Tiffany. Both artists released debut albums the same year (1987). Although Tiffany's self-titled debut album was a success, her journey to get there was different from Gibson's. Tiffany showed interest in music as a child and performed in front of crowds as early as the age of 11. Her manager George Tobin got her signed for a record deal, but the single that was released to promote it, *Danny,* failed to get radio play. Tobin then arranged a mall tour that kicked off in Paramus, New Jersey, for the young singer. Tiffany also appealed to a female teen fan base since she was close to them in age and sang about issues of romantic love and first relationships. In conjunction with the hype surrounding the mall tour, a new single—"I Think We're Alone Now"—debuted and peaked at the number one spot on Billboard. The song is a remake of a popular tune from the 1960s band *Tommy James & the Shondells.*

Although the two young performers never knew one another during the height of their careers, the media created a perception that the two feuded over whose record was selling more or was getting more appearances on the covers of teen-marketed magazines like *Teen Beat.* The media often creates or exaggerates this type of conflict because historically it has worked to generate interest in whatever product is being sold—records, movies, TV shows, etc. It is almost always directed at women and plays on preexisting stereotypes of women being emotional and insecure. It exploits biases and at the same time reinforces negative perceptions about how women deal with competition or challenges. Seldom do these types of comparisons get made when discussing two male artists who appeal to similar audiences. This happens routinely with TV shows and movies that feature predominantly or exclusively female casts. Speculation rises as to how the women get along on the set and there are frequent suggestions of petty jealousies and rivalries among the costars.

Debbie Gibson's sophomore album, *Electric Youth* (1989), went double-platinum and generated another smash hit single, "Lost in Your Eyes." The artist also shared an award that year with rock icon Bruce Springsteen—both received recognition from American Society of Composers, Authors and Publishers for Songwriter of the Year honors. Another single from the album *Electric Youth* reached number 11 on the charts. The title of the album explicitly states the focus of both the music and the intended teen audience, as does much of the lyrical content.

Gibson continued making music and recording albums, releasing four studio albums in the 1990s. Although none of them had the same commercial success as her first two records, she remained popular in the industry and branched out into work on Broadway. Gibson has appeared in *Les Miserables, Beauty and the Beast, Grease, Funny Girl*, and *Cabaret*. Gibson continues recording music today and also has appeared in film and television, most notably as a celebrity contestant on the 2005 season of *Dancing with the Stars*. She and former pop superstar Tiffany joined forces and began a "Journey through the 80s" tour in 2011. The nostalgia factor has enabled Gibson and Tiffany to reward their longtime fans and at the same time dispel myths about their fictionalized battle that became tabloid fodder in the 1980s.

See also: 1970s: *Grease*; 1980s: Blondie; Lauper, Cyndi; Madonna; 1990s: Spice Girls; 2000s: Rihanna; Spears, Britney; Swift, Taylor

Further Reading

Locker, Melissa. 2016. "Debbie Gibson Is Not Just an '80s Throwback." *Elle*, August 29. http://www.elle.com/culture/movies-tv/interviews/a38839/debbie-gibson-summer-dreams-interview/.

Schoemer, Karen. 1991. "POP MUSIC; The Perils and Perishability of a Teen Idol." *New York Times*, March 10. http://www.nytimes.com/1991/03/10/arts/pop-music-the-perils-and-perishability-of-a-teen-idol.html?pagewanted=all.

HUGHES, JOHN, FILMS OF

No name is more closely associated with 1980s teen comedies than John Hughes. The Michigan born writer-director-producer achieved phenomenal popularity and success with his humorous—and often angst-ridden—take on teenage life in America. Although Hughes enjoyed success with many adult-themed films such as *Planes, Trains and Automobiles, National Lampoon's Vacation*, and the box office juggernaut franchise of the *Home Alone* movies, he is most closely tied to a string of memorable productions that examined the trials and tribulations of the American teenager during the Reagan era.

To understand the enduring popularity and effect of these movies, it's important to examine them within the context of the social, economic, and political culture of the time in which they were made. The 1980s was a decade of an explosion of wealth, but not for everyone. Although wealthy Americans largely saw their earnings and net worth escalate, the same was not true for the middle class. While the rich enjoyed the benefits of a robust stock market and other financial gains, those in the middle saw wages stagnate. This, added to significant price increases in the housing market, kept many Americans immobilized. The reality for the working poor was alarming: in a six-year period between 1983 and 1989, their net worth plummeted almost 40 percent.

The increase in wealth for the upper echelon fueled rampant and conspicuous consumerism. One only has to view lifestyle images of fashion and popular culture during this period to see the hyperfocus on excess and extravagance. The term "power dressing" referred to both men and women in the corporate workplace. With its emphasis on sharp angles (via padded shoulders in jackets and boxy, double-breasted suits) and bright colors and designs, this style correlated with the importance of real or perceived financial success within the business world.

The protagonists and supporting characters of most of Hughes's teen films reflected to some degree the socioeconomic divide of the times. A recurring theme in his films—especially in *The Breakfast Club*, *Pretty in Pink*, and *Some Kind of Wonderful*—is that of the lower- or middle-class youths striving to gain either acceptance or approval from a higher-class individual or peer group. Rejection is reality in most teens' lives, and Hughes covers that territory in a humorous and sometimes poignant way.

Pretty in Pink (1986) follows the story of Andie Walsh (Molly Ringwald) and her attraction to a "preppy" boy at her high school. Andie lives in a modest house with her underemployed father, Jack. Blane (Andrew McCarthy) and his gang of friends come from wealthy homes and flaunt their sense of entitlement through trendy clothes and house parties. Several conflicts prevent Andie and Blane from getting together. In addition to the obvious socioeconomic issues, Andie's friend, Duckie (Jon Cryer) pines for her but cannot articulate his feelings due to fear of being rebuffed. As Andie and Blane begin dating, class issues become problematic when Blane's friends tease and antagonize him about dating a girl from the "wrong side of the tracks." Duckie becomes more and more agitated about the situation as he attempts to convince Andie her relationship with Blane is doomed. After a series of arguments and fights, Andie and Blane reunite at the prom and Duckie finds potential love in the arms of an attractive girl expressing interest in him. The prom is the perfect setting for this sort of melodrama as it is a universal rite of passage for teens and a ritual that the majority of them participate in—its relevance in their lives at the time it happens is ripe for exploration within media productions.

Some Kind of Wonderful (1987) is largely a retelling of the *Pretty in Pink* story with the gender roles reversed. Keith Nelson (Eric Stoltz) is the working-class teen enamored with the rich girl, Amanda Jones (Lea Thompson). His best friend, Watts (Mary Stuart Masterson), is protective of him because she has romantic feelings that she finds difficult to express. The resolution in this story is different in that the two "misfits" end up together while the primary love interest (Amanda) musters the strength to leave her arrogant boyfriend. Once again, Hughes tapped into the anxieties of teenagers with respect to romantic notions and the emotional impact on them when they are rejected or passed over in favor of someone else.

The Breakfast Club (1985) is arguably the best critically received film of Hughes's. Instead of a plot focusing on two individuals from different worlds, this one focused on a group of teens all serving out detention at their school on a Saturday. Each character is assigned a label (reflected in the film's movie poster) of jock, brain, basket case, princess, and criminal. Since the group is physically restricted to the library in which they are completing their punishment, they are forced to interact with one another on some level.

The story explores the hidden and sometimes not so hidden pain of teenagers who feel forced to present themselves to the world in a very specific way even when that conflicts with their own sense of self. Claire and Andy (Molly Ringwald and Emilio Estevez) are the targets of many of the arguments from the rest of the group. Since they are the most popular teens at detention, they receive criticism and rebukes from their peers. Especially angry John (Judd Nelson) lashes out at Claire and pokes fun at her diamond earrings and superior attitude. Throughout the course of the day, each character reveals their struggles with unrealistic or demanding expectations from parents and the relentless peer pressure to conform to whichever group they are linked with. At the film's end, they have formed a bond, though the question is reasonably posed as to whether this will continue once they all see one another at school again on Monday morning. Social castes are so prevalent in many high schools, and this film explores the emotional effects on teens who are struggling with their identities while dealing with complex and sometimes conflicting messages from parents, educators, and peers.

Another Hughes favorite is 1986's *Ferris Bueller's Day Off*. The plot of this one centers on the charming and cunning title character and his intricate plot to skip a day of school by feigning illness. He is joined by girlfriend, Sloane (Mia Sara), and introverted best friend Cameron (Alan Ruck) on a series of adventures and misadventures around the Chicago area. The primary conflict involves Ferris's attempts to keep the charade a secret from his parents, combative sister Jeanie (Jennifer Grey), and determined principal Rooney (Jeffrey Jones). These conflicts are well received by teens that often argue and fight with their siblings and also may resist authority figures such as school principals at a time when they are becoming more autonomous and independent.

Unlike the emotional turmoil of *Pretty in Pink* and *The Breakfast Club*, this one is played primarily for laughs. Adults in the film appear mainly dimwitted or apathetic, and although the climax of the film showcases a race for Ferris to beat home his suspicious sister, parents, and fixated principal, the audience knows the outcome before it happens. Ferris represents a sneaky yet likable teen who apparently can routinely outsmart authority figures in his life with little to no consequence. The trope of having ineffectual adults outwitted by a clever teen taps into the struggle with authority figures that young people identify with at this life stage. Music played an integral part in all of these films. Hughes was keenly aware of the importance of matching images and motion to songs. During a period of MTV mania, he capitalized on this by linking both lyrics and sound to themes within his films. New Wave music featured prominently and included hits such as Spandau Ballet's "True" from *Sixteen Candles*, the title track from *Pretty in Pink* by the Psychedelic Furs, "Don't You Forget about Me," the anthem from *The Breakfast Club* by Simple Minds, and a plethora of others. Lyrics in these songs also tapped into emotional and romantic struggles surrounding independence, romantic love, and other issues that teens deal with during the high school years and beyond.

The soundtrack from *Pretty in Pink* has been recognized by both the Huffington Post and *Rolling Stone* magazine as one of the best movie soundtracks of all time. The film is also referenced in multiple TV shows and films including *Dawson's Creek* and *Psych* and even the network comedy *Two and a Half Men*, which stars Jon Cryer.

Although he died in 2009, John Hughes's legacy is still felt today through the timeless popularity of his films as viewed by their original fans and a new generation who appreciates his serious and mostly sensitive telling of their universal experiences.

See also: 1980s: *Dirty Dancing*; *Risky Business*; *Say Anything . . .*; 1990s: *Clueless*; *She's All That*; 2000s: *Juno*; *Mean Girls*; *Princess Diaries, The*

Further Reading

Clarke, Jaime. 2007. *Don't You Forget about Me: Contemporary Writers on the Films of John Hughes*. New York: Gallery Books.
Zaleski, Annie. 2016. "Why 'Pretty in Pink' Ensures: John Hughes' Classic Is More Than Just Another Teen Movie." Salon, February 12. https://www.salon.com/2016/02/12 /why_pretty_in_pink_endures_john_hughes_classic_is_more_than_just_another _teen_movie/.

IT

Among the numerous books that prolific author Stephen King (1947–) has written, *It* (1986) is one of his most well known. This story of a group of young misfits who confront their greatest terrors terrified readers with its uncanny ability to tap into deep childhood fears. The close-knit group of friends, known as the Loser's Club, resides in Derry, a small fictional town in Maine that has a disturbing history of young children who are killed or otherwise seem to vanish.

King has always had a flair for the macabre, but he is also recognized as a creator of strong characters in many of his books. In *It,* the book is divided into two sections—the first dealing with the children and their united fight against the evil that permeates their community, and the second part that deals with their attempts as adults to once again return to their hometown and vanquish the monsters that haunted their collective childhood. The evil in the story, then, manifests itself as the greatest fear of each individual character. Since the childhood portion of the novel is set in the 1950s, various film monsters such as Frankenstein and the Wolf Man are manifested. The members of the club—William "Bill" Denbrough, Benjamin "Ben" Hanscom, Beverly "Bev" Marsh, Richard "Richie" Tozier, Edward "Eddie" Kaspbrak, Michael "Mike" Hanlon, and Stanley "Stan" Uris—band together, and slowly begin to unravel the mystery surrounding the deaths and uncover the dark and deadly history of the town that has created and nurtured an evil force.

A recurring apparition of evil in the book is that of Pennywise the Clown. King exploits existing fears and phobias about clowns and uses them to terrorize the characters in the story, and by default, the reader. The first child victim of Pennywise is Bill's younger brother, Georgie, who is murdered after chasing his paper boat down the street during a rainstorm. Usually, the clown is a symbol of childhood innocence and joy. However, smaller children are often scared of clowns and other characters that use elaborate makeup, costumes, or disguises because they fear the unknown. What is beneath the mask or makeup? That question allows fear and dread to fester within the mind as the possibilities seem endless. King uncannily tapped into deep-rooted children's fears for full nightmarish effect.

What sometimes eludes discussion or analysis of King's novel are the "smaller evils" that pepper the narrative. In addition to the menace of Pennywise and his various incarnations are human-based horrors: Bev is the victim of physical abuse at the hands of her father; Eddie has an overprotective mother who acts out her fears by inventing an illness for her son that he doesn't have, and Mike and his family are victims of racism. It's not certain if these human-based evils are the source of the supernatural horror that consumes the town, or if Pennywise is only allowed to exist and thrive because other transgressions go unnoticed or unpunished in Derry. Perhaps that which is unnamed—*It*—is a literal manifestation of Derry.

Teen readers gravitated toward the book largely because of its examination of fears and anxieties especially relevant to youths. Pennywise can easily symbolize any number of issues that afflict teens: fear of rejection, isolation, the uncertainty associated with the transition to young adulthood, and so on. The author also demonstrated insight and respect for his young characters; they weren't presented as stupid kids. Their outcast status was relatable to many readers who may also have identified with the struggles of the Losers Club in terms of the quest for popularity or just acceptance from peers.

It was developed into an ABC miniseries that aired over two nights and clocked in at four hours. Given the length of the book (more than 1,000 pages), several subplots were jettisoned and content was pared to a minimum. Although it did well in the Nielsen ratings, many core fans of the book felt slighted. Critical reception to the TV miniseries was mixed with most critics noting that the "adult" segment of the production wasn't as strong as the "children's" story line. One source of agreement, however, was the performance of Tim Curry as Pennywise. He was praised for his terrifying turn as the murderous clown, and it has become an iconic role for him that has endured for decades.

Fans rejoiced in 2009 when plans were announced for a theatrical remake of *It*. Unlike the miniseries, the film would remain more faithful to its source material. Like the miniseries, though, it would be split into two parts. The first film would cover the story line of the Loser's Club and the second film that of the adults after leaving Derry behind but returning at the behest of Mike. *It: Chapter One* opened in wide release in September 2017. The movie broke box office records and quickly grossed more than $274 million worldwide. Because it was a theatrical release, the graphic content was able to remain in the film. The timeline in the new film shifted from the 1950s to the 1980s. This was due to several factors, not the least of which is nostalgia; those teens who read the book in the 1980s are now adults who have sentimental associations with that time period. Also, setting it in the 1980s allowed for an update of the monsters that scare viewers.

Although production hasn't started yet on the second film, creators of *It: Chapter One* indicate that the sequel will be set in the present and will include the younger stars in flashback sequences.

See also: 1960s: *Twilight Zone, The*; 1970s: *Carrie*; *Jaws*; 1990s: *Buffy the Vampire Slayer*; *Craft, The*; *I Know What You Did Last Summer*; *Scream*; 2000s: *Twilight*; *Vampire Diaries, The*

Further Reading

Smyth, James. 2013. "Rereading Stephen King, Chapter 21: It." *The Guardian*, May 28. https://www.theguardian.com/books/series/rereading-stephen-king.

Veres, Bence. 2017. "Stephen King's Memorable 'It' Taps into Childhood Fears." Reading Eagle, August 8. http://www.readingeagle.com/voices/article/stephen-kings-memorable-it-taps-into-childhood-fears.

LAUPER, CYNDI

The 1980s pop icon Cyndi Lauper (1953–) is credited with bringing a punk aesthetic to the mainstream with her colorful wardrobe and hit records. While rockers like Joan Jett and Pat Benatar displayed the toughness of women within the 1980s musical landscape, Lauper brought freshness and playfulness, and a hit song that would go on to become a feminist anthem. While Madonna was shocking both fans and critics with her overt sexuality and disco-influenced dance music, Cyndi Lauper broke out from the pack with her revolutionary song, "Girls Just Want to Have Fun." Written originally as a celebration of a man's sexual conquest of multiple women, Lauper toyed with the lyrics and reengineered the tune into a unifying anthem of the diversity of women that celebrated differences, but also was non-threatening to potential critics.

The song's popularity was fueled by the energetic and eye-dazzling optics of its accompanying music video, which begins with Cyndi dancing through the streets of her New York neighborhood while on her way home. It's early morning by the time she arrives, and, once there, she is scolded by her mother, apparently for being out all night. She is later reprimanded by her father when she gets a phone call late in the evening. She and her girlfriends are also seen chatting on the phone together.

These images were relatable to teen fans as common experiences while living at home. The video was revolutionary for its depiction of diversity among the young women as well. At a time when white artists were still primarily featuring white actors in their videos, Lauper's included an African American female, a Hispanic female, and at least one woman whose appearance at the time might be described

1980s pop superstar, Cyndi Lauper. Known for her unconventional personal style and catchy lyrics, the singer-songwriter has evolved into a Broadway lyricist and advocate for LGBT youth. Her smash 1983 hit, "Girls Just Want to Have Fun," went on to become a feminist anthem. (Dave Hogan/Hulton Archive/Getty Images)

as "tomboyish." At the end of the video, the girls are all dancing through the streets as onlookers join in and follow them. By the finale, Cyndi brings everyone back to her house and invites them into her room where they dance and frolic.

Lauper contends that the song was relevant because of its simple but powerful message that women want the same things that men do, and, more importantly, that they should be afforded the opportunities to get them.

Her debut album, *She's So Unusual*, was a commercial and critical success, and spawned three additional hit singles after the release of "Girls Just Want to Have Fun." Her follow-up single, "Time after Time" was praised as a poignant love song and demonstrated her range both as an artist and a songwriter (Rob Hyman cowrote the song). Its popularity had endured and it has appeared on lists that include *Rolling Stone* and MTV's "100 Greatest Pop Songs" of all time. The next single, "She Bop," was also a hit, peaking in the third position on Billboard. This song, however, ignited controversy, as the song is about female masturbation. The lyrics aren't explicit enough to make it obvious to a casual listener, but the reference to a popular gay pornographic publication at the time was an indicator. This edgy subject matter resonated with teens who were beginning to explore their own sexuality.

The song was suggestive enough that it angered the Parents Music Resource Center, and it was instrumental in the creation and implementation of a "Parental Advisory Sticker" that was placed on records deemed inappropriate for minors. The sticker's purpose was to alert parents to the questionable content of music being purchased by their children. Many believed that this action only heightened the allure of the material to teen listeners, making the forbidden desirable.

The fourth and final single from the album, "All through the Night" was also a hit. At the time, this set a new record for a female artist having four hit singles in the Billboard Top 5 from one album.

Lauper's personal style and carefree persona had huge appeal to young listeners. The content of "She Bop" aside, Lauper was deemed "safer" by parents than counterpart Madonna. Where Madonna sported more physically revealing garments and exuded a raw sexuality, Lauper embodied a playful punk persona. Her hair bright red and shaved on one side, she favored vintage prom dresses with men's hats. Fashion-wise, she and Madonna both made elements of punk style accessible to the masses. Young girls adapted these looks during the 1980s. Ironically, once these types of "unique" styles are adapted on a mass scale, they no longer become expressions of individualism.

Lauper's sophomore effort, *True Colors*, was a solid album that furthered her popularity. The album enjoyed three hit singles and was certified double platinum (sales of at least 2 million units). She received two Grammy Award nominations and two MTV Music Video Award nominations for her work on the album.

While Lauper has continued making music since her initial rise in the 1980s, she is now focusing more on writing music for Broadway. She won the 2013 Tony Award for Best Original Score for *Kinky Boots*. She also ventured into acting and won an Emmy Award in 1995 for Outstanding Guest Actress in a Comedy Series for *Mad about You*.

The artist has also become passionate about fighting for equality and established the True Colors organization in an effort to combat homelessness among LGBTQ youths. Lauper has always been outspoken about her beliefs. One need only look back at the song and video for "Girls Just Want to Have Fun" to be reminded that she celebrated the underdog and provided a voice for the disenfranchised or nonconformist even at the onset of her celebrated career.

See also: 1980s: Blondie; Boy George; Gibson, Debbie; Madonna; 1990s: Spice Girls; 2000s: Rihanna; Spears, Britney; Swift, Taylor

Further Reading

Kaplan, Sarah, and Justin William Moyer. 2015. "Cyndi Lauper and the Secret Feminist History of 'Girls Just Want to Have Fun.'" *Washington Post*, April 30. https://www.washingtonpost.com/news/morning-mix/wp/2015/04/30/cyndi-lauper-on-capitol-hill-and-the-secret-feminist-history-of-girls-just-wanna-have-fun/?utm_term=.6b807c9b02a6.

Lauper, Cyndi, and Jancee Dunn. 2012. *Cyndi Lauper: A Memoir*. New York: Atria Books.

LESS THAN ZERO

Less Than Zero, the 1985 best-selling novel by Bret Easton Ellis (1964–) shocked readers and critics alike with its dark depiction of drug and alcohol abuse, casual sex, and moral decay among a group of young friends living in Los Angeles, California. The plot centers on Clay, the protagonist of the book, who is on winter break from his freshman year at college. After a few endless nights of partying at clubs, he decides to look up his ex-girlfriend from high school, Blair, and best friend, Julian. He discovers that Julian is now a heroin addict and has been forced into prostitution to pay off a significant drug debt.

Clay and his friends apparently are shocked by nothing and have become numb to their emotions. For example, in one passage, they stumble upon the body of an overdose victim in the back alley of a nightclub. Not only does no one make an attempt to contact law enforcement, but one of the characters places a cigarette into the mouth of the corpse. Later, Clay and the others witness an underage sex slave being held hostage by an acquaintance; Clay makes a half-hearted attempt at persuading the man to release the girl, but the man refuses to let her go. After witnessing at a party the sexual assault that no one other than him objects to, Clay decides it's time to leave his friends and California and head back to school.

Parents in the novel are either absent or woefully detached from their children's lives. This may explain the sense of emptiness and desperation the characters experience, as well as the rampant substance abuse and recreational sex. Clay and other characters struggle with their physically or emotionally absent parents, but rather than viewing adults disdainfully, they instead express an implicit longing for attention, if not some sort of discipline. Several times in *Less Than Zero*, Clay attempts to shock his parents with the revelation that he's on drugs. Neither parent expresses concern.

Ellis wrote the novel while in college. He and several contemporaries such as Jay McInerney and Donna Tartt write about disaffected youths in their novels in an explicit and oftentimes shocking style. Wealth and materialism figure in prominently, and most of the characters come from rich families and fixate on brand names and lavish lifestyles.

Less Than Zero was wildly popular with readers who were coming of age when it was released. The major appeal to young readers was the "forbidden" element: sex, drugs, and casual violence feature prominently throughout the book. Although the novel is ultimately a cautionary tale of sorts, it also glamorizes to some extent the decadent lifestyles of some of its characters.

Less Than Zero was pegged as the first MTV novel. This referred primarily to its style, as it's written in short sentences and fragments, not unlike the editorial style of early videos featured on MTV. It's also written in a style that reflects the characters' lives: flat and devoid of feelings and emotions. Although these characters are from wealthy families, the universal feelings of confusion, isolation, and emptiness are ones that many teens can relate to regardless of the fictional setting and circumstances.

The film version of *Less Than Zero* sanitized the character of Clay. In the book, Clay randomly sleeps with boys and girls and takes drugs, just as his friends do. In the film, Clay (Andrew McCarthy) is the de facto moral authority of the group, who is shocked and saddened by the drug usage of his friends. He also is stripped of his bisexuality. The studio behind the film felt that the material was too depressing and wouldn't connect with audiences. To that end, significant changes were made to the story line that enabled Clay to be seen as a hero who desperately wanted to rescue his girlfriend and best friend from the evils of a drug subculture. Clay frees Julian (Robert Downey Jr.) from his dealer, Rip (James Spader). Then, Clay, Julian, and Blair (Jami Gertz) drive off into the desert in a last-ditch effort to help Julian kick his habit and begin anew. But, in the end, Julian dies in the car, and Clay then convinces Blair to leave California with him and head back east. The film was lambasted my most critics who felt it was lackluster and predictable. Robert Downey Jr.'s performance, however, was praised for its authenticity and grittiness. There has been some speculation that the film might be remade by Quentin Tarantino, but there hasn't been confirmation of that rumor.

Ellis went on to write several other popular novels including *Rules of Attraction* and *American Psycho*. *Rules of Attraction* also focused on college-aged characters dealing with romantic entanglements and sexual attraction. All three books were adapted into films, though Ellis initially distanced himself from the film version of *Less Than Zero* and expressed dissatisfaction with the adaptation due to significant plot changes made by the filmmakers. Viewing the film now, however, the author has expressed that he can appreciate it on its own merits. The sequel to *Less Than Zero*—*Imperial Bedrooms*—was published in 2010.

See also: 1950s: *Catcher in the Rye, The*; 1960s: *Bell Jar, The*; 1970s: *Go Ask Alice*; 1980s: MTV; 1990s: *Kids*

Further Reading

Bollen, Christopher. 2010. "Bret Easton Ellis." *Interview,* June 2. https://www.interviewmagazine.com/culture/bret-easton-ellis.

Curnutt, Kirk. 2001. "Teenage Wasteland: Coming of Age Novels in the 1980s and 1990s," *Critique* 43: 93.

MADONNA

Few celebrities in history are recognized by first name only—Elvis, Beyoncé, and Cher being notable examples. Madonna Louise Ciccone (1958–)—a.k.a. Madonna—is another member of that exclusive club. Although Madonna continues to release records and tour, she is most closely associated with the 1980s in terms of defining not just popular music but fashion and style as well. Born and raised in Bay City Michigan, Madonna moved to New York City after attending school in Michigan. Her goal was to pursue a career in modern dance. After joining and then leaving two bands, Madonna pursued a solo career and primarily performed at popular New York City nightclubs. Noticed by a DJ and record producer, she was given a singles deal with Sire records. Two songs became dance/club hits, prompting Madonna to begin recording her first self-titled album. Unhappy with the musical direction of her initial producer from Warner Brothers, the singer sought assistance from her then boyfriend John "Jellybean" Benitez.

The album was released in 1983 and produced three hit singles: "Holiday," "Borderline," and "Lucky Star." Each of the videos for the songs featured Madonna's unique style at the time: black fingerless fishnet gloves accompanied with multiple bracelets and a large hair bow. Throngs of teenage girls emulated her signature style. The "look" was accessible and affordable due to it being thrift-store-chic; young girls could find most of the items at resale shops.

Madonna's next album and single, "Like a Virgin" were also huge hits. Her performance of the song at the 1984 MTV Video Awards stirred controversy with some religious organizations who claimed that the song promoted premarital sex. Years later, Madonna replied that the song's lyrics weren't meant to be taken so literally and that she was expressing the feeling of rejuvenation and "newness" that one experiences when doing something exciting and rewarding. Given the provocative title and connection to sexual activity, it proved to be another hit with teen listeners, especially younger girls. The rite of passage associated with first time sexual encounters resonated with this audience.

The criticism of Madonna's overt sexuality would become a constant through much of her career. Something that set her apart from earlier female performers: she consistently intertwined sexuality with religion—most conspicuously in her use of the crucifix as a fashion statement. Examining images of the pop superstar from the early days of her career, she is photographed wearing a crucifix on numerous occasions. Author José Prieto-Arranz emphasizes that most of the lyrics in Madonna's early work were not sexually explicit, but the look and style and demeanor of the singer often was.

Teenage girls gravitated toward the singer because of her self-confidence, her dance-oriented music, and her message of sexual awareness and exploration. She also tackled issues like teen pregnancy in the hit single "Papa Don't Preach." The song revolved around a young woman who becomes pregnant and decides to keep her baby rather than have an abortion or give the child up for adoption. Her rebellious nature against male authority figures and patriarchal institutions including the Catholic Church tapped into teenage girls' identities and struggles as they figured out their life goals and desires. In short, she gave them permission to be comfortable with their bodies and also to realize their potential in a male-dominated society.

There is, of course, a history in the Catholic Church (and within Christianity itself) of desexualizing female figures, and Madonna has made very strong verbal and nonverbal statements about gender and sexuality and religion. A preferred reading of her video for "Like a Prayer" is the portrayal of a young devout Catholic woman who, because of her love for Christ, is compelled to right an injustice after witnessing a crime. Critics of it, however, seized on the singer's attire and a brief kiss with a dark-skinned man who was meant to represent a saint. It seemed that even when Madonna was attempting to create a morality play as art, her critics were determined to reject and vilify it as corrupt.

Although the star's recording career in the 1980s was hugely successful, her foray into acting has had mixed results. Although she had a small role in the 1985 film, *Vision Quest,* her first major role was in 1985's *Desperately Seeking Susan.* Madonna's popularity at the time outweighed that of seasoned actress Rosanna Arquette so much that most of the marketing and advertising for the movie focused on the singer rather than her costar. The film was a moderate commercial and critical success.

She recorded and released several best-selling albums in the 1990s including *Erotica* (1992), *Bedtime Stories* (1994), and *Ray of Light* (1998). All three were successful and sold millions of copies.

She has been an ally and advocate for a variety of LGBT issues throughout her career as well. This attracted and retained a significant young, gay male fan base that began amassing in the 1980s and has continued throughout her long career. At the height of the AIDS crisis, when gay men were subject to increasing discrimination, Madonna used her public platform and mainstream popularity to be a visible supporter of that community.

Madonna's longevity can largely be attributed to her ability for reinvention. As the singer ages, much of her audience ages along with her. Young girls who listened to her as teens in the 1980s continue to follow her career. And just when the media or the public think they have her figured out, she suddenly reappears with a new look, and many times a new sound as well.

Madonna has sold more records than any other female artist in history. She's been inducted into the Rock and Roll Hall of Fame and *Rolling Stone* magazine included her in their list of both the "100 Greatest Artists of All Time" and the "100 Greatest Songwriters of All Time." Her dominance in the musical and pop cultural landscape of the 1980s made her an icon among teenage girls as she influenced music, fashion, and female empowerment via her musical genius and overt and unapologetic sexuality. The international pop icon continues to record music and tour today and has also written five children's books.

See also: 1950s: Presley, Elvis; 1960s: Doors, The; Joplin, Janis; Rolling Stones, The; 1970s: Devo; Led Zeppelin; Queen; 1980s: Blondie; Duran Duran; Gibson, Debbie; Lauper, Cyndi; MTV; 1990s: Green Day; Morissette, Alanis; 2000s: Cyrus, Miley; Rihanna; Spears, Britney; Swift, Taylor

Further Reading

Simone, Alina. 2016. *Madonnaland: And Other Detours into Fame and Fandom.* Austin: University of Texas Press.

Smith, Nathan. 2015. "Madonna: A Rebel with a Cause." Huffington Post, March 7. https://www.huffingtonpost.com/nathan-smith/madonna-a-rebel-with-a-cause_b_6804412.html.

Sullivan, Caroline. 2015. *Madonna: Ambition. Music. Style.* London: Carlton Books.

Taraborrelli, Randy J. 2007. *Madonna: An Intimate Biography.* New York: Simon and Schuster.

MTV

The pop cultural significance of MTV may have begun in the early 1980s, but its influence continues today through its youth-oriented programming. MTV (an abbreviation for Music Television) launched in the summer of 1981 and dramatically altered the way that music videos were conceived and produced, and, most importantly, received by fans. The concept seemed simple: broadcast music videos 24 hours a day and 7 days a week on a cable television channel. With some notable exceptions that include groups like the Beatles, the Monkees, and Queen, music videos prior to the advent of MTV were visually unimpressive and unengaging with fairly low production values. So, while the idea for music videos was not a new one, MTV would provide a viable venue for them. This platform would quickly become one of the most popular and effective marketing tools for artists and bands to promote their music.

MTV was a youth-oriented venture that catered primarily to teens and young adults. The channel was hosted by five VJs (video jockeys) when it began: Nina Blackwood, Mark Goodman, Alan Hunter, J. J. Jackson, and Martha Quinn. They would introduce videos, interview singers and bands, and promote concert tours. While MTV featured established artists such as David Bowie, Aerosmith, and Billy Joel, it literally launched the careers of lesser-known bands at the time, including Men at Work, Duran Duran, Culture Club, and the Eurythmics. Within a few years of its premier, it had become commonplace for most artists and bands to contribute to this growing medium. The videos themselves were becoming more sophisticated in content and style. In a pre-Internet and pre-DVR era, world premiere videos of popular bands were an event, with much hype and publicity surrounding the airings of them.

Bands like Duran Duran and the Eurythmics especially gained notoriety from MTV. Music videos such as "Hungry Like the Wolf" and "Love Is a Stranger" benefited from high production values and heavy rotation (the number of times a video was shown within a 24-hour period). Superstars like Michael Jackson and Madonna were able to maintain their relevance with eye-catching videos that supported their albums and singles. Both artists appear in a list of the most expensive music videos ever produced, with Madonna's 1989 "Express Yourself" coming in at $5 million dollars (more than most low-budget independent films at the time) and Jackson's revolutionary 1991 "Black or White" coming in at $4 million dollars.

MTV became a major source of influence on the latest music, fashion, and lifestyle trends for youths. Teenagers especially would tune into it to see their favorite artists, but the phenomenon extended beyond the music videos. Live interviews with bands and popular artists also attracted young viewers. Viewing world premier videos became event programming. Groups of teens would gather together at a central location to watch the first airing of a music video and then discuss it and watch it numerous times afterward. And when there was major news in the entertainment world, MTV was the go-to source for adolescents.

While the very first video aired on MTV was "Video Killed the Radio Star" by the Buggles, perhaps the most famous and emblematic music video of the 1980s that shows the power of MTV exposure is Michael Jackson's "Thriller." The 14-minute mini-movie is an homage to popular 1950s horror films that feature ghouls and werewolves. As with a feature film, there is scripted dialogue and a story with a beginning, a middle, and an end. It showcases Jackson's iconic dancing skills and trademark moves. "Thriller" is arguably the most well-known music video of all time and is still referenced and copied today with tributes and simulations of it taped and uploaded to sites like YouTube.

This exposure also had a significant monetary impact on Jackson's album of the same name. The phenomenal success of the video reignited interest in *Thriller*, which had already sold millions of copies. Rather than leveling off, sales of the album increased after the release of the video.

MTV didn't just feature pop and dance-oriented artists. Rock bands like ZZ Top, Asia, and Bon Jovi reaped rewards as well. African American artists like Tina Turner, Herbie Hancock, and Prince also stayed current by making videos in support of new albums and singles. The network also aired live concerts such as Live Aid and created its own music formatted shows such as *Yo! MTV Raps* and *MTV Unplugged*. Although some diversity among artists existed in terms of representation on MTV, the channel was primarily marketed toward a white youth demographic.

MTV and 1980s popular culture had a symbiotic relationship. During a decade where teens enjoyed significant buying power, the cable channel exemplified a life-style that catered to the rampant consumerism of the times. Young viewers discovered new bands and artists, many of them touting new styles and emerging sounds that would define genres like New Wave and expose listeners to music they might not otherwise have had easy access to. It was common for teens to copy fashions and hairstyles seen on MTV and to discard one look for another as styles changed. MTV became a primary influence on album and concert spending and attire for youths throughout the country.

Although music videos were still popular in the 1990s, they slowly began to wane. MTV responded to this by producing original shows like the animated *Beavis and Butt-head* and reality shows such as *The Real World* and *Road Rules*. MTV also was not the only venue anymore for music videos. Launching a few years after MTV, VH1 featured music videos for an older demographic and narrowed its appeal to those who enjoyed pop but were unlikely to watch rock or rap videos.

For most currently under the age of 30, their familiarity with the channel most likely comes from reality programs like *Jersey Shore, The Hills,* and *Teen Mom.* The channel continues to adapt to demographic and societal changes as it attempts to stay relevant to young viewers. Additionally, MTV has long been a target of parent and religious groups that feel it promotes teenage sexuality and drug usage in its programming.

The future of MTV is unknown, but its monumental impact on music, movies, and even fashion has been significant and equal to that of the advent of both radio and the phonograph/record player from a historical perspective.

See also: 1960s: Beatles, The; Monkees, The; 1970s: Queen; 1980s: Boy George; Duran Duran; Lauper, Cyndi; *Less Than Zero*; Madonna; 1990s: Backstreet Boys; Green Day; Morissette, Alanis; Nirvana; Salt-N-Pepa; *Scream*; Smashing Pumpkins, The; Spice Girls; 2000s: Cyrus, Miley; Lavigne, Avril; My Chemical Romance; Rihanna; Spears, Britney; Swift, Taylor

Further Reading

Flynn, Mark, and Sung Yeon Park. 2015. "'Where Do I Belong, from Laguna Beach to Jersey Shore?' Portrayal of Minority Youth in MTV Docusoaps." *Howard Journal of Communications* 6(4): 381–402.

Tannenbaum, Rob, and Craig Marks. 2012. *I Want My MTV: The Uncensored Story of the Music Video Revolution*. New York: Plume.

Williams, Cameron. 2017. "How MTV Changed the World with Its Industry of Cool." *SBS*, February 13. https://www.sbs.com.au/guide/article/2017/02/13/how-mtv-changed -world-its-industry-cool.

REVENGE OF THE NERDS

Revenge of the Nerds (1984) is a comedy movie that played out the revenge fantasy of miscasts against their antagonists in a college setting. The "nerd" emerged as a social archetype in the 1950s when the term was first used. At the time, it described a male who dressed and behaved in a manner that was counter to the accepted norms of the time. Specifically, nerds were depicted in the media as socially awkward but academically superior to their contemporaries. They were frequently interested in math and science and seemed particularly clumsy around members of the opposite sex.

In the film, friends Lewis Skolnick and Gilbert Lowe (Robert Carradine and Anthony Edwards) begin their academic journey at the fictional Adams College as incoming freshmen. They are computer science majors; as computers became more widely used and computer programming grew as a viable occupation, this discipline became more timely fodder for the depiction of nerds relative to their skill set and area of interest. The pair find themselves unceremoniously booted from their dormitory after a fire at a fraternity house displaces a group of fraternity brothers. Dean Ulich (David Wohl) compensates for the disruption by allowing Lewis, Gilbert, and some of their friends to pledge campus fraternities, but predictably they are not accepted.

Lewis and Gilbert and the rest of the nerds in the movie find an ally in Lambda Lambda Lambda fraternity president U. N. Jefferson (Bernie Casey). The Tri-Lams are a black fraternity organization that initially are resistant to allowing the nerds to be part of their group. After witnessing firsthand the discrimination and bullying that the nerds endure at the hands of the Alpha Betas, Jefferson assists them and commissions their charter for installation on campus.

Stories of underdogs that rise up and become victorious often connect with teenage audiences. Given the persistent and enduring themes of alienation and teen angst in films and other media, the formula is reliable and also can speak to issues of diversity and acceptance. Covering these themes and ideas within the text of a comedy sometimes can be more effective since the tone is informal and less didactic. The evolution of how nerds are portrayed within media is interesting from a cultural perspective, but, during the 1980s, nerds were still deemed very uncool and undesirable.

At stake in the movie is the opportunity to influence campus life via the Greek Council. The winner of the Greek Games is able to place a member of their chapter into the role of president of the Council. The Tri-Lams are able to use their superior technical skills and deliver a winning musical performance in the talent portion of the contest. Their victory secures a win for both the fraternity and Gilbert, who is elected president. The Alpha Betas retaliate by destroying the Tri-Lams' fraternity house, but the violation only brings the group closer together, even winning over new allies. At the film's conclusion, Gilbert encourages everyone who has been bullied or discriminated against to join the group onstage, and Dean Ulich does so, admonishing the Alpha Betas and their negative behavior and telling them that they can now reside in the school gym.

The aspect of inclusion is important in the film as demonstrated by the Tri-Lam member Lamar Latrell (Larry B. Scott). A gay African American fraternity brother, Lamar isn't technically a nerd, but he is clearly an outsider. His talents and abilities are instrumental to the Tri-Lam's victory in the Greek Games and reiterate the film's message about the value of those who are discounted or dismissed by the majority.

The film interested teens for several reasons. Media vehicles focused on college life typically have a built-in teen audience simply because of the setting and same or similar age characters. Plots involving conflicts between the "in crowd" and the "outsiders" hold tremendous appeal as they can reflect real-life struggles that many viewers might be currently experiencing or have experienced in the past. The added allure of first-time sexual activity and budding romances intrigues the typical teen moviegoer as well.

After this film, the popularity of the nerd within media productions grew. In 1980s television, both Screech from *Saved by the Bell* and Urkel from *Family Matters* are featured. Additionally, Lisa Simpson from Fox's *The Simpsons* is the quintessential nerd, routinely displaying her intellectual prowess while enduring the idiocy of others including her own brother Bart and father Homer. The 1990s brought a modified nerd, exemplified by the character of Ross (David Schwimmer) in the mega-smash sitcom, *Friends*. Ross was as intelligent as most media nerds who preceded him, but he was also desirable and less socially awkward as evidenced by his romance with the physically attractive and outgoing Rachel (Jennifer Aniston). And in the 2000s and beyond, there's an entire show that focuses exclusively on nerds: CBS's *The Big Bang Theory*. While these characters vary in age, the appeal is especially strong with younger viewers who can identify more to the plight of feeling as though they are many times isolated or excluded from the "popular crowd."

Revenge of the Nerds spawned three sequels: *Revenge of the Nerds II: Nerds in Paradise* (1987), *Revenge of the Nerds III: The Next Generation* (1992), and *Revenge of the Nerds IV: Nerds in Love* (1994). The first sequel was a theatrical release and the other two were made-for-television movies.

See also: 1970s: *National Lampoon's Animal House*; 1980s: Hughes, John, Films of; *Saved by the Bell*; 1990s: *American Pie*; *Clueless*; *She's All That*; 2000s: *Mean Girls*; *Napoleon Dynamite*

Further Reading

Fox, Jesse David. 2013. "The Evolution of the TV Nerd, from Potsie to Urkel to Abed." Vulture, March 12. http://www.vulture.com/2013/03/evolution-of-the-tv-nerd-screech -urkel-abed.html.

Melendez, Angel. 2016. "The Evolution of the Nerd: From Geek to Cool Kid." *Miami New Times*, January 13. http://www.miaminewtimes.com/arts/the-evolution-of-the -nerd-from-geek-to-cool-kid-8173816.

RISKY BUSINESS

Risky Business (1983), a cinematic comedy, is an examination of Western capitalism as seen through the lens of its protagonist, high school student Joel Goodsen (Tom Cruise). While Joel's parents are away on a trip (a familiar plot device in many "teens gone wild" films), he is convinced by friends to loosen up and enjoy the temporary freedom he is afforded by their absence. The usually straight-laced Joel decides to hire an escort through an advertisement in the newspaper. When a man dressed in women's clothing arrives at the front door and confronts him, Joel is given the name and phone number of another escort who apparently meets his criteria much better. Lana (Rebecca De Mornay) makes a dramatic entrance later that night and she and Joel have sexual intercourse. The next morning, Joel discovers that his adventure will cost $300, so he goes to the bank and cashes in a savings bond to pay the debt. Things escalate when Lana's pimp, Guido, gets involved. Angered by Joel's relationship with Lana and threatened by the loss of revenue from her work, Guido steals furniture from Joel's house along with an expensive glass egg that his mother prizes. To complicate matters, Joel takes out his father's Porsche and ends up accidentally sinking it in Lake Michigan.

The issues of materialism, class differences, sex as a commodity, and other relevant themes propel *Risky Business* into a more clever and revealing realm of work than its contemporaries at the time such as *My Tutor* and *Private Lessons*. Those films, which focus almost exclusively on teenage boys' sexual coming of age, forfeit an opportunity to dig beneath the surface for deeper significance. Instead, Joel learns a great deal about business and entrepreneurship through his relationship with Lana and Guido. He also experiences the inherent conflict of falling for someone whose career requires her to have sex with other men for money. Additionally, people differ on the overarching message of the film, as it could be read as a critique on the corrosive effects of capitalism, or a celebration of capitalism's material riches.

Joel is a very anxious character. He is controlled by fear and an overarching need to conform to what is expected from him. Although his parents only appear in the film in a few scenes, one can draw reasonable assumptions about his upbringing. His obsession over standardized test scores and gaining acceptance into a "good school" most likely reflect the values and goals instilled by his parents. The stress and pressure coming from parents relative to academic success and future career endeavors is relatable to teen viewers as they prepare to leave high school for college and take on more adult responsibilities. Although Joel's adventure is extreme, the loss of control and "walk on the wild side" that he experiences can be cathartic for teens, as they can experience the thrills onscreen without any real-life risks.

The home and furnishings in the Goodson house are material representations of economic success. That beloved Porsche of his father's is emblematic of status and hierarchy, and when it is destroyed, Joel must take extreme and even dangerous action to restore it.

Writer-director Paul Brickman offers viewers a complex and satirical look at American consumerism linked to sexual politics and an overriding need to succeed. Although all ends well for Joel (he gets back the furniture and his mother's beloved glass egg, and he also gets accepted into Princeton), the film ends on a slightly ambiguous note, forcing the audience to examine their own values as they relate to the plot, though that ending was much more positive than the original, scrapped ending.

The original ending of the film gives clues to the director's possible vision. In the theatrical release, the final scene ends with Joel and Lana walking in a park and talking about the future. Their discussion leaves open-ended the likelihood of them ending up together at some point. Teen boys especially were intrigued by Joel's sexual relationship with Lana. As a prostitute, her sexual experience and physical appearance enticed them and was a noteworthy detour from most teen sex comedies that ignored or discounted the emotional component of sex and played it strictly for laughs.

In the original version that was not released theatrically, Joel and Lana are having lunch together. Joel wonders aloud where they might both be in 10 years. Lana gives a very general response that she thinks they'll both do well (the implication being monetary). Joel goes further and asks Lana whether what they had together was real or simply transactional. She reassures him that it was more than that, but Joel seems unconvinced. A voice-over from Joel tells us that he deals in "human fulfillment" and ends with "ain't life grand?"

This conclusion is darker than the original and reinforces some of the bleaker earlier critique of the film with respect to capitalism. While Joel may have gotten into an Ivy League college, he's clearly distraught at losing Lana. Brickman was allegedly so upset with the studio's decision to tack on a happier ending that he didn't direct another film for seven years.

The film was a huge box office success and catapulted Tom Cruise into becoming a Hollywood star. The film appeared on *Entertainment Weekly*'s list of the 50 Best High School movies, and the iconic scene of Cruise dancing in his underwear around his parent's home after they leave has been parodied and copied multiple times in various media productions.

See also: 1980s: *Dirty Dancing*; *Fast Times at Ridgemont High*; *Say Anything . . .*; 1990s: *Clueless*; *Dazed and Confused*

Further Reading

Pirnia, Garain. 2017. "12 Old Time Facts about Risky Business." Mental Floss, August 5. http://mentalfloss.com/article/67263/13-old-time-facts-about-risky-business.

Spitz, Marc. 2014. "'Fast Times' and 'Risky Business' Created the '80s: How These Iconic Teen Films Led the Way to 'Heathers' and John Hughes." Salon, September 2. https://www.salon.com/2013/09/02/risky_business_director_some_people_like_the_visibility_i_dont/.

SAVED BY THE BELL

Saved by the Bell (1989–1992) was an unexpected hit TV show for the NBC network. The series originated on the Nickelodeon channel under the title *Good Morning, Miss Bliss*. The production was revamped with the elimination of several of the original characters and the addition of a few new ones. In the reboot, the focus was taken away from the teacher and placed on the students. The show revolved around a group of teenagers at the fictional Bayside High in California. The cast of characters consisted of the following archetypes: good looking troublemaker Zack Morris (Mark-Paul Gosselaar), on again/off again girlfriend and cheerleader, Kelly Kapowski (Tiffani-Amber Thiessen), sidekick jock A. C. Slater (Mario Lopez), passionate activist Jessie Spano (Elizabeth Berkley), Samuel "Screech" Powers (Dustin Diamond), and the clueless school principal Mr. Belding (Dennis Haskins). Even though the series was widely panned by critics, it was a ratings hit and connected with its target teen audience. The focus of the show was on Zack's constant attempts to pull off some sort of scam or scheme without getting caught. As with many teen-centered movies and shows in the 1980s, parental figures were either absent or clueless, like Mr. Belding.

Because *Saved by the Bell* was a daytime show it had to meet compliance regulations of the Federal Communications Commission; the show had to include "educational content." This forced the producers to cram conspicuous messages into the episodes where blatant moral lessons were shared with viewers. One particularly obvious example of this is the now-famous episode where Jessie becomes addicted to caffeine pills in order to have enough energy to study and maintain her scholastic commitments.

Negative stereotypes permeate the show. For example, Jessie is depicted as a feminist who is constantly railing against male oppression. The character is so annoying, however, that she becomes a caricature of feminism. And when her values are put to the test, as they are in an episode where a female athlete vies for a spot on the male wrestling team, she fails miserably. In that specific story line, Jessie at first vocalizes support for the young girl. When she discovers that the girl might have her sights on Jessie's boyfriend, however, she quickly abandons her feminist principles and condemns gender equality in varsity team sports. Without critical analysis of the content, the average teen viewer is left with an inauthentic, even cartoonish impression of feminism.

The boys on the show don't fare much better. Zack and A. C. are in perpetual competition with one another for girls. They treat women essentially as trophies to be brandished in a display of victory, and then tossed aside shortly thereafter. Since the show depicts Zack and A. C. as protagonists who are just "boys being boys," it reinforces negative cultural stereotypes of women whose primary purpose is to please men. Further, it fails to hold men responsible for their sexist behavior. Due to the show's lack of nuance and the abundance of one-dimensional characters, its superficiality allows teens to dismiss its potentially harmful stereotypes as "mindless" fun.

Saved by the Bell is noteworthy for a few other reasons. Most of the show's lead actors have moderate success within the television industry after their time on the show. Mark-Paul Gosselaar starred in ABC's *NYPD Blue* and had a recurring role on CBS's *CSI*. Tiffani-Amber Thiessen starred in the popular teen show *Beverly Hills 90210*. Additionally, Elizabeth Berkley salvaged her career after starring as a stripper in the much maligned 1995 film, *Showgirls*. The actress gained professional credibility when she took smaller roles in independent films and also guest starred on popular TV crime procedurals such as *Law & Order: Criminal Intent* and *CSI*.

Actor Dustin Diamond is infamous for exploits in his personal life. After the series ended, Diamond tried his hand at stand-up comedy. He penned a tell-all book entitled *Behind the Bell* in 2009. The confessional work painted a very negative picture of the cast and crew of the show, and Diamond later refuted much of it and claimed a ghostwriter embellished many of the stories in order to make the book more provocative. Most scandalously, Diamond was convicted of two misdemeanor crimes and sentenced to four months in prison in 2015 for a bar fight that he was involved in the previous year. Diamond's posttelevision exploits embody the "child actor gone bad" narrative that affects a significant number of child or teen television and movie stars who, for a variety of reasons, seem unable to successfully transition into more adult roles, or to follow another career path after their early media successes end.

The impact of *Saved by the Bell* on popular culture is impressive. The show spawned two spin-offs: *Saved by the Bell: The College Years* and *Saved by the Bell: The New Class*. It also inspired a very adult-themed musical spoof entitled *Bayside! The Musical!* which was a *New York Times* Critic's Pick in 2013. Comic and late night TV talk show host Jimmy Fallon is a huge fan of the show and featured the cast in a 2015 sketch that had all of them in their original roles.

See also: 1970s: *Welcome Back, Kotter*; 1980s: *Facts of Life*; *Revenge of the Nerds*; *Sweet Valley High*; *Wonder Years, The*; 1990s: *Boy Meets World*; *Clarissa Explains It All*; *Freaks and Geeks*; 2000s: *Friday Night Lights*; *Glee*; *High School Musical*

Further Reading

Blistein, Jon. 2014. "Mark-Paul Gosselaar Slams 'Negative' Dustin Diamond 'Saved by the Bell' Book." *Rolling Stone*, August 7. https://www.rollingstone.com/tv/news/markpaul -gosselaar-slams-negative-dustin-diamond-saved-by-the-bell-book-20140807.

Brodeur, Michael Andor. 2015. "The Secret History of Saved by the Bell's Insane Caffeine Pill Episode." Thrillest, November 2. https://www.thrillist.com/entertainment/nation /im-so-excited-im-so-excited-im-so-scared?ref=twitter-869.

Massengale, Jeremiah. 2013. "School Was Cool in 'Saved by the Bell.'" Pop Matters, November 11. https://www.popmatters.com/176322-its-all-right-saved-by-the-bell-the-complete -collection-2495709925.html.

SAY ANYTHING . . .

Say Anything . . . (1989) starring John Cusack (1966–) has become iconic due primarily to a memorable scene where the lead character, Lloyd Dobler, stands in the yard outside his girlfriend's bedroom window and blasts the Peter Gabriel song, *In Your Eyes* on a large boom box that he holds over his head. The plot centers on the blooming relationship between average high school student Lloyd Dobler and his intellectually superior classmate, Diane Court (Ione Skye). The two begin dating shortly after graduation; while Lloyd's academic and career ambitions are vague, Diane's are clear as she's been awarded a scholarship to study abroad in England.

The conflict in the film centers on Jim's (Diane's father) disapproval of Lloyd. He views Lloyd as someone with no ambitions or future plans and attempts to persuade his daughter to end the relationship. To complicate matters, Jim is under investigation by the IRS for alleged tax violations tied to his personal business.

In most teen films centered on the angst of their protagonists, this movie, while following the predictable formula of boys meets girl/boy loses girl/boy gets girl back, does manage to portray the father as somewhat more complicated—or at least more three-dimensional—than most of its contemporaries. Jim genuinely cares for Diane, and they have a very close and mutually respectful relationship.

Say Anything . . . is an examination of the transition from adolescence into adulthood. As teenagers, individuals are preparing for important decisions involving the future, such as where they will go to college, what they will study, and how they will shape their future. In one notable scene in the film, Lloyd eats dinner with Diane and her father, and Jim grills Lloyd about his future plans. He rattles off a list of things that he doesn't want to do but is hard pressed to name a specific job or career path that interests him. This scene shows the uncertainty that so many teens experience as they are forced to choose a path in life that will direct them to higher education or straight to work. Lloyd's inability to specify a plan is viewed as evasiveness, but he's simply giving an honest answer as to where he is in that exact moment. Many teens can relate to this dilemma and the expectations from parents, teachers, and society in general.

The trope of star-crossed young lovers has been popular since Shakespeare penned the play *Romeo and Juliet*. Lloyd and Diane are clearly mismatched, and they are both aware of this at some level. The audience, however, is rooting for them, or at least for Lloyd's pursuit of Diane. The audience is meant to identify with Lloyd regardless of age or socioeconomic differences. He represents the quintessential underdog, but he also represents the naïveté of youth.

What the film conveys very effectively is the intensity of first love and all of the emotions and experiences associated with it. Many people experience their first love or "crush" during high school, and *Say Anything . . .* offers a protagonist who professes his love in clear and undeniable terms. Lloyd doesn't try to "play it cool" or minimize his affection for Diane as many male teen characters do in films like this.

The film ends with Lloyd and Diane reconciling after a brief split. Jim has been sent to prison, and Lloyd visits him and informs him that he will be accompanying Diane overseas when she leaves for college. This reinforces the romantic myth that the "guy gets the girl" despite all odds against him. This occurs almost universally in romantic comedies and perpetuates the notion that no obstacle is insurmountable when true love is at stake.

Critics largely praised the film for its intelligence and sensitivity in handling issues that were dismissed or discounted in many similar films during the 1980s. Chicago critic Roger Ebert lauded the film for being "one of those rare movies that has something to teach us about life. It doesn't have a 'lesson' or a 'message,' but it observes its moral choices so carefully that it helps us see our own" (Ebert 1989).

Some, however, found the plot formulaic. In a 1989 *New York Times* article, critic Caryn James contends that the character of Lloyd Dobler is less a nonconformist and more a rehash of the stock teenage film character that is quite average but imagines himself to be a hero. She contends that the film and others in the same vein perpetuate a myth that the underdog is always rewarded with the popular boy or girl of his or her dreams despite all odds.

Entertainment Weekly ranked *Say Anything . . .* #11 on their list of the 50 best high school movies ever. It is recognized today as an iconic teen film right alongside *The Breakfast Club*, *Pretty in Pink*, and others. The film was written and directed by Cameron Crowe, who also created the teen hit *Fast Times at Ridgemont High* based on his own best-selling book.

See also: 1970s: *American Graffiti*; 1980s: *Fast Times at Ridgemont High*; Hughes, John, Films of; 1990s: *Clueless*; *She's All That*

Further Reading

Bailey, Jason. 2014. "Was 'Say Anything . . .' the End of a Teen Movie Era?" Flavorwire, April 14. http://flavorwire.com/451435/was-say-anything-the-end-of-a-teen-movie-era.

Ebert, Roger. 1989. "Say Anything . . ." Roger Ebert, April 14. https://www.rogerebert.com/reviews/say-anything-1989.

Holmes, Linda. 2014. "'Say Anything' at 25: Nothing Bought, Sold or Processed." NPR, April 13. https://www.npr.org/sections/monkeysee/2014/04/13/302712465/say-anything-at-25-nothing-bought-sold-or-processed.

SWEET VALLEY HIGH

Sweet Valley High, a series of paperback books, was conceived by author Francine Pascal, but she hired a team of ghost writers to pen the teen-marketed novels. The stories are set in the fictional town of Sweet Valley, California. Twins Elizabeth and Jessica Wakefield are the two central characters, and they have an older brother named Steven who also figures into some of the plots. Although the genre falls under romance, the majority of story lines evoke traditional soap opera themes: cheating boyfriends, class snobbery and gossip, competition over desired mates, on again/off again relationships, and so on.

Although largely dismissed by critics as superficial in areas of character development and literary merit, the books were immensely popular with their teen readers. With more than 150 titles, there were 34 million *Sweet Valley High* titles in print in 1989. In 1985, *Sweet Valley High: Perfect Summer,* became the first young adult (YA) novel to ever appear on the *New York Times'* best-selling books list.

Sweet Valley High became a franchise, spawning a TV series that ran for four seasons, spin-off book series including *Sweet Valley Junior High*, *Sweet Valley Twins*, *Sweet Valley Kids*, and the *Unicorn Club* (itself a spin-off from Sweet Valley Kids). Merchandising proved to be a successful enterprise as well, with items like puzzles, board games, and CD soundtracks from the TV series. The marketing aspect of the books was very specific in terms of aesthetics: pastel colors, portraits of the main characters on the front cover, and perhaps most notably a "hook" at the end of each title intended to garner interest and purchases of the subsequent book in the series. Teen girls gravitated toward the titles largely based on these visuals.

It's difficult to determine exactly what facilitated the massive appeal of the books, but several studies and surveys conducted during the height of their popularity provide some insight. Many of the loyal readers significantly identified with the characters in the novels. Most notably, there was a positive reaction to stories where the male love interest went from being a dominating, sometimes insensitive individual to a caring and empathetic one who communicates effectively and often with his girlfriend. This type of story line appeals to teen girls' notions of romantic love and the myth that behavior can be changed if only the boy finds "the right girl" to teach him what love means.

With a series like *Sweet Valley High*, the scope of its appeal raises questions about its readers and their fierce loyalty to the books. The stories are written in a very melodramatic style, which seems fitting given the audience. Without a frame of reference, middle-school girls may wonder what the high school experience will be like. The adventures of Elizabeth and Jessica must seem very exciting and even intriguing to young readers. These readers are far less likely to be influenced by book reviews than they are by what their friends are reading.

At a core level, these books are entertaining, and perhaps not intended to be taken very seriously. But media is critical in the development of self-identity for adolescents, so the impact is significant. And, given the sheer volume of titles, they do have a cumulative effect on the reader. However, many original fans of the series are now adult women, and some have been very vocal about their disapproval of the books and the messages inherent in them. A common complaint from the now adult readers is that they felt the books glamorized the high school experience and didn't offer great role models for young girls. Additionally, from a quality perspective, many of them now see how formulaic the books are, with little to no originality in either plot or characters.

Regardless of perceived quality, the phenomenal commercial success of the series paved the way for future titles from other authors. Since so many media productions are derivative of what came before them, it's doubtful that without *Sweet Valley High*, there would have been a *Gossip Girl* or a *Pretty Little Liars*. And Paramount Pictures has greenlit a movie version of *Sweet Valley High*. This, of course, will be an effort both to attract a new generation of potential fans and to evoke the nostalgia factor for young women who read the books as tweens and teens. Screenwriters Kirsten "Kiwi" Smith and Harper Dill will develop the story line and screenplay.

See also: 1960s: *Patty Duke Show, The*; 1970s: Blume, Judy; 1980s: *Dirty Dancing*; 1990s: *Clarissa Explains It All*; 2000s: *Gossip Girl*; *Mean Girls*; *One Tree Hill*; *Pretty Little Liars*; *Sisterhood of the Traveling Pants, The*

Further Reading

Henriquez, Cristina. 2014. "Confessions of A Former 'Sweet Valley High' Addict." NPR, July 13. https://www.npr.org/2014/07/01/327248188/blonde-bombshells-escaping -into-sweet-valley.

Pattee, Amy S. 2011. *Reading the Adolescent Romance: Sweet Valley High and the Popular Young Adult Romance Novel*. New York: Routledge

21 JUMP STREET

The crime drama *21 Jump Street* (1987–1991) featured a young group of undercover police officers who were able to infiltrate various organizations in order to investigate crimes committed by and/or against young adults. The title comes from the address of the location from where the characters work when not undercover. Given the popularity of police procedurals with middle-aged viewers, the idea behind this show was to keep the genre and its conventions intact while focusing on teenaged and young adult characters in order to attract and retain that market segment. The show was cast to reflect a sense of diversity both within the characters and (hopefully) viewers: Officer Tom Hanson (Johnny Depp), Sergeant Judith "Judy" Hoffs (Holly Robinson), Officer Douglas "Doug" Penhall (Peter DeLuise), Sergeant Harry Truman Ioki/Vinh Van Tran (Dustin Nguyen), and Captain Richard Jenko (Frederic Forrest).

Youth marketing was especially important at this time for television. When *21 Jump Street* debuted, there were no satellite or dish networks, no streaming services like Hulu or Netflix, and no social media. That desirable demographic wasn't really being served well on network television, at least not with respect to the genre of crime dramas.

The series covered significant social issues at the time and often included a public service announcement at the end tied to a topic covered in the actual episode. Among topical themes covered in the show: abortion, AIDS, drug addiction,

Johnny Depp, Peter DeLuise, and Dustin Nguyen in a publicity portrait for the television series 21 Jump Street. The show featured a group of young undercover police officers and appealed to a target demograph of teens and young adults. (Fox Network/Getty Images)

and child abuse. These issues were especially resonant with teens and young adults as they were dealing with issues of sexual activity and its repercussions during the peak of the AIDS crisis. As with most police procedurals, the issue is handled and resolved within the show's 60-minute time frame and almost always included a moral lesson for the viewer. It also featured an episode that dealt sensitively with the issue of gang rape that devoted more time to its origins and causes than other shows would have tackled at the time.

The only network television show that preceded this and appealed to a similar demographic was the ABC crime drama *The Mod Squad* (1968–1973). That show featured Michael Cole as Peter "Pete" Cochran, Peggy Lipton as Julie Barnes, Clarence Williams III as Lincoln "Linc" Hayes, and Tige Andrews as Captain Adam Greer. Its premise was similar in that young recruits were used to investigate crimes in locales where they could blend in and avoid attention. Since this was the late 1960s, the three leads in the show were emblematic of societal issues at the time—the young woman, Julie, was fierce and independent; Linc was arrested during racial riots, and Pete was a disaffected young man from a wealthy family who'd turned to crime as a form of rebellion. Although the characters on *The Mod Squad* were a bit older than the ones on *21 Jump Street,* they focused on crimes involving youths and also put perspective on issues of the day such as domestic violence, illiteracy, and the antiwar movement.

Debuting on the new Fox network, the show was the first series on Fox to win its time slot against competing shows on the other big three networks: ABC, CBS, and NBC. In addition to casting for diversity, producers hoped for at least one breakout star that would connect significantly with its younger audience. That hope came in the form of actor Johnny Depp. Featuring a young attractive male star was not coincidental. Police procedurals are typically more popular with male viewers; having a young physically appealing male character was part of an effort to lure young female viewers to the show.

Though this was early in his career, Depp was noticed by viewers and quickly became a fan favorite. He had his professional sights on feature films, though, and felt constrained both within the medium of television and within a program that was teen-centric. In a 2014 *Today Show* interview, Depp joked about trying to get fired from the show so that he could move on to bigger career challenges.

In the second season, a new character was brought on to the show. Dennis Booker (Richard Grieco) quickly became the next heartthrob character and was spun-off into his own series, *Booker,* which lasted only one season. This ill-fated spin-off proved that it takes more than physical appeal to attract and retain a teen audience.

21 Jump Street connected with teenagers due to its relevant story lines and its cast. Teens were able to see characters their age with adult jobs. They were competent at their work but were also relatable as they had the same or similar personal struggles as many of their viewers. The excitement of police work as depicted in the show also added to its allure for teen viewers as a potential career path in the not-too-distant future.

Like many popular TV series that later become adapted into a theatrical vehicle (*Charlie's Angels, Starsky & Hutch, Dukes of Hazzard,* etc.), a *21 Jump Street* movie was released in 2012 and starred Channing Tatum and Jonah Hill. Former high school students Morton Schmidt (Hill) and Greg Jenko (Tatum) meet up years after graduation at the police academy and end up working together undercover in order to infiltrate the spread of a synthetic drug making the rounds at various high schools. The film was comedic in tone and scored big at the box office. It spawned a sequel, *22 Jump Street,* and both films featured cameos from some of the stars of the television series.

See also: 1970s: *Starsky & Hutch*

Further Reading

Cavender, Gray, and Nancy C. Jurik. 2017. "Feminist Themes in Television Crime Dramas." *Criminology and Criminal Justice.* http://criminology.oxfordre.com/view/10.1093/acrefore/9780190264079.001.0001/acrefore-9780190264079-e-17.

Inhat, Gwen. 2017. "21 Jump Street Did More Than Just Make Johnny Depp Famous." *AV/TV Club,* April 10. https://tv.avclub.com/21-jump-street-did-more-than-just-make-johnny-depp-famo-1798260689.

WONDER YEARS, THE

The Wonder Years (1988–1993) was a hit network comedy that ran for six seasons from 1988 to 1993. It centers on the teen protagonist, Kevin Arnold (Fred Savage), who is growing up against the background of the late 1960s and early 1970s, and all of the historic events that occurred during that time period. Kevin's family—his mom (Alley Mills), dad (Dan Lauria), older brother, Wayne (Jason Hervey), and older sister, Karen (Olivia d'Abo)—figure in prominently to many of the plots, as does his friend Paul (Josh Saviano). But the show's most popular story

Considered by many critics and fans to be one of the best television series ever created, *The Wonder Years* examined the lives of several young friends and their families. The show focused on both personal relationships and life events that helped shape them. (Bettmann/Getty Images)

line involved Kevin's romantic crush on classmate Winnie Cooper (Danica McKellar).

The novelty of the show largely had to do with its format. Much of the action was narrated by an "adult" Kevin (voiced by actor Daniel Stern) reminiscing about events from his childhood. The creators of the show—husband and wife team Neal Marlens and Carol Black—credit much of the show's success to its ability to make the mundane memorable. Most of the show's teen story lines are events that are largely relatable regardless of the era in which they occur: asking a classmate to a school dance, sibling rivalries, and a burgeoning sense of one's own body and sexual curiosity.

Some have compared the show to the 1950s sitcom *Leave It to Beaver*. There are certainly structural similarities since both focus on the "average" American family and the trials and life lessons of a male tween with an older brother, mother and father, and several nerdy friends. The main difference between the two is the backdrops against which they are set. In *Leave It to Beaver,* the outside world rarely if ever intrudes upon the inner world of the Cleaver household.

The 1970s loom large in the Arnold household. There are references to the Vietnam War, even in the pilot episode, when Winnie's older brother is killed in combat. Karen is interested in the women's movement, part of a bigger social issue relating to equal rights. Another story line followed housewife Norma Arnold (Kevin's mom) as she returns to college later in life to pursue a technical degree and eventually goes to work for a software company.

The romantic ups and downs of Kevin and Winnie were featured throughout much of the show's run as they fought, broke up, and then got back together more than once. Teen girls were especially drawn to this story line. Teen viewers were also able to see themselves—or at least elements of themselves—in the young characters on the show.

The Wonder Years evoked nostalgia among its viewers like few shows did at the time. Setting the show approximately 20 years earlier than the time in which it was produced allowed baby boomers to enjoy the show on two different levels. They could easily envision themselves and/or their friends as Kevin and his gang. Since coming-of-age stories usually contain some universal truths and commonly shared experiences, adult viewers relived some of their youthful activities. Just as importantly, though, these same viewers could now relate to the adult characters on the show. Many or most baby boomers were now parents and likely dealing with their own children who were going through puberty.

Keeping in mind that this show aired at a time when cable and streaming shows were not yet an option for the masses, its inventiveness and authenticity should be praised. The 30-minute sitcom format had been in place for decades prior to this, but *The Wonder Years* evoked the same sense of quality that some theatrical films do. It also wasn't afraid to treat its young characters with respect and not merely as the punch lines to jokes or the objects of parody. It was also a well-balanced show. Kevin's parents were able to become fully developed characters in their own right as opposed to simple authority figures as foils for the exploits of their children. Additionally, Winnie wasn't portrayed as a one- or even two-dimensional character. She was just as, if not more, complex, than the others characters on the show. She also had a purpose beyond being the object of Kevin's affection. Winnie was a powerful and positive role model for teen girls. This made the series finale especially heartbreaking, but also painfully realistic, when the two encounter one another at an airport and realize their lives had changed dramatically since they had last seen each other.

One particular noteworthy element of the show is that, while it took place in another era, the issues and themes explored on *The Wonder Years* weren't mutually exclusive to that time. Where current TV sitcoms like *The Goldbergs* place an undue emphasis on the aesthetics of the time period (the 1980s), *The Wonder Years* didn't overly rely on visuals to capture and hold the attention of their viewers. It examined universal truths about adolescence that resonated with its teen and adult viewers.

The show won an Emmy award for Best Outstanding Comedy Series in 1988 and was recognized in 1989 with a Peabody Award for its groundbreaking approach to a sitcom and its inventiveness in format. The show won 22 awards during its network run and is considered one of the best comedy series of the 1980s.

See also: 1950s: *Adventures of Ozzie and Harriet, The*; *Father Knows Best*; *I Love Lucy*; *Leave It to Beaver*; 1960s: *Patty Duke Show, The*; 1970s: *Happy Days*; 1980s: *Back to the Future*; *Cosby Show, The*; *Facts of Life, The*; *Family Ties*; *Full House*; 1990s: *Boy Meets World*; *Clarissa Explains It All*; *Freaks and Geeks*; *7th Heaven*; 2000s: *Friday Night Lights*

Further Reading

Dupuis, Julia, and Claire Dwyer. 2015. "Two Views of the Wonder-ful Years." Bolt Online, April 7. https://lightningboltonline.com/2015/04/07/two-views-of-the-wonder-ful-years/.

Hill, Libby. 2015. "A Show Focused Wholly on the Past, the Wonder Years Was Still Ahead of Its Time." *AV Club*, January 29. https://tv.avclub.com/a-show-focused-wholly-on-the-past-the-wonder-years-was-1798276068.

The 1990s

DECADE OVERVIEW

Economically, the 1990s were wildly successful. Starting with an increase in gross domestic product (GDP) in 1991, the U.S. economy boomed for the entire decade until 2001 when the dot-com "bubble" finally burst, as technology-based companies suffered serious monetary losses. Bill Clinton was elected president of the United States in 1992 and again in 1996 in strong victories for the Democratic Party. Although he was and still remains a popular president, he is one of only two presidents to ever have been impeached by Congress. Although not found guilty by the U.S. Senate, Clinton's impeachment is widely known due to the scandalous details of the charges. Clinton was charged with perjury and obstruction of justice charges related to a sexual affair that he had with White House intern Monica Lewinsky.

In popular culture, the family comedy *Home Alone* was the top-grossing film of 1990. However, a sleeper hit named *Pretty Woman* was also a box office smash, raking in more than $175 million and launching the career of actress Julia Roberts. On television, top 10 shows included *Roseanne, Cheers,* and *Murphy Brown.* Horror writer Stephen King ruled the *New York Times* Best Seller list with three different titles.

Teen pop bands and artists were incredibly popular throughout the 1990s. Groups like Backstreet Boys and NSYNC dominated the radio and sales charts for part of the decade. Additionally, female superstars such as Britney Spears and all-girl group Spice Girls skyrocketed to fame and sold millions of records. The decade also offered more serious fare with female singer-songwriters like Liz Phair, Tori Amos, and Alanis Morissette. Alternative rock and grunge also shared popularity with younger listeners, with bands like Pearl Jam, Nirvana, and Alice in Chains receiving both critical and commercial attention.

"Third-wave feminism" originated during the 1990s. The term was coined by writer Rebecca Walker in an article written by her for *Ms.* magazine. Although there are different definitions of the term depending on who is asked, common themes include individualism and diversity. This new brand of feminism also focused on sexual freedom for women and a rejection of cultural shaming of sexually active females. There was also a focus on intersectional feminism, which highlighted the need to include women of color in continuing efforts for equality in a variety of areas.

More women joined the ranks of Congress as senators between 1992 and 1993. Ruth Bader Ginsburg, the second woman ever to be placed on the U.S. Supreme Court, was appointed by President Clinton. This rise of "girl power" was reflected in many media depictions as well. Three popular television series showcased strong and independent young women in lead roles: *Charmed, Buffy the Vampire Slayer,* and *Sabrina the Teenage Witch*. Young women of color also made an impact in the music business as artists like Missy Elliott and groups TLC and Destiny's Child broke barriers in a white, male-dominated business.

Reality television became a staple on cable stations like MTV with the premier of *The Real World*. Each season featured a cast of young people, and the show was set in various large cities like New York, Los Angeles, and Seattle. Though contrived and formulaic, the show is now recognized as bringing relevant cultural issues such as abortion, sexuality, AIDS, and religion into the national dialogue. Although commonplace now on both cable and network channels, the show was considered revolutionary at the time that it first aired.

The evolution of technology exploded in the 1990s. Personal computers became standard in many American households as knowledge and use of the devices became more common. The first generation of wireless/cellular phones debuted, and millions of Americans began "surfing" the World Wide Web. The societal impact of this was significant as previous barriers to communication were broken down. Texting on wireless devices was still fairly new at this time, but the lasting impact of these technologies is still being felt today.

The first *Harry Potter* book was published in 1997, and, by 1999, TV shows like *Frasier, Friends*, and the nighttime game show *Who Wants to Be a Millionaire* dominated the Nielsen ratings.

Pop superstar Prince's hit song "1999" struck a chord with many as the year 2000 approached. Widespread panic erupted due to a formatting issue with the date/year on computer programs as many believed the technology would be unable to distinguish between the year 1900 and 2000 and wreak havoc upon technology. What became known as the "Y2K bug" ultimately resulted in an overhyped nonevent.

Each of these 25 entries discusses the nuanced experience of growing up in the 1990s. The rise of girl power is covered in many of the television shows, music, and films discussed in this section. The 1990s had more women out front in popular culture than in previous decades, though the status quo was still present in the movies, video games, and books of the era.

Further Reading

Cooper, Gael Fashingbauer, and Brian Bellmont. 2013. *The Totally Sweet 90s: From Clear Cola to Furby, and Grunge to "Whatever," the Toys, Tastes, and Trends That Defined a Decade*. New York: Perigee.

Davidson, Telly. 2016. *Culture War: How the '90s Made Us Who We Are Today Whether We Like It or Not*. Jefferson, NC: McFarland.

Oxoby, Marc. 2003. *The 1990s: American Popular Culture through History*. Westport, CT: Greenwood Press.

AMERICAN PIE

American Pie (1999), a teen sex comedy, was a surprise blockbuster hit that spawned two theatrical sequels. The male-centric comedy focuses on a group of friends at West Michigan High who pledge to lose their virginity before graduation. The characters follow fairly standard archetypes: Jim (the nerd), Chris "Oz" (the jock), Kevin (group leader), Paul (the intellectual/sophisticate), and Steve Stifler (Seann William Scott), the school stud who has already lost his virginity, rounds out the gang. After a series of misadventures leave the boys in various states of confusion, embarrassment, humiliation, and despair, all four of them end up fulfilling the pledge by having a sexual encounter on prom night.

The film relies largely on sight gags for laughs: Jim (Jason Biggs) has a sexually humiliating experience with a foreign exchange student that is captured and broadcast to the entire school via webcam. Also, desperate to experience simulated sex, Jim experiments with a dessert and is caught by his father. Paul (Eddie Kaye Thomas) is given a laxative by Stifler and has an "accident" that is witnessed by other students at school. This type of "gross out" humor is aimed at a male teen audience and has roots going back to earlier teen sex comedies such as *Porky's* (1981).

Kevin's (Thomas Ian Nicholas) dilemma in the film centers on his efforts to convince his girlfriend, Vicky (Tara Reid), that he's not simply using her for sex, even though his ultimate goal is to lose his virginity to her on prom night. Oz's (Chris Klein) attempts to find a girlfriend involve him joining the school jazz choir where he meets Heather (Mena Suvari). Feedback from an earlier romantic attempt with a college girl pushes him toward trying to become a more sensitive boyfriend.

American Pie's explicit content nearly earned it an NC-17 rating. Several scenes had to be edited or reshot in order for the MPAA to assign it an R (Restricted) rating. In order to widen the audience appeal of the film to women and girls, several of the female characters were made to be sexually bolder than what was typically depicted in this genre—at least at the time it was made. The foreign exchange student, for example, masturbates on Jim's bed when she discovers a trove of pornographic magazines hidden in his room. Michelle, a "band geek," ends up sleeping with Jim, but when he awakes the next morning, she is gone and has left a note. Apparently, she only wanted him for sex. This reversal of typical gender norms suggests that girls have the same physical desires that boys do and are not always focused on relationship potential when it comes to sex.

Given the taboo nature of sexuality in our culture, it's no surprise that this type of film is successful with its target audience. Films like this can be viewed several different ways, but given the natural sexual curiosity of teens during this period of their lives, it makes sense that they would gravitate toward media productions that reflect the issues and events in their own lives. How effectively or accurately a film like *American Pie* reflects these experiences is, of course, subjective.

The theme of women as sexual objects has historically been the norm in countless films. The makers of *American Pie* may have been attempting to update this formula by fleshing out female characters that are as sexually curious or active as their male counterparts. In addition to the two already mentioned, there is also Stifler's mother (Jennifer Coolidge). She is absent through most of the film, which allows Stifler to throw wild parties in an unsupervised house. Toward the end of the film, Finch, who is without a potential partner, retreats to the basement of Stifler's home where he finds the mother. She is physically attracted to him, and he reciprocates her feelings. The two end up having sex on the pool table, which is where Stifler finds them the next morning. Whether or not this is progress or provocation is open for discussion, but, in terms of character development (or lack thereof), it is conspicuous that the role of Stifler's mother isn't even assigned a first name. Her character is listed in the film credits as "Stifler's mother."

When viewing *American Pie* through the lens of a teenager, it can be seen as a pseudo tutorial on sexual education. Even with its raunchy humor and fixation on bodily functions, the film isn't so much rebellious or even subversive as it is traditional. Teenagers glean much of what they learn sexually from popular media. While sexual education curriculum may still exist in most high schools, it is often delivered with moral as well as sexual instruction. Whether it's an abstinence only program or a more typical curriculum that includes basic information on issues like menstruation and pregnancy, it is designed as a one size fits all program and must adhere to strict guidelines and approval from authority figures. Media, then, can often fill in the gaps.

An examination of beliefs and values within the film should be considered in conjunction with its sequels, *American Pie 2* and *American Wedding*. As the characters in the original mature—especially the male characters—there is an acknowledgment and even confirmation of traditional societal norms with respect to sex and marriage. Sexual pranks and "dirty talk" aside, the characters in this trilogy follow traditional Western culture's road map of marriage and even monogamy as ideals that are to be valued and upheld. Even Stifler, the woman-izing playboy, redeems himself (somewhat) in the conclusion of the trilogy by proving to be a dependable friend, and—perhaps more importantly—he seems open to the idea of settling down with one woman after witnessing the vows of Jim and his new wife.

For all of its superficial shock value, the message of the *American Pie* films ulti-mately clings to conservative and patriarchal ideology with respect to male–female relationships. Although the film was largely dismissed by critics, its commercial appeal was widespread, earning the first film in the series more than $100 million and inspiring four direct-to-DVD spin-offs.

See also: 1970s: *National Lampoon's Animal House*; 1980s: *Fast Times at Ridgemont High*; Hughes, John, Films of; *Revenge of the Nerds*; *Risky Business*; *Say Anything . . .*; 1990s: *Clueless*; *Dazed and Confused*; *She's All That*; 2000s: *Bring It On*; *Mean Girls*

Further Reading

Mallan, Kerry, and Sharyn Pearce. 2003. *Youth Cultures: Texts, Images, and Identities*. Westport, CT: Greenwood.

Rosenberg, Alyssa. 2012. "The Lost Sexual Equality Legacy of 'American Pie.'" Think Pro-gress, April 9. https://thinkprogress.org/the-lost-sexual-equality-legacy-of-american -pie-2f575671c7c5/.

Sims, David. 2014. "Virgin Territory: 'American Pie's' Confusing Sexual Legacy." *The Atlantic*, July 7. https://www.theatlantic.com/entertainment/archive/2014/07/virgin-territory-american-pies-confusing-sexual-legacy/374032/.

BACKSTREET BOYS

Popular boy band the Backstreet Boys wasn't formed in the traditional method where singers and musicians come together and choose to form a musical group. Rather, Backstreet Boys was the brainchild of producer Lou Pearlman, a native New York businessman and record producer who created and then promoted the band via a talent search in Florida. Pearlman apparently was fascinated with the financial success of earlier boy band, New Kids on the Block, who rose to fame in the early 1990s. He believed he could duplicate that success—or even surpass it— by following the same formula: a group of young attractive men in their late teens or early 20s, a mass-marketed "pop" sound, and the incorporation of synchronized dance moves. None of the members could look "rough" or threatening. To have mass appeal, it was required to package a look and sound that would appeal to its target audience while not alienating or angering parents. That mix was found with members A. J. McLean (1978–), Howie Dorough (1973–), Nick Carter (1980–), Kevin Richardson (1971–), and Brian Littrell (1975–).

The Backstreet Boys skyrocketed to success in the United States after recording and releasing music in Europe, where they enjoyed commercial success with the single, "We've Got It Goin' On." The song peaked in the Top Five in several countries including France and Germany. This international breakthrough allowed them to tour overseas and to record their first album, *Backstreet Boys*. After selling hundreds of thousands of albums internationally and reaping noteworthy success particularly in Germany, where they earned their first platinum selling album, the group decided to test the waters in America.

The band's third studio album, *Millennium* (1999), was released in the United States with heavy promotion. The album spawned four Top 40 singles and ended up selling more than 40 million copies worldwide. An equally successful national tour highlighted the group's wide appeal and significant fan base. Product tie-ins and target marketing aimed at young girls via youth-oriented magazines and other media helped maintain the group's popularity even though it might not have been the image or career trajectory the band members had envisioned.

A lot of planning and calculations go into the formation of boy bands. Producers and record executives realize the importance of having a group of young men who will appeal to as many fans as possible. One way to do this is to expand the allure beyond the market segment typically associated with boy bands: young girls. By the mid- to late 1990s, it was fairly evident that this type of group could also have widespread appeal with young gay men, too.

Appealing to these two demographics requires market-savvy skills. The product—in this case, an all-male pop band—has to adhere to specific standards to be successful. For example, making lyrics or dance movements too sexually suggestive risks alienating the parents who are often the people purchasing the music, concert tickets, and so on. At the same time, however, there needs to be some subtext or "reading" of the content that can be relatable to young gay men. In short, they need to feel that they are either represented to some extent by the band members—or at least one of them—or perhaps fans can project themselves as objects of the band's attention, affection, or both. Young girls are especially prone to being attracted to groups like this because the carefully constructed image of the group's members appeals to their notions of what romantic love and physical attraction look and feel like. To that end, one fairly easy method of appealing to the two primary target audiences here is to have band members who are fairly androgynous in appearance. Although three of the five band members have darker hair and often sport facial hair, two of the members—Brian Littrell and Nick Carter— are blonde, and have features and builds that would typically be considered less traditionally "masculine."

The youngest member, Carter, was arguably the main focus of the band's first videos. In the video for the song, "Quit Playing Games (with My Heart)," Nick is set apart from the other band members. They shoot hoops in the pouring rain; he watches from the bleachers. He frequently hangs his head down in the video, avoiding watching the other boys play. Nick is shown playing with his hair and frequently has his head thrown back with closed eyes, a gesture that cinematically implies sexual release. Whether one reads any gay subtext into any of this is clearly subjective, but Carter also appeared on the cover of *xy*, a gay teen-oriented magazine, to promote the single and album. It is noteworthy too that no girls or women appear in this video, unlike their previous ones. Also, the lyrics to "Quit Playing Games (with My Heart)" don't assign a gender to the heartbreaker. The song could be written for anyone and sung by anyone then.

The band is still together after several reinventions and a temporary departure by Kevin Richardson. While none of their subsequent musical efforts reached the success they had with *Millennium,* they have had success touring and have capitalized on the nostalgia factor as the majority of their original fans are now adults, many with their own young children. Their original producer and man who undeniably launched their career, Lou Pearlman, pleaded guilty to a number of white-collar crimes and was sentenced to a lengthy prison term; he died in federal custody in 2016. Nick Carter has had several successful solo efforts as recently as 2015.

See also: 1960s: Beach Boys, The; Beatles, The; Monkees, The; Rolling Stones, The; 1970s: Bee Gees, The; Clash, The; Led Zeppelin; Osmonds, The; Queen; 1980s: Blondie; MTV; 1990s: Green Day; Nirvana; Smashing Pumpkins, The; Spice Girls; 2000s: My Chemical Romance

Further Reading

Battan, Carrie. 2017. "The State of the Boy Band in 2017, According to Two New Reality-TV Shows." *New Yorker*, July 31. https://www.newyorker.com/culture/culture-desk/the -state-of-the-boy-band-in-2017-according-to-two-new-reality-tv-shows.

Carter, Nick. 2013. *Facing the Music and Living to Talk about It*. Los Angeles: Ghost Mountain Books.

Stec, Carly. 2013. "What Boy Bands Can Teach Your Business about Effective Marketing Practices." Impact. December 12, 2013. https://www.impactbnd.com/blog/what-boy -bands-can-teach-your-business-about-effective-marketing-practices.

BOY MEETS WORLD

Boy Meets World (1993–2000), an ABC sitcom, featured Ben Savage (1980–) in the title role of Cory Matthews. The show follows Cory and his circle of friends from middle school to college, careers, and marriage. Standard themes and plots were covered, including peer popularity, budding romances, sibling rivalry, academic pressures, and eventually important life decisions such as choosing a major or profession, and finding a permanent partner or spouse. The show was popular among teen viewers, who gravitate toward material that reflects their own lives, and these themes reflect common events in the lives of adolescents.

Much of the conflict in the show comes from the sibling rivalry between Cory and his older brother, Eric Matthews (Will Friedle). Eric struggles academically and doesn't do well on tests, which makes his post–high school existence potentially uncertain. In one episode, he even admits to cheating on tests with the help of a tutor. Additionally, Eric's focus is primarily on girls and not school. As with many sitcoms, the "dim bulb" archetype is played mainly for laughs. Whether his faltering grades are due to lack of intellect or motivation or both, he is constantly involved in schemes and pranks that further his reputation as a joker and not someone who should be taken seriously.

The brothers argue quite a bit and even get physical sometimes. In shows that depict sibling conflicts, boys typically get physical and girls get verbal. A quick content analysis of a show like *Modern Family* illustrates this. Sisters Haley (Sarah Hyland) and Alex Dunphy (Ariel Winter) bicker with one another constantly. Haley is the "girly girl" who is consumed with her appearance and is fixated on boys and romance. Alex is academically gifted and frustrated with the superficiality and lack of depth of her older sister. For every slight that Haley gets in on Alex, her younger sibling lobs an equally stinging one back at her. The show does a nuanced job of showing dimensions of each of the sisters rather than reducing them to flat caricatures.

On *Boy Meets World,* Cory and Eric also spar verbally, and often, it doesn't take long to escalate into physical fighting; this is evidenced in an episode where Eric is leaving home and attempts to take an item that Cory claims is his. Before long, the two are shoving one another and hitting before the parents come into the room to break things up. These types of conflicts resonate with teen viewers, especially when they deal with the shifting nature of relationships as siblings age and move into new situations, and experience rituals such as moving away from home or going to college.

One of the most beloved characters on *Boy Meets World* is educator Mr. Feeny (William Daniels). This character is intended as a tough but caring individual who constantly challenges his students, especially Cory and his friend Shawn (Rider Strong), to do better. He is prone to giving advice on issues that go beyond the schoolroom and helps his students navigate the tricky world of adolescence.

After the boys graduate high school—where Mr. Feeny becomes their principal—and head off to fictional Pennbrook University, he arrives there first as a student and then later becomes an instructor. These sorts of plot contrivances are routine in many television sitcoms and dramas in order to keep characters together and allow for interaction. Although Cory and Shawn resist Mr. Feeny's advice and guidance most of the time, they grow to appreciate and respect him for his dedication to their development. The final scene in the series features Cory, Shawn, and Topanga (Danielle Christine Fishel), Cory's wife, back in Mr. Feeny's classroom reminiscing about their times together and the impact he had on their lives.

Once Shawn and Cory graduate high school and start college, the focus of the show shifts to their adjustment to higher education. This too is a common element of TV shows that feature young men and women going away to college and all of the changes that this entails. Issues examined on this show and others like *Felicity* (1998–2002) revolve around grades and final exams. For competitive students, there is a comparative element to this. While a B- or C might be acceptable to one student, another student may feel disappointed with that grade. Additionally, final exams or "finals" supply endless potential for drama or comedy in TV shows. In both *Boy Meets World* and *Felicity*, for example, finals are represented as significant markers for students that can affect their future opportunities. They are highly stressful and influence behavior and attitudes. This is relevant for adolescent viewers, as studies have indicated that incoming college freshmen are influenced by representations of the college experience within popular media. While socioeconomic factors heavily influence expectations of college, so too do films and TV shows that depict the experience.

A spin-off of *Boy Meets World* debuted in 2014 on the Disney Channel. *Girl Meets World* focused on Cory and his wife Topanga and their two children—daughter Riley and son Auggie. That show ended in 2017 after three seasons.

See also: 1950s: *Adventures of Ozzie and Harriet, The*; *Father Knows Best*; *I Love Lucy*; *Leave It to Beaver*; 1960s: *Patty Duke Show, The*; 1970s: *Carrie*; *Happy Days*; *Welcome Back, Kotter*; 1980s: *Back to the Future*; *Cosby Show, The*; *Facts of Life, The*; *Family Ties*; *Full House*; *Saved by the Bell*; *Wonder Years, The*; 1990s: *Clarissa Explains It All*; *7th Heaven*; 2000s: *Friday Night Lights*

Further Reading

Leigh, Megan. 2014. "Chick Like Me: Gender Equality in Boy Meets World." *Pop Verse*, June 6. http://pop-verse.com/2014/06/06/chick-like-me-gender-equality-in-boy-meets-world/

Quiñónez, Ariana. 2015. "Why Shawn and Angela from 'Boy Meets World' Were the Most Groundbreaking Teen Power Couple of the '90s." Hypable, June 19. https://www.hypable.com/shawn-angela-boy-meets-world/

BUFFY THE VAMPIRE SLAYER

Buffy the Vampire Slayer (1997–2003), an innovative supernatural teen drama created by Joss Whedon, featured a strong female heroine named Buffy Summers (Sarah Michelle Gellar) who battled a variety of monsters that included vampires, werewolves, and demons. A somewhat typical high school student on the surface, Buffy is actually endowed with mystical powers and supernatural strength that help her in her battles. She is also part of a rich tradition of vampire slayers—whether she likes it or not. Unlike previous slayers, though, Buffy doesn't go it alone; she enlists the aid of her friends: Willow Rosenberg (Alyson Hannigan), Xander Harris (Nicholas Brendon), and Cordelia (Charisma Carpenter). Willow is smart and nerdy; Xander is a typical teen boy who desperately wants to be noticed by a girl; and Cordelia Chase is a popular cheerleader who reluctantly becomes part of the inner circle but ultimately proves herself to be a solid friend and ally.

Unlike adults in other teen centric shows, the adults in *Buffy the Vampire Slayer* directly support the efforts of the teenagers. Rupert Giles (Anthony Stewart Head) is a librarian who mentors Buffy; his role is that of a "Watcher." It is his primary duty to oversee Buffy's activities and help her in any way that he can. Joyce Summers (Kristine Sutherland), Buffy's mother, is nurturing and supportive as well. One of the strongest elements of the show is the importance of community. Buffy relies heavily on her friends and family to thwart evil together as a strong group.

The topic of romance and sexual desire is dealt with on the show in an authentic manner. Buffy meets and falls in love with a young man named Angel (David Boreanaz). Unfortunately, he is a vampire. The supernatural element of this pairing aside, the feelings and conflict that Buffy endures is typical of a girl her age. She is deeply attracted to Angel but knows that the consequences of a relationship with him could be seriously problematic—even fatal. Her dilemma over whether to sleep with him plays out over many episodes, creating sexual tension and angst. When the two finally do have sex, the results are disastrous. Angel reverts back to being a demon and loses the human soul he was given by a gypsy.

Each decade from the 1950s through today has featured shows about teenagers. Generally, these shows reflect current social issues and themes within our culture. The 1950s reflected the paternalism and authoritarianism of the times, showing children and teens who desperately needed discipline and structure from parents and other authority figures in order to survive. The 1960s and 1970s reflected the changing cultural landscape with the roles of women and minorities evolving, while the 1980s focused on the modern family that many times had two full-time working adults. By the time that *Buffy the Vampire Slayer* debuted on television, teens were savvier than before. They had seen the effects of high divorce rates, the AIDS crisis, and a significant growth of women within corporate America. And while the show did feature supernatural elements, it resonated among the cynical yet vulnerable teens of the 1990s.

High school has always been fertile ground for melodrama in popular culture. As teens struggle with their identities and their place in the world, they are dealing many times with romantic relationships and breakups, academic challenges as they prepare for college, and uncertainty about the future. Though all of these issues have been covered in previous shows, books, and movies, *Buffy the Vampire Slayer* took it one step further: all of those fears and struggles manifested themselves as literal monsters. The notion that high school is "hell" isn't a terribly original one, but turning that into a literal reality with threats from otherworldly creatures on a weekly television series was. In the series, Sunnydale High is built on top of a "Hellmouth," a portal for demons.

The format of the show was similar to another supernatural series of the 1990s, *The X-Files*. On that show, each episode featured an alien or monster that the two protagonists had to deal with, but there was a larger story arc involving government conspiracies about aliens and the protagonists' role in that story line. On *Buffy the Vampire Slayer*, a typical season featured a monster that Buffy and the gang battled, but there were also interpersonal relationship dramas that grounded the show in reality and made it relatable, including LGBT relationships.

The WB series was based on a 1992 theatrical film of the same name that received mediocre critical reviews and less-than-stellar box office sales. Whedon found producers who were receptive to the idea of translating the movie into a television series that focused on the primary character's everyday high school struggles, as well as her circle of friends. What had been missing in the theatrical version of his material was given new life in a weekly television series. Whedon was heavily involved in the writing of the show and also was given a lot of creative control.

Buffy the Vampire Slayer was widely praised by critics. Its portrayal of a strong female warrior connected on a deep level with fans, especially female fans who sought representation in media. Its ability to work as both a supernatural action series and an intimate interpersonal drama is still noteworthy today. Although the show never won Emmy Awards in any major categories, it has appeared on multiple "Best TV Shows Ever" lists and attracted and retained a loyal following of fans.

See also: 1950s: *Blob, The*; *I Was a Teenage Werewolf*; 1960s: *Addams Family, The*; *Slaughterhouse-Five*; *Twilight Zone, The*; 1970s: *Carrie*; *Six Million Dollar Man, The*; 1980s: *Back to the Future*; *It*; 1990s: *Charmed*; *Craft, The*; *Harry Potter*; 2000s: *Divergent*; *Hunger Games, The*; *Twilight*; *Vampire Diaries, The*

Further Reading

Beaudoin, Julianna. 2015. "Exploring the Contemporary Relevance of 'Gypsy' Stereotypes in the Buffyverse." *The Journal of Popular Culture* 48 (2).

Holder, Nancy, and Lisa Clancy. 2017. *Buffy the Vampire Slayer Encyclopedia: The Ultimate Guide to the Buffyverse*. New York: Harper Design.

Magee, Sara. 2014. "High School Is Hell: The TV Legacy of Beverly Hills, 90210, and Buffy the Vampire Slayer." *Journal of Popular Culture* 47 (4).

CHARMED

Charmed (1998–2006) was a popular supernatural TV series that aired on the WB channel. The show features three modern-day witches living together in a family mansion in San Francisco. In *Charmed*, sisters Prue (Shannen Doherty), Piper (Holly Marie Combs), and Phoebe (Alyssa Milano) join forces to fight evil but try to keep their supernatural powers secret from others. Doherty's departure from the show after season three forced the writers to introduce half-sister Paige Matthews (Rose McGowan) who took Prue's place in order to maintain their abilities through the "Power of Three."

The term "witch" is fraught with images and connotations. For some, the word conjures the image of fictional witches that are associated with Halloween: the black pointy hat, the broomstick as flying device, green skin, and bubbling cauldrons. The very real history of witches and witchcraft, however, is quite disturbing in terms of its misogyny and violence. The Salem witch trials provide ample evidence of this. In the late 1600s in Salem, Massachusetts, mass hysteria broke out after accusations that several local women had displayed odd behaviors that were believed to have been linked to supernatural powers. The accused were brought before a council that was governed exclusively by men and determined to be either innocent or guilty of witchcraft. Even though the "evidence" in the trials was spectral (unsubstantiated testimony about dreams and visions), 19 people were convicted and hanged for their "crimes."

The witches in *Charmed* have much more in common with Wiccans than they do with those accused of witchcraft in the 1600s or the fictional witches of films like *The Wizard of Oz*. Wicca is a relatively new religion, though with ancient roots, that has gained considerable popularity over the past few decades. Unlike most formal religions, Wicca doesn't prioritize a central authority or singular deity. It's much more focused on the relationship between the individual and nature than between the individual and a sole, all-powerful, and all-knowing god. There are elements of magic within Wicca, but there is also a core belief that any harmful or malicious acts perpetrated against others will be revisited upon the perpetrator threefold. This relates to the three elements of the human: mind, body, and spirit. The producers of the show strived for authenticity and even had a licensed demonologist on staff to ensure that story lines were accurate based on occult beliefs and practices.

Teen girls are a receptive audience for the ideas and practices of Wicca because it views both genders equally, demonstrates concern and respect for the Earth, and offers a more inclusive and less restrictive worldview around areas of sexual behavior and orientation. In short, it's not oppressive and punitive with respect to personal choices.

Unlike some of their female counterparts in the "battling evil" business, witches are somewhat unique in their proactive nature and actions. Unlike the female protagonists in vampire-based stories such as *Twilight* and *True Blood*, witches tend to be assertive socially and even physically when necessary. They typically don't stay in the background and wait for a man to handle the problem. Witches typically tend to be more internally aware as well. Although, for example, the sisters in *Charmed* have romantic lives, they also focus on interpersonal relationships with one another. It's for these reasons and others that the term "witch" is often directed at strong-willed and powerful women in our culture. Teen girls connected with the strength and confidence of the three female leads.

Although the Haliwell sisters each have unique powers that enable them to fight evil forces, they are forced to keep these secret. Their special talents are invisible to the rest of the world. This, of course, can be viewed as a plot device to create and further subplots with possible male suitors and law enforcement personnel, but it can also be viewed as a metaphor for the work that women do that goes unnoticed or unrecognized within society as well. Additionally, Wicca has been subject to stigma throughout history, so some practitioners may keep their religious beliefs a secret.

Although *Charmed* featured strong-willed, independent young women who just happen to possess supernatural powers and abilities, there are sometimes reminders within the framework of the narrative that men are still in charge. In an episode entitled "Crimes and Witch-Demeanors," the sisters are forced to sit before a tribunal that will determine whether they are allowed to continue using their special powers or not due to alleged abuse. Although they ultimately aren't stripped of their collective magic, Phoebe is reprimanded and her powers are removed because she used some of them to advance her personal goals. She is reassured that she can regain these powers if she behaves. Rather than voice her opposition to this, she acquiesces and accepts it without a fight.

Charmed lured teen fans with its hip, updated depiction of witches living in a fashionable West Coast city. They were young, attractive, and had careers as well as romantic entanglements. Female teen viewers were intrigued with the lifestyles of the sisters and their exciting adventures. Much of the appeal was rooted in the strong family tie between them. Aesthetics were also important. Each sister had her own distinct personal style, and teens could identify with this and even be influenced to some degree by clothing choices made by the characters.

Since *Charmed* ended its network run in 2006, witches have become even more mainstream. The popular cable network FX featured an entire season of its hit show *American Horror Story* devoted to witches living in modern day Louisiana. *American Horror Story: Coven* examined issues of racism and relationships between women interwoven with a revenge tale that included voodoo and the casting of spells that resulted in violent deaths. The show portrayed both good and evil witches and created some empathy for the witches' plight by depicting them as descendants of those who survived the Salem witch trials.

Charmed developed a loyal following and spun-off into other media including novels, comic books, and soundtracks. A reboot of the show is currently under development at two separate networks.

See also: 1950s: *Blob, The*; *I Was a Teenage Werewolf*; 1960s: *Addams Family, The*; *Slaughterhouse-Five*; *Twilight Zone, The*; 1970s: *Carrie*; *Six Million Dollar Man, The*;

1980s: *Back to the Future*; *It*; 1990s: *Buffy the Vampire Slayer*; *Craft, The*; 2000s: *Divergent*; *Hunger Games, The*; *Twilight*; *Vampire Diaries, The*

Further Reading

Feasey, Rebecca. 2005. "The 'Charmed' Audience: Gender and the Politics of Contemporary Culture." *USC*, Fall. http://cinema.usc.edu/assets/097/15720.pdf.

Gibson, Megan. 2013. "Witches Are the New Vampires—and That's a Good Thing." *Time*, November 11. http://entertainment.time.com/2013/11/11/witches-are-the-new-vampires-and-thats-a-good-thing/.

Kelly, Kim. 2017. "Are Witches the Ultimate Feminists?" *The Guardian*, July 5. https://www.theguardian.com/books/2017/jul/05/witches-feminism-books-kristin-j-sollee.

CLARISSA EXPLAINS IT ALL

Clarissa Explains It All (1991–1994) was a teen-centered sitcom on the popular children's television network, Nickelodeon. The show focused on the exploits of the title character and her family and friends. Clarissa Darling (Melissa Joan Hart, 1976–) is a high school student living in a small town in Ohio. She has an annoying younger brother, Ferguson (Jason Zimbler), who frequently gets into squabbles with her, and parents Janet and Marshall (Elizabeth Hess and Joe O'Connor) who are portrayed as socially and environmentally conscious middle-aged hippies. The series received a lot of attention when it premiered because it was one of the first shows on the network that featured a teenage girl as the lead character. In addition, the network also produced two other female-centric shows, *As Told by Ginger* and *Nick News*. The former was another situational comedy and the latter was a news show focused on children's issues and produced and hosted by seasoned journalist Linda Ellerbee.

The 1990s were the decade of "girl power." Although that term was originally intended to reflect the internal strength and talents and abilities of women, some argued that it became more of a marketing slogan to sell products to young women under the guise of self-empowerment. Some of this criticism was directly aimed at the all-girl pop group, the Spice Girls, whom some believed to be nothing more than a gimmicky and manufactured product created to exploit young girls' needs to feel represented within the media.

In that light, it's worth noting that *Clarissa Explains It All* made inroads for feminists and provided positive female gender portrayals within media productions. Many shows featuring young girls historically tended to make their central theme one of "How do I get a boy to notice me?" or "How do I land a boyfriend?" However, that was not central to this show. For one, Clarissa's best friend is a boy, but he's not her boyfriend. This may not seem terribly significant, but it was progressive. Analyses of sitcoms that include teen girls prior to this typically define friendships as exclusive between two women or girls. When boys are introduced to a plot, it's usually to generate romantic interest or tension.

As for her personality, Clarissa is quirky, but she's also clever and verbal. She is smart and does not have to rely on men to help her navigate challenging situations or avert crises. Additionally, Clarissa routinely breaks the fourth wall and addresses the audience directly. This allows audience members to feel closer to the character as she shares her thoughts and ideas directly with them. In a nod to another contemporary, female-centric sitcom, Clarissa references *Murphy Brown* in an episode entitled "The Last Episode." *Murphy Brown* was a popular network sitcom that featured actress Candace Bergen as an assertive, self-confident television reporter. This episode's focus was on the difficult choice that Clarissa has to make between accepting an internship offer from a newspaper or going off to college. Presenting this type of story line can be viewed as positive because it demonstrates that women—or more specifically, young girls—have professional options. They have value outside of the home and are able to make their own decisions regarding their futures. Clarissa was relatable to teen girls as she embodied many of their desires and aspirations beyond boys and high school.

One argument that has been made against *Clarissa Explains It All* is that a series like this cannot further feminism because it's a commercial product or commodity designed for a mass audience. This viewpoint stems from the very real differences between second- and third-wave feminism. Second-wave feminism contends that mainstream media largely ignores women and women's issues, and, when it isn't ignoring them, it's exploiting them for commercial gain. Third-wave feminism doesn't necessarily subscribe to this belief. While *Clarissa Explains It All* can certainly be categorized as a mainstream media production, it is produced on a network that regularly features young girls and women in positive roles. Those subscribing to third-wave feminism don't necessarily view mass media as the enemy. Instead, they see it as an opportunity for women to have a platform. Ideally, women are involved in all stages of the process from creation and development of content to producing and directing and starring in these presentations.

Much of this debate centers on a key question: can women be part of a system that historically has relegated them to secondary positions? Is the concept of "girl power" real or is it simply a fad that is inextricably linked to market segmentation and profitability?

Perhaps the most revolutionary part of *Clarissa Explains It All* was its popularity with young male viewers. Conventional wisdom has always contended that, while young girls might be interested in watching shows with young boys as lead characters, the reverse simply wasn't true. This spoke to the crossover appeal of the title character.

After the show ended its run, Nickelodeon produced other shows featuring young women as leads: *The Secret World of Alex Mack*, *The Amanda Show*, and *The Mystery Files of Shelby Woo*.

See also: 1950s: *Adventures of Ozzie and Harriet, The*; *Father Knows Best*; *I Love Lucy*; *Leave It to Beaver*; 1960s: *Patty Duke Show, The*; 1970s: *Happy Days*; *Welcome Back, Kotter*; 1980s: *Back to the Future*; *Cosby Show, The*; *Facts of Life, The*; *Family Ties*; *Full House*; *Saved by the Bell*; *Wonder Years, The*; 1990s: *Boy Meets World*; *7th Heaven*; *Spice Girls*; 2000s: *Friday Night Lights*

Further Reading

Hart, Melissa Joan. 2013. *Melissa Explains It All: Tales from My Abnormally Normal Life*. New York: St. Martin's Press.

Rankin, Sieja. 2016. "How Clarissa Explains It All Started TV's Girl-Power Movement." *E News*, March 3. http://www.eonline.com/news/745102/how-clarissa-explains-it-all -started-tv-s-girl-power-movement.

Vagianos, Alanna. 2015. "'Clarissa Explains It All'—Even White Supremacy." Huffington Post, January 12. https://www.huffingtonpost.com/2015/01/12/clarissa-explains-it-all -white-privilege-meme_n_6443048.html.

CLUELESS

Clueless (1995), a comedy loosely based on the classic novel *Emma* by Jane Austen, follows the adventures of a wealthy Beverly Hills teen named Cher Horowitz (Alicia Silverstone). Cher and her friend Dionne (Stacey Dash) are two of the most popular girls at their high school. Attractive and spoiled, they spend their time and energy shopping for the latest fashions at the mall and seem relatively clueless to the world around them. In a self-serving move, Cher attempts to play matchmaker for a pair of teachers, with the ulterior motive being the desire to have a poor grade renegotiated. The scheme works, but it triggers an internal conflict in Cher that forces her to reexamine her own sense of values.

Now on a spiritual mission to do something truly kind, Cher embarks on yet another project, this one involving a new and unpopular girl at school named Tai Frasier (Brittany Murphy). She and Dionne take on the task of giving Tai a makeover, which isn't just a physical makeover; their efforts extend into Tai's behavior and even her romantic life. After a series of adventures and missteps, Cher realizes that she is actually attracted to her ex-stepbrother, Josh (Paul Rudd), a nonmaterial idealist

Alicia Silverstone as pampered teen Cher Horowitz in *Clueless*. The '90s comedy, an updated re-telling of Jane Austen's *Emma*, chronicled the romantic misadventures of Cher and her materialistic friends. (Paramount Pictures/Getty Images)

who visits when he's home from college. By film's end, Cher embraces the relationship as she discovers that Josh has similar feelings.

Clueless spawned a number of teen films in the late 1990s that were based on classic texts and marketed successfully toward a youth market. These stories were updated and set in modern times and took liberties with plot points, but the central theme or message remained intact. Without *Clueless*, it's doubtful there would have been films like *She's All That* (1999) or *Cruel Intentions* (1999). Additionally, these films prompted teen interest in their source material as many students—especially female students—expressed that seeing films like *Clueless* sparked interest in seeking out the classic novels on which they were based.

In *Clueless*, there is much attention paid to optics. In addition to the stylish and pricey clothes worn by Cher and Dionne, Cher's home is impressive; its size and furnishings are far more lavish than a typical teen's home. Cher is given whatever she wants by her wealthy litigator father, Mel Horowitz (Dan Hedaya), and lacks for nothing—except a romantic partner of her own.

The reach of *Clueless* extended far beyond movie theaters. Originally conceived as an ill-fated television show, *Clueless* became a catalyst for additional media products. The film spawned a TV series by the same name that ran for four seasons split across two different networks. It also produced 16 novelizations of the show that followed Cher and other characters into new situations and settings. Dolls based on the two central characters soon followed. National retail chain Wet Seal even created a line of clothes for their stories that were tie-ins to the fashions from the TV show. This multimedia strategy is noteworthy because these types of franchises have historically been limited to male-centric media vehicles. *Clueless* demonstrated that female-centric, teen films could be financially successful when marketed and promoted successfully. Furthermore, it proved that its fans would continue to follow the characters across other platforms and even purchase items associated with the film. Whether or not characters like Cher and Dionne empower young women is debatable, but what is not debatable is that films with female-focused casts and plots can generate box office profits and garner a fan base that is willing to spend money on associated products.

Language is a key element of *Clueless*. Part of the film's enduring appeal is its innate ability to mimic how a certain segment of teens speak (or did at the time the film was made). Filmmaker Amy Heckerling devoted significant research to making this aspect of the film authentic by observing teens in hangouts including malls, skate parks, and even high schools. Additionally, Cher's father likely had an impact on her astute vocabulary given his occupation. She is prone to hyperbole and frequently overdramatizes mundane events. She and her friends use terms and phrases that parents and authority figures presumably would not be familiar with. This is used to create much of the comedy in the film. Additionally, for a teen film, *Clueless* relies heavily on verbal references for laughs as opposed to physical comedy. The film's dialogue is so revered by fans that "quote along" screenings have taken place where audience members recite lines from the film along with the characters. Some of the more memorable quotes include Cher's description of individuals who are attractive from a distance but not as much on closer inspection (a "Monet") and boys who are physically attractive ("Baldwins").

Clueless received overall positive reviews with most critics noting its witty dialogue and appealing performances. Alicia Silverstone received accolades in the role of Cher and won several awards including *National Board of Review's* Best Breakthrough Performer and Best Female Performance at the MTV Movie Awards. Heckerling's script also was nominated for several national awards.

See also: 1970s: *National Lampoon's Animal House*; 1980s: *Fast Times at Ridgemont High*; Hughes, John, Films of; *Revenge of the Nerds*; *Risky Business*; *Say Anything . . .*; 1990s: *American Pie*; *Dazed and Confused*; *She's All That*; 2000s: *Bring It On*; *Gossip Girl*; *Mean Girls*

Further Reading

Chaney, Jen. 2015. *As If: The Oral History of Clueless as Told by Amy Heckerling and the Cast and Crew*. New York: Touchstone.

Leppert, Alice. 2014. "'Can I Please Give You Some Advice?' Clueless and the Teen Makeover." *Cinema Journal* 53 (3).

O'Meara. Jennifer. 2014. "We've Got to Work on Your Accent and Vocabulary: Characterization through Verbal Style in Clueless." *Cinema Journal* 53 (3).

CRAFT, THE

The Craft (1996), which was directed by Andrew Fleming, was one of several movies and television shows about witches in the 1990s. It focused on a group of four high school girls who banded together in order to maximize their supernatural powers. A new transfer student, Sarah Bailey (Robin Tunney) arrives at her new high school after she and her father and stepmother move from San Francisco to Los Angeles. Sarah is warned by classmates about a trio of girls known as "the b****** of Eastwick" and is advised to stay away from them. Sarah, of course, gravitates to them, and they quickly become friends. Bonnie (Neve Campbell), Nancy (Fairuza Balk), and Rochelle (Rachel True) inform Sarah that they have special powers and worship a god named Manon who controls the universe. Sarah reveals that she also has powers—she was born with them as she inherited them from her mother—and when she collaborates with the other girls, they soon discover that their power is significantly magnified.

While many earlier media treatments of witches were either humorous or overtly evil, this film depicted them in a straightforward style, acknowledging the typical challenges that teenage girls face. Sarah is humiliated by Chris (Skeet Ulrich) for whom she has romantic feelings; Bonnie suffers from low self-esteem and body image issues due to severe scarring from burns; Rochelle is the target of racist bullying by a classmate; and Nancy is poor and abused by her stepfather. These are problems that many teenagers deal with, which made the four characters sympathetic. These are not the menacing witches with pointy hats and rotten teeth and warts that inhabited earlier works of fiction, especially in children's fairy tales.

Rather, the witches in *The Craft* feel isolated and confused about how to navigate through adolescence. And while they face the same issues that many of their more earthly counterparts do, they are afforded opportunities otherwise unavailable once they discover and capitalize on their newfound cumulative powers.

By working together all of their obstacles are overcome: they place spells on both their enemies and their objects of affection. But as their magic is resoundingly successful, things start to backfire. For example, Rochelle feels sorry for her bully, and Chris can't manage his emotions for Sarah and attempts to rape her. As things dissolve, Nancy becomes obsessed with retaining and even strengthening her powers, doing things that Sarah objects to. However, after she kills Chris, the group starts to splinter, and Nancy, Rochelle, and Bonnie all turn on Sarah, trying to convince her to commit suicide. Ultimately, Sarah defeats them and Nancy ends up in a psychiatric hospital, apparently stripped of her special powers. She is last seen restrained, ranting, and raving, while a nurse prepares an injection to calm her.

On the one hand, the film seems to celebrate the outcast status of these young women, and presents them as powerful and able to determine their own destinies. In a culture where men still dominate and predefined gender roles still exist, it's refreshing to see women in the role of the powerful as opposed to the powerless. However, things soon revert back to the status quo when the girls turn on each other and cease working together. Rather than harnessing their collective power for good, egos override cooperation. One can argue that this is merely a teen-targeted thriller and the plot, while predictable, isn't antifemale or antifeminism. An oppositional viewpoint, though, is that the girls are punished when they are able to gain power. To take that even further, a possible reading of the film is that girls are *unable* to control power once they possess it. One possible takeaway is that only good, well-behaved girls are deserving of power. Still, putting four young women at the center of a movie who find success together shows the power of female friendship.

The Craft, in order to have an accurate and authentic depiction of Wicca, hired a Wiccan consultant to ensure that they were on point; while it depicts a fictionalized view of Witchcraft, or Wicca, it also drew on a number of actual practices that witches use. Wicca is a nature-oriented religion practiced by many men and women; some practice alone, and others practice together in covens as the girls in the movie do. Some practitioners have a less formal approach and consider it a loose form of spirituality. However, other practitioners have a set and ordered spiritual practice. Additionally, practitioners utilize objects that either have power or represent power: candles, salt, incense, athames, and so on. As in the film, there are rituals, including the casting of spells, which practitioners believe have spiritual prayer, as Christians do with prayer.

The Craft, along with TV shows like *Sabrina the Teenage Witch* and *Charmed*, presented witches and Wicca in a more normalized manner than their predecessors, arguably changing the genre. Furthermore, previous Hollywood renderings of witchcraft focused on the individuals and did not consider Wicca in context. Story lines—especially in the media presentations mentioned above—examined how self-discovery empowered these witches to take control and solve problems, large and small. These characters had personalities both separate from and related to their powers.

The Craft was a surprise box office hit, raking in more than $50 million and produced on a budget of approximately $15 million. A straight-to-DVD sequel was tentatively planned but was never produced.

See also: 1950s: *Blob, The*; *I Was a Teenage Werewolf*; 1960s: *Addams Family, The*; *Slaughterhouse-Five*; *Twilight Zone, The*; 1970s: *Carrie*; *Six Million Dollar Man, The*; 1980s: *Back to the Future*; *It*; 1990s: *Buffy the Vampire Slayer*; *Charmed*; 2000s: *Divergent*; *Hunger Games, The*; *Twilight*; *Vampire Diaries, The*

Further Reading

Lagace, Lisa. 2016. "How 'The Craft' Changed the Game for Female-Driven Teen Films." *Marie Claire*, October 27. http://www.marieclaire.com/culture/news/a23254/the-craft-female-driven-teen-films/.

Stubbins, Sinead. 2016. "'We Are the Weirdos, Mister': The Craft and the Year of the Teen Witch." *AV Club*, May 3. https://film.avclub.com/we-are-the-weirdos-mister-the-craft-and-the-year-of-1798246863.

VanArendonk, Kathryn. 2017. "Why the Witch Is the Pop-Culture Heroine We Need Right Now." *Vulture*, October 25. http://www.vulture.com/2017/10/why-the-witch-is-the-pop-culture-heroine-we-need-right-now.html.

DAZED AND CONFUSED

Although it was a commercial disappointment when originally released theatrically, *Dazed and Confused* (1993) has gone on to become a cult hit with fans. The comedy takes place over a single day in the lives of a large group of teenagers on their final day of school. One of the film's primary characters, Randall "Pink" Floyd (Jason London), is being coerced into signing a pledge that forbids him from taking drugs in solidarity with the high school football team, for which he is the star player. Other subplots include naive freshman Mitch Kramer (Wiley Wiggins) who drinks and smokes pot for the first time, a revenge scheme to punish a mean senior who delights in hazing incoming students, and several budding romances.

Director Richard Linklater is known for his unstructured style of storytelling. Born in Austin, Texas, the filmmaker has built his career on a unique approach to making movies. Rather than being drawn to big-budget spectacles, Linklater has focused on films that showcase life's "smaller moments." Even in his early efforts, the director expressed interest in minimalism with respect to the technicality of film. His trademark in the film industry is that of experimentation. Two of his moves, *Waking Life* and *A Scanner Darkly*, employed innovative techniques that blended live action with animation to produce a unique visual experience for audiences. Furthermore, Linklater is regarded as a visionary filmmaker. This is noteworthy because he often tells stories that seem to have little if any direction but almost always provide insight into the minds of their characters.

As with most of Linklater's films, the plot isn't as relevant as the implied bigger issues, the central one being the issue of challenging authoritarianism. The appeal of defying authority is always a popular theme within teen-oriented productions. A major example of this in the film is whether or not Randall will succumb to the demands of his coach—hence the school's power structure—and refrain from doing drugs. If he does take drugs, it could be that he is succumbing to peer pressure, or perhaps because he feels he is "thumbing his nose" at adult authority. It's also possible that he would do it simply because he's a teenager and wants to experiment, another issue relevant to teen audiences.

Although the film takes place in Austin, Texas, *Dazed and Confused*—along with many coming-of-age films—is largely independent of the locale in which it was set. Much of the film takes place a local pool hall called the Emporium. When activity there winds down, the action moves to an outdoor keg party where a fight occurs. Randall is confronted there by another player about his refusal to sign the pledge. Then, near the end of the film, Randall and several of his friends end up smoking marijuana on the 50-yard line of the school's football field. These locales represent typical teen hangouts for a large portion of the country and are especially relatable for Midwestern and Southern teen audiences.

The symbolism of this act of defiance taking place on school grounds and, more specifically, at the location of the football games is fairly obvious. And as it turns out, the rebellion does not go unnoticed. After the police are called, they contact the football coach, who is subsequently in touch with Randall. Randall then tells him that, although he may continue to play on the team, he will not sign the anti-drug pledge. This assertion of his autonomy and refusal to cave in to an authority figure is an indicator of his growth as an individual. This independence and rebellion especially resonates with younger viewers who are discovering their own identities and voices during this transitional time.

Although the film fared poorly at the box office, it garnered glowing reviews from a wide range of critics. *Rolling Stone* awarded the film a perfect rating (four out of four stars), and *Entertainment Weekly* bestowed an "A" grade upon it. Once released on video, the movie found a wider audience and eventually reached cult status. Among its breakout stars was a young Matthew McConaughey, who played the role of David Wooderson, a friend of Randall's in his 20s who still hangs out with high schoolers. Another rising star was Ben Affleck who played the role of Fred O'Bannion, a doltish senior who revels in the hazing tradition that torments younger students.

The film has appeared on several prominent "Best of" lists and continues to attract new viewers even 20 years after its theatrical release.

See also: 1970s: *National Lampoon's Animal House*; 1980s: *Fast Times at Ridgemont High*; Hughes, John, Films of; *Revenge of the Nerds*; *Risky Business*; *Say Anything . . .*; 1990s: *American Pie*; *Clueless*; *She's All That*; 2000s: *Bring It On*; *Mean Girls*

Further Reading

Gleiberman, Owen. 1993. "Dazed and Confused: EW Review." *Entertainment Weekly*, September 24. http://ew.com/article/1993/09/24/dazed-and-confused-4/.

Lambie, Ryan. 2015. "A History of Stoners in Film." Den of Geek, http://www.denofgeek .com/movies/movie-stoners/36744/a-history-of-stoners-in-film.

Stone, Rob. 2013. *The Cinema of Richard Linklater: Walk, Don't Run*. London: Wallflower Press.

Travers, Peter. 1993. "Dazed and Confused." *Rolling Stone*, September 24. http://www .rollingstone.com/movies/reviews/dazed-and-confused-19930924.

FREAKS AND GEEKS

Freaks and Geeks (1999), a network comedy, aired for only one season on NBC. But like other shows that find a second life years (or even decades) later, it has become a cult favorite on DVD and streaming services. The show heavily reflects the experiences of its creator, Paul Feig. Feig grew up in a small Midwestern town; the series is set in the fictional town of Chippewa, Michigan. The series' two main characters were siblings Lindsay (Linda Cardellini) and Sam Weir (John Francis Daley). Lindsay is a star pupil who is determined to change her image, so she starts hanging out with a group of students known for being problematic. Her younger brother Sam navigates the social universe of high school with his nerdy group of friends. Both characters are very relatable for adolescent audiences.

Feig envisioned a show that was honest about the pain of the high school experience. Rather than focusing on popular kids and predictable rites of passage in a proven format, the plan was to develop characters that the average high schooler could relate to. *Freaks and Geeks*, then, was not created for the jocks or the cheerleaders; it was created for the outcasts and those struggling just to make it through high school before pursuing other life goals. However, Feig's insistence on creating authentic high school characters and plots that didn't gloss over the harsh realities of high school life made for clashes with the network after a management change at NBC.

The show's executive producer, Judd Apatow, fully supported Feig and his approach to storytelling. The two were amazed that the show was bought by the network as is. Feig felt that the show's characters should be shown failing at things just as people do in real life. However, this commitment to authenticity fell on deaf ears, as the management at NBC didn't seem to understand the public high school experience. Although there are several reasons that might explain the show's low ratings and swift cancellation, Feig and Apatow both contend that the network never supported it or made any real efforts to promote it effectively.

Freaks and Geeks covered familiar terrain: a teen smoking pot for the first time, school bullying, underage drinking, vandalism, love triangles, academic struggles, and so on. Although the show takes place in the early 1980s, the themes are universal. A recurring theme of the show is that of disappointment: disappointment in parents' faltering marriage, disappointment when one's talents aren't as great as one had hoped, disappointment in discovering that the object of one's desire is boring or unappealing. The show didn't flinch from the ugliness and awkwardness of trying to find one's own voice during a very difficult life stage. Because of this, many teen viewers saw characters who were very much like themselves on the show, many of whom had not had that experience before. The focus of the series on those existing within the margins, rather than the traditional popular crowd, offered deeper insight into the lives of young characters who are often overlooked or discounted. This made the show a favorite for many.

Feig and Apatow survived the failure of the show to get renewed beyond its initial season. NBC ran 15 of the 18 completed episodes; the final 3 were shown on another network. Despite this, the show launched the careers of several well-known actors including James Franco, Seth Rogen, and Jason Segel. Linda Cardellini went on to star in the hit show *ER* on the same network. Judd Apatow has gone on to become one of the most commercially successful directors in film comedies. His hit films include *The 40-Year-Old Virgin*, *Knocked Up*, and *Trainwreck*. Feig directed several smash hit movies including *Bridesmaids*, *The Heat,* and *Spy*. Many of these films are extremely popular with young audiences.

The legacy of *Freaks and Geeks* is evident in the critical acclaim it has received since its short life on network television. *TV Guide* included it in its list of "The 60 Greatest Dramas of All Time" and also crowned it as the number one show that was canceled too soon. It also received accolades from a variety of magazines and newspapers for being a quality program. The series was also nominated for three Primetime Emmy Awards and two Television Critics Association Awards, though Apatow has expressed disappointment that the show never found its audience when it initially aired on NBC. The release of the series on DVD and streaming platforms has allowed for renewed interest in the show and has opened it up for a whole new audience to appreciate.

See also: 1980s: Hughes, John, Films of; *Revenge of the Nerds*; *Saved by the Bell*; *Say Anything . . .*; *Wonder Years, The*; 1990s: *Boy Meets World*; *Clarissa Explains It All*; *Freaks and Geeks*; 2000s: *Friday Night Lights*; *Juno*; *Napoleon Dynamite*

Further Reading

Koski, Genevieve. 2012. "Paul Feig Walks Us through Freaks and Geeks." *AV Club*, April 9. https://tv.avclub.com/paul-feig-walks-us-through-freaks-and-geeks-part-1-of-1798230923.

Lloyd, Robert. 2012. "2 Good 2 Be 4Gotten: An Oral History of *Freaks and Geeks*." *Vanity Fair*. https://www.vanityfair.com/hollywood/2013/01/freaks-and-geeks-oral-history.

Stiernberg, Bonnie. 2014. "On Freaks and Geeks, the Most Relatable High-School Show of All Time." *Paste Magazine*, October 3. https://www.pastemagazine.com/articles/2014/10/on-freaks-and-geeks-the-most-relatable-high-school.html.

GRAND THEFT AUTO

The *Grand Theft Auto* (*GTA*) video game series is one of the most popular series in the history of gaming. The original *Grand Theft Auto* was released in 1997 for MS Windows, and later was adapted for other operating systems and devices such as

PlayStation. It was a resounding success and has since spawned multiple entries in its series, enhancing both the visual and storytelling elements with each new addition. The series features excessive violence and criminal activities in a variety of fictional settings that resemble American cities. In the first few entries in the series, there was very limited character/avatar development, but in later installments, story lines and characters are more fully fleshed out.

The *GTA* series is an "open world" game where the player has a lot of autonomy and can make decisions that alter the trajectory of the game and the experience. For example, although the primary objective may be to rise through the ranks of organized crime in order to avenge an enemy, all sorts of secondary options exist throughout the narrative journey. Although the main story line is linear, players can detour into other activities that include car racing and various criminal acts such as theft and assault.

GTA and similar games hold strong appeal for teenage boys. There are various theories as to why they are drawn to these types of games, but many of the elements are historically steeped in gender stereotypes. Many young men become fascinated with fast cars and rebellious activities as they develop. There has long been a link between fast cars and the dangerous activity of drag racing. Although it started in the 1950s, it's still popular today among fans of NASCAR and other auto racing. Adding in elements of violence and property crimes enhances the appeal of the game to rebellious young men; some teens may feel empowered while playing these games when they aren't empowered in other aspects of their lives such as at school or home.

Although the origins of video games can be tied directly to the U.S. military, where they were designed and used primarily for training purposes, people have argued that now they have blurred the lines between virtual reality and the material world. Technological advances have enabled these games to become more and more realistic in their depictions of violent acts and sexual activities. To that end, the effect of violent video games on both teens and adults remains a topic of extensive academic research. While numerous studies have focused on causality—i.e., does exposure to violent video game content actually cause or contribute to violent behavior—not as many studies have focused on how this activity might affect criminal *thinking*.

One study (Crosby, Porter, and Shaw 2014) related to the issue of the potential effects of exposure to violent video game content on players failed to prove an explicit connection. The primary hypothesis of the study—"that criminal media would alter explicit criminal thinking, was not substantiated. Both criminal news clips and video gameplay did not produce a significant change in self-reported criminal thinking patterns." However, there was some indication that there may be *implicit* effects.

The results of the study seem to indicate that individuals exposed to even short periods of time playing violent video games may engage in "me"-centered criminal thinking. The researchers used four groups: Group 1 viewed neutral news content, Group 2 viewed news content with references to violence, Group 3 played a nonviolent version of *Grand Theft Auto*, and Group 4 played the version of *Grand Theft Auto* with violent content. To differentiate between the two versions, participants were given a specific task to *accomplish*. For example, when a Group 3 player might be told to speak to a shop person, a Group 4 player would be told to physically assault the shop person.

There were limitations to this study as there are in any study. However, the results are in sync with many other formal studies that have previously been done. It is a very different experience to watch or witness a violent act than it is to participate in one, even if done so virtually. In order to act out a violent behavior in a video game, the player must be willing to suspend a moral code or to agree to participate in antisocial behavior. Again, this in no way implies a causal effect or contends that exposure to violent video games like *Grand Theft Auto* is a reliable indicator of future violent acts, but it does raise relevant questions about the quantity of time spent playing these types of games and their cumulative possible effect on an individual's propensity to describe their actions with criminal adjectives.

Grand Theft Auto and the virtual realities created by the franchise have strong ties to Hollywood gangster films. *Grand Theft Auto: San Andreas* especially has origins in earlier movies related to gang activity such as *Boyz N the Hood* and *Menace II Society*. This may explain in part the series's popularity with tween and teenage boys. The depiction of physical and mental toughness and propensity to solve problems with violence perpetuates long-standing myths about how men are expected to behave within our culture and what it means to be a "man" in Western society. In *GTA: San Andreas*, the primary character, Carl Johnson, is the victim of police brutality and is framed for murder. The mission of the game is to help him find remaining family members, bring them to safety, and reestablish order in his old neighborhood. This character detail is significant because Carl doesn't begin the story as a criminal, but, because of circumstances, he is prompted into committing criminal acts in order to survive.

The *Grand Theft Auto* franchise, while financially successful and lauded for its game design, continues to be a source of controversy because of violent, misogynist, and racist content. The original entry in the series was condemned internationally for its violent content, and multiple lawsuits have been brought against its publisher, Rock Star Games. Perpetrators in several violent crimes referenced the game as a source of influence on or inspiration for their behavior. More research undoubtedly will occur in the area of violent video games and their potential negative effects on their players. In the meantime, the audience for *Grand Theft Auto* and other similar games doesn't appear to be waning.

See also: 2000s: *Call of Duty*

Further Reading

Crosby, Kimberly, Stephen Porter, and Julia Shaw. 2014. "The Impact of a Video Game on Criminal Thinking: Implicit and Explicit Measures." *Simulation and Gaming* 45 (6).

Garrelts, Nate. 2006. *Meaning and Culture of Grand Theft Auto: Critical Essays*. Jefferson, NC: McFarland.

Morris, Chris. 2013. "New 'Grand Theft Auto' Finds New Ways to Outrage Critics." CNBC, September 19. https://www.cnbc.com/2013/09/19/new-grand-theft-auto-finds-new-ways-to-outrage-critics.html.

GREEN DAY

Green Day, a punk and pop hybrid band, was formed in 1986 by friends Billie Joe Armstrong (1972–) and Mike Dirnt (1972–). Since then, Green Day has become synonymous with the term "protest music," and with the production of the Broadway musical *American Idiot* (based on their multiplatinum album of the same name), they have reached an entirely new audience that is receptive to the group's political messages. Other band members include drummer Frank Edwin Wright III (1972–), also known as Tré Cool, and guitarist Jason White (1973–), who has been a touring member with the band since 1999.

The band got its start in the punk rock scene in Berkeley, California. They recorded several studio albums with the independent label Lookout! Records before earning widespread acclaim and popularity with the release of their first major studio album, *Dookie*. Aided by heavy video promotion for the singles "Longview" and "Basket Case" on MTV and significant airplay on radio stations, the album soared in sales and the singles reached number one on Modern Rock charts. The group's overall look and sound appealed to teen listeners, and the theme of malaise examined in the single "Longview" was tailor made for discontented youths.

The band's musical influences range from punk rock and alternative rock groups like Hüsker Dü and the Replacements to classic rock bands like the Who and the Kinks. Although *Dookie* contained songs about apathy and angst that were clearly aimed at a young audience, the songs were largely apolitical. The band's popularity grew quickly, and *Dookie* eventually reached Diamond status in sales (10 million copies). The follow-up record, *Insomniac,* was released in 1995 and sold approximately 2 million copies. Although the album won critical accolades for its dark tone, it lacked the melodic playfulness of the band's earlier effort. As with *Dookie,* though, it was nominated for several Grammy awards and American Music Awards.

In subsequent years, the band released several studio albums to mixed commercial and critical success. They remained popular, but it seemed uncertain that they would ever again achieve the success or "buzz" of that first major studio release. Although the band retained some level of pop cultural relevance, album sales declined and it looked as though Green Day might fade into relative obscurity. But things turned around quickly when the band released its fourth studio album, *American Idiot,* in September 2004, a few months prior to the American presidential election and reelection of George W. Bush.

American Idiot can be described as a punk rock opera in a similar vein to the Who's rock opera, *Tommy*. The album is an arc of connected songs that tells a story.

Known for their politically geared music, American punk rock group Green Day first gained recognition in the 1990s but have continued to remain popular. Their career-defining album, *American Idiot* was adapted into a hit Broadway musical in 2010. (Photo by Robert Knight Archive/Redferns/Getty Images)

It follows the journey of Jesus of Suburbia, a fictional character, who attempts to make sense of his environment and relationships in the midst of turmoil and confusion. Additionally, the album was filled with voices of disillusionment, anger, and apathy. It spoke to teenagers who felt their voices hadn't been heard and their concerns had been minimized or dismissed. These were individuals who felt they had been indoctrinated into fervent patriotism after the terrorist attacks of September 11 and the resulting wars that America became embroiled in shortly thereafter. Their futures seemed uncertain as they struggled to acclimate to a new normal of global terror alerts. The American economy was roaring back to life, but discontent and heightened tensions dominated the cultural landscape during this period, and many teens especially felt unsettled. *American Idiot* was for them a source of solace and understanding.

Although the album produced several hit singles, it was much more ambitious than anything the group had done previously, and this is illustrated especially by the inclusion of the nine-minute song, "Jesus of Suburbia." Given the business and practical implications of producing hit records, a format is followed within the industry. Songs played on terrestrial (nonsatellite) radio must adhere to specific rules: they are free from profanity and generally are three minutes or less in length. "Jesus of Suburbia" breaks both of these rules.

American Idiot was a phenomenal commercial and critical success for the band, selling more than 16 million copies worldwide. It reinforced the punk rock credibility of Green Day but also broadened the band's appeal with a concept album that touched on the divided state of the nation in 2004. The effort stemmed partly from a desire on the part of Armstrong and other band members to create memorable lyrics that would stand the test of time—relevant enough to connect with listeners but not so narrow that they might later seem dated.

Armstrong had become politically outspoken by the time *American Idiot* was being recorded and released and was very vocal about his opposition to both the Iraq War and policies of George W. Bush. Even though Green Day had always self-identified as a punk band, this album cemented their place in musical history in terms of its breadth and depth and its ability to give voice to a generation of disillusioned young men and women. Politically motivated teens began to gravitate toward the group. Among fans, it was suddenly fashionable to be interested in politics and socioeconomic issues even though many of them might not have been old enough to vote at the time the record was released.

The single "American Idiot" was a direct criticism of what Armstrong believed to be a culpable and lazy media who failed to speak truth to political power and the mindless citizenry who allowed a false sense of patriotism to cloud their judgment regarding what was happening within the country at that time. Other hit singles from the album included the title track, "Wake Me Up When September Ends," "Boulevard of Broken Dreams," and "Holiday." The album won Best Rock Album at the 2005 Grammy Awards and also snagged a win for Record of the Year for the single, "Boulevard of Broken Dreams."

The album was adapted into a successful Broadway musical in 2010 and there are plans for a film adaptation in 2017 from HBO. Green Day continues to tour and record music. Their most current studio album, *Revolution Radio*, was released in 2016.

See also: 1960s: Doors, The; Rolling Stones, The; 1970s: Clash, The; Devo; Led Zeppelin; Queen; 1980s: Blondie; Boy George; Duran Duran; Madonna; MTV; 2000s: My Chemical Romance

Further Reading

Fricke, David. 2014. "'Dookie' at 20: Billie Joe Armstrong on Green Day's Punk Blockbuster." *Rolling Stone*, February 3. http://www.rollingstone.com/music/news/dookie-at-20-billie-joe-armstrong-on-green-days-punk-blockbuster-20140203.

Myers, Ben. 2005. *Green Day: American Idiots and the New Punk Explosion*. New York: Disinformation Books.

Spitz, Mark. 2007. *Nobody Likes You: Inside the Turbulent Life, Times, and Music of Green Day*. New York: Hachette.

HARRY POTTER

Few book series in the history of publishing have had the pop cultural impact that the *Harry Potter* series has. Although author J. K. Rowling (1965–) didn't necessarily have a target age demographic in mind when she wrote the original novel, the publisher immediately recognized a significant opportunity to market the book to a youth audience. Published in Great Britain shortly before it was published in the United States, Scholastic turned the novel and its subsequent titles into phenomenal best sellers, garnering critical praise and unprecedented popularity among its legions of fans.

The fantasy series of novels—seven in all—follow the journey of Harry and his friends Ron Weasley and Hermione Granger, all three attending Hogwarts School of Witchcraft and Wizardry. Each novel covers one year in Harry's life as he and his fellow students experience a number of adventures. The primary villain in the saga is Lord Voldemort, an evil wizard who plans to become immortal and reign over both wizards and muggles (humans with no supernatural abilities).

Since the novels deal in a fantasy world with magical beings and mysticism, they were met with derision and condemnation by some conservative religious groups. Some critics argued that the books promoted witchcraft and Satanism and were heretical to organized religion, specifically Christianity. But other religious scholars and followers argue that the *Harry Potter* books actually reflect values and lessons adhered to by traditional Christians. They argue that, while formal religion may be losing ground among millennials, *Harry Potter* fans still have a strong interest in spirituality and connections with their fellow human beings. Readers of Harry Potter are able to navigate spiritual issues and seek answers within the realm of fiction that they might not otherwise investigate or challenge. Furthermore, the case has been made that religious leaders and followers shouldn't reject works like *Harry Potter* simply because they operate in a fantasy realm.

The *Harry Potter* books operate both within the material world and a parallel magical world. While wizardry and other supernatural occurrences take place within the latter, the former is also an important setting within the tales. The first story begins with Harry living in the material world with Uncle Vernon and Aunt Petunia and their impish son, Dudley. Harry is treated poorly by his relatives and largely relegated to chores and housework. Upon his 11th birthday, Harry is enlightened about his magical powers and learns the truth about the murder of his parents by Lord Voldemort. Teenagers often connect with tales that involve familial discord or parental conflict and loss as they relate to the plight of the protagonist and can imagine themselves in the same or similar situations.

Once at Hogwarts, Harry is able to see a much broader world than the one he has previously experienced. He learns the importance of community through his friendships with Ron and Hermione, but, even more significantly, he learns about self-sacrifice for the greater good. It's important that the books always remained grounded in the interactions of Harry and his friends, as these interpersonal relationships are universal to the teen experience of finding others with common interests and values and experiencing a sense of community.

All three central characters—Harry Potter, Ron Weasley, and Hermione Granger—deal with universal coming-of-age issues in the novel. Harry struggles with his identity and with being an orphan; he longs for strong personal relationships and finds them with both Ron and Hermione. His relationship with his

Uncle Sirius Black provides him with a sense of family that has been absent from his life. His bravery and selflessness shine through in *Harry Potter and the Chamber of Secrets* when he shows a willingness to sacrifice himself for the safety of another person.

Hermione is more mature than either of her male friends and tends to overcompensate in order to prove her self-worth. She is instrumental in several of the stories in terms of devising solutions to obstacles and threats. Ron comes from a large family and thirsts for the type of attention he receives from Harry and from being associated with Harry. In *Harry Potter and the Goblet of Fire*, he becomes envious of Harry to the point that their friendship is damaged, but he eventually realizes that they need each other and can learn from one another.

These themes of community and a de-emphasis on material possessions in lieu of valuable relationships is central to the teachings of Jesus Christ and ones that are embodied throughout the Bible. It is at Hogwarts—an institution promoting supernatural activities—that Harry finds his spiritual center and life's purpose. Rowling's message of unity and the triumph of good over evil align with both Christianity and secularism.

Harry Potter has been a cultural phenomenon. The last four books in the series made history by becoming the fastest-selling books ever. The final book in the series, *Harry Potter and the Deathly Hallows*, sold 15 million copies in the first 24 hours of its release. Book release parties were held at bookstores throughout the United Kingdom and the United States for several of the series titles. Tweens and teens enjoyed these immersive events by dressing up as characters from the books and playing games associated with the novels. The events were festive gatherings for fans where they could come together and celebrate free from criticism of those who might have considered the series "nerdy" or uncool.

Although critical reception to the books was mixed, there was no denying the impact on young readers as many praised the fact that the series sparked an insatiable desire among children and teens to devour the action-packed tales. Books in the series have won several Children's Writing Awards including the Hugo Award for Best Novel (*Harry Potter and the Prisoner of Azkaban*) and Whitbread Children's Book of the Year Award (*Harry Potter and the Philosopher's Stone*). The books were adapted into a series of box office smash films starring Daniel Radcliffe in the title role.

See also: 1960s: *Addams Family, The*; 1970s: Blume, Judy; 1990s: *Buffy the Vampire Slayer*; *Charmed*; *Craft, The*; 2000s: *Twilight*; *Vampire Diaries, The*

Further Reading

Anatol, Giselle Liza, ed. 2009. *Reading Harry Potter Again: New Critical Essays*. Santa Barbara, CA: Praeger.

Beach, Sara Ann, and Elizabeth Harden Willner. 2002. "The Power of Harry: The Impact of J. K. Rowling's Harry Potter Books on Young Readers." *World Literature Today* 76, no. 1 (Winter): 102–106. Web, March 9, 2014.

Bell, Christopher E. 2016. *From Here to Hogwarts: Essays on Harry Potter Fandom and Fiction*. Jefferson, NC: McFarland.

Chanda, Kaustav. 2014. "What Lies Deep in the Unconscious: A Psychoanalytical Scrutiny of Harry Potter in J. K. Rowling's Harry Potter Series." *International Journal of Multidisciplinary Approach and Studies* 1 (6).

Feldt, Laura. 2016. "Contemporary Fantasy Fiction and Representations of Religion: Playing with Reality, Myth and Magic in His Dark Materials and Harry Potter." *Religion* 46 (4).

Lesperance, Alice. 2018. "Living through Death with Harry Potter." *The Atlantic*, January 23. https://www.theatlantic.com/entertainment/archive/2018/01/living-through-death -with-harry-potter/550445/.

Rowling, J. K. 2006. *Harry Potter Paperback Boxed Set*. London: Bloomsbury Children's.

I KNOW WHAT YOU DID LAST SUMMER

The commercial success of 1995's *Scream* spawned a flurry of slasher films targeted at a teenage audience, most notably *I Know What You Did Last Summer*. This 1997 film capitalized on *Scream*'s formula of casting popular young actors and actresses in the lead roles and building on the "teens in peril" story line. Based loosely on a popular 1973 young adult novel by Lois Duncan, the film centers on a group of four teens, who, while out having fun after high school graduation, accidentally hit a man on a dark, winding road. Fearful of being charged with a crime and going to prison, they decide to dispose of the body by dumping it in the water. At a local dock, the man who they thought had died revives briefly, but ultimately he falls into the sea and presumably dies.

The film then flashes forward one year as one of the central characters, Julie (Jennifer Love Hewitt) returns home from college for the summer. She receives a note in the mail that states, "I know what you did last summer." She panics and quickly informs her cohorts, Ray (Freddie Prinze Jr.), Helen (Sarah Michelle Gellar), and Barry (Ryan Phillippe) about the mysterious message. An ominous figure begins appearing to them, wearing a bright yellow rain slicker and wielding a hook. After a series of misleading clues lead the group in circles, Barry is killed along with Helen and her sister Elsa (Bridgette Wilson) in the dress shop owned by their parents.

Casting young and famous television actresses Sarah Michelle Gellar and Jennifer Love Hewitt ensured that the film would attract preexisting teen audiences. Gellar played the title character in *Buffy the Vampire Slayer,* and Hewitt was part of the ensemble of the hit TV show *Party of Five*. Actors Freddie Prinze Jr. and Ryan Phillippe also guaranteed that adolescents would want to see the film.

I Know What You Did Last Summer follows a tested formula that works with its intended teen audience. The one-dimensional characters serve mostly to advance the plot and are not heavily developed. Additionally, audiences for these types of films typically expect significant gore and sex, whether implied or explicit. Writers and directors also plant several red herrings to throw the less sophisticated viewer off the track of the real culprit.

Slasher movies have their roots going back to the 1970s. Even though horror films and suspense films predate this by several decades, the genre of the slasher film in American pop culture is generally attributed to John Carpenter's 1978 film, *Halloween*. That film's focus on a psychotic killer who is loose in a small Midwestern town thrilled moviegoers who enjoyed its suspense and simple plot. The killer—Michael Myers (Tony Moran)—escapes from a mental asylum shortly before Halloween and makes his way back to his hometown, where he brutally murdered his older sister years before. Zeroing in on three teenage friends, he stalks and murders two of them and is ultimately foiled by his court-appointed psychiatrist, Dr. Loomis (Donald Pleasance). The low-budget film was a surprise success and was largely praised for its innovative camerawork and chilling musical score. Its financial success spawned a glut of copycat films that adhered to the basic elements of *Halloween*'s plot: a killer who reappears years or decades after an initial murder or traumatic event to exact revenge, a close-knit group of teenage friends, violent and bloody deaths, and an ending that is open-ended and leaves ample opportunity for sequels. Ironically, there is very little gore in the original *Halloween* film. Its filmmakers felt that focusing on the terror and suspense elements of the story would create a more terrifying experience for the viewer. The countless sequels and imitations that followed continued to ratchet up the body count and the gruesome nature of the killings.

I Know What You Did Last Summer, produced almost 20 years after *Halloween*, remains true to this formula. In the finale of the film, Julie and Ray battle the killer aboard his boat. After Ray wounds him and the killer plunges into the water, they believe they are finally safe. The final scene shows Julie entering a locker room shower at her school where she spies a note hanging on a mirror: "I still know." A figure crashes through the mirror, presumably as a final act of terror.

In a glaring example of how Hollywood likes to "update" book to movie translations in order to tailor to their target market, the film adaptation of the young adult book *I Know What You Did Last Summer* bore scant resemblance to its source material. Besides changing the setting of the story from New Mexico to a seaside village (a fairly benign modification), the film contained graphic violence that never occurred in the book. The book's villain is not a rain slicker clad boogeyman who appears out of nowhere to decapitate and eviscerate his victims. When Lois Duncan saw the film at a screening, she was shocked at the liberties that had been taken with her work. Given that she had been kept at a distance during filming and not invited to provide any sort of feedback (as she had been during at least one other film adaptation of one of her books), she was jolted by the excessive gore and violence in the film.

I Know What You Did Last Summer produced two sequels: *I Still Know What You Did Last Summer* (1998) and the direct-to-video *I'll Always Know What You Did Last Summer* (2006). Neither were commercial or critical hits.

See also: 1950s: *Blob, The*; *I Was a Teenage Werewolf*; 1960s: *Twilight Zone, The*; 1970s: *Carrie*; 1980s: *It*; 1990s: *Scream*; 2000s: *Pretty Little Liars*

Further Reading

Nowell, Richard. 2010. *Blood Money: A History of the First Teen Slasher Film Cycle.* London: Bloomsbury.

Parkinson, Hannah Jane. 2014. "My Guilty Pleasure: I Know What You Did Last Summer." *The Guardian*, April 11. https://www.theguardian.com/film/filmblog/2014/apr/11/my -guilty-pleasure-i-know-what-you-did-last-summer.

Willoughby, Vanessa. 2017. "Turning 20: The Final Girl Is Still as White as Ever." Bitch Media, November 13. https://www.bitchmedia.org/article/turning-20/white-final-girls -slasher-films.

KIDS

Kids (1995), a gritty, low-budget independent film directed by Larry Clark (1943–), gained notoriety for its shocking depiction of disaffected youths living in New York City during the aftermath of the initial AIDS crisis. The movie follows a small group of friends throughout the course of a single day. The central character, Telly (Leo Fitzpatrick), is a sexual opportunist who is on a quest to have sexual intercourse exclusively with virgins. He and his friend Casper (Justin Pierce) enjoy skateboarding and doing drugs. After a violent encounter with a passerby in Washington Square Park, the duo flees when they suspect they may have killed the stranger during a severe beating. Concurrently, a group of young girls are shown explicitly discussing sex and the dangers of unprotected sex. Ruby (Rosario Dawson) and Jennie (Chloë Sevigny) share that they both recently were tested for HIV/AIDS. Ruby tested negative for the virus; Jennie tested positive even though she has only had sex with one person: Telly. For the remainder of the film, Jennie goes in search of Telly in an effort to prevent him from infecting other partners.

Although this was Clark's first feature film, his background in photography was well established by the time he directed the film. Clark showed an early interest in photography that grew during and after his time serving in the military in Vietnam. He chronicled drug use by fellow soldiers, and this theme carried over into his work dealing with teenagers. His stark black-and-white photography is featured in two books: *Tulsa* and *Teenage Lust*. While artists such as Martin Scorsese have voiced admiration for Clark's raw and unfiltered style, others have expressed serious concern over his seeming fascination with teens having sex and using illegal drugs.

Clark himself has indicated that he has an unyielding interest with youth culture. During his 50s, he could be found hanging out with teens at skate parks and observing their language and behavior. This keen interest led him to develop the idea for *Kids*. As with any media presentation that is controversial, the inevitable question arises as to its cultural value. Some prominent critics praised the film and felt it could be viewed as a very strong antidrug film that also shows the ease with which HIV can be contracted when safe sex is not practiced. Even members from some politically conservative groups such the Media Research Center lauded the film's brutal and tragic view of unsupervised teens, feeling that the film would send a strong message about the perils of this type of lifestyle.

An oppositional viewing of the film, however, has a different takeaway. Jennie is the only woman in the film who has contracted HIV; other female characters evade the illness. The film ends when Jennie tracks down Telly at a party but then passes out after a drug she was given at a club earlier takes effect. She is then raped by Casper, who exposes himself to the virus. Some argue that this follows the trope of "innocent" girls being punished for having sex.

The graphic nature of *Kids* earned it an NC-17 rating, initially; this rating almost guarantees that a film will be a commercial failure. Although the film did well in large markets like New York, it was barely seen in other cities. Although the issues examined in the film are relevant to a teen audience, the rating of the film precluded many of them from seeing it. It was rereleased later with no rating after a studio change, and it still failed to reach a wider audience. Given that the budget for the film was less than $2 million, the $7 million plus that the film grossed at the box office made it a modest financial success.

The threat of contracting HIV and dying of AIDS loomed large in the mid-1990s, and many young people were diagnosed with the disease during this time period. From a historical perspective, then, it was certainly a good time to address the issue. Whether this was an effective media presentation to do that still seems to be open for debate and discussion.

Kids was nominated for several Film Independent Spirit Awards including Best First Feature and Best First Screenplay. Justin Pierce (Casper) won an award for Best Debut Performance. *Kids* propelled the careers of actresses Rosario Dawson (Ruby) and Chloë Sevigny (Jennie). Larry Clark has made several other independent films since *Kids* that include *Another Day in Paradise* and *Bully*. More recently, he directed the 2014 film *The Smell of Us*.

See also: 1960s: *Clockwork Orange, A*; 1970s: *Go Ask Alice*; 1980s: *Less Than Zero*

Further Reading

Brathwaite, Les Fabian. 2013. "And the Films Played On: 17 Essential Movies about HIV/AIDS." Queerty, December 1. https://www.queerty.com/and-the-films-played-on-16-essential-movies-about-aids-20131201.

Hynes, Eric. 2015. "'Kids': The Oral History of the Most Controversial Film of the Nineties." *Rolling Stone*, July 16. http://www.rollingstone.com/movies/news/kids-the-oral-history-of-the-most-controversial-film-of-the-nineties-20150716.

Locker, Melissa. 2015. "Harmony Korine on *Kids*: It Would Be Impossible to Make That Film Now." *The Guardian*, June 22. https://www.theguardian.com/film/2015/jun/22/harmony-korine-kids-20th-anniversary.

MCDANIEL, LURLENE

Although more recent young adult literature has focused on topics ranging from vampire love triangles to survival in a dystopian society, author Lurlene McDaniel (1944–) dominates the subgenre of "teen sick lit." McDaniel is a prolific author who has written more than 70 books, most of them focusing on a young female

protagonist with a serious, oftentimes fatal, illness. The titles of many of these indi-
cate the plots and themes very conspicuously: *Mother, Please Don't Die*, *Why Did She Have to Die*, *Baby Alicia Is Dying*, and *Somewhere between Life and Death*.

When an author or artist is preoccupied with a specific topic or theme, many times it's a response to a personal issue, or even a crisis. McDaniel's son was diagnosed with juvenile diabetes at the age of three. In interviews, she says this is primarily what triggered her interest in writing on the topic of illness and death from a young adult's perspective. Although she can fuel the emotion and plotlines, she does interview doctors and other medical personnel in an effort to lend as much authenticity to the content as possible.

Some find it puzzling that her books are so successful with teens given the weighty and sometimes depressing issues of life and death covered in the stories. On closer examination, however, the appeal becomes evident. In many of McDaniel's novels, the sick or disabled female protagonist has romantic interest in a young boy. The focus in many of these stories is on both the physical and emotional lengths that the protagonist will go in order to find love or to at least attract the attention of the object of her desire. There is a strong connection in these stories between sickness, romance, and youths.

The female protagonists are often consumed with their feelings of unattractiveness or physical disabilities due to an illness. They adhere to and reaffirm cultural notions of what beauty means in Western culture. While sick boys in these stories "fight through" their illnesses with participation in sports, sick girls restrict their focus to the physical: fascination with their bodies and the effect an illness has had on them, most often resulting in feelings of inadequacy. They are also encouraged to use makeup and do whatever they can to make themselves more physically appealing to the opposite sex.

This conformity to traditional standards of beauty is taken to an extreme in the novel *So Much to Live For*. The protagonist, Dawn Rochelle, is in remission from leukemia and working as a camp counselor with other sick children. One of her wards is Marlee Hodges, an angry tomboy who refuses to cooperate with the other campers and shows no interest in dressing in "girly" fashions. Dawn makes it her mission to make Marlee see the error of her ways and change her fashion and mannerisms to that of a typical young woman. Even after a contentious showdown where Marlee admits that she is unwilling to apply makeup because the results of her attempt to do this earlier were disastrous, Dawn doesn't relent. She instead points to other accomplishments that Marlee has achieved and insists that this one can also be won. Dawn is portrayed as the injured party in this exchange and Marlee as the ungrateful girl who just doesn't understand that Dawn and the other girls are going out of their way to help her so that she can attract a boy. While it's understandable that some young girls would rely on traditional stereotypes of beauty for a frame of reference, the nonconforming gender character (Marlee) is treated in a demeaning manner while the conforming gender character (Dawn) is viewed as the prototype on which other sick girls should model their appearance and behavior.

The appeal of these stories relies on several elements: a sense of pity or sadness for the character(s) with the illness, a relatability on the part of the reader to the tragic situation of the character, especially as it relates to the desire for physical love with a looming possibility of death, and a reassurance that while things in the book may not turn out well for the protagonist, the reader is unaffected in the real world by the plight of the characters. A simpler explanation for the popularity of these types of novels is the soap opera effect; viewers actively enjoy reading about (or watching) melodramatic events unfold within a fictional world. Even though the topic of physical illness and death may be unappealing on the surface for most readers, the addition of romance and the urgency of the situation can be quite compelling. Some parents and educators also see the possibility of "learning through tears" for young readers who can absorb the emotion of these novels and translate that into empathy and compassion for others in their own lives.

McDaniel's novel *Six Months to Live* was so popular among readers that it was placed in a time capsule at the Library of Congress and is scheduled to be opened in 2089. Readers nominated it as their favorite young adult novel through an essay contest sponsored by Pizza Hut: Reading Is Fundamental. McDaniel continues to write novels and her latest, *Somebody's Baby*, was published in July 2017.

See also: 1970s: Blume, Judy; 2000s: *Divergent*; *Hunger Games, The*; *Twilight*

Further Reading

Elman, Julie Passanante. 2012. "'Nothing Feels as Real' Teen Sick-Lit, Sadness, and the Condition of Adolescence." *Journal of Literary and Cultural Disability Studies* 6 (2).

Op de Beeck, Nathalie. 2004. "'Sixteen and Dying': Lurlene McDaniel's Fantasies of Mortal Endangerment." *Children's Literature Association Quarterly* 29 (12) 62–89. http://www .longwood.edu/staff/miskecjm/381sicklit.pdf.

Whitfield, Jamie. 2000. "Lurlene McDaniel: Missions of Mercy Inspire Lurlene McDaniel's Angelic Series." Bookpage, July. https://bookpage.com/interviews/8063-lurlene -mcdaniel#.WiWMvkqnHIU.

MORISSETTE, ALANIS

Canadian born singer Alanis Morissette (1974–) exploded into the American music scene in 1995 with the release of her phenomenally successful album, *Jagged Little Pill*. Prior to the album's release, Morissette had been a teen pop star in her native country and was known as Canada's version of Debbie Gibson. Her first two records were released exclusively in Canada where they produced several hit singles. Frustrated by the limits of her target demographic and wanting to grow as an artist, Morissette sought other options and outlets for her songwriting and singing. The commercial failure of her second album also left her without a record company to promote her work.

After meeting producer Glen Ballard, the two worked together on a new set of songs that would comprise *Jagged Little Pill*. The first single from the effort, "You

Oughta Know" quickly gained wide popularity with radio listeners—especially young women—and became a smash hit. Vastly different in tone and content from her prior songs, "You Oughta Know" is a scathing rebuke to a former boyfriend. The song's raw lyrics and Morissette's vocal stylings on the record convey anger, confusion, and even rage. In contrast to her pop music roots, this new sound was rock-oriented and showed a depth of analysis lacking in her previous songs. It was in three different top 10 music charts at the same time in the United States. Other popular singles from the album included "Hand in My Pocket," "You Learn," and "Ironic," and they all made it onto the record charts and propelled sales of *Jagged Little Pill.*

Morissette connected with music fans on a very personal level. Few popular songs reach the level of notoriety that "You Oughta Know" did. It became an anthem for young women betrayed by boyfriends and partners. Moreover, the song made no apologies for its anger, which legitimized anger as valid for young women. The singer resisted efforts to tone down the song when it was originally presented as a potential song on the album. Morissette recorded the song in one take, presumably as a method for keeping the urgency and rawness of it intact. Fellow musicians Dave Navarro, who was the guitarist on the song, and bassist Flea from the rock group Red Hot Chili Peppers added their rock flair instrumentally to boost the song's sound as well.

Morissette spawned a new genre of music that featured young women singing about life and relationships. They were vocal. They were angry. Perhaps most important, they didn't feel compelled to ask permission to feel this way. Although the songwriting aspect and success of Morissette and other female artists in the mid- to late 1990s mirrored to some degree that of earlier 1970s artists such as Joni Mitchell, Kate Bush, and Carole King, there was a newfound confidence and unapologetic message—*we don't want your sympathy.*

This created or at least built upon the archetype of the Angry Young Woman. The Angry Young Woman is sexually confident while still emotionally vulnerable. The feelings and experiences expressed by Morissette, especially in that first juggernaut of a hit single, demanded attention. Not attention for attention's sake, but attention as a valid and authentic voice within the music business. Additionally, relationship issues covered in her songs resonated with teenage girls who were experiencing not only their first crushes or romantic relationships but, perhaps more poignantly, their first breakups. Being able to connect those feelings and emotions within a larger context and within a media presentation resulted in a significant response to the material.

Alanis Morissette's lyrics certainly have something in common with other female artists during this time period—P. J. Harvey (1969–), Courtney Love (1964–), and Tori Amos (1963–). However, these artists didn't enjoy the same commercial success. The music business is first and foremost a business. Record sales speak louder than worldviews. Some doubted Morissette as a genuine article and pointed to her pop star roots as proof or indication that her motives were suspect with regard to female empowerment and post feminism.

The types of songs made popular by Morissette and subsequently by other female artists coined the term "Bitchpop." This wasn't intended as an insult. This subgenre of music alluded to songs by empowered young women expressing anger, hurt, and confusion while still retaining control of their destinies. The 1997 hit song "Bitch" by Meredith Brooks would likely have never been recorded were it not for predecessors like Morissette. That song, with lyrics like "I'm a bitch, I'm a tease, I'm a goddess on my knees" easily made its way onto Top 40 radio stations and was used in several movies and television shows.

Alanis Morissette released five additional studio albums since *Jagged Little Pill*, but none of them matched its commercial success. *Under Rug Swept*, released in 2002, was well-received critically and produced the hit single "Hands Cleans." She is still regarded as a talented artist within the recording industry and has actually broadened her work into television and film, appearing in movies that include *Dogma* and *De-Lovely*. A 20th anniversary edition of *Jagged Little Pill* was released in 2015 that included all of the original songs and 10 demo tracks that had never been released previously.

See also: 1960s: Doors, The; Joplin, Janis; Rolling Stones, The; 1970s: Devo; Led Zeppelin; Queen; 1980s: Blondie; Duran Duran; Gibson, Debbie; Lauper, Cyndi; Madonna; MTV; 1990s: Green Day; 2000s: Lavigne, Avril

Further Reading

Anderson, Kyle. 2015. "Alanis Morissette's Jagged Little Pill oral history."

Cantin, Paul. 1998. *Alanis Morissette: A Biography.* New York: St. Martin's Griffin. *Entertainment Weekly*, October 9. http://ew.com/article/2015/10/09/alanis-morissettes-jagged-little-pill-oral-history/.

Gibsone, Harriet. 2015. "Is 'Jagged Little Pill' the Most Feminist Album of the 90s?" *The Guardian*, June 15. https://www.theguardian.com/lifeandstyle/womens-blog/2015/jun/15/jagged-little-pill-alanis-morissette-most-important-album-90s.

Morissette, Alanis. 2016. "Alanis Morissette: Feminism Needs a Revolution." *Time*, March 8. http://time.com/4215897/alanis-morissette-feminism/.

Roberts, Michael Reid. 2014. "What Everybody Gets Wrong about Alanis Morissette's 'Ironic.'" Salon, May 8. https://www.salon.com/2014/05/08/what_everybody_gets_wrong_about_alanis_morissettes_ironic_partner/.

NIRVANA

The arrival of rock band Nirvana onto the American music scene was as explosive as the British Invasion or the Punk Rock movement. The Seattle-based band had enjoyed local success in the 1980s as they went through several band members and formed a loyal but relatively small following. Before adopting the name Nirvana, the band went briefly by several other names including Skid Row, Pen Cap Chew, and Bliss. Popular with college radio stations and having moderate success touring, the band released its first album, *Bleach*, under the Sub Pop record label. Founding member and lead singer Kurt Cobain (1967–1994) grew dissatisfied

1990s rock band Nirvana arguably defined the grunge era of music. Lead singer Kurt Cobain embodied teen angst and alienation through songs like "Smells Like Teen Spirit." The 1994 suicide death of the artist shocked fans who deeply connected to the band's material. (Martyn Goodacre/Getty Images)

with the limited reach and interest generated by Sub Pop and began looking for a major record label that could buy out the band's remaining contractual obligations. The other original founding member of Nirvana is Krist Anthony Novoselic (1965–). The band had a succession of drummers, but the one who remained longest with Nirvana was Dave Grohl (1968–).

Nirvana was and is most closely associated with the term "grunge rock." Originating in Seattle in the 1980s, this musical style drew on existing rock and punk influences and then added its own unique touches in order to form something new and different. This sound added and built on two specific elements: repetition of a simple verse/lyric within the song and a tempo that begins slowly and builds into a louder—even raucous—crescendo. This style of music was extremely popular among adolescent listeners.

The term "grunge" also applies to aesthetics. It connotes a distinctly Pacific Northwest style of clothing and lifestyle: plaid shirts and a generally disheveled appearance, sometimes coupled with casual drug use and lower socioeconomic status. Musically, labeling Nirvana as grunge is oversimplified. Nirvana incorporated several styles into their music and clearly had other influences outside of rock and punk that contributed to their sound.

Their first major studio album, *Nevermind*, dramatically surpassed sales expectations for the band. Upon its release, less than 50,000 copies were shipped to record stores. Comparing the potential sales of *Nevermind* to actual sales of other "indie rock" bands' first major albums, studio executives and insiders were cautiously optimistic that it might eventually hit gold status (500,000 copies sold) over an extended period of time. The album's first single, "Smells Like Teen Spirit" became a smash hit on both radio stations and in sales. The accompanying video portrayed a familiar high school image: cheerleaders and students at a pep rally. This familiar setting added to the appeal of the song to its young audience. Starting off in a niche or specialty slot in MTV, the accompanying music video soon began playing on the cable channel in heavy rotation. Less than a year after its release, *Nevermind* was selling several hundred thousand copies per week and replaced Michael Jackson's iconic *Thriller* album on the Billboard charts. Several hit singles including "Lithium" and "Come As You Are" followed as sales of the album continued to rise.

As with most bands, the lead singer was focused on the most by the media and fans. Cobain rose to stardom quickly after the success of *Nevermind*. Raised by working-class parents, Cobain fit the model of disenfranchised youth. Unpopular as a teenager, he expressed an interest in punk rock music. Given his family's socioeconomic status and his feelings of marginalization, Cobain gravitated toward music that voiced alienation, anger, and dissatisfaction with the status quo.

Insight into Cobain's creative process and his internal struggles was revealed with the release of his personal journals in 2002. These were purchased from his widow, Courtney Love (1964–). The journals are filled with everything from random doodlings to political observations to scrawled song lyrics. Most notable was Cobain's obsession with bodily functions and the state of his own body. His slight frame became even more conspicuous after he began using heroin. He also suffered from severe gastrointestinal problems that caused nausea and vomiting on a regular basis. Scoliosis further added to his chronic pain. Cobain's physical appearance and build added to his identification as an outsider and most likely appealed to other young fans who weren't physically gifted or prone to athletic prowess within school sports.

Also evident in these journals was Cobain's identification as an outsider. Due in large part to his small physical size and his many ailments, he often compared himself to a rampant "jock" culture among high school and college-aged men. He drew self-portraits in his journals that depicted him as skeletal. His obsession with this extended into his worldview as he often associated jocks with bullies and oppressive authoritarians. Some of this was based on personal experience and some was a hyperextension of that.

Cobain's emotions and thoughts on this made their way into Nirvana's music most conspicuously through screaming. A standard element of many punk rock and metal songs includes screaming and expressing emotions through guttural sounds and lyrics that are many times obscured or distorted by grunts and other primal sounds. One may view this in several different ways. Cobain reflected on authenticity on a routine basis. He expressed a strong desire that his music be viewed as genuine and not something mass produced and marketed to the widest possible audience. He also experienced physical pain that may have found something of an outlet in performing. Even when *Nevermind* was being recorded and edited, he and other band members were very vocal in their desire that the sound be kept as raw and organic as possible. They were leery of their work sounding overproduced.

The band's second major effort *In Utero* was also a huge success but kept the band's signature sound, prompting the hit singles "Heart Shaped Box" and "Rape Me." For this record, they worked with producer Steve Albini. The band continued touring and doing television appearances to promote the new album. They also appeared on MTV Unplugged, and the special was immensely popular among teenage viewers.

After continuing bouts of drug addiction and mental health issues, Kurt Cobain committed suicide in 1994, widowing Courtney Love and their young daughter, Frances Bean Cobain. Drummer Dave Grohl formed the rock band the Foo Fighters, which still continues to tour and produce studio albums. *Nevermind* has sold more than 30 million copies worldwide and is included on both *Time* magazine's and *Rolling Stone*'s list of the Greatest Albums of All Time.

See also: 1960s: Rolling Stones, The; 1970s: Clash, The; Devo; Led Zeppelin; Queen; 1980s: Blondie; Duran Duran; MTV; 1990s: Green Day; Smashing Pumpkins, The; 2000s: My Chemical Romance

Further Reading

Azerrad, Michael. 1993. *Come As You Are: The Story of Nirvana*. New York: Three Rivers Press.
Cobain, Kurt. 2003. *Journals*. New York: Riverhead Books.
Cross, Charles R. 2001. *Heavier Than Heaven: A Biography of Kurt Cobain*. New York: Hachette Books.
True, Everett. 2007. *Nirvana: The Biography*. Cambridge, MA: De Capo Press.

SALT-N-PEPA

Salt-N-Pepa, the only all-female rap/hip-hop group to ever reach platinum record sales, was a trio of women from New York City. The original configuration of the group consisted of Cheryl James/"Salt" (1966–), Sandra Denton/"Pepa" (1964–), and Latoya Hanson (1971–). The band formed in the mid-1980s, later replacing Hanson with Deidra Roper/"DJ Spinderella" (1971–) in 1986, shortly before their first hit single, "Push It" was released and went platinum. The album that included the single ultimately went on to platinum status as well; *Hot, Cool & Vicious* sold nearly 1.5 million copies. Many of their fans were teenagers and adolescents, though they were popular across a variety of demographics

Salt-N-Pepa made an indelible mark upon the hip-hop genre and created new opportunities for future female rappers in the industry. Although "Rapper's Delight" is considered to be the first mainstream rap song to cross over into popular culture, many artists before this wrote, produced, and recorded rap songs. Rap originated in New York City and grew from minority communities that experienced economic despair. These artists yearned to express themselves, and, from that creative urge, a new genre of music evolved. Hip-hop gave artists a new way to vent about the struggles and frustrations that were embedded into the daily lives of many blacks and Latinos, especially youths, living primarily in the Bronx area of New York City.

As with other genres of music, male artists had distinct advantages in terms of being given opportunities typically not afforded to female artists. More so than in other genres, there was also an inherent bias toward women breaking into this growing art form. Not only do well-known male rappers still outnumber their female contemporaries but also the musical genre itself has largely attached itself to a male perspective. Although this has changed in recent years and continues to progress, there is the equivalent of a "good ole boys" network operating within the industry still.

Although earlier female rap artists had made some musical inroads, Salt-N-Pepa were able to cross into the mainstream and get exposure on radio stations across the country. Their success wouldn't have been possible, however, were it not for previous rappers and deejays like Queen Lisa Lee, Teena Marie, and Puerto Rican, Jewish MC, Brenda K. Starr. Since these women won wider exposure and recognition, an act like Salt-N-Pepa was able to break through and secure a record deal.

Female rap artists in the mid- to late 1980s were often introduced to their audiences via an established male rap star. Chuck D from Public Enemy promoted Sister Souljah; Sean "Puffy" Combs introduced Mary J. Blige, a performer who mixed rap with soul music. A multitude of female rappers who would become successful in their own right were launched by male artists who had the access and resources to pave the way for them.

Rap music enabled women primarily from the black community to voice their concerns about a variety of issues, many of them personal. Although some spoke to larger sociopolitical challenges and inequities, most used the platform to speak out on relationship issues such as unfaithful men, abusive relationships, and sexual self-empowerment. For fans, this came with an authenticity lacking in other formats. There was a rawness and immediacy communicated in many of these songs that connected with listeners. Although they may not have explicitly labeled themselves as feminists, their music gave voice to many women who felt silenced or invisible. The genre is complicated as well since some female rappers have been accused of reinforcing the same negative sexual stereotypes about themselves that many male rappers have been accused of doing.

The success of Salt-N-Pepa and other female artists served to empower young women about issues related to their bodies, such as their sexual autonomy and freedom. Perhaps more importantly, Salt-N-Pepa served as role models for young girls by making inroads into a male-dominated musical genre and demonstrating that they could produce hit music while retaining their own sense of style, purpose, and individuality. References to sexual activity resonate in part because they lower teens' inhibitions or feelings of awkwardness about sexuality and sexual activity. Other influences also factor into this, but rap and hip-hop music especially have lessened or removed many taboos about suggestive or sexually explicit topics. This also comes across in the fashions worn by many female rap artists. Historically, there was more of a tendency in this genre to dress provocatively and showcase physical attributes than in some other genres, though those differences are eroding today within pop and country genres as well.

Rap and hip-hop music appeals to and is focused on a youth market. Although Salt-N-Pepa may have spoken about issues universal to women, the genre itself is most popular with those under 30. This is mainly due to the typical lifestyle embodied in much of the work—i.e., partying, having sex, and speaking out against the status quo and oppression.

Where artists like Foxy Brown and Lil' Kim released sexually explicit songs, Salt-N-Pepa's work was more playful and suggestive. A single from their third studio album, *Blacks' Magic,* "Let's Talk about Sex" became a smash hit and reached number 13 on the Billboard charts. At a time when male rap groups like 2 Live Crew released sexually explicit albums that were accused of being pornographic, the lyrics of "Let's Talk about Sex" were tame in comparison. The song was rerecorded later as "Let's Talk about AIDS" and released for radio promotion to enhance public awareness and dialogue about the disease. The original version was nominated for a Grammy Award for Best Rap Performance by a Duo or Group. The song furthered their influence on the teen market as HIV and AIDS grew within demographic groups other than gay men in the 1990s.

The group reached the pinnacle of their success in the 1990s and officially disbanded in 2002. In 2005, they were honored on VH1 and the following year performed their hit single, "Whatta Man" with En Vogue. Since then, they have reunited for several shows, and the individual group members have had solo projects on their own. In 2014, they appeared in a commercial for Geico, featuring their hit song "Push It."

See also: 1980s: MTV; 2000s: Rihanna; Spears, Britney

Further Reading

Brown, Stacia L. 2015. "It's Time to Tell the Stories of Women in Hip-Hop." *New Republic,* August 26. https://newrepublic.com/article/122611/its-time-tell-stories-women -hip-hop.

Orcutt, K. C. 2016. "First Ladies of Rap: Salt-N-Pepa." *The Source*, March 10. http:// thesource.com/2016/03/10/first-ladies-of-rap-salt-n-pepa/.

Weingarten, Christopher R. 2017. "Salt-N-Pepa: Our Life in 15 Songs." *Rolling Stone*, September 5. https://www.rollingstone.com/music/lists/salt-n-pepa-our-life-in-15-songs -w500728/lets-talk-about-sex-1991-w500784.

SCREAM

Scream (1996) is credited with resurrecting the "teen slasher" film genre, which had faded from popularity in the late 1980s and early to mid-1990s. In the late 1970s and 1980s, Hollywood saw the birth and growth of a movie genre that had the potential for huge profitability and low production costs. Films like *Texas Chainsaw*

Massacre and *Halloween* were made on shoestring budgets and reaped big returns at the box office. Both of these films expanded the generic "slasher" film to focus on teenage victims, primarily young women. The age and situations of the lead characters appealed to young ticket buyers. The standard teen slasher film usually features a villain that is superhuman in terms of strength or indestructibility. This applies to Michael Myers from *Halloween*, Freddy Krueger from the *Nightmare on Elm Street* series and Jason Voorhees from the *Friday the 13th* franchise.

By the time that *Scream* was made, the teen moviegoer was much more sophisticated with respect to knowledge and familiarity with traditional horror and slasher film conventions. A very strong frame of reference existed among these potential ticket buyers that created a challenge for filmmakers intent on reviving the genre. It would no longer be possible to produce profitable films that relied solely on resurrecting preexisting formulas that had been depleted of surprises and shocks. The creative team behind *Scream* and its sequels realized the need to incorporate this inescapable reality into their story lines. Rather than ignoring their target audience's ambivalence or boredom with teen slasher film content, they would make the cynicism part of the story.

Scream revolves around a masked killer known as Ghostface. He terrorizes a small town in California by murdering teens in a gruesome fashion with a large hunting knife. His primary target is high school student Sidney Prescott (Neve Campbell), a teen whose mother was murdered years earlier. While other victims are dispatched, Sidney manages to elude Ghostface. There are several potential suspects, and Sidney eventually joins forces with news reporter Gale Weathers (Courteney Cox) to try and unmask Ghostface and return order to the small town of Woodsboro.

Scream is notable within its genre for several reasons. As already mentioned, it is responsible for reviving the slasher flick. While horror and slasher films are generally viewed with disdain among movie critics and academicians, the film elevated the genre by featuring well-known actors such as Drew Barrymore and Courteney Cox in central roles. The screenwriter, Kevin Williamson, was fascinated with horror films from his youth and believed there was still fresh material to be mined from the genre. Williamson also created the popular TV series *Dawson's Creek*, so he was familiar with and skilled at tapping into teen themes and issues for media material. He partnered with famed horror director Wes Craven, who had helmed the *Nightmare on Elm Street* series and other popular films.

In earlier incarnations of the teen slasher film, there was an archetype identified as "the Final Girl." This was literally the last remaining character in the film who survived after the murderer had been killed. The Final Girl was almost always a virgin. Another common element of teen slasher films from the 1970s and 1980s was the vicious killing of female characters that has just had sexual intercourse. It became an expectation and reality in these stories that once a female character loses her virginity or engages in sexual activity, she would die on screen shortly thereafter. Another consistent element in these films is that the Final Girl, while resilient, was always rescued or saved at the end of the film by a male character. Notably, this doesn't occur in *Scream*; Sidney Prescott has intercourse with her boyfriend, Billy Loomis (Skeet

Ulrich), and escapes from Ghostface again. Another twist on the Final Girl element is that *Scream* features two female protagonists. Gale Weathers, while not a teenager, is a central figure to the story. She is assertive and opinionated and makes no apologies for her career ambitions. Her character is not punished (killed) for these traits that are traditionally associated with dominant male authority figures. Perhaps most important, Sidney and Gale prove capable of taking care of themselves and are able to overcome the killers at the conclusion of the film without male assistance or rescuing. This female empowerment twist held special appeal for young female viewers who typically might usually have an aversion to teen slasher films.

Scream has all the ingredients of a teen date movie: young attractive stars, sex, violence, and the comfort of knowing that once the film ends, all has returned to normal—at least in the real world where the viewer lives. The visceral thrills experienced while watching the film are not unlike the adrenaline rush of riding a roller coaster or visiting a haunted house.

Scream's villain isn't supernatural, in another departure from earlier teen slasher films. In fact, it isn't a single villain; the plot reveals two killers working in tandem and taking turns with the murders. Creators felt that presenting a very real evil would make for a scarier filmgoing experience: the killers in *Scream* are members of the protagonist's circle of friends, and one of them is her boyfriend. This heightens the sense of fear and dread as Sidney realizes that the very person she has depended on for comfort is one of her assailants.

During the violent finale of the film, the killers—Billy and Stu Macher (Matthew Lillard)—reveal their motives to a certain extent. Sidney's mother and Billy's father had an affair, causing Billy's parents to divorce. His motive is simple revenge. Stu's motives are less clear and more disturbing. Although he jokes about peer pressure and the influence of media violence on real-life violence, he just enjoys the act of killing. Having murderers who are trusted individuals that the victims interact with on a regular basis is more terrifying than an unknown supernatural evil because it's more credible.

Although it didn't start off strongly when released, *Scream* went on to become a box office sensation and also received overall positive praise from many film critics. It spawned three sequels: *Scream 2, Scream 3,* and *Scream 4.* It even inspired a TV show by the same name that is slated for a third season on MTV in 2018. *Scream* grossed close to $375 million worldwide and breathed new life into a genre that had been written off due to a depletion of fresh ideas and poor-quality sequels that most times bypassed theatrical release and went straight to DVD.

See also: 1950s: *Blob, The*; *I Was a Teenage Werewolf*; 1960s: *Twilight Zone, The*; 1970s: *Carrie*; 1980s: *It*; MTV; 1990s: *I Know What You Did Last Summer*

Further Reading

Guzman, Rafer. 2015. "How Wes Craven's 'Scream' Defined the 1990s." *Newsday*, September 21. https://www.newsday.com/entertainment/movies/how-wes-craven-s-scream -defined-the-1990s-1.10796871.

Lisi, Jon. 2014. "The Rules of Reviving a Genre: 'Scream' and Postmodern Cinema." The Artifice, August 20. https://the-artifice.com/scream-postmodern-cinema/.

Reilly, Kaitlin. 2016. "Why This Scream Character Was So Good for Women." Refinery 29, December 16. http://www.refinery29.com/2016/12/130121/sidney-prescott-scream-movies-heroine.

7TH HEAVEN

7th Heaven (1996–2007), which followed the chronicles of the Camden clan in fictional Glenoak, California, was the most watched television series on the WB network. Producers from the network, upon determining that there was an unfulfilled niche for family friendly content, greenlit the production of the show. It featured father and husband Eric Camden (Stephen Collins), who was a preacher, and his wife and stay-at-home mother Annie Camden (Catherine Hicks), whose primary responsibility was seeing to the care of her husband and children. Although the premise may have seemed quaint at the time, the show became a smash hit and received praise from a wide variety of critics and family groups who appreciated its straightforward style of storytelling that was meaningful without being overwrought or preachy.

The Camdens in some way represent a throwback to the "nuclear family," a term that originated in the 1920s to describe a specific type of family unit. The original definition of nuclear family was restricted to two parents and their children. This, of course, excluded single parent households, as well as the more recent evolution of households that are headed by same-sex parents. It also didn't include extended family members or nontraditional family configurations where, for example, children might be raised by grandparents or even aunts and uncles. It is a term closely associated with socially conservative individuals, though the definition has expanded due to the broadening of nontraditional households over the past decades.

Regardless of political viewpoints or ideologies, the show depicted a family that struggled with modern-day issues in a compassionate manner. It tackled timely issues related to coming of age, such as sex and sexuality, teen pregnancy, and addiction. Although it still adhered to largely traditional views of what constitutes a family unit and expected gender roles within society, the series was lauded for its nonpartisan approach to problem solving. For example, one episode that resonated universally with parents and children was one that focused on financial responsibility. In it, the eldest daughter, Mary (Jessica Biel), does something stupid at school and loses a college scholarship. Overreacting to this, she decides to forgo college altogether and work instead. After her parents refuse to buy her a car, she buys one herself. It is too expensive and far beyond her means. After realizing that she cannot afford car payments and insurance, she gets into trouble with her creditor, whom she cannot pay. To make matters worse, she raids a brother's savings and squanders it on nonessential items. She is eventually sent off to stay temporarily with her grandfather, John "The Colonel" Camden (Peter Graves), who will straighten her out on these and presumably other matters.

7th Heaven followed the ups and downs of the Camden clan in a fictional California town. Although the father and husband of the family was a preacher, the storylines focused primarily on widely relatable family issues and was a smash hit for the WB network. (Barry King/Getty Images)

In the text of this episode, Mary is awakened to the realities of payroll taxes, social security deductions, and the loss of value of automobiles postpurchase—all hallmarks of the financial reality of adulthood. This was helpful for audiences, as responsible money management is an important life skill. If this lesson is absorbed to some degree by children and teens watching a fictional character struggle with it, then a valuable service has been provided.

Another episode with coming-of-age themes dealt sensitively with menstruation. In many media presentations, this topic is either used for laughs or simply glossed over or ignored. In some cases, such as in the horror film *Carrie*, it is depicted through the lens of young girls who have no knowledge of it and are understandably confused and even terrified when it occurs. In the episode, middle child Lucy (Beverley Mitchell) is anticipating her first menstrual period. Many of her friends have already gotten their first periods, and she is worried that she is lagging behind them. Unlike the typical treatment of menstruation, which excludes men altogether by either omission or commission, her father is also anxious for her to experience this rite of passage. He doesn't become embarrassed when menstruation is discussed—rather, he initiates some of the discussion himself. Additionally, Mary is also nonplussed by this physical occurrence. When Lucy does get her period, her father congratulates her, and Lucy, Mary, and Mom go out to dinner to celebrate. While Dad has been supportive and positive, he realizes that it's time to allow some space for female camaraderie. This episode was important for viewers, as this experience is literally universal for cisgender tween and teen girls, and it was examined in a sensitive and age-appropriate manner.

The positive legacy of the show was overshadowed in 2014, when a leaked audiotape was given to the media that included an alleged confession of actor Stephen Collins to several instances of indecent exposure and molestation of female minors. The tape was released and did serious damage to the actor's career and reputation. Even though the alleged incidents occurred prior to the actor's time on the series, it was still especially scandalous given the role of his character as a preacher on the show and his regular interaction with young actresses on the show.

Overall, *7th Heaven* managed to provide morality lessons without being overly religious; the morality of the characters might have been rooted in their faith, but their relatable struggles resonated with a wide audience that included secular fans. Although the show never won any Emmy Awards, it was nominated for multiple Teen Choice Awards, Kids' Choice Awards, and Family Television Awards. After the show announced its final season on the WB for 2006, another network that was formed by a merger between UPN and the WB (CW) picked it up for an additional season that ended in the spring of 2007.

See also: 1950s: *Adventures of Ozzie and Harriet, The*; *Father Knows Best*; *I Love Lucy*; *Leave It to Beaver*; 1960s: *Patty Duke Show, The*; 1970s: *Carrie*; *Happy Days*; 1980s: *Back to the Future*; *Cosby Show, The*; *Facts of Life, The*; *Family Ties*; *Full House*; *Wonder Years, The*; 1990s: *Boy Meets World*; *Clarissa Explains It All*; 2000s: *Friday Night Lights*; *One Tree Hill*

Further Reading

Glover, Nathan. 2016. "Religion Is Becoming a More Popular Subject for TV Shows." *World Religion News*, July 4. http://www.worldreligionnews.com/religion-news/religion-is-becoming-a-more-popular-subject-for-tv-shows.

Kepnes, Caroline. 2002. "Why '7th Heaven' Is as Great as 'The Osbournes.'" *Entertainment Weekly*, May 1. http://ew.com/article/2002/05/01/why-7th-heaven-great-osbournes/.

Meltzer, Marissa. 2006. "7th Heaven Goes to Heaven." *Slate*, May 8, 2006. http://www.slate.com/articles/arts/television/2006/05/7th_heaven_goes_to_heaven.html.

SHE'S ALL THAT

Some films by their very titles indicate that they have been produced and marketed in order to "cash in" on a trend that is current at the time the film is being made. *She's All That* (1999) is one such film. Translated from slang, the title means "a physically attractive woman." In this instance, the young woman is a nerdy high schooler named Laney Boggs (Rachael Leigh Cook). The audience knows that she is nerdy because she wears glasses and paints dark and strange things in the school art room. After being dumped for a faded reality star by his popular and gorgeous girlfriend, equally popular student Zack Siler (Freddie Prinze Jr.) accepts a bet that not only can he get any girl in school to go to the prom with him but also that she'll be named prom queen. What follows is predictable. Zack attempts to woo Laney. She introduces him to her world, and he slowly begins to fall in love with her. Laney, of course, transforms into a beautiful and popular young woman—though given the fact that not much happens other than having her remove her glasses and put on a bit of a makeup, the revelation isn't very dramatic to anyone who has paid attention earlier.

This film, along with other "makeover" films, is squarely targeted at a teen audience. The plot is simple as is the formula: good looking and popular boy is dumped by equally good looking and popular girl. Popular boy takes on a "project" to confirm or validate his appeal but then discovers he has feelings for the "project" and drama ensues. All ends well as the "project" forgives the popular boy for the intended prank and consequences of the elaborate scheme are minor or nonexistent.

Films like this largely reinforce negative stereotypes about women. Stripping away the humor and likable stars who populate these types of movies, the inherent message is that women are objects and that they exist largely for the pleasure of the male. In *She's All That*, the filmmakers attempt to make Zack sympathetic by saddling him with a controlling father who is fixated on having Zack attend the same college that he did. Laney lives with her father, who is a pool cleaner. She is clearly an intelligent student, but as in most films like this, that is viewed as a strong negative in high school landscapes when it comes to social interactions and romance.

This film and others in the same subgenre are often referred to as "Pygmalion" films. This refers to the work of writer George Bernard Shaw, who wrote the play *Pygmalion*. In that story, a dialect expert accepts a bet that he can take a young woman from lower socioeconomic status and train and coach her into speaking proper English and passing herself off as a member of high society. The issue with this comparison, though, is that the focus in *Pygmalion* is more interior. The male protagonist, Henry Higgins, is intent on changing flower seller Eliza Doolittle into a "proper" member of society by changing her dialect, vocabulary, and manners. Although part of this transformation relies on new clothes and a change in physical appearance, the emphasis is on behavior. With *She's All That,* the focus is more on aesthetics, which sends a strong message about the significance of physical beauty within our culture.

What Henry is not prepared for is Eliza's strong-willed determination. He is also changed by this experiment, and that is something lacking—or at least weaker in Zack's story arc in *She's All That*. Again, the emphasis is on the (mainly) physical change in the female character and not on growth in the male character.

Both pieces begin with a wager that is insensitive and both rely on stereotyped gender roles to further their plots and themes. However, it's important to take into account that *Pygmalion* was written in the 1930s and takes place in England. *She's All That* takes place more than 60 years later in America, but its inherent worldview implies that things haven't changed much for women and their perceived value within society. In short, *Pygmalion* can largely be attributed as a product of its time with respect to the plot and underlying worldview.

Pygmalion was adapted into a film and later into the Broadway musical, *My Fair Lady*, which also became a musical film.

The film was a box office hit, reaching the number one slot and making more than $100 million at the U.S. box office. It was produced on a $10 million budget. It received largely mixed reviews with many critics zeroing in on its predictable plot and sexist premise.

See also: 1970s: *National Lampoon's Animal House*; 1980s: *Fast Times at Ridgemont High*; Hughes, John, Films of; *Revenge of the Nerds*; *Risky Business*; *Say Anything . . .*; 1990s: *American Pie*; *Clueless*; *Dazed and Confused*; 2000s: *Bring It On*; *Mean Girls*

Further Reading

Breslaw, Anna. 2015. "13 Pop Culture Stereotypes about Women That Need to Die." *Elle*, April 6. http://www.elle.com/life-love/a27645/pop-culture-tropes-about-women-that -need-to-die/.

Garis, Mary Grace. 2016. "13 Beloved Cliches from Your Favorite '90s Teen Films." Bustle, April 6. https://www.bustle.com/articles/152249-13-beloved-cliches-from-your -favorite-90s-teen-films.

Hentges, Sarah. 2014. *Pictures of Girlhood: Modern Female Adolescence on Film*. Jefferson: McFarland.

SMASHING PUMPKINS, THE

Alternative rock band the Smashing Pumpkins is typically included along with Nirvana and Pearl Jam when discussing the most influential and successful bands of the 1990s. Although the band formed in the late 1980s, they didn't record or release any studio albums until the early 1990s. Their second album, *Siamese Dream,* was released after significant turmoil during the recording process. In what was to become a recurring theme throughout the career of the band, conflicts and upheaval among the group's members made their producers nervous about their ability to deliver a product on time and at or under budget. The original group consisted of founder and front man Billy Corgan (1967–), guitarist James Iha (1968–), bass guitarist D'arcy Wretzky (1968–), and drummer Jimmy Chamberlin (1964–).

Corgan was rumored to be a perfectionist and was blamed for much of the distress within the band initially. He often played multiple instruments on recorded songs (minus the drums) in response to producer Butch Vig's wishes. This created tension and contributed to ongoing issues with the band. Although the process to get *Siamese Dream* into record stores was difficult, it was met with critical and commercial success. The album was a top 10 hit on the Billboard chart and sold approximately 4 million copies.

As discussed in other entries within this book, the issue of musical categorization can be problematic since the tendency is to oversimplify or force a group into a rather narrowly defined category that is many times arbitrarily created to begin with. This is especially true with respect to the Smashing Pumpkins. Unlike other 1990s bands like Nirvana and Pearl Jam, both of whom were inextricably linked to the "grunge" movement, Smashing Pumpkins drew on a variety of musical genres and styles to come up with something that was perceived as quite unique. Elements of pop, heavy metal, punk, and even electronica permeate their songs. Corgan has referenced a wide variety of groups that have influenced him creatively, ranging from New Order to Boston to Judas Priest.

The success of both Nirvana and Pearl Jam inspired something else within Corgan—suicidal thoughts. In a podcast interview, he confessed that the unexpected success of both those bands triggered in him significant feelings of uncertainty and inadequacy. Part of this may have been triggered by the endless comparisons by music critics of all three bands. Although some embraced the eclectic mish-mash of sounds and styles in the music of the Smashing Pumpkins, others considered them less creatively authentic than Nirvana or Pearl Jam.

"Today," one of the group's most well-known hit singles from *Siamese Dream* was a by-product of Corgan's depression. He discusses how the dark period of his life when he began giving away possessions and planning his own eulogy eventually pushed him to the precipice. One day while ruminating on all of this, he had the idea for the song "Today." It was a declaration of his decision to determine the state of his own mind. The refrain of the song "today is the greatest day. . ." reflected a catharsis he experienced when he realized that since he felt things could not get worse at a particular moment, anything beyond that was going to be an upswing.

Teens are often drawn to media content that speaks directly to or alludes to themes of depression and suicide. Because emotions are heightened for adolescents during this transitional stage to adulthood, material that speaks to feelings of sorrow, self-doubt, and overall angst resonates with younger fans. Communicating the status of being an outsider or someone who doesn't fit in with the status quo effectively connects with teens when the message is received as authentic.

Whatever remaining inadequacy Corgan might have been feeling would be tempered with the staggering success of the follow-up to *Siamese Dream*. *Mellon Collie and the Infinite Sadness* was the band's ambitious double-album release that contained 28 tracks. The sprawling record was more diverse in sounds than their previous release and had massive crossover appeal. In addition to debuting at the number one spot on Billboard, it had four radio friendly hit singles: —"1979," "Zero," "Tonight, Tonight," and "Bullet with Butterfly Wings." Most critics praised its depth and scope; *Time* magazine named it the "Best Album of the Year" for 1995. These hit singles and accompanying videos increased the band's popularity with teens; tapping into themes of romantic struggles, alienation, and nostalgia furthered the Smashing Pumpkins' reputation as bona fide rock stars. The record was nominated for multiple Grammy Awards and MTV Music Video Awards. It eventually sold more than 10 million copies.

Drug use and its effects on the band were widely reported within the media. Temporary keyboard player, Jonathan Melvoin (1961–1996), died of a heroin overdose shortly before the band's planned American tour to promote *Melon Collie and the Infinite Sadness*. Drummer Jimmy Chamberlin was arrested for drug possession. These issues coupled with the interpersonal and unresolved conflicts within the group created more division and disharmony. Melvoin's passing was one in a long list of heroin-related deaths and addictions that affected groups such as Nirvana, Hole, and Blind Melon. Bands that struggle with drug abuse are not unique, but there is still an aura of danger and rebellion associated with it, and younger fans tend to view this less negatively than older ones.

The band's fourth studio album, *Adore,* was praised by critics but failed to connect with many fans. As with many successful groups who have consecutive hit albums whose sales continue to skyrocket, the band found its future uncertain. After the departure of several original band members including Chamberlin, the Smashing Pumpkins never regained momentum within the business. As late as 2016, however, Corgan has indicated tentative plans for the group to release new music, but no details were provided.

See also: 1960s: Rolling Stones, The; 1970s: Clash, The; Devo; Led Zeppelin; Queen; 1980s: Blondie; Duran Duran; MTV; 1990s: Green Day; Nirvana; 2000s: My Chemical Romance

Further Reading

Hyman, Dan. 2014. "Billy Corgan Remembers Adore, the Smashing Pumpkins' Most Misunderstood Album." *Esquire*, September 23. http://www.esquire.com/entertainment/music/interviews/a30155/billy-corgan-interview/.

Hyman, Dan. 2012. "Q&A: Billy Corgan Looks Back on the Smashing Pumpkins' 'Mellon Collie and the Infinite Sadness.'" *Rolling Stone*, November 19. http://www.rollingstone.com/music/news/q-a-billy-corgan-looks-back-on-the-smashing-pumpkins-mellon-collie-and-the-infinite-sadness-20121119.

Reyes, Matthew. 2016. "Smashing Pumpkins' 'Mellon Collie' was Alt-Rock's Swan Song." *Medium*, October 3. https://medium.com/cuepoint/smashing-pumpkins-mellon-collie-was-alt-rock-s-swan-song-7f6c52f10132.

SPICE GIRLS

The Spice Girls quickly became one of the most commercially successful recording groups in history several years after they burst upon the scene in 1994. In an effort to compete with popular boy bands who dominated the record charts during this period in the United Kingdom, managers and record executives began looking for the young female equivalent of groups like Take That and East 17. Responding to an advertisement in a trade publication, hundreds of young female performers auditioned for five slots in an all-female pop group to be developed by a male management team and male financier. After months of training and recording musical tracks, the original group of girls bolted from Heart Management and began

Girl Power! The Spice Girls pose for the cameras at the 1997 MTV Music Awards. The all-female British pop sensation rose to fame and popularity on a message of female empowerment. (The LIFE Picture Collection/Getty Images)

promoting themselves to other producers and executives. In September 1995, the group adopted the name Spice Girls, was signed by Virgin Records, and began touring parts of the western United States. The group was composed of Melanie Brown /"Scary Spice" (1975–), Melanie Chisholm/"Sporty Spice" (1974–), Emma Bunton/"Baby Spice" (1976–), Geri Halliwell/"Ginger Spice" (1972–) and Victoria Beckham, née Adams/"Posh Spice" (1974–). Each member had a very distinct style and personality, though they were all complementary to one another.

In 1996, the group released their first single, "Wannabe," in the United Kingdom. It was a huge hit and quickly raced up the record charts. In addition, the accompanying video played in heavy rotation on the youth-oriented TV show *The Box*. Media outlets amplified the group's popularity by playing up the all-girl angle. The single soon hit number one on the charts and remained there for almost two months. More impressively, it reached number one in almost 40 other countries and went on to become the biggest selling single of all time for a female group.

The Spice Girls received an equally impressive reception within the states. "Wannabe" debuted at number 11 on the American record charts—at the time, it was the highest scoring debut single by a non-American artist or group. The single sold millions of copies, and the debut album *Spice* quickly became the best-selling album of 1997, reaching platinum status seven times over (7 million copies sold). It was evident that this type of success within a short period of time spoke to the immense popularity of the group and their wide-range appeal.

The music was standard pop material and nothing revolutionary by any standard, so other factors contributed to their success. Spice Girls' motto was "girl power." Although the phrase may seem simple and perhaps even banal, it resonated among the young women in Great Britain when the group became popular. Additionally, the band's clothing and overall physical appearance was playful and captured the attention of fashion-conscious teens and adolescents. Embedded within the aesthetics was a simple message of self-acceptance and female empowerment. The group became fashion icons and heavily promoted various brands of clothing and accessories targeted toward their audience. As with many pop idols and bands, their influence was significant, and they quickly became style setters for a teen demographic willing to spend money to emulate their favorite female band and be part of the "girl power" movement.

In the same election cycle that saw Tony Blair come into power as prime minister of Great Britain, a record number of female members of Parliament (MPs) had been elected. There is a photograph that shows all the new female civil servants surrounding Tony Blair, presumably to tout this new wave of female representation within the government. Also at this time, a resurgent effort to energize Great Britain's popular culture was under way. Fashions designers, singers, and other celebrities were associated with this, and leading the way was the Spice Girls.

Some argue that this carefully created and marketed pop band was an important part of the postfeminist landscape. Views on this are diverging and merit more analysis than is allowed for here, but there is no denying that they had captured the attention of the world; certainly they were able to create dialogue about gender politics and the evolution of female power and appeal within the entertainment business.

One observation about the Spice Girls is that they were sexual without being overly attention-seeking or provocative along the lines of other female artists like Madonna. In interviews and more importantly in some of their music videos, they present themselves as sexually confident and playful, and not necessarily monogamous. They were vocal about empowering young girls to be themselves—to embrace their authenticity whatever that might be. Given that the members of the group represented a variety of archetypes, from the athletic (Sporty) to the upscale fashion plate (Posh), it's possible this was intended to extend beyond the superficial; this can be viewed as either merely enforcing stereotypes, or as making a statement about individuality and choices. If the latter is true, then the message of "girl power" resonates as genuine. Teens witnessed a powerful but simple representation of young women taking charge of their professional and personal destinies, and it connected with them. But people with more historical or traditional views on feminism viewed the Spice Girls warily and discounted or dismissed their message as one that was artificially constructed or marketed as a commodity: "feminism" via consumerism.

The 1997 film *Spiceworld*, featuring the members of the group along with more established actors, was a significant box office hit, grossing more than $75 million worldwide. To illustrate the popularity of the group in the United States, the film opened over Super Bowl weekend and still managed to gross close to $11 million, a record debut for a movie opening on what is traditionally a low-grossing weekend for ticket sales.

The Spice Girls' success continued as more hit records were released and tour dates sold out. Then, in 1998, member Geri Halliwell left the group. Remaining band members continued touring and making records, and even won several music awards including MTV's Europe Music Awards for Best Pop Act and Best Group. After a few follow-ups that could not match the financial success of their first few albums and hit singles, the band announced a hiatus in 2000. Since then, there have been several successful reunion tours along with a musical based on the group's songs entitled *Viva Forever!* In 2016, a video was released online that celebrated the 20th anniversary of the release of "Wannabe." The musical impact of the Spice Girls can be seen today as they paved the way for other all-female groups such as the Pussycat Dolls and Fifth Harmony. Their commercial success and influence on popular culture is significant.

See also: 1960s: Beach Boys, The; Beatles, The; Monkees, The; Rolling Stones, The; 1970s: Osmonds, The; 1980s: Blondie; Madonna; MTV; 1990s: Backstreet Boys; 2000s: Rihanna; Spears, Britney; Swift, Taylor

Further Reading

Armstrong, Jennifer Keishin. 2016. "Spice Girls' 'Wannabe': How 'Girl Power' Reinvigorated Mainstream Feminism in the '90s." *Billboard*, July 15. https://www.billboard.com/articles/news/features/7439005/spice-girls-wannabe-girl-power-feminism.

Blay, Zeba. 2015. "It's Time to Give the Spice Girls the Credit They Deserve." Huffington Post, August 6. https://www.huffingtonpost.com/entry/spice-girls-feminist-history_us_55c36cafe4b0923c12bbb16f.

Sinclair, David. 2008. *Spice Girls Revisited.* London: Omnibus Press.

THAT '70s SHOW

That '70s Show (1998–2006) ran for eight seasons on the Fox network. It was one of Fox's most successful television shows of all time, and it helped launch the careers of several then-unknown actors including Topher Grace, Mila Kunis, and Ashton Kutcher. The show takes place in the fictional town of Point Place, Wisconsin. It focuses on a group of high school peers and chronicles their typical adolescent experiences. Although the series ran for eight seasons, its timeline within the show itself is concentrated from 1976–1979. Had the series covered one TV year for each calendar one, it would have extended into the 1980s. Just as *Happy Days* (1974–1984) did in the 1970s and 1980s, *That '70s Show* capitalizes on nostalgia. While *Happy Days* featured characters and events from the 1950s, *That '70s Show*, as evidenced by its title, focused on a time period from approximately 20 years earlier than the time of its airing.

Since the show takes place in the 1970s, important socioeconomic issues that were relevant during the decade are covered. These issues include sexism and gender roles, economic struggles due to recession, and teenage drug use. A recurring theme in the show is that of financial struggles for the Forman family. The show's main character, teen Eric Forman (Topher Grace), is exposed to the results of a downturn in the economy when his father, Red (Kurtwood Smith), has his hours cut at his job at the auto parts plant. Eric's mother and Red's wife, Kitty (Debra Jo Rupp), is a nurse, but she also has the gender-prescribed role of family nurturer.

While assorted subplots among the group of teens occur on the show, a budding romance between Eric and friend Donna Pinciotti (Laura Prepon) is an ongoing focus. Supporting characters that flesh out the show include: superficial Jackie Burkhart (Mila Kunis), "dim bulb" Michael Kelso (Ashton Kutcher), best friend Steven Hyde (Danny Masterson), and foreign exchange student Fez (Wilmer Valderrama).

Because casual drug use was fairly common in this decade, especially among younger people, the show's producers came up with a creative way to include this in the show without making it explicit. Scenes featuring various characters sitting in a circle in the Forman basement and having discussions became a staple of the show. Although no one is ever shown smoking pot, it is implied by the use of showing thick clouds of smoke and including frequent heavy coughing.

One interesting way to analyze a show like *That '70s Show* is to examine its cultural representations for accuracy. In terms of gender roles and expectations, the show depicts men as the primary wage earners. Furthermore, factory and other blue-collar jobs were much more prevalent in that decade than they are now. Although women certainly were part of the professional workforce in the 1970s, there were still a large number of women who worked at home and whose primary focus was on caring for the needs of the family.

The character of Fez is interesting to examine from a Western perspective. Throughout the show, Red often refers to him by the wrong name. This running gag is intended to poke fun at the "otherness" of those not born in the United States. Another recurring joke of the show is that Fez's birth country is never revealed. Each time he is about to announce it, a distraction occurs. This allows the viewer to maintain a generic view of his origin—specifically, he's not associated with a country that the United States may have antagonistic relations with.

Viewing the show from the worldview of another culture can also provide insight. In Middle Eastern countries, the role and importance of family is paramount. Shows like *That '70s Show* depict average American teens as inclined to spending their free time with friends rather than parents and siblings. Moreover, time spent with parents and siblings is many times combative, filled with arguments and disagreements. Teens in America are also depicted as being obsessed with sex. Most of their energies are directed at finding access and opportunity to engage in sexual activity. Last, there is a casual attitude toward drug use and underage drinking. All of these behaviors and attitudes run counter to those of Middle Eastern culture. Although media representations are dramatized and exaggerated for effect, many times other cultures draw wider conclusions about other countries and their beliefs and values based on what they see in TV shows, movies, videos, and so on.

Although the show lasted eight seasons, like many other series, it seemed to be running out of fresh ideas and materials. Also, several of its stars, notably Topher Grace and Ashton Kutcher, were enjoying success in film and were likely anxious for the show to end. *That '70s Show* was a commercial success for Fox. It scored solid TV ratings over the course of its run and was nominated for 16 Primetime Emmy Awards, winning only one for costume design.

See also: 1970s: *Happy Days*

Further Reading

Adams, Erik. 2014. "That '70s Show Took TV Adolescence Down into the Basement (Where It Belongs)." *AV Club*, July 30. https://tv.avclub.com/that-70s-show-took-tv-adolescence-down-into-the-baseme-1798270795.

Zushi, Yo. 2017. "Time Travelling with That '70s Show." *New Statesman,* August 11. https://www.newstatesman.com/culture/tv-radio/2017/08/time-travelling-70s-show.

The 2000s

DECADE OVERVIEW

The decade began with a chaotic and unprecedented national election. The presidency of the United States of America would end up being decided in a courtroom rather than a voting booth as Democratic contender Al Gore (who served as vice president under Bill Clinton in the preceding decade) won the popular vote of the American people but ultimately lost the election to Republican opponent George W. Bush due to contested results from the state of Florida. The margin of error for the popular vote in Florida was razor-thin (less than 1 percent), so the case went to the Supreme Court of the United States where the victory was given to Bush in a 5–4 decision. This outcome would set the stage for a decade of deeply divisive politics among both elected officials and the citizenry of the country.

In popular culture, the top-grossing film of 2000 was *How the Grinch Stole Christmas*. Other box office hits the same year included *Gladiator*, *Cast Away*, and *What Women Want*. The spillover of reality television programs that started in the prior decade continued gaining momentum and resulted in the CBS phenomenon of *Survivor*. Other popular shows included *ER*, *Friends*, and *Law & Order*.

Rap artist Eminem became the best-selling artist of the decade, narrowly defeating a group that had disbanded decades earlier. The Beatles enjoyed renewed popularity with the release of their hit singles on an album entitled *1*, which sold more than 31 million copies. As the industry moved away from physical records and toward digital downloads, the best-selling digital album of the decade was Coldplay's *Viva La Vida*. Bands that spoke to teen angst and were popular among coming-of-age youth included Dashboard Confessional, My Chemical Romance, blink-182, and Panic! at the Disco.

In the publishing world, authors like John Grisham, Danielle Steel, Mary Higgins Clark, James Patterson, and John Sandford dominated book sales. The staggering success of the *Harry Potter* series would continue unabated for author J. K. Rowling throughout the decade as well. But *Harry Potter* wasn't the only fictional teen to enjoy soaring literary popularity. Young adult novels would enjoy staggering levels of success in this decade, with the two most recognizable series being Stephenie Meyer's *Twilight* and *The Hunger Games* trilogy. They each featured female protagonists, but with very little in common.

Technology continued to make advances at record pace. One of the most significant innovations was the introduction of texting by AT&T in late 2000. Already popular in Europe, this service, which was used on wireless phones, would become a common practice among Americans—especially among teens and tweens. As with any proliferation of technology within a culture, there were concerns. Parents worried that their children would engage in "sexting," or sending nude pictures of themselves to others. Another concern that is still paramount today is the amount of time that tweens and teens spend on their devices on a daily basis, known as screen time.

The defining moment of this decade was, without question, the terror attacks on September 11, 2001. In addition to the Twin Towers in New York City, other targets included the Pentagon and Washington D.C. Commercial planes, highjacked by foreign terrorists, crashed into buildings in both New York City and Virginia. A third plane headed toward D.C. crashed in a field in Pennsylvania after a group of passengers thwarted the hijackers. A horrified and grief-stricken nation turned toward the commander-in-chief for reassurance and leadership, and, for a brief time, much of the country seemed to be united under a common goal and purpose: to find and punish the terrorist group that masterminded these violent attacks. But that cohesion soon fell away as the country became enmeshed in two wars—one in Iraq and the other in Afghanistan. Once again, basic ideological differences created a wedge among Americans. This combative opposition would continue through George W. Bush's second term. The 2008 election of Barack Obama did nothing to quell the divide or tensions in the country. Many believed that the election of the first black president proved that we now lived in a post racial America. By the end of his first term, however, it was evident that deep cultural and political divisions still remained.

There was a voracious appetite for stardom during the 2000s; everyone from celebrity debutantes like Paris Hilton to gossip bloggers like Perez Hilton vied for media attention and monetary rewards. A "perfect storm" of reality television, 24-hour news cycles, social media platforms like Facebook and Twitter, and a never-ending obsession with the cult of celebrity created a generation of attention seekers whose "talents" were many times questionable.

By the end of the decade, recording artists like Lady Gaga, Taylor Swift, Katy Perry, and Justin Bieber were ruling radio airplay and record sales, proving the timeless appeal of pop music to a young audience. The youth market also reigned at the box office in 2010 as four of the five top-grossing films appealed primarily to tweens and teens: *Alice in Wonderland*, *Iron Man 2*, *The Twilight Saga: Eclipse*, and *Harry Potter and the Deathly Hallows Part 1*.

Women and girls continued to enjoy growing media representation in the books, films, and television shows analyzed in this section. Although dystopias and supernatural realities reigned supreme in the 2000s, traditional depictions of life held strong during the decade as well. Americans may have been gripped by the fear of terror, but ordinary coming-of-age anxieties were depicted alongside their newer counterparts.

Further Reading

Batchelor, Bob. 2008. *The 2000s: American Popular Culture through History*. Westport, CT: Greenwood Press.

Corrigan, Timothy, ed. 2012. *American Cinema of the 2000s: Themes and Variations.* New Brunswick, NJ: Rutgers University Press.

Melnick, Jeffrey. 2009. *9/11 Culture.* Malden, MA: Wiley-Blackwell.

BOOK THIEF, THE

The historical novel *The Book Thief* (2005), written by Markus Zusak (1975–), takes place in Germany during World War II. It fast became an international best seller and was adapted into a film in 2013. The story's protagonist, Liesel Meminger, goes to live with her adoptive parents, Hans and Rosa Hubermann, after her brother dies and her mother gives her up for adoption due to political necessity (the mother is a Communist). Liesel and Hans' relationship grows as he teaches her to read in secret. At one particularly dramatic point, the Hubermanns take in the son of a friend and Jewish refugee, Max Vandenburg, and hide him in their home. As Liesel comes of age, she finds herself exposed to the horrors of the Nazi regime.

Within the novel, access to books is a privilege afforded the wealthy. So, in addition to reading being a hobby of the formally educated, it is also an indicator of status within society. But because Liesel's mother does work for the mayor and his wife, Liesel is given access to the couple's library, where she can choose from a vast collection of books. She then takes her newfound love of language and reading and uses it to steal books. In addition to stealing books that have been banned by the Nazis, Liesel begins employing her own skills and starts to write her own stories.

Neighbor Rudy Steiner has a crush on Liesel, but she views him solely as a friend. Though he is German, Rudy doesn't subscribe to Nazi beliefs and is simply trying to carry on with his life in as normal of a fashion as is possible during wartime. Adding an element of romance to this coming-of-age story makes the young characters more relatable to young readers, demonstrating that even in extreme and

Author Markus Zusak promotes his novel *The Book Thief*, a young adult story that became a publishing sensation. The coming-of-age tale takes place during the Holocaust and focuses upon young protagonist Liesel Meminger. (Gilbert Carrasquillo/Getty Images)

horrifying circumstances, emotions and feelings of love are a normal part of growing into adulthood.

Tackling an issue like the Holocaust within young adult literature is fraught with issues. First and most obvious is the issue of death. More specifically, the deaths of millions of Jewish people at the hands of a dictator and carried out by the country's military. Although these horrors are documented historically, how much detail can or should an author expose young readers to? There exists a natural tendency on the part of parents and educators to prevent children from seeing disturbing images or reading about them. However, if the goal of a narrative is to convey the true horror of an event like the Holocaust, isn't it advisable to avoid "sugar coating" it? How does an author use fiction to communicate ideas and beliefs and actions that are deeply disturbing to young readers without watering down the impact in order to balance storytelling with truth?

A device used in *The Book Thief* to attempt this delicate navigation is point of view. Although the central character is grade school–aged Liesel, the primary narrator of the story is Death. Using Death to speak directly to the reader accomplishes two things: it makes real the inevitability of dying but also shields the young reader from witnessing visceral brutality. Second, and perhaps most important, this narrative device lends a supernatural element to the story: Death speaks about "rescuing" souls after they have been killed. This spiritual piece provides comfort to young readers, but is it fair? Does it lessen the pain and finality of death? Does it minimize the physical and emotional agony endured by its victims?

Other books dealing with the Holocaust aimed at teens and preteens include, of course, the renowned *The Diary of a Young Girl* by Anne Frank. Since that is a published diary and not a work of fiction, it is more internal. By nature of its format and its narrator, it is unable to explore the more graphic elements of the daily horrors of concentration camps and gas chambers. Some school programs promote the reading of both of these texts for literature or even history courses, feeling that this allows for solid comparisons and contrasts in content and themes. The rationale behind this is partly due to an inclination in some academic circles to discount or even dismiss newer works that fall under the category of "young adult." Some argue that incorporating newer books into the curriculum will prompt these same readers to seek out earlier books ("classics") that cover the same or similar terrain.

The Book Thief is ultimately about hope and love in times of unthinkable horror and despair. With death and hatred consuming her country, Liesel is able to build trust and forge meaningful relationships with her family and Max. Although marketed in the United States as a young adult novel, it is just as popular with adult readers.

The novel won numerous awards in 2006 including *Publishers Weekly*'s Best Children's Book of the Year, National Jewish Book Award for Children's and Young Adult Literature, *School Library Journal*'s Best Book of the Year, and *Book Sense*'s Book of the Year Award for Children's Literature. The 2013 release of the film adaptation of *The Book Thief* was less enthusiastically received both by critics and moviegoers.

Many critics noted that, while the performances in the film were engaging, it distilled the horrors of war and the Holocaust into something bland and safe rather than provocative or even thought provoking.

See also: 1960s: *To Kill a Mockingbird*

Further Reading

Abele, Robert. 2013. "Review: 'The Book Thief' Robs the Truth from an Evil Time." *Los Angeles Times*, November 8. http://articles.latimes.com/2013/nov/08/entertainment /la-et-mn-the-book-thief-review-20131108.

Pauli, Michelle. 2014. "Markus Zusak: The Book Thief Film's Biggest Hurdle Was Death." *The Guardian*, February 25. https://www.theguardian.com/childrens-books-site/2014 /feb/25/book-thief-markus-zusak-interview.

Zusak, Markus. 2005. *The Book Thief*. New York: Knopf.

BRING IT ON

The sports comedy *Bring It On* (2000) stars Kirsten Dunst and focuses on the fierce competition and rivalry within the world of high school cheerleading. It was directed by Peyton Reed and written by Jessica Bendinger. The plot revolves around primary character Torrance Shipman's (Kirsten Dunst) desire to lead her cheerleading team to their sixth consecutive national title.

When newcomer Missy Pantone (Eliza Dushku) arrives at school and joins the Rancho Carne Toros, she notices that their routines bear an uncanny resemblance to a competitor team from her previous high school. At first defensive and unconvinced of this, Torrance accompanies Missy to Los Angeles to witness it firsthand. The East Compton Clovers, a black cheerleading squad, are indeed performing the same routines that Torrance inherited from her predecessor on the Rancho Carne squad. Clovers leader, Isis (Gabrielle Union,) informs Torrance that her predecessor did videotape their routines and then use them herself to train the Toros. She also explains that the Clovers are a superior squad to the Toros and can easily beat them in competition. In the end, the Clovers triumph at Nationals and the Toros come in second place.

Cheerleading has often been the subject of mockery and denigration in comedic media presentations. The historical and cultural stereotype of what cheerleaders look like and what their purpose is doesn't typically conjure images of empowerment and liberation for young women. This is a bit misleading, however, if one doesn't know the entire historical context of the sport. Many are surprised to learn that cheerleading began as a men's athletic activity in the late 1800s and early 1900s. At that time, it was considered to be a worthy extracurricular activity that showed strong character and school spirit. It was generally practiced at "upper crust" schools by privileged white men. Although girls began to infiltrate the sport in the late 1920s and early 1930s, it was still viewed as a male pastime. But during World War II, more women gained access to the sport while young men were off fighting in the military. As men returned home in the 1950s, however, they began to reclaim this terrain. Some schools enforced actual bans against women within the cheerleading ranks at this time.

In the 1960s and early 1970s, the typical image of a female cheerleader included the short skirts and the pom-poms and an overall appearance that put aesthetics ahead of athleticism. Things began to change culturally as the women's liberation movement gained ground, and, by the time the 1980s arrived, cheerleading began to resemble a much more physical endeavor that relied on intensive training and acrobatic stunts and risky routines that highlighted the athletic prowess of its participants. By the 1990s, cheerleading had reinvented itself as a sport. The focus now was on choreography and synchronicity and stunts. Practices were constant and they were grueling. Special coaches were hired to "beef up" teams as competitive cheerleading squads grew in schools across the country.

Bring It On, though presented as a garden-variety teen comedy, is really more of an attempt to deal with the issue of cultural appropriation in an entertaining fashion. Films with teen characters and high school settings clearly target that same demographic for ticket sales, but this film elevated the topic of competition and sidestepped many of the clichéd aspects of teen films that covered similar terrain. It also featured a group of girls who showed the same level of dedication and prowess at their chosen sport as is usually shown for young men relative to theirs.

Cultural appropriation has strong historical context and goes back even further than the accusations leveled against Elvis Presley and other white entertainers who arguably mined styles and material from minority populations. At the heart of cultural appropriation is the allegation that a dominant group "borrows" an art form from a traditionally disenfranchised group, uses it for profit, and doesn't give credit (or a share of profits) to the community from which it was lifted. Because Torrance wants a level playing field, she convinces her father to financially sponsor the Clovers so that they can compete at the national finals. Isis rejects the offer and instead convinces a popular talk show host with ties to East Compton to finance the trip.

An important element of *Bring It On* is the way that is subtly debunks myths about the "Angry Black Woman" archetype. Isis is a very physically and mentally confident adversary, but she isn't presented as out of control with anger or vengeance. She simply wants a shot for her team, which they've earned. Torrance grows from the experience as well because she is forced to step out of her comfort zone and learn and train her squad on new material in a brief amount of time. Most important, a mutual bond of respect is fostered between the two rivals that can easily be viewed as intersectional feminism among young women in action.

A potentially easy "cop out" of the film would have been for the Toros somehow to overcome their challenges and defeat the Clovers, presumably teaching a universal lesson on hard work and determination and overcoming odds. Instead, the better team, which comprised young black women, won.

Bring It On was a box office success and received mixed reviews, though most agreed that Dunst and Union delivered solid performances. The film spawned five direct-to-video sequels and a stage musical that has toured nationally and includes music by Lin-Manuel Miranda of *Hamilton* fame. None of the original cast returned for any of the film sequels.

See also: 1980s: *Fast Times at Ridgemont High*; Hughes, John, Films of; *Say Anything . . .*; 1990s: *American Pie*; *Clueless*; *Dazed and Confused*; *She's All That*; 2000s: *Mean Girls*

Further Reading

Betancourt, Manuel. 2015. "15 Years Later, 'Bring It On' Remains Our Most Surprisingly Feminist Teen Movie." *Mic,* August 25. https://mic.com/articles/124224 /bring-it-on-15th-anniversary-feminist-cheerleaders#.IIZPtX6ac.

Duca, Lauren. 2015. "The Death of the Cheerleader." Huffington Post, August 20. https://www.huffingtonpost.com/entry/the-cheerleader-in-pop-culture-bring-it-on _us_55ba55f1e4b0af35367a859a.

Rush, Tyree. 2015. "5 Things 'Bring It On' Taught Us about Intersectional Feminism." Huffington Post, August 25. https://www.huffingtonpost.com/tyree-rush/bring-it-on -intersectional-feminism_b_7064800.html.

CALL OF DUTY

Call of Duty was released in 2003 by Activision. The game is a "first person shooter" style format that takes place during World War II. Various battlefield scenarios unfold as the player reacts to them in real time, and the game incorporates situations from three different viewpoints: American, British, and Soviet. This game emphasized squad level behavior and tactics rather than the "lone wolf" approach commonly used in previous war games.

The 2000s built on the popularity of gaming that exploded in the 1990s. Whereas the visuals and narratives of video games from the 1990s were limited largely to two-dimensional optics, the new wave of video games introduced in the late 1990s and into the 2000s expanded on these items and offered more robust experiences for gamers. This new generation of video games was more immersive in both style and content—sharper and clearer images made for a more realistic setting, but players were now much more directly involved with the action. Along with this new look and feel came heavy criticism from media and parents' watchdog groups. The new wave of games offered story lines steeped in profanity, excessive violence, and sexuality that many felt were inappropriate for children and teens.

Before delving into specifics of this video game, it's important to discuss the unique relationship between teenage boys and violent video games. Teenage boys undergo hormonal changes, especially during the ages of 13–15. Increases in testosterone can fuel aggressive behavior; the exposure to violence within video games can exacerbate this. More so than in a violent movie or TV show, the violence in video games is repetitive over a long period of time. Many "gamers" tend to play frequently and repeatedly unlike a film or TV series that is watched once. Additionally, many violent video games reinforce gender stereotypes where the male is the hero or aggressor and the female is the victim. These factors combined with the glorification of and desensitization to the violence in the game contribute to a potentially unhealthy view of violence in general.

Considering that *Call of Duty* is a response to the earlier game *Medal of Honor*, it's easy to see where influences originated from and how they impacted both style and subject matter in the *Call of Duty* series. *Medal of Honor* launched in 1999. It is connected to—more likely inspired by—Hollywood juggernaut Steven Spielberg. During postproduction of his commercial and critical hit film, *Saving Private Ryan*, the director approached the company who eventually launched *Medal of Honor*. Spielberg believed that video games connected to war, particularly World War II, could become more realistic by incorporating more Hollywood style tools into their narratives instead of primarily relying upon flashy visuals. The proliferation of war films, most of which feature young actors in the roles of soldiers, contribute to the timeless fascination with combat. Recruiters for the various military branches understand and capitalize on this. For example, enlistment into the Air Force increased after the popular film *Top Gun* was released. In some cities, recruiters even set up information tables outside of the theater, taking advantage of the adrenalin rush that some younger male audience members may have experienced while watching the film and making them more likely to consider signing up for service.

Call of Duty dramatically altered the experience of gamers from *Medal of Honor* in two significant ways: *Medal of Honor* showcased the individual soldier as the main attraction. The gamer identified with this lone individual, and it reinforced a worldview of the important contributions of a sole fighter. *Call of Duty*, by allowing for the British and Soviet soldier experiences, literally forced the gamer to adapt to other settings and cultures and soldiers. Expanding this universe geographically and culturally also prompted gamers to perhaps expand their own knowledge and understanding beyond the safe and familiar.

One of the most controversial issues to stem from the dramatic increase in violent video games is that of exposure and potential influence on behavior. In short, does prolonged and consistent exposure to violent images within these games increase the likelihood of violent acts by those who absorb them? As one can imagine, it isn't quite that simple. Although direct cause and effect has always been complex and difficult to address here, various studies have certainly supported the notion that violent video games and repetitive exposure to them can strongly influence actions and decisions made within the gaming environment by players. Within the modern battlefield setting in war video games, an absence of civilians propels the idea of a "free for all" with respect to taking out one's enemies.

The laws that would apply within civilian society respective to violence—especially that of gun violence—are nonexistent in *Call of Duty*. Soldiers can (and do) shoot at anyone who isn't on their side. This is referred to as "encouragement of crime." Teen boys especially may absorb this message and even extend it into the real world with respect to how violence is viewed and processed. Dehumanization of the enemy also allows the soldier to take whatever steps are deemed necessary to achieve objectives. This encompasses not just killing but also physical and psychological torture. When a human being is reduced to an object, it is much easier to attack and even destroy him without justification or remorse. Methods are unimportant as long as the end goal is achieved. This aligns with the concept of "war aims" or campaign objectives.

Opportunity is a third influential factor. In real life and within society, actions have consequences. Within a battlefield setting, this becomes murky. Given that the end goal is all important and that methods to achieve it are secondary to outcomes, there is a freedom to break the rules. More importantly, there are little to no consequences for doing so. This also appeals to teenage boys who may feel rebellious toward parents and other adults in power.

Social and psychological factors weigh in to this equation as well. Obedience—even blind obedience—to the unit is expected and demanded. Individuality is not only discouraged with respect to decision making, it is punished. Therefore, an individual soldier—or gamer—is released in some sense from moral obligations relative to killing another human being. He is simply following orders and doing the same thing that all of the other soldiers in the unit are doing.

Call of Duty has become a profitable franchise that has expanded beyond its original World War II setting. Later games in the series focus on modern battlefield scenarios. A spin-off series of games entitled *Call of Duty: Black Ops* returns to the World War II format. Sales figures from 2016 support the video game series selling more than 250 million copies.

See also: 1990s: *Grand Theft Auto*

Further Reading

Ramsay, Debra. 2015. "Brutal Games: Call of Duty and the Cultural Narrative of World War II." *Cinema Journal* 54 (2): 94–113.

Stanton, Rich. 2016. "Do Video Games Make Children Violent? Nobody Knows—and This Is Why." *The Guardian*, March 9. https://www.theguardian.com/technology/2016/mar/09/do-video-games-make-children-violent-nobody-knows-and-this-is-why.

CYRUS, MILEY

Miley Cyrus (1992–) shot to fame on the *Hannah Montana* series that aired on the Disney Channel for four seasons before cancellation. The show revolved around the title character, Miley Stewart, an "average" teen by day and singing phenomenon, Hannah Montana, by night. Cyrus's real-life father, country-western star Billy Ray Cyrus, also starred as her father in the show. The show was popular with young viewers and spawned two theatrical releases and a soundtrack.

The singer-actress's career has been rife with controversies. Just as Britney Spears received unrelenting media attention during the earlier years of her career, Cyrus seems to also be a magnet for tabloid fodder and social media analysis. However, the two artists both have noncontroversial origins; Cyrus began her career on the Disney Channel, and Spears began her career on *The All-New Mickey Mouse Club* as a fresh-scrubbed adolescent. This, of course, was a reboot of sorts of the original

Singer-actor Miley Cyrus at the 2006 VH1 Awards. The former teen star has created controversy with her reinvented image and edgy projects since leaving behind her family-friendly Hannah Montana persona. (Aaron Settipane/Dreamstime.com)

show, which began in the 1950s. Other notables from the revival that started in 1989 include singer-actor Justin Timberlake, actor Ryan Gosling, and pop superstar Christina Aguilera.

Once the show ended, Cyrus was faced with the same challenge that all child/teen stars must contend with—what now? It is difficult to make a transition from childhood to adulthood for anyone; it's even more difficult to do that in front of the public. For Cyrus, the transition was in the music industry. The first few non–*Hannah Montana* studio records she released were commercially successful. Her first breakout hit was the single, "The Climb" (2009), which crossed over in popularity with both country-western and pop music fans. Cyrus also landed a clothing deal with mass retailer Wal-Mart and as part of that promotional campaign, Cyrus released her next single, "Party in the USA." It was pop/dance-oriented and clearly targeted at a teen/tween demographic.

Over the next few years, Cyrus had a few studio albums produced and released to mediocre sales. She guest starred in a few TV shows including *Two and a Half Men* and several theatrical films that were commercial and critical failures.

Cyrus's fourth studio album, *Bangerz,* signaled clearly to fans and critics that she was intent on divorcing herself from the Hannah Montana persona that arguably limited her creative options since the show ended. She utilized producers including Pharrell Williams and will.i.am, both known for their expertise in hip-hop and dance-oriented music. The album's first single, "We Can't Stop," was a bona fide hit and reached number two on the Billboard Hot 100 chart. The follow-up, "Wrecking Ball," became her first number one hit and created a renewed interest in the singer. The video for the song skyrocketed in popularity, becoming the fastest video to reach the number one spot on Vevo, and also snagging the 2014 Video of the Year award on the MTV Video Music Awards (VMAs).

Prior to her win in 2014 at the VMAs, her live performance there one year earlier with singer Robin Thicke raised eyebrows and garnered negative coverage of both artists. Cyrus performed two songs at the ceremony, "We Can't Stop" and Thicke's provocative hit, "Blurred Lines." During their performance of the Thicke song, Cyrus stripped down to a flesh colored bikini, and the two groped and grinded their way in front of a confused and awkward audience. Several factors contributed to the stunned reaction among media and the global online community. There was, of course, Cyrus's squeaky clean beginning as Disney star Hannah Montana. Thicke's song "Blurred Lines" was the target at the time of much criticism. Many feminists and women's rights groups leveled accusations of misogyny and promotion of rape culture against Thicke because of the lyrical content. Thicke was also a married man at the time, and many viewed his participation in the performance as unsavory and bordering on pedophiliac.

Talk and criticism of the performance dominated social media and the news cycle for several days. Cyrus brought the term "twerking" into the mainstream. This refers to a style of dance (usually performed by women) where the buttocks bounce in time to the beat or rhythm of music, typically rap or hip-hop. The physical movement has a historical and social context linked to New Orleans and Mardi Gras. The first music video that directly employed this technique is DJ Jubilee's "Do the Jubilee All" in 1993. At that time, it was referred to as a "bounce" video. Prior to that, groups of young African American men and women would often engage in this activity at social events. It gained traction and awareness on a broader scale as it became popular in strip clubs and nightclubs.

The negative reaction to Cyrus as she morphed from child star into adult artist can be seen as reflective of our cultural ideals and values. Although everyone transitions from childhood at some point, we are many times uncomfortable seeing this occur with our celebrities, especially when they are female. Young girls who aren't celebrities aren't watched by millions of people while they evolve into adulthood. Every statement or action is scrutinized and criticized. Seeing them become sexual beings makes many people uncomfortable.

Part of this may be due to the inability or unwillingness of the public to reconcile that childhood persona with a young adult one. Perhaps parents view the burgeoning sexuality of their own offspring and link it to the celebrity's maturation. Sexuality is a complex and many times complicated topic. Culturally, we tend to oversimplify this and attempt to place people and behaviors into categories that don't allow for what we perceive as contrasts or contradictions.

The issue of sexism and selective outrage also cannot go unchallenged. When a young male singer such as Nick Jonas changes his musical style and image or appearance, he is not criticized for presenting himself as a sexual creature. The fact that male singers rarely attract the amount or depth of critical analysis when singing about sexual experiences or longing is an indicator of a double standard. Robin Thicke is a rare exception, and that is an extreme example given the circumstances.

Cyrus recently wrapped a season on *The Voice* as one of the judges/coaches and released a single from her sixth studio album. The single, "Malibu," has currently peaked at the number 10 spot on Billboard.

See also: 1960s: Joplin, Janis; 1980s: Blondie; Gibson, Debbie; Madonna; MTV; 1990s: Backstreet Boys; 2000s: Rihanna; Spears, Britney; Swift, Taylor

Further Reading

Gaunt, Kyra D. 2015. "YouTube, Twerking and You: Context Collapse and the Handheld Co-Presence of Black Girls and Miley Cyrus." *Journal of Popular Music Studies* 27 (3): 244–273.

Jones, Jaleesa M. 2016. "Miley Cyrus Talks Gender, Pansexuality and Coming Out to Her Parents." *USA Today*, October 11. https://www.usatoday.com/story/life/entertainthis/2016/10/11/miley-cyrus-talks-sexuality-gender-identity-for-variety-power-of-women-issue/91900640/.

Spanos, Brittany. 2017. "Miley Cyrus' 10 Biggest Scandals." *Rolling Stone,* May 8. https://www.rollingstone.com/music/lists/miley-cyrus-10-biggest-scandals-w481179.

Summers, Kimberly Dylan. 2009. *Miley Cyrus: A Biography*. Westport, CT: Greenwood Press.

DIVERGENT

Divergent, a popular trilogy of novels penned by author Veronica Roth (1988–) is set in a dystopian future where society has been divided into five separate and distinct factions: Candor, Abnegation, Dauntless, Amity, and Erudite. Each of these factions dedicates itself to the nurturing of a specific virtue in its members. For Candor, it's honesty that matters most; for Abnegation, selflessness is paramount; Dauntless focuses on bravery; Amity fosters peace; Erudite nurtures intelligence. The protagonist of the story, Tris Prior, discovers that she is actually "Divergent," meaning that she doesn't fit exclusively into the existing categories or factions. Eventually, she is then selected to train with other Divergents to become physically and mentally stronger in order to do battle for their survival. To be a Divergent in their society threatens the status quo and makes them targets of a totalitarian government.

After having her test results faked to shroud the fact that she is Divergent, Tris chooses the Dauntless faction and struggles significantly to prove herself and be accepted into that group. A transfer instructor, Four, takes an interest in Tris and aides her as she moves through the various tests and challenges of the faction. She makes the final cut and she and Four begin a romantic relationship. Tris becomes aware of a takeover plot that is being orchestrated by leaders in both the Dauntless and Erudite factions; they plan on eliminating the Abnegation faction. Tris shares this with her brother Caleb, who is an Erudite, but he doesn't believe what she tells him. After Tris is captured when it's discovered that she is a Divergent, her mother Natalie rescues her and she escapes. Her mother is killed and her father later sacrifices himself in order to protect her.

While dystopian-themed novels are nothing new within the realm of young adult (YA) literature, the phenomenal success of *The Hunger Games* series inspired many similar stories, and the *Divergent* trilogy is one of the more conspicuous ones. In order to determine possible reasons why these types of narratives connect so strongly with their target audience, it's important to look at significant events that have affected the lives of those who consume this type of media. This material resonates with teens because of its dark and cynical take on government and issues of mass control and subjugation. Several studies focusing on millennials indicate that a significant reason for their alleged apathy on important issues relates to their distrust of the political process itself. Since they feel alienated or ignored within the process, they don't necessarily feel compelled to get involved to the level others expect of them. So, while they may not be interested in engaging directly with politics and political issues, they might be seeking other avenues in which these issues are explored.

It's possible that some millennials may be engaged with important issues through fictional narratives such as *The Hunger Games* and *Divergent*. After all, these stories directly deal with issues of social injustice, Fascist governments, and the importance of taking a moral stand on the condition of our society. It doesn't hurt that the protagonists of these stories are young and are also experiencing universal struggles of self-identity and dealing with romantic conflicts. These elements of the novels appeal to their readers by offering characters that are relatable in terms of their internal struggles.

Although data suggest that the wide popularity of these dystopian novels among millennials suggests an interest in political engagement, it certainly cannot be proven. With the exception of the 2008 presidential election and the short-lived Occupy Wall Street movement, nothing quantifiable indicates a widespread "awakening" of social awareness and civic engagement since these novels have been released. An argument can be made, however, that reading novels that deal with important issues can spark conversation and debate, and that can be a starting point for other actions. If young people are inspired or motivated to become more aware and engaged in political issues after being exposed to media presentations like *Divergent*, then it has served an important purpose regardless of literary merit.

Although the screen adaptations for the first two books in the series did well at the box office, the third installment failed to live up to the studio's hopes. Modeling the approach of *The Hunger Games*, the third and final book of the *Divergent* series was split into two separate films. The third film adaptation, *Allegiant,* didn't indicate a strong finish for the series, so the fourth and final film adaptation of the series will be released as a television movie and not a theatrical one.

The film *Divergent* (2014) won several Teen Choice and People's Choice Awards, but overall critical reception to the film was lukewarm. Many movie reviewers felt the plot was predictable and the story line uninvolving.

In what might be seen as a real-life parallel of rebellion, actress Shailene Woodley, who played the role of Tris, was arrested in 2016 for her protest against the proposed access to the Dakota pipeline. She wrote a lengthy public statement about the arrest and spoke about the abuse perpetrated against Native Americans within the United States. Woodley has been very vocal about her position on this, but few celebrities are willing to go to jail for their political beliefs. The actress was charged with trespassing and engaging in a riot.

See also: 1960s: *Slaughterhouse-Five*; *Twilight Zone, The*; 1980s: *Back to the Future*; 1990s: *Harry Potter*; 2000s: *Hunger Games, The*; *Twilight*; *Vampire Diaries, The*

Further Reading

Berlatsky, Noah. 2014. "The Glorious Incoherence of *Divergent*." *The Atlantic*, March 24. https://www.theatlantic.com/entertainment/archive/2014/03/the-glorious -incoherence-of-em-divergent-em/284605/.

Dockterman, Eliana. 2014. "Why Hollywood Desperately Needs Shailene Woodley." *Time*, March 18, 2014. http://time.com/27165/why-hollywood-desperately-needs -shailene-woodley/.

O'Hehir, Andrew. 2014. "'Divergent' and 'Hunger Games' as Capitalist Agitprop." Salon, March 22, 2014. https://www.salon.com/2014/03/22/divergent_and_hunger_games _as_capitalist_agitprop/.

FRIDAY NIGHT LIGHTS

Friday Night Lights (2006–2011), a popular network TV series, was based on a theatrical film of the same name that was released in 2004 starring Billy Bob Thornton and Derek Luke. That film is based on a 1990 book entitled *Friday Night Lights: A Town, a Team, and a Dream* by H. G. Bissinger. The source material for both the film and the TV show is a nonfiction book of sports journalism that follows the Permian Panthers, a high school football team from Odessa, Texas. The book follows the team's journey to the Texas state championship. Though the original intent was to highlight the game and its players, the book ultimately is viewed as a criticism of the town in which it takes place.

Actor-director Peter Berg saw strong potential for adapting the film into a weekly television series as he felt that the constraints of a two-hour film severely limited the depth of character exploration that could be accomplished. By moving the location to the fictional town of Dillon and adding multiple fictional characters to flesh out the themes and story lines, Berg hoped to expand the focus of the book and film into an examination of issues affecting Middle America.

The series centers on the Taylor family: Coach Eric Taylor (Kyle Chandler), wife Tami (Connie Britton), and daughter Julie (Aimee Teegarden). The show chronicles various team members and follows their personal challenges and struggles, including a serious injury that derails the talented quarterback, Jason Street (Scott Porter), paralyzing him. Due to the economic instability of the town and grim prospects for most of its residents, football is seen as not just a sport or entertainment, but as a religion, giving salvation and possible freedom for the players, and subsequently for the town's inhabitants. By featuring story lines about the Taylor children and the local football team, the intention was to appeal to a teen demographic. Sports shows that focus on high school athletics feature younger actors and typically include plots that teens can relate to and become invested in over an entire season and beyond.

Fans, both in the show and in life, often spend a lot of money and invest a lot of emotional energy into supporting their home team(s). The emotional investment can be especially fervent when it's at the local level. Teens and their parents attend games together and become deeply invested in game outcomes because of the feelings of membership and community generated when fans know the players personally. The teams become extensions of the town and its inhabitants.

American sports are embedded in myth and hero worship. Even in professional sports where most of the fans never know the players personally or interact with them in any direct way, there is nonetheless a perceived connection between them on the part of the fan. Additionally, there is an inherent belief of fairness among fans relative to sports. Specifically, there is a strong view that good players and teams are rewarded with success. They win games; they win championships. Bad players and bad teams do not. Poor sportsmanship is viewed negatively. This is restricted most times, however, to behavior on the field or court, as most fans don't want to know what goes on in player's personal lives—at least not anything unsavory or negative. When players are caught using performance-enhancing drugs, for example, most players and the media point to the behavior as grossly unfair and unsportsmanlike. At some level, though, athletes, fans, and the media know that this occurs. They also know when professional athletes commit crimes or break the law.

Friday Night Lights struggled in the ratings and was on the "chopping block" for cancellation each season. Several cross promotions were done the first season that involved potential scholarships and other appealing items for the target audience as an incentive to watch the show, but it didn't happen. One possible reason for the show's low ratings: viewers expected a "feel good" experience about a high school football team. Viewers who tuned in were instead treated to a serious examination of issues such as poverty, abortion, and racism. Although these issues affect teens, a disconnect between the marketing focus of the show and the actual content proved to be problematic. Although elements of the show highlighted traditional coming-of-age themes, the intended viewers largely ignored the show.

Critics praised the show for its writing, direction, and performances. Unlike other scripted series, cast members were given leeway with the script. They were allowed to add or modify their lines based on their interpretation of character authenticity. This lent an added element of reality to the show. Rehearsals were not done, and actors most times did scenes in one take. Again, the producers and director felt this offered a more unique and rewarding experience for viewers.

Although the show developed a small but loyal fan base, it was canceled after five seasons (two seasons on NBC and three on a DirectTV network). In that short time, it won a Peabody Award, a Humanitas Award, and several technical Emmy Awards. In 2011, star Kyle Chandler won an Emmy for Outstanding Lead Actor for a drama series, and the show won an award for writing as well.

As with many shows that garner low ratings on their initial network run, *Friday Night Lights* has found a new audience with syndication and release of the series on DVD. President of NBC at the time of the show's run, Kevin Reilly, has expressed regret that the show was marketed to the wrong audience as he feels that it should have been geared toward a female demographic as opposed to teen sports fans.

See also: 1950s: *Adventures of Ozzie and Harriet, The*; *Father Knows Best*; *I Love Lucy*; *Leave It to Beaver*; 1960s: *Patty Duke Show, The*; 1970s: *Happy Days*; *Welcome Back, Kotter*; 1980s: *Back to the Future*; *Cosby Show, The*; *Facts of Life, The*; *Family Ties*; *Full House*; *Saved by the Bell*; *Wonder Years, The*; 1990s: *Boy Meets World*; *Clarissa Explains It All*; *7th Heaven*; 2000s: *One Tree Hill*

Further Reading

Bissinger, H. G. 2015. *Friday Night Lights, 25th Anniversary Edition: A Town, a Team, and a Dream*. Boston, MA: Da Capo Press.

Garber, Megan. 2016. "Friday Night Lights Democratized TV Drama." *The Atlantic,* October 3. https://www.theatlantic.com/entertainment/archive/2016/10/friday-night-lights-helped-turn-tv-into-literature/502604/.

Phillips, Benjamin P. 2014. "Clear Eyes, Full Hearts, Can Lose: Friday Night Lights and the Myth of the Rewarding of Morality in Sports." *Journal of Popular Culture* 47 (5).

GLEE

Glee (2009–2015) is a successful musical comedy-drama that aired on the Fox network for six seasons. The story revolves around a group of students and faculty at fictional William McKinley High School in Ohio. The main characters are members of a "glee" club or show choir that engages in competitions at the state, regional, and national level. The group is led by Spanish teacher Will Schuester (Matthew Morrison). His archnemesis is cheerleading coach Sue Sylvester (Jane Lynch) who routinely sabotages his efforts and mocks the group to the point of cruelty. Originally conceived by one of its three original writers as a feature film, the series focused primarily on the trials and travails of its teenage members as they struggled with issues of personal identity, sexuality, and a host of other topics normally associated with coming-of-age stories. Primary members of the glee club include: Kurt Hummel (Chris Colfer), Rachel Berry (Lea Michele), Artie Abrams (Kevin McHale), Santana Lopez (Naya Rivera), Tina Cohen-Chang (Jenna Ushkowitz), Mercedes Jones (Amber Riley), Brittany Pierce (Heather Morris), Finn Hudson (Cory Monteith), Quinn Fabray (Dianna Agron), and Noah "Puck" Puckerman (Mark Salling).

The identities and characteristics of the main characters in the show fall along familiar lines with Kurt as the effeminate gay teen who loves musical theater, Rachel as the talented "diva," "Puck" as the womanizing athlete, Finn as the dimwitted jock, Artie as the dorky and awkward kid with a disability, Santana as the sexually provocative cheerleader with Brittany as her academically challenged sidekick, Tina as the Asian American student, and Mercedes as the confident and assertive African American girl.

One of the most groundbreaking aspects of this show was its honest and straightforward depiction of teenagers dealing with their burgeoning sexuality. While other TV series have addressed issues of sexuality in various forms and to varying degrees, *Glee* was a trailblazer in that it focused on LGBT issues not as secondary story lines, but as deserving of serious attention and treatment. A popular and ongoing story line centered on Kurt and his more gender-conforming boyfriend Blaine, who was also a member of a glee club at another high school. The show presents their romance in much the same vein as that of their heterosexual counterparts. Portraying these characters as equals to their heterosexual classmates and club members allowed audience members, some of whom may have had pre-existing biases, to see them as "typical" teens struggling with all of the same fears and foibles that most young adults struggle with.

The Kurt–Blaine story also segued to topical themes such as the process of LGBT youths "coming out" to their parents and the bullying of LGBT teens by classmates. One story line that stemmed from the Kurt–Blaine romance was that of a closeted football player at McKinley who bullies Kurt because he is gay. In a later episode, the bully kisses Kurt as he struggles to come to terms with his own sexuality. It was an attempt to show the negative effects of internalized homophobia and how that sometimes manifests itself.

Another unique aspect of featuring these types of story lines on the show was the real-time opportunity for viewers to react among friends and acquaintances. *Glee* was a show that appealed to group viewings. Friends on college campuses and elsewhere would gather to watch it together and discuss it as events on the series unfolded. The level of fandom associated with the show was and is impressive. As with almost all TV series, there were fan favorites, and with existing social media platforms in place, dedicated viewers often took to sites like Twitter and Facebook to express their views.

Beyond the casual viewing and discussions that might take place during or after a viewing of the show, these group gatherings allowed for insight into the views held by those watching the series. A 2011 study examined (in part) how groups of college students reacted to story lines and how (or if) plotlines dealing with LGBT issues affected these viewers, half of whom identified as gay. In tandem with this, researchers examined how viewers outside of this group responded to the show on social media sites such as Twitter. A variety of methodologies were utilized for this part of the study, looking at the use of specific hashtags and trending topics relative to the show.

One of the more interesting findings of the study related to the correlation between those who had overall positive feelings about the show in general and their likelihood of either being LGBT or LGBT accepting. In other words, the posts and comments from viewers were seen to be an indication to others of how accepting or unaccepting these individuals were of people who identified as lesbian, gay, bisexual, or transgender. Taking this a step further, group gatherings to view the show were sometimes seen as "safe spaces" where fans felt they could be themselves and not worry about judgment or bullying from classmates or dorm-mates. Some even saw this as a potential opportunity to meet others whom they could have friendships or even possibly romantic relationships with.

The show was not without controversy. Although embraced by progressive and LGBT groups, it received criticism from religious groups who felt its portrayal of premarital sex and openly gay characters was immoral. One particular episode raised the ire of several religious groups when it focused on the Lady Gaga gay anthem "Born This Way" and a message of acceptance of the LGBT community. Political groups also criticized the show for an episode that featured comedienne Kathy Griffin as a right-wing ideologue who was portrayed as mean-spirited. They felt the show promoted values not in sync with Middle America and glorified teenage sexuality.

Glee is somewhat of a rarity in that it was a transmedia vehicle. The show expanded far beyond its network airings. Songs from the show were released weekly on iTunes, a 3-D *Glee* movie was released, and countless social media accounts and YouTube channels were devoted to it. The show crossed multiple platforms to connect with fans, and at its peak it was highly rated and generally well regarded by media critics.

After two successful seasons, ratings began to decline for the show. This can be attributed to a variety of issues: the novelty of the show seemed to begin waning, favorite characters moved on beyond the high school setting and new characters were introduced, many felt that the quality of the writing declined after one of the original creators, Ryan Murphy, stopped writing for the show.

Glee won numerous awards including Golden Globes, Emmys, and even the Screen Actors Guild. Perhaps most significantly, it received the GLAAD Media Award in both 2010 and 2011.

See also: 1970s: *Grease*; 2000s: *High School Musical*

Further Reading

Ananny, Mike, Mary L. Gray, and Alice Markwick. 2014. "Dolphins Are Just Gay Sharks: Glee and the Queer Case of Transmedia as Text and Object." *Television and New Media* 15 (7).

Balser, Erin. 2010. *Don't Stop Believin': The Unofficial Guide to Glee*. Toronto: ECW Press.

Meyer, Michaela D. E., and Megan W. Wood. 2013. "Sexuality and Teen Television: Emerging Adults Respond to Representations of Queer Identity on Glee." *Sexuality and Culture* 17: 434–448.

GOSSIP GIRL

Gossip Girl (2007–2012) is a teen drama that ran for six seasons on the CW network. It focuses on a group of pampered teens living in the Upper East Side of Manhattan, New York. The episodes are narrated by an anonymous blogger who delves into the lives of the group and exposes all of their secrets. The show's primary characters include "It" girl Serena van der Woodsen (Blake Lively), her best friend and sometimes nemesis Blair Waldorf (Leighton Meester), and a host of male and female supporting players with various story lines, most of which are connected to the main characters. The series opens with Serena returning to New York after a mysterious absence. Soon thereafter, relationships and histories are established for the benefit of the viewers. Love triangles and rivalries dominate the show.

Blair, the undisputed Queen Bee of Constance Billard School for Girls, spends much of her time planning details of her first sexual encounter with boyfriend

Nate Archibald (Chace Crawford). Nate, however, has stronger romantic feelings for Blair's best friend, and he constantly finds ways to avoid any erotic encounters. Serena has an on again/off again relationship with scholarship student, Dan Humphrey (Penn Badgley), an aspiring writer from Brooklyn who is the perennial outsider among the group of spoiled socialites. Mating rituals, dating, and sex are ripe topics for teen-centered dramas. At its core, though, *Gossip Girl* is about identity and authenticity in the digital age.

Some shows utilize their settings or locations to the extent that the locale becomes a character in and of itself. Given the lifestyles of its characters, it seems obvious that *Gossip Girl* would be filmed in New York City. The cost of filming there, however, is quite expensive. When originally pitched to TV executives, there was an initial plan to film in a Los Angeles sound studio and re-create the setting of numerous

Teen-centric *Gossip Girl* featured attractive and wealthy high school students living in New York. Blake Lively (pictured) starred as the fashionable and mysterious Serena van der Woodsen. (James Devaney/WireImage/Getty Images)

locales in New York City. Just as *Sex and the City* utilized the Big Apple to maximum effect, *Gossip Girl* did as well, featuring shots of famous nightclubs, restaurants, and hotels. Even the exterior shots of the show's fictional high school were filmed outside the Museum of the City of New York. The superficial appeal of the characters' lifestyles was also a big draw for teen girls; seeing how the "other half" lives is always intriguing, especially when it's portrayed in glamorous settings.

Although rites of passage for teenagers haven't changed much through the ages, culture and technology have. The characters in the show live in a universe where their every move is monitored and reported. Although much of this is via the ongoing Gossip Girl website where activities are reported for public consumption, everyday access to and use of social media sites can be sufficient to destroy friendships, wreck romances, and instigate and perpetuate intense rivalries. No matter how carefully public personas are crafted and nurtured, one negative post/Tweet/blog entry can create chaos and degrade reputations. Nowhere is this better demonstrated than the havoc caused for Blair. She painfully maps out every aspect of her life with the desire to achieve maximum success. Although she controls her narrative in real life, entries from the blog disrupt this on a regular basis. Social media usage and technology is especially prevalent and significant to teens, so this aspect of the show also resonates with the target audience.

This excessive exposure begs the question: how does one reconcile the public with the private persona? Is it even possible? In a society that relies more and more upon social media to disseminate "news" (the current president of the United States regularly uses Twitter to communicate national and even international issues that are traditionally handled via news outlets and formal media statements), how do individuals identify truth or facts and distinguish them from opinion or even gossip?

Another aspect of technology relative to *Gossip Girl* is its reach beyond television. Although ratings for the show dipped consecutively each season, it had a strong following on *Second Life*, an online "virtual playground" that allows *Gossip Girl* viewers to experience life on the Upper East Side. Gamers can sit in Central Park and people watch, or shop at exclusive retail stores featured on the series. The CW maximized the relationship between advertisers and the show, capitalizing on the appeal of marketer's products seen being used by the show's popular characters. Brands such as Verizon, VitaminWater, and L'Oréal all had product placement in the show. The psychology of this is fairly obvious: fans can vicariously live through their favorite series characters (to an extent) by wearing the same or similar clothes, drinking the same beverages, hanging out—albeit online—in the same spaces, and so on. Although *Gossip Girl* wasn't the first show to use product placement or utilize online extensions of the show's experience for viewers, it did so masterfully, prompting several publications including the *New York Times* to remark that it may have been the first show that was created in part to promote specific types of fashion and promote them accordingly within its production.

Gossip Girl, while primarily an entertainment vehicle, illustrates the dangers and damage done when access to technology is married to malicious intent. Whether the lead characters deserve to be "outed" online for their duplicitous activities is a question for another discussion. The issue here is that the ability to do this in the first place creates and fosters an atmosphere of negativity and likely abuse. With the proliferation of online bullying, this topic is especially relevant for teens and tweens.

Gossip Girl is based on a series of young adult books by author Cecily von Ziegesar (1970–). The show won multiple *Teen Choice Awards* in 2008, 2009, 2010, and 2011. It received mainly positive critics' reviews, especially for the first few seasons. The series was met with much negative criticism from the Parents Television Council and was referred to in one article as a "nasty piece of work." Its depiction of teen sex and other issues were deemed inappropriate by some of the same vocal critics who decried story lines on the series *Glee*. *Gossip Girl* spawned several international adaptations produced and distributed in both Turkey and Mexico.

See also: 1980s: *Sweet Valley High*; 1990s: *Clarissa Explains It All*; 2000s: *Mean Girls*; *One Tree Hill*; *Pretty Little Liars*; *Sisterhood of the Traveling Pants, The*; *Vampire Diaries, The*

Further Reading

Grant, Tracy. 2011. "'Gossip Girls, Psycho Killer' Sends Bad Message to Teens." *Washington Post,* October 19. https://www.washingtonpost.com/lifestyle/advice/gossip-girls-psycho-killer-sends-bad-message-to-teens/2011/10/03/gIQAkH7AyL_story.html?utm_term=.c221c48a7502.

Jaeger, Marley. 2016. "How 'Gossip Girl' Is Feminist as Hell." *Odyssey*, August 23. https://www.theodysseyonline.com/gossip-girl-feminist.

Orenstein, Hannah. 2017. "23 Ways 'Gossip Girl' Would Be Different in 2017." *Seventeen*, September 19. http://www.seventeen.com/celebrity/movies-tv/a41417/how-gossip-girl-would-be-different-in-2016/.

HIGH SCHOOL MUSICAL

High School Musical (2006), a Disney Channel Original Movie, was the most successful premier in the channel's history, producing two sequels and generating a best-selling soundtrack. It also created cross media products that included video games, books, and even an ice show that premiered in New York City before its global tour. The movie appeals primarily to tweens and teens, but it can also be watched with parents. The story focuses on teens Troy Bolton (Zac Efron) and Gabriella Montez (Vanessa Hudgens). Troy is a popular jock and Gabriella a math and science whiz kid. They share a passion for musical theater, and when they both audition for leads, a schism is created among the student body. Troy and Gabriella predictably overcome any obstacles thrown in their path, even that of jealous rival Sharpay Evans (Ashley Tisdale). One noteworthy aspect of the film is its racial diversity in casting, not something typically associated with Disney films. Chad Danforth (Corbin Bleu) is Troy's best friend, and Taylor McKessie (Monique Coleman) is Gabriella's friend; both are African American. Chad is a jock and Taylor is an academic, and the two become romantically involved.

Disney doesn't have a strong history or reputation for diversity, and many of its shows and movies have typically centered on white characters. Even when Disney has featured non-white characters in some of their animated films, they've been the target of criticism with regard to authenticity issues, although the 2017 film *Coco* was well received. So, featuring two important characters who are African American is significant, especially since their race isn't important or integral to the story line—they just happen to be friends with the lead characters and they happen to not be white. It's a significant move forward for Disney and shows the importance of representation in film and television for people of color.

The setting of *High School Musical* has universal appeal, and the cast has just enough diversity to satisfy both viewers and critics while maintaining the squeaky image that Disney has built a media empire on. There are themes of unity and community within the production; the finale even culminates in a song entitled "We're

All in This Together." Many have noted the conspicuous similarity to the final song in the musical *Grease,* entitled "We'll Always Be Together."

To understand how this made-for-television production became a pop cultural phenomenon, it's necessary to understand the state of the music industry in 2006. With the proliferation of technology and a move away from buying physical records (the current trend of vinyl record sales notwithstanding), the music industry has changed in the way it produces, markets, and distributes records. More importantly, where there used to be differentiated market segments for different genres of music, there is now more of an overlap, specifically with respect to children's interest in popular music and buying power. Historically, children haven't been directly targeted with pop music. Their primary exposure to music has been via television shows like *Sesame Street* and Disney animated films like *Beauty and the Beast* and *The Lion King.*

Music executives quickly realized that there was an untapped market for popular music: tweens. This age group generally includes children from the age of 9 through 12. Historically, there had always been a downward influence with respect to music—i.e., adult musicians and groups influence teens and children with respect to musical taste. Typically, a child is exposed to music at different stages of development; she or he may begin with lullabies, music on TV shows, and movies geared specifically toward children. As the child progresses into adolescence, she or he often begins to listen to more mainstream popular music and then eventually gravitates toward one or more specific genres, be it country-western, pop, rock, electronica, and so on. Acts like Miley Cyrus (during her Hannah Montana days) and the Jonas Brothers demonstrated that the reverse could happen: adolescents having an influence on popular music that is typically targeted toward adults. *High School Musical,* then, was explicitly marketed to tweens and teens and was successful in that demographic in large part because of the music.

High School Musical builds off earlier works such as *West Side Story.* That famous musical centered on two rival gangs, the Jets and the Sharks. Although there are no gangs in *High School Musical*, the pairing of Troy and Gabriella creates a conflict among students, splitting pupils into one of two camps: pro-jock or pro-academic. This has wide appeal for a teenage audience since it mirrors (to some degree) the perpetual conflict between the popular crowd and the "brainy" crowd. This allows the filmmakers both to indulge in an age old story line about the battle among high schoolers for social status and to challenge it. With respect to the love story between the two leads, elements of *Romeo and Juliet* are present, and again, teen fans become invested in the outcome of the story and are especially intrigued with plots involving a couple with different backgrounds who inevitably are brought together against all odds.

In addition to the original made-for-television musical, *High School Musical* spawned two sequels: *High School Musical 2* and *High School Musical 3: Senior Year.* Unlike its predecessors, *High School Musical 3: Senior Year* was released theatrically and grossed more than $90 million in the United States. The staggering success of the *High School Musical* franchise not only demonstrated the buying power and influence of the tween market, it solidified once again the Disney corporation's immense business savvy relative to creating and nurturing media productions that successfully cross other media platforms. Both the *High School Musical* soundtrack and the DVD were also hugely successful. It also launched the career of actor-singer Zac Efron, who has gone on to star in several R-rated comedies including *Neighbors* and *Dirty Grandpa.*

See also: 1970s: *Grease*; 2000s: *Glee*

Further Reading

Leszkiewicz, Anna. 2016. "Extracurricular Angst: How Does *High School Musical* Look Ten Years After Its Release?" *New Statesman*, January 20. https://www.newstatesman.com/culture/film/2016/01/extracurricular-angst-how-does-high-school-musical-look-ten-years-after-its.

Potter, Anna. 2011. "It's a Small World After All: New Media Constellations and Disney's Rising Star—The Global Success of *High School Musical*." *International Journal of Cultural Studies* 15 (2).

Rodosthenous, George. 2017. *The Disney Musical on Stage and Screen: Critical Approaches from 'Snow White' to 'Frozen.'* London: Methuen.

HUNGER GAMES, THE

The Hunger Games, a popular trilogy of young adult books written by Suzanne Collins (1962–), was adapted into an equally popular series of theatrical films. *The Hunger Games* is the first installment of a series that takes place in the future and chronicles a reality TV like "show" that features groups of children and teenagers competing against one another for physical survival. The story takes place in the fictional country of Panem, which has been divided into 12 districts and the Capitol, which houses President Snow and wealthy citizens. Residents of the districts all live in varying degrees of poverty, especially in the outer districts. Due to an uprising against Snow and the Capitol by citizens of the now defunct District 13, an event called the Reaping takes place each year, where a boy and girl from each district are selected by lottery to compete in the Hunger Games. The televised show is intended to be a reminder to the districts of their failed attempt at revolt and to dissuade them from any inclinations to repeating that effort.

The novel focuses on protagonist Katniss Everdeen, a young woman from the poorest district (12) who lives with her mother and younger sister, Prim. Her father was killed in a coal mine accident. Katniss is adept at hunting; she is the food provider of the family. She has honed the use of a bow and arrow to a demonstrable skill that impresses everyone in the district, including her friend, Gale Hawthorne. When her younger sister is chosen to be a tribute (contestant) in the annual Hunger Games event, Katniss immediately volunteers to go in her place. The male tribute is Peeta Mellark, a baker who harbors a long-term crush on Katniss.

The *Hunger Games* is very dark material for books aimed at a young adult demographic. The very notion of children competing in a televised fight to the death is remarkable in its morbidity. The larger narrative, though, is one of political and social oppression. District residents live in squalor and literally struggle to survive daily while elites in the Capitol enjoy lavish lifestyles in a picturesque setting. Until Katniss enters the game and understands the machinations and tyranny of President Snow and those who support him, she trudges through daily existence with a sole focus on physical survival. This, of course, is intentional. With the population relegated to second-class status, they are prevented from focusing on bigger issues of independence and equality.

The reality TV show element of both the novel and the film(s) reflect our culture's continued obsession with this form of entertainment. For one, Collins was inspired to write the novels while switching between coverage of the war in Iraq and reality television. Additionally, both network and cable television networks continue to churn out this type of programming for several reasons: it's cheaper to produce than scripted shows, it doesn't need stellar ratings to turn a profit, and it clearly serves some role with the viewing public based on its popularity. One need only examine a TV show like *Survivor* to understand the manipulation of both contestants and viewers. Although participants in that show are not expected to kill one another, they are certainly encouraged to "do whatever it takes" to win. Lying, cheating, and stealing are all acceptable. Emotional manipulation is expected and allegedly encouraged by the show's producers. Just as the contestants in *The Hunger Games* are manipulated by President Snow and his inner circle, the "show" they are on is just as manufactured and controlled as *Survivor*.

Katniss demonstrates throughout these novels—particularly in the first one—that she is media literate. Given that the Capitol/President Snow actively engages in misinformation and disinformation campaigns, Katniss shows an innate ability to use logic and critical thinking to see how the government uses and manipulates media to control the citizenry. For example, she realizes that in order to win the Hunger Games, she must deceive viewers into believing a narrative that she has concocted along with Peeta. They will pretend to be star-crossed lovers, thereby drawing in viewers to their manufactured romance. Although Peeta does have genuine feelings for Katniss, she is confused about her feelings for him as she harbors deep-seated emotions for Gale, her longtime friend and hunting partner from home. The love triangle within the story line appealed to teen fans by allowing them to "root" for their favorite young man and hope that Katniss ended up with him.

Although Katniss and her sister attend school within the district, her main focus due to poverty has always been hunting and survival. She is, however, able to determine exactly how to play the game—not just physically, but emotionally as well. When she and Peeta appear to have won the contest, the Capitol reinstates the rule they previously revoked that would have allowed a boy and girl from the same district to win. Rather than concede, they fake a suicide pact by pretending to eat poison berries (shades of *Romeo and Juliet*), knowing that the government will not allow the fan favorites to go out in that fashion.

Having a teen heroine attracted a teen audience and depicted a strong-willed, smart protagonist that young girls could especially relate to. The rebellion aspect of the story is also critical to its popularity; Katniss represents the evolution of a young woman who grows out of her apathy or reluctant acceptance of the status quo into a fierce warrior who defends her family and community at great risk to her own safety. It also connects with some readers at a political level and might prompt them to take a greater interest in social issues.

Katniss becomes a hero and symbol of revolt to the citizens of the districts as further adventures occur in the sequels *Catching Fire* and *Mockingjay*. There is the element of children outwitting and outlasting their adult oppressors, providing a theme that resonates with the target audience of the books and the film adaptations. Additionally, Katniss has to deal with a myriad of issues as the story progresses, including posttraumatic stress, the continued barbarousness of President Snow, the demolishment of District 12, and the loss of her younger sister, Prim. At the end of the final novel many years later, Katniss and Peeta have married and had children, but Katniss still struggles with the trauma of the games and notes that she will for a long time.

The *Hunger Games* book series has been critically lauded and financially successful. The series has sold at least 65 million copies. The series was adapted to four theatrical films and stars Oscar winner Jennifer Lawrence in the role of Katniss Everdeen, Josh Hutcherson as Peeta Mellark, Liam Hemsworth as Gale, and Donald Sutherland as President Snow. Each film in the series enjoyed significant box office success and set opening day and opening weekend records. The films have grossed close to $3 billion worldwide.

See also: 1960s: *Slaughterhouse-Five*; *Twilight Zone, The*; 1980s: *Back to the Future*; 1990s: *Harry Potter*; 2000s: *Divergent*; *Twilight*; *Vampire Diaries, The*

Further Reading

Collins, Suzanne. 2008. *The Hunger Games*. New York: Scholastic

Holmes, Linda. 2013. "What Really Makes Katniss Stand Out? Peeta, Her Movie Girlfriend." NPR, November 25. https://www.npr.org/sections/monkeysee/2013/11/25/247146164/what-really-makes-katniss-stand-out-peeta-her-movie-girlfriend.

Latham, Don, and Jonathan M. Hollister. 2014. "The Games People Play: Information and Media Literacies in the Hunger Games Trilogy." *Children's Literature in Education* 45 (1): 33–46.

Scarlet, Janina. 2015. "The Psychology of Inspirational Women: Katniss Everdeen." Mary Sue, March 26. https://www.themarysue.com/the-psychology-of-inspirational-women-katniss-everdeen/.

Zeitchik, Steven. 2015. "The Katniss Factor: What the 'Hunger Games' Movies Say about Feminism, and War." *Los Angeles Times*, November 20. http://www.latimes.com/entertainment/movies/moviesnow/la-with-hunger-games-mockingjay-part-2-theaters-katniss-feminism-lawrence-20151119-story.html.

JUNO

Juno (2007), which was produced by an independent studio and shot on a shoe-string budget, became one of the biggest commercial and critical hits the year that it was released. The story focuses on an unplanned pregnancy. Its protagonist, high schooler Juno MacGuff (Ellen Page), becomes pregnant after a sexual encounter with her friend, Paulie Bleeker (Michael Cera). Initially planning to have an abortion, Juno abruptly changes her mind after a visit to a local women's clinic. After speaking with her parents about the situation, Juno decides to give the baby up for adoption. She finds an interested and ideal couple in Mark and Vanessa Loring (Jason Bateman and Jennifer Garner). At the film's conclusion, Juno decides to allow Vanessa to raise her baby alone after Mark has bolted from the marriage. This decision demonstrates that Juno has grown and is able to make adult decisions that reflect personal responsibility.

Teen pregnancy is a familiar topic in Hollywood films. Traditionally, films that have explored the topic concentrate on the turmoil and emotional upheaval associated with it. There are predictably shocked parents and school administrators usually blame "irresponsible" children for having premarital sex. Protagonists in these films are many times painted as one extreme or another—an innocent victim who fell prey to the charms of a young man, or a "bad girl" who knew exactly what she was doing, perhaps even with the hopes of getting pregnant so that she could manipulate the father into a long-term commitment, most times marriage. Juno is neither of these. She is an intelligent and witty young woman who isn't sure exactly how she feels about Paulie. Furthermore, her parents support her decision to carry the pregnancy to term and then allow the child to be adopted by the Lorings. Juno, while clearly realizing the significance of her situation, is still a teenage girl. She is still discovering who she is and has the same struggles that most teenage girls have relative to self-identity, sexuality, and independence.

Teen pregnancy and abortion are potentially weighty topics for a comedy. One notable aspect of *Juno* is in how it was received by both pro-life and pro-choice groups and individuals. Generally speaking, the film appealed to both sides of the issue. Pro-lifers applauded the decision that the character made to give birth while pro-choice advocates viewed the decision as an individual one—i.e., Juno wasn't forced to carry her baby to term; she made herself aware of the options and chose the one that felt right to her.

Although the issues examined in *Juno* are serious ones, it is still a traditional coming-of-age story in several respects. Although Juno engages in clever banter with those around her and exudes a jaded take on most things, she realizes that she does indeed have feelings for Paulie. These emotions rise to the surface when she discovers that he has asked another girl to the school prom. In this scene, Paulie reminds Juno that it was she who suggested they go no further with anything romantic so as not to complicate matters further.

Things begin to sour between the Lorings as the film progresses. Viewers initially are empathetic toward the character of Mark, an arrested adolescent who bonds with Juno over their shared love of horror films. Vanessa is presented as the stereotypical overachieving female career woman who must have every aspect of her life perfectly managed and maintained. Juno discovers, however, that Mark is not being honest with his wife about his unwillingness or inability to commit to being a parent. In an awkward and inappropriate moment, Mark even makes a sexual advance upon Juno, another indication of his immaturity and fascination with youth.

One cannot view *Juno* without taking into account religious, political, and media influences on teen sexuality. After the social and political upheaval of the 1960s and 1970s, the 1980s saw a return to traditional beliefs about gender roles and sexuality within our culture. Conservatism returned with the election of President Ronald Reagan and the rise of the Moral Majority, led by televangelist Jerry Falwell. This political movement mobilized millions across the country to become involved in sociopolitical issues and to support causes and candidates who reflected conservative Christian beliefs. Although the group was dissolved at the end of the decade, their influence still reverberated throughout the country.

This movement was reignited to a degree when George W. Bush ran for (and won) the presidency in 2000. His campaign exploited fears and concerns over issues such as marriage equality and reproductive rights for women. Culture wars were reignited, and hordes of conservative men and women were put into cabinet positions during Bush's administration. Politics and religion became intertwined. This resulted in how sexuality was treated within the media, especially within teen-centric media. While religious and political groups were promoting abstinence-only sexual education programs in schools, and railing against the evils of premarital sex, popular culture was promoting women's sexual liberation through popular programs like *Sex and the City* and *Gossip Girl*.

Putting aside the explosive topic of teen pregnancy and abortion, Juno is in many ways an average teenage girl attempting to navigate the expectations of male–female relationships in the 21st century. In order to do this, she must deal with the onslaught of media exposure that is put forth regularly, much of which contains mixed messages about sexuality and gender roles.

Juno was nominated for four Academy Awards. It won for Best Original Screenplay (Diablo Cody). The film received countless accolades from film critics and grossed more than $230 million at the box office worldwide.

See also: 1980s: Hughes, John, Films of; *Revenge of the Nerds*; *Say Anything . . .*; *Wonder Years, The*; 1990s: *Freaks and Geeks*; 2000s: *Gossip Girl*; *Napoleon Dynamite*; *Teen Mom*

Further Reading

Cardamenis, Forrest. 2015. "The Misunderstood Feminism of Diablo Cody." *The Week*, August 20. http://theweek.com/articles/572789/misunderstood-feminism-diablo-cody.

Lowen, Linda. 2017. "What 'Juno' Says about Teen Pregnancy, Abortion and Choice." ThoughtCo, May 23. https://www.thoughtco.com/what-juno-says-about-teen-pregnancy-3534249.

Ralph, Kaylen. 2015. "Pregnancy on Film: Ranking the Good, the Bad, the Ugly." *The Riveter*, July 21. http://www.therivetermagazine.com/pregnancy-on-film-ranking-the-good-the-bad-the-ugly/.

LAVIGNE, AVRIL

Avril Lavigne (1984–), a "punk pop" singer-songwriter from Canada was pegged by the media as the "anti-Britney" when she burst into the American music scene in 2002 with her debut album *Let Go*. The album spawned three top 10 hits: "Complicated," "Sk8ter Boi," and "I'm with You." The album reached six time platinum status and was the best-selling album of 2002. Lavigne also snagged something just as important in the music business as sales recognition: she won the 2002 MTV Music Video Award for Best New Artist. Despite her commercial success as a pop artist, Lavigne's roots are more country-western than pop or punk.

Lavigne's big musical break came when she won a radio contest that allowed her to share the stage at an event with country music superstar, Shania Twain. After that performance, she got noticed by record executives, who expected her to fit into a country music mode. Initial attempts to force this aesthetic on her were unsuccessful, and Lavigne ended up working with producers who understood and accommodated her true passion for making pop music with an edge.

Canadian singer-songwriter Avril Lavigne was marketed as a musical alternative to contemporaries such as Britney Spears. Lavigne appealed to teens that connected with her casual personal style and relationship-focused songs. (Tim Roney/Getty Images)

The Canadian born singer-songwriter quickly gained a reputation within the music business as being strong-willed and outspoken. She routinely battled with stylists and photographers on magazine shoots. They allegedly tried to steer her into the predictable "girl next door" image with pink T-shirts and shorter skirts; she rebelled and instead insisted on wearing what she liked and what she felt comfortable in. Her authenticity resonated with young fans who admired her refusal to conform to societal expectations relative to what a "young lady" should look and behave like.

When Lavigne entered the popular music market in 2002, consumers had been under a steady diet of artists like Britney Spears. The music and images associated with Spears and her contemporaries often capitalized on burgeoning sexuality and a focus if not fixation on the female body. However, Lavigne bucked this trend, favoring baggy clothes, men's neckties, and a style that was more aligned with punk rock or grunge than traditional attire worn by young female pop stars. This divergence from the norm attracted young female fans that may not have identified with Spears's brand of sexual confidence and physicality. The music was markedly different as well. While Spears and other contemporaries sang of sexual longing and titillation, Lavigne focused more on the angst and confusion of first relationships. The passion and emotion she effused into her songs connected with young girls who were in touch with these emotions as they came of age. In other words, Lavigne's songs spoke more to the typical female adolescent that may have felt awkward or unsure of how to navigate romantic relationships.

All of Lavigne's albums did well commercially. She peaked on Billboard with multiple hit singles and remained a top-selling artist both within the United States and the United Kingdom. She became the second best-selling artist from Canada, right behind legendary balladeer Celine Dion.

As discussed throughout this book, media often relies on categorization of artists and content. Oftentimes, the label applied may not be an accurate reflection of the artist's work or talents, but it allows people to quickly identify a genre. Record producers and other executives, of course, do the same thing. To market their products effectively and efficiently, they place their artists into existing categories and subcategories. It is much easier to promote a new artist or band as being similar to an existing artist for point of reference. The expectation is that if consumers of Product X are told that Product Y is similar but new, they are more inclined to sample it than if Product Y has no existing association to another product. This works the same for books, movies, TV shows, and so on. Lavigne had to contend with this over the course of her career.

Though Lavigne never explicitly defined her music as "punk pop," that label stuck. Given that she enjoys skateboarding and would wear sporty clothes inspired by the punk aesthetic, it seemed like an easy way to define her, but the artist herself has avoided self-identifying as "punk." Additionally, she has never delved into social or political issues like many punk rock artists do. While her fans adored her and praised her individuality and apparent refusal to succumb to expected standards, others accused the singer of being nothing more than a poseur—an individual capitalizing on a current trend but lacking authenticity or credibility.

After achieving musical success, Lavigne tried her hand with a few acting projects, including voicing a character in the animated film, *Over the Hedge*. She also appears in the independent film, *Fast Food Nation,* directed by Richard Linklater. Her style has evolved over the years, and she collaborated with Disney on a line of clothes inspired by the film *Alice in Wonderland*. Lavigne also branched out into the world of designer fragrances with the introduction of her scent Black Star. Most of these efforts outside of music were marketed to her large teen fan base.

Avril Lavigne continues to record new music. Throughout her career, she has expressed disappointment in what she feels has been a dismissal of her songwriting abilities. Part of this she alleges is due to her age and the suspicion that she wasn't taken seriously as an artist. To complicate this, songwriting trio the Matrix accused the singer of passing off her three hit singles from *Let Go* as hers, but they assert that they penned the bulk of the lyrics. Lavigne denied the charges and insisted that she was the primary songwriter for those songs.

See also: 1960s: Doors, The; Joplin, Janis; Rolling Stones, The; 1970s: Devo; Led Zeppelin; Queen; 1980s: Blondie; Duran Duran; Gibson, Debbie; Lauper, Cyndi; Madonna; MTV; 1990s: Green Day; Morissette, Alanis; 2000s: My Chemical Romance; Spears, Britney

Further Reading

Copsey, Robert. 2013. "Avril Lavigne Talks 'Sexual' New Album Track 'Hello Kitty.'" *Digital Spy*, October 15. http://www.digitalspy.com/music/news/a523644/avril-lavigne-talks-sexual-new-album-track-hello-kitty/.

Kotarba, Joseph A. 2013. *Understanding Society through Popular Music*. Abingdon: Routledge.

Zulch, Meg. 2016. "Why Avril Lavigne Has Been Crucial to My Masculine Identity." Bustle, June 30. https://www.bustle.com/articles/169351-why-avril-lavigne-has-been-crucial-to-my-masculine-identity.

MEAN GIRLS

Mean Girls is a 2004 teen comedy that stars Lindsay Lohan and was written by *Saturday Night Live* alumna Tina Fey. It is loosely based on a nonfiction book entitled *Queen Bees and Wannabes* by Rosalind Wiseman. The film tells the story of shy and intellectual Cady Heron (Lindsay Lohan), a teenager who has moved with her scientist parents to the suburbs of Illinois after a 12-year stay in Africa. Attending her first public school, Cady is taken in by a pair of outcasts, Janis Ian (Lizzy Caplan) and Damian Leigh (Daniel Franzese). They educate her on the school's caste system and warn her specifically about a small but influential trio of "mean girls" known as the "Plastics" who rule the school socially. The group is led by Regina George (Rachel McAdams), a popular and attractive student who holds power and influence over followers Gretchen Wieners (Lacey Chabert) and Karen Smith (Amanda Seyfried). Perhaps out of curiosity, the trio befriends Cady and she soon finds herself a part of their inner circle, much to the dismay of Janis and Damian.

The teen comedy is a popular genre that typically employs a number of familiar themes and situations that resonate with its target audience. Although teen comedies have historically focused on the male experience, female-centric stories are becoming more commonplace for a variety of reasons. Examining gender roles and norms and identities in this format allows filmmakers to present and challenge pre-existing beliefs while staying rooted in the familiar plotlines and characterizations. In other words, these can be ideal vehicles in which to test gender and social constructs while still being entertaining and holding the interest of the target audience.

Mean Girls effectively examines the perils and rewards of being female and socially aggressive. In Western culture, men are viewed as and conditioned to be physically aggressive while women are traditionally viewed as and conditioned to be physically nonaggressive. Although not all individuals conform to this imposed standard, stereotypes of expected behaviors are deeply entrenched within our culture. In following with Albert Bandura's social cognitive theory, media messages significantly influence how receivers interpret and subsequently acquire these beliefs. Extending this theory, individuals observe how certain behaviors between the genders are received and rewarded in terms of outcomes.

Social aggression differs from physical aggression and that is one of the focuses of the film; specifically, what it looks like when a woman—or a group of women—behaves in a socially aggressive manner. Focusing on negative relationships rooted in romantic rivalries and petty conflicts between young women highlights preconceived gender role stereotypes. Research doesn't support the notion that women are significantly more socially aggressive than men, but one wouldn't know that when looking at media representations of women, especially younger women. If anything, research suggests that female friendships are more complex than male friendships and they may also be more supportive overall.

In the film, Cady is asked to be part of a revenge scheme concocted by outsider Janis Ian. Janis has a long-held grudge against Plastics leader Regina George who has routinely tormented her in school. Cady is uninterested in becoming involved until Regina retaliates against her for showing interest in Regina's ex-boyfriend, Aaron Samuels (Jonathan Bennett). At this point, Cady participates in a series of pranks and calculated actions designed to humiliate Regina and presumably dethrone her from her position of power and prestige at school.

Extending beyond the immediate group of main characters, *Mean Girls* attempts to examine to some degree the moral universe of high school. In addition to the social hierarchy at the film's center, there are also issues of sex education and the ineffectiveness of well-intentioned educators and authority figures. As evolving young adults, high school students struggle with their identities and place within community. Although the public school setting seems like an ideal location in which "community" can be achieved, the likelihood of that happening, at least in this film, is thin. To a large degree, the school is presented as a cut-throat environment in which one must put one's own survival and well-being ahead of any sense of community cohesion.

In her efforts to remove Regina as a threat, Cady becomes the very "mean girl" that she initially rejected. After the release of a "burn book" that contains slanderous comments about fellow students and faculty alike, Cady finally sees her way to falsely confess and take responsibility for the tome in an effort to put an end to all of the vitriol. More importantly, this happens from a plot perspective in order to restore Cady's likability with the students and by extension the audience. Regina is injured after being hit by a school bus, so there is an implication that punishment is the most effective tool when dealing with bullies.

Order appears to be restored at the film's conclusion, but it's short lived. Cady observes a new group of "mean girls" arriving at the high school exhibiting the same destructive behavior as those who came before them. She imagines them being hit by a school bus, suffering the same outcome that Regina did. The suggestion, of course, is that regardless of what happens, the patterns of hurtful behavior continue.

Mean Girls was a box office smash, grossing almost $130 million dollars globally. It was widely praised by critics with many taking note of the breakout performances of its young stars. It spawned a direct-to-DVD sequel called *Mean Girls 2*, and a stalled related project called *Mean Moms* has yet to be produced.

See also: 1980s: *Sweet Valley High*; 1990s: *She's All That*; 2000s: *One Tree Hill*; *Pretty Little Liars*; *Sisterhood of the Traveling Pants, The*; *Vampire Diaries, The*

Further Reading

Brody, Richard. n.d. "Why Mean Girls Is a Classic." *New Yorker*. https://www.newyorker .com/culture/richard-brody/why-mean-girls-is-a-classic.

Piper, Alana. 2015. "The Myth That Women Secretly Hate Each Other Has a Long History." *News Minute*, September 26. http://www.thenewsminute.com/article/myth-women -secretly-hate-other-women-has-long-history-34663.

Simpkins, Jennifer. 2014. "'You Can't Sit with Us!'—How Fourth-Wave Feminism Became 'Mean Girls.'" Huffington Post, March 21. http://www.huffingtonpost.co.uk/jennifer -simpkins/feminism-fourth-wave-became-mean-girls_b_4616597.html.

MY CHEMICAL ROMANCE

Allegedly inspired by reaction to the 9/11 terrorist attacks, founding band member and front man Gerard Way (1977–) formed My Chemical Romance (2001–2013) in his home state of New Jersey. Other band members include guitarists Ray Toro and Frank Iero, bassist Mikey Way, and drummer Bob Bryar. The band is perhaps best known for their third studio album, *The Black Parade*. This is a concept album similar to Green Day's *American Idiot*. The work focuses on a fictional character known simply as "the patient" who is dying of cancer. The work examines depression, death, and reflections on the afterlife. Four singles were released from the album, with "Welcome to the Black Parade" reaching number one in the United Kingdom. The single weighs in at number 17 in *Rolling Stone's* 100 Best Songs of 2006 and ranked in the number one spot for MTV's 50 Greatest Music Videos of the 21st Century.

One single from the album, "Teenagers," was a departure for the group musically—it had a simple melody and refrain—but the lyrical message was just as dark as their other material. The song deals with school shootings and is sung from the point of view of an adult. Lead singer Way was apparently inspired to pen the song after an incident on a subway where he was surrounded by teenagers. It sparked some introspection about being an adult and the realization that he was looked at differently by adolescents due solely to his age. It was also a statement about the rash of school shootings in the country and the violence and danger in an institution that used to be viewed as a physically safe space for children.

The band's music certainly struck a chord with fans. Their single, "I'm Not Okay (I Promise)" adroitly zeroed in on feelings of teen alienation, fear, and anxiety in the age of mass shootings, cyberbullying, and wars. They relied on costumes and makeup to also communicate visually with their fans, often donning marching band uniforms, bulletproof vests, and heavy doses of eyeliner.

My Chemical Romance doesn't necessarily fall neatly into a predefined musical genre. However, although broadly identified as an American rock band, their music can reasonably be labeled as postpunk or even "emo." Emo music grew out of the punk music movement and has its roots in 1980s Washington, D.C. As with most new musical movements or styles, it morphed and was reinvented into something more mainstream as time passed. The primary distinction between punk rock and this outgrowth from punk rock is in its lyrics. Where punk rock focused on rage and violence, emo turned inward, producing songs centered on feelings of isolation and angst. Rather than fixating on external forces, emo music examines internal struggles and despair.

Given the challenging and at times tumultuous rites of passage associated with being a young adult, emo bands like My Chemical Romance have a special allure for teenagers; the music deals in emotions. At a time when many young people are entering into their first romantic relationships or experiencing their first breakups, the themes communicated in emo songs resonate with teen listeners. The music also speaks to feelings of alienation and disillusionment. Although some parents and other authority figures might worry that this type of music can trigger or exacerbate depression in youths, there's nothing to support that theory. Teens might turn to this kind of music because it's a reflection of their emotions at a given time, but their feelings are not caused by the songs.

The irony of this is that My Chemical Romance has explicitly distanced itself from emo music and claims it does not qualify for that categorization. Gerard Way profanely dismissed emo music in a 2007 statement where he referred to the genre in unflattering terms and dismissed the connection made between emo music and his band.

Some traditional rock fans have mocked bands like 30 Seconds to Mars and My Chemical Romance. The reason for the criticism is the way band members subvert traditional gender norms. Emo bands and their members are viewed negatively due to both the content of their music and their performance style and appearance. Derogatory terms used for gay men are often hurled at these bands, and there is an overt hostility aimed at them that largely seems to be based on regressive views. Teens are less likely to subscribe to these beliefs than their elders, however, and are more likely to gravitate toward music that speaks to them on a personal and emotional level. They also tend to be more evolved with respect to flexible gender roles. The fashions and physical appearance of the band members along with the lyrics in their songs resonated with LGBT and non–gender conforming youths. The freedom of expression and embrace of those who might be considered on the "margins" within teen social hierarchies was a welcome change from artists and bands that adhered to gender conformity and produced garden variety pop music for the masses.

The band received negative attention after the suicide of a 13-year-old fan in the United Kingdom in 2008. Apparently, teen Hannah Bond had become fascinated with emo music and lifestyle and had begun cutting her wrists as part of an "initiation" into the lifestyle weeks before she took her own life. The band responded on their website and emphasized that their music is designed to comfort those who feel alienated and abandoned and expressed sorrow for the teen's death.

See also: 1960s: Doors, The; Joplin, Janis; Rolling Stones, The; 1970s: Devo; Led Zeppelin; Queen; 1980s: Blondie; Duran Duran; Madonna; MTV; 1990s: Green Day; Morissette, Alanis; 2000s: Lavigne, Avril

Further Reading

Branstetter, Gillian. 2016. "The Overlooked Link between Emo Music and a Mental Health Crisis." *The Week*, August 2. http://theweek.com/articles/639360/overlooked -link-between-emo-music-mental-health-crisis.

Bryant, Tom. 2014. *Not the Life It Seems: The True Lives of My Chemical Romance.* Boston, MA: De Capo Press.

Gordon, Jeremy. 2016. "10 Years Later, My Chemical Romance's The Black Parade Still Speaks to Emo Internet Kids." *Spin,* October 24. https://www.spin.com/featured/my -chemical-romance-the-black-parade-10th-anniversary-emo/.

Haydn, Reinhardt. 2008. *My Chemical Romance: This Band Will Save Your Life.* Medford, NJ: Plexus.

NAPOLEON DYNAMITE

Napoleon Dynamite, a critically and commercially successful 2004 comedy, features a title character who both embodies and defies the term "nerd" as it has been created and depicted in American popular culture. Napoleon (Jon Heder) is a socially awkward Midwestern teenager who lives with his older brother Kip (Aaron Ruell), a lazy adult who spends countless hours in Internet chat rooms, flirting with strangers and dreaming of becoming a famous cage fighter. Napoleon routinely insults Kip and points out to everyone that he doesn't have an actual job. The brothers are cared for by their grandmother (Sandy Martin) and their sometimes sleezy Uncle Rico (Jon Gries), as there is no mother or father apparent in their lives.

Popular movies like *Revenge of the Nerds* and TV's *Big Bang Theory* depict nerds in a variety of ways, but the more common attributes are: intellectually above average, obsessed with sex, socially awkward, and most times unaware or unconcerned about fashion and physical fitness. While there are some variations in these representations, nerds are almost always shown as individuals who lack self-confidence with respect to romantic relationships. This is usually played for laughs as the nerd struggles to connect with the object of their affection. The character of Napoleon Dynamite certainly embodies some of these traits: he is socially awkward and lacking in fashion sense. He is not, however, academically gifted nor does his self-confidence suffer. He performs onstage in front of his school, showing off his dance moves. He also pursues a popular and pretty girl Trisha (Emily Kennard) by asking her to attend the prom with him.

Napoleon befriends a fellow student named Pedro Sanchez (Efren Ramirez), a transfer student from Mexico. Napoleon envies Pedro's calm but confident demeanor. The two of them befriend Deborah "Deb" Bradshaw (Tina Marjorino), an unpopular teen who dresses in retro 1980s fashion, and sells arts and crafts to raise money for college tuition. Unlike Napoleon and Pedro, Deb doesn't possess self-confidence.

Having Both Napoleon and Pedro either unaware or apathetic about their lack of social standing in school was a new twist for nerd tropes. Napoleon is often sullen and even combative when dealing with other students or members of his family. In this, he defies the stereotype of the shy and quiet nerd. Pedro, also a fashion victim, displays an understated sense of confidence that also goes against more typical depictions of nerds.

The surprise success of *Napoleon Dynamite* had many in the movie business befuddled. While it was clearly targeted toward a teen demographic, it was utterly lacking in profanity, sex, and gross-out humor. Instead, the film relied on the appeal of its lead stars and humor that was largely based on characters rather than sight gags. Part of this may be tied to the film's producers, who are Mormon. Notably, the novel *Twilight* was penned by a writer who is also Mormon, and it also avoided vulgarity and overt sexual content. Though the author denied that her religion influenced her writing, it's worth noting that both of these media vehicles were aimed at a teenage demographic, and both were commercially successful in spite of the exclusion of graphic content.

The timeline of *Napoleon Dynamite* confused audiences. It's set in 2004, but many of the visual references in the film seem rooted in earlier decades. Deb sports a sideways ponytail and Napoleon wears moon boots, both remnants from the 1980s. There's also archaic technology, including a Sony Walkman and Kip's dial-up Internet connection. While there may be several reasons for these seeming contradictions, they mesh perfectly with the oddball aura of the picture as a whole.

Equally absurd is the subplot in which Kip meets a woman on the Internet who later becomes his girlfriend. Lafawnduh arrives by bus, and when she steps off, she is an extremely attractive and well-dressed black woman. Regardless of her beauty and social intelligence, she is crazy about Kip, and the two fall completely in love. The final sequence of the film, after the credits, takes place at their wedding, during which her family is shown visibly distraught by the union.

The film's producers and its director Jared Hess adhered to a microbudget for a major motion picture: $400,000. In order to keep costs down, they filmed in Southeastern Idaho and used friends and locals as "extras." The original idea for the film stemmed from lead actor Heder and director Hess who attended college together in Utah. They created a short movie for a film class entitled *Peluca* that was shot in black and white and focused on a nerdy high schooler named Seth.

Napoleon Dynamite received generally positive reviews and grossed more than $46 million worldwide, though some critics didn't connect with its quirky humor or bizarre subplots. It became such a popular movie that it achieved cult status and even spawned a variety of merchandise that included shirts and pins stating "Vote for Pedro." The film even spawned an animated series in 2012 that was canceled after only six episodes. Additionally, the movie won three MTV Movie Awards, including one for Jon Heder for Breakthrough Male Performance and Best Movie. It also snagged four Teen Choice Awards, including one for Choice Movie: Hissy Fit for Jon Heder.

See also: 1980s: Hughes, John, Films of; *Revenge of the Nerds*; *Saved by the Bell*; *Say Anything . . .*; *Wonder Years, The*; 1990s: *Freaks and Geeks*; 2000s: *Juno*

Further Reading

Borrelli-Persson, Laird. 2016. "Gosh! Napoleon Dynamite Is the Man of the Moment." *Vogue*, November 7. https://www.vogue.com/article/industry-icons-napoleon-dynamite.

Duca, Lauren. 2014. "How 'Napoleon Dynamite' Became a Cultural Phenomenon (and Then Reached Critical Mass)." Huffington Post, June 10. https://www.huffingtonpost .com/2014/06/10/napoleon-dynamite-anniversary_n_5440587.html.

McCray, N. D. 2014 "Napoleon Dynamite: Ten Years Later." Paper, August 14. http://www .papermag.com/napoleon-dynamite-ten-years-later-1427368183.html.

ONE TREE HILL

One Tree Hill (2003–2012) was a popular, teen-based drama on the WB/CW network that featured two competitive half-brothers who play on the same high school basketball team. The series, originally envisioned as a theatrical film about a high school basketball team, was instead produced as a television series on the network known for creating shows popular with the youth market. The central drama in the show centers on half-brothers Lucas Scott (Chad Michael Murray) and Nathan Scott (James Lafferty). The first season emphasizes their rivalry on and off the court. In addition to both of them vying to be the better athlete, romantic conflicts entangle them as well. Nathan's girlfriend Peyton Sawyer (Hilarie Burton) is sought after by Lucas. Nathan is attracted to Lucas's best friend Haley James (Bethany Joy Lenz).

While the first season focused primarily on the Scott brothers and their athletic and romantic entanglements, the second season expanded to additional characters and also delved into topics like bisexuality and lesbianism. One of these story lines follows siblings Felix and Anna Tagaro (Michael Sowell Copon and Daniella Alonso) who arrive as new students to One Tree Hill's high school. It seems that Anna was involved in something scandalous at her previous boarding school, so the family decided to relocate and give her a fresh start at a new school. Anna soon becomes friends with Peyton, but several misunderstandings and tensions create conflict between them. After Peyton makes an innocent gesture toward Anne at a school dance, Peyton arrives at school the following day to find the word "dyke" spray painted on her locker. It is actually Anna who is bisexual but afraid to come out publicly, she advises Peyton to dismiss the incident. Peyton refuses and instead shows her support for her LGBT peers by wearing a T-shirt to school that has the word "dyke" spray painted on it. Anna feels pressured to come out but isn't sure how to deal with the issue. Unsure of Peyton's sexual orientation, she kisses her. Peyton tells her that she's not interested but also isn't offended by it.

Without exploiting the nature of Anna's sexual identity and treating it as something unusual, the series instead showed how sexual identity and orientation is part of the natural transition from adolescence to adulthood. Anna gets more support from Peyton than she does from her own brother. After he reveals that he is the one who spray painted Peyton's locker at school to deflect attention away from Anna, she reports him to the administration and he leaves for military school. Anna eventually gets back in touch with her friend Darby (Sprague Grayden) from her previous school. Darby is out as a lesbian and helps Anna both come to terms with her sexuality and come out to her parents. At the conclusion of the story line, Anna decides to return to her former school and presumably be open about her sexual identity.

One Tree Hill, while following the tropes of the average teen soap opera, showed young women who were sexually active and not demonized because of it. Additionally, female characters on the show were also not limited to their appearance in terms of worth. As the show progressed and these characters got older, they went on to have careers and follow their passions. This is important because studies have shown that many teens use fictional narratives to help them navigate issues of identity in their own lives. In some instances, these media presentations may be the primary or sometimes sole source of information for them. When positive reinforcements are lacking in the social structure for a teen, seeing characters on TV dealing with the same or similar issues can be beneficial for their identity development.

Other story lines on the show delved into romantic complications in various relationships, family struggles with siblings and parents, and medical illnesses. Love triangles are always appealing in dramatic productions, and *One Tree Hill* capitalized on this to maximum effect. The show excelled at heightening emotions and raising the stakes of character conflicts, drawing their teen fans in season after season. The show also dealt with timely issues such as school shootings, reflecting real-life events and weaving them into the fictional narrative. Fans of the show developed such an attachment to the characters that a parasocial relationship existed, an occurrence that typically exists between fans and celebrities where fans invest time and energy into following famous people who are unaware of their admirers' existence.

The structure of the show differed from other teen dramas in that it jumped forward in time and showed how the characters' lives were evolving post–high school and college as they navigated through early career and relationship choices. This strategy kept viewers interested and rewarded their loyalty with a "pay off" of seeing their favorite characters mature and move into new situations and face new challenges. *One Tree Hill* received mixed reviews during its network run, but the network attracted and retained a loyal base of viewers with this show and other teen-centric dramas such as *Dawson's Creek, Beverly Hills 90210, The O.C,* and others.

See also: 1980s: *Sweet Valley High*; 1990s: *7th Heaven*; 2000s: *Friday Night Lights*; *Gossip Girl*; *Pretty Little Liars*

Further Reading

Associated Press. 2008. "Ardent Fans Push 'One Tree Hill' to Sixth Season." *Denver Post*, September 11. http://www.denverpost.com/2008/09/11/ardent-fans-push-one -tree-hill-to-sixth-season/.

Martin, Dennis. 2009. "'One Tree Hill's' Strong Roots." *Los Angeles Times*, October 5. http:// articles.latimes.com/2009/oct/05/entertainment/et-onetreehill5.

Whitney, Alyse. 2015. "One Tree Hill's Cast and Creator Reveal Where Their Characters Would Be Now." *Glamour*, May 21. https://www.glamour.com/story/one-tree -hills-cast-and-creato.

PRETTY LITTLE LIARS

Pretty Little Liars, which aired on the ABC Family network (2010–2017), is a teen-centered drama based on a series of young adult novels by author Sara Shepard (1977–). The plot of the show revolves around the disappearance of Alison DiLaurentis (Sasha Pieterse), the leader of a small group of friends. Approximately one year after she disappears, the remaining four members of the clique, Spencer Hastings (Troian Bellisario), Aria Montgomery (Lucy Hale), Hanna Marin (Ashley Benson), and Emily Fields (Shay Mitchell) begin receiving ominous and threatening messages exposing secrets that they wish to keep hidden.

The show combines elements from several genres: mystery, teen romance, supernatural, and drama. At the onset of the series, the five girls are presented as "typical teens" doing what typical teens do—shopping, flirting with boys, and participating in rites of passage like underage drinking. The tagline for the show is "Never trust a pretty girl with an ugly secret." This telegraphs much of what the viewer can expect. All five girls are physically attractive and are very consumed with beauty rituals. The opening credits of the show are a montage of images including high-heeled shoes and makeup and nail polish being applied. There is also an emphasis on both music and fashion. The soundtrack to *Pretty Little Liars* features artists like Pink, Lady Gaga, and Florence and the Machine. These artists and groups have significant appeal to a teen demographic.

Critics have wondered whether *Pretty Little Liars* is an exercise in postfeminism or a repackaging of existing gender stereotypes presented in a slick format. Some feel that the show empowers young women to make their own decisions about their sexuality and not be shamed or judged for it. Others feel that the hyperfocus on the superficial and physical aspects of the characters' lives confines them to being viewed largely as objects vis-à-vis the male gaze. In terms of the feminist element of the show, the five main characters are all white and live an upper-class existence. Their challenges or problems certainly don't include socioeconomic woes. In terms of diversity, one of the characters, Emily Fields (Shay Mitchell), does come out as a lesbian. Given that New Wave feminism focuses more on the individual than broader political issues, it could be argued that *Pretty Little Liars* contains some of this but doesn't extend—at least in its story lines—to issues of intersectionality, how the media defines women, or addressing institutional patriarchy.

Pretty Little Liars is derivative of other teen media vehicles including *I Know What You Did Last Summer* and *Heathers*. The show is also reminiscent of the television series *Twin Peaks*. That show (which has recently been rebooted on Showtime) focused on the disappearance and murder of a popular teenager in a small town. It also contained unexplained supernatural events and a portrayal of older men as sexual predators of younger women. *Pretty Little Liars* has a subplot involving an affair between Aria and her English teacher, Mr. Fitz (Ian Harding). There is even a character in the show named Agent Cooper, the same name as the lead detective on *Twin Peaks*.

"Quality" is a subjective term with respect to art. It should be noted that while a show like *Twin Peaks* is widely lauded as "edgy" and praised for its production elements and content, *Pretty Little Liars* is largely written off as a "guilty pleasure." Although both contain very similar elements, a question looms as to whether *Pretty Little Liars* is discounted in terms of worth or value because of its teen focus and target audience. For example, one critic of the show dismissed it based on the pilot episode that he felt was too cinematic. The show had paid homage to famed Hollywood director Alfred Hitchcock in a few episodes and even toyed with film noir in the episode "Shadow Play." This is not to argue which show is better—rather, it's simply an observation that some critics tended to dismiss the show outright based on preconceived notions of what it should be and what it should not be. There is a paradox of sorts in having low expectations for a media vehicle that is arguably marketed as a guilty pleasure and then criticizing it for showing ambitions beyond that category.

Pretty Little Liars' story lines asks fans to suspend disbelief in a series of incredulous plots involving murder, mistaken identities, and faked deaths. At its core, it is a teen soap opera. Media productions featuring teen cliques hold special appeal to their audiences regardless of genre. Viewers typically identify with one or more of the characters (even when the characters have exaggerated qualities), which makes the content more relatable.

The show won numerous Teen Choice Awards in multiple categories and also several People's Choice Awards as well. Although critics were certainly mixed in their assessment of the show, it developed a loyal following throughout its seven seasons. A spin-off show entitled *Ravenswood* aired on the same network but was canceled after airing 10 episodes.

See also: 1990s: *I Know What You Did Last Summer*; 2000s: *Gossip Girl*; *Mean Girls*; *One Tree Hill*

Further Reading

Bradley, Laura. 2017. "How That Bonkers *Pretty Little Liars* Ending Came Together." *Vanity Fair*, June 28. https://www.vanityfair.com/hollywood/2017/06/pretty-little-liars-series-finale.

Green Emma. 2014. "How *Pretty Little Liars* Redeems the Pop-Culture Mean Girl." *The Atlantic*, January 7. https://www.theatlantic.com/entertainment/archive/2014/01/how-i -pretty-little-liars-i-redeems-the-pop-culture-mean-girl/282877/.

Hallisey, Maura. 2014. "'Pretty Little Liars': The Queer Feminist Drama You Might Just Have Missed." *IndieWire*, June 10. http://www.indiewire.com/2014/06/pretty-little -liars-the-queer-feminist-drama-you-might-just-have-missed-214096/.

PRINCESS DIARIES, THE

The Princess Diaries, a 2001 theatrical film helmed by famed director Garry Marshall (*Pretty Woman*), catapulted actress Anne Hathaway's career and possesses all of the tropes that viewers have come to expect from a long line of Disney "princess" movies. The film tells the story of uber-awkward teenager, Mia Thermopolis (Hathaway), and how her world is altered dramatically when she discovers that her grandmother (Julie Andrews) is a queen and she is heir to the throne of Genovia. Mia is a bright student but is socially awkward and desperately vies for the attention of Josh Bryant (Erik von Detten). He doesn't reciprocate those feelings and spends much of his time mocking and ridiculing her, accompanied by his cheerleader girlfriend, Lana Thomas (Mandy Moore).

The Disney Corporation has a long history of producing children's films that feature princesses: *Snow White*, *The Little Mermaid*, *Beauty and the Beast*, *Mulan*, and *The Princess and the Frog* among them. While the plots and characters may differ, the themes and ideals in the films remain fairly constant. In order to understand the reach and impact of what is now referred to as "princess culture," it is necessary to examine the psychology behind it. Peggy Orenstein, author of the 2011 nonfiction book, *Cinderella Ate My Daughter,* examines the origins of this culture and the very obvious commercial agenda behind it. She noted that this obsession with all things pink (literally) seems to start with most young girls around the age of four. It is at this age that children are mostly concerned with the exterior in terms of having an identity—i.e., their toys, clothes—largely define who they are at this stage. Orenstein contends that the origins of this hyperfeminine stage that advertisers capitalize on has its roots in child beauty pageants, wherein young girls are sexualized, dressed up with hair and makeup more befitting a grown woman than a toddler. An outgrowth of this manifests itself in the creation and marketing of vast arrays of products that are intended to set the standard for how young girls dress and even behave. This creates an inflexible ideal of what it means to be a girl at this age, and it is determined by marketers and manufacturers based solely on gender stereotypes.

In the film, one of the first things that is done to Mia in preparation for her new role as a princess is to undergo an extreme physical makeover. She is turned over by her grandmother to a melodramatic hairdresser named Paulo (Larry Miller) and his two chic female assistants. In what is intended to be a comedic scene, Paulo straightens her curly hair with a flat iron. Before that, however, he breaks off a comb in her hair. After asking her about the use of eye contacts, he breaks her glasses in half in order to force her to use contacts over eyeglasses. Once the transformation is complete, Mia is then presented to her grandmother who observes that the "new" Mia is an improvement over the old one. This scene, of course, resonates with young women due to the very reasons that Orenstein lays out in her book: they perpetuate the cultural myth that a woman's value is determined primarily by her physical appearance. Indoctrinated from a young age by saturated media images coordinated with a fashion industry effort to standardize what is considered appropriate "female attire," teen girls view this "makeover" as perfectly normal and even desirable.

While maintaining one's appearance and having a desire to be found physically attractive is fine, it is the emphasis on this *above all else* that creates less-evolved or independent female characters. Although Mia is not portrayed as a helpless victim like so many other *animated* Disney princesses who came before her, she ultimately seeks self-validation through the approval and love of a male suitor. Although *The Princess Diaries* was marketed as a "modern"-day fairytale, is it all that different from its predecessors in terms of outcomes?

Although Mia may complete a dramatic arc within the film and grow as an individual, the audience is still reassured at the end of the film that male attention is the ultimate reward. Romantic love is worthy, but if messages of self-worth and autonomy are to be communicated to young girls in a media production, why does the "happy ending" always equate to the ultimate goal of landing a boyfriend or husband? At the finale of the film when her crush, Michael (Robert Schwartzman) kisses her, the implication is that this is what completes her or makes her whole as opposed to the character development that has given her newfound confidence and conviction.

The film succeeds largely with its target audience because it adheres to rather than deviates from cultural and gender stereotypes. *The Princess Diaries* was a box office hit and grossed more than $160 million. The reviews for the film were mixed, with many critics citing that although it was a pleasant enough diversion, there wasn't anything particularly original about its plot or execution. *The Princess Diaries 2: Royal Engagement* was released as a sequel in 2004. In spite of its negative reviews, the film grossed more than $120 million at the box office.

See also: 1990s: *She's All That*

Further Reading

Orenstein, Peggy. 2011. *Cinderella Ate My Daughter: Dispatches from the Front Lines of the New Girlie-Girl Culture*. New York: Harper.

Salyer, Kirsten. 2016. "Are Disney Princesses Hurting Your Daughter's Self-Esteem?" *Time*, June 22. http://time.com/4378119/disney-princess-effect-on-girls/.

Sun, Maggie. 2015. "Disney Princesses, de Beauvoir, and Media Depictions of Women." *Stanford Freedom Project*. https://stanfordfreedomproject.com/what-is -freedom-new-essays-fall-2014/1190-2/.

RIHANNA

Robyn Rihanna Fenty (1988–), a Barbados-born singer, has become one of the world's most popular recording artists. She has sold hundreds of millions of albums and has received numerous awards and accolades. She has the distinction of being the youngest solo artist to have 14 number one hit singles on the Billboard Hot 100. Rihanna enjoyed modest success with her two first albums, but when her third studio release, *Good Girl Gone Bad*, came out in 2007, her popularity soared. The single, "Umbrella," became an international hit, and it sold over 8 million copies. Three additional hit singles emerged from the album, and Rihanna was heralded as a bona fide pop icon.

Rihanna's name recognition increased dramatically in 2009, but not for reasons she wanted. Tabloid website TMZ released photos of the singer after she had been assaulted by then boyfriend and hip-hop star, Chris Brown. Suddenly, the pop and dance music superstar was fodder for not just celebrity gossip sites and shows but also mainstream news shows and publications where details of the assault crept in. As in many scenarios where young celebrities are involved in unsavory situations,

Recording artist Rihanna has sold millions of records and maintained her popularity and fan base for more than a decade. She became the unwilling face of domestic violence in 2009 after an incident with her then boyfriend Chris Brown was widely reported by the media. (Kevin Winter/Getty Images)

there was a predictable outcry from many that Rihanna was serving as a poor role model for young girls. People could not fathom how anyone, let alone a rich celebrity with access to resources that others could not afford, would "side" with her attacker. Victim blaming escalated around her as news got out that she wasn't pursuing criminal charges against Brown.

Part of this strong response might be a reaction to the singer's revelations that she has an interest in sexual bondage and discipline. She has presented herself as a sexually confident woman in her musical performances and in interviews. Additionally, she has appeared in cover photos for magazines such as *Vogue,* decked out in thigh-high denim boots and tops that partially reveal her breasts. This is perceived differently by different audiences, but it likely isn't received well by some conservative men and women. However, many young girls find this empowering and absorb the message of being proud of one's body and not shameful about female sexuality.

Rihanna showed no indication of appeasing her critics when the studio album that was released less than a year after the assault incident contained songs focusing on sex and violence. *Rated R* includes songs that make direct reference to Chris Brown and explore relationships involving domestic violence. Her duet with rapper Eminem, "Love the Way You Lie," especially infuriated some critics. Centering on a fictional couple with a volatile relationship, the song ends with the woman being burned alive at the hands of her abuser. Rather than convey a message of survival and female empowerment, the song and video seem to explore the dichotomy between intimacy and physical violence. Given the history of her coartist on the song (Eminem has a history of domestic violence with his ex-wife), the choice seemed perplexing to women's rights advocates and survivors of abuse.

Approximately three years after the assault, Rihanna and Brown reunited much to the dismay of a baffled public and questioning media. The reunion was brief, but it reignited many of the same arguments that surfaced shortly after news of the assault was made public. It's possible, though, that some young girls who have been in abusive relationships might have felt a kinship with the artist on this volatile issue and may not have judged her the same as adults and those in the media.

Rihanna showed once again that she had no interest in appeasing her critics with the release of the 2015 single, "B**** Better Have My Money." The song's lyrics and musical style were a departure from much of her earlier work, and the accompanying video was dark and violent. Younger fans, especially female fans, view her as a rebel who does what she wants and dismisses criticism when she makes unconventional choices.

The scandal hasn't hurt Rihanna's career. In 2007, Rihanna became the face of Cover Girl cosmetics. This reinforced her status and influence as a style icon and demonstrated that young girls were interested in her not just as a singer but also as an influencer of beauty product consumption. Publications like *Teen Vogue* have followed her closely and featured pieces on her hair, makeup, and clothing choices. In 2017, she launched the inclusive makeup line Fenty Beauty as well.

She has released several best-selling albums that have sold millions of copies. She has hit single after hit single and continues to show an ability to retain her fan base while stretching as an artist. Her musical influences range from Madonna to Bob Marley to Celine Dion. Her eighth studio album, *Anti,* became her first in the United States to reach number one on Billboard. She's won eight Grammy Awards and 12 Billboard Music Awards. The singer starred in an all-female reboot of the *Ocean's Eleven* film series, entitled *Ocean's Eight,* which was released in the summer of 2018.

See also: 1960s: Joplin, Janis; 1970s: Summer, Donna; 1980s: Blondie; Gibson, Debbie; Madonna; MTV; 1990s: Backstreet Boys; 2000s: Cyrus, Miley; Spears, Britney; Swift, Taylor

Further Reading

Cragg, Michael. 2016. "Rihanna Review—Like Watching a Different Artist." *The Guardian,* June 24. https://www.theguardian.com/music/2016/jun/24/rihanna-review-wembley-stadium-anti.

Edgar, Amanda Nell. 2014. "R&B Rhetoric and Victim-Blaming Discourses: Exploring the Popular Press's Revision of Rihanna's Contextual Agency." *Women's Studies in Communications* 37: 138–158.

Friedman, Vanessa. 2017. "Rihanna and the Fashion X Games." *New York Times,* September 11. https://www.nytimes.com/2017/09/11/fashion/rihanna-fenty-diane-von-furstenberg-new-york-fashion-week.html.

SISTERHOOD OF THE TRAVELING PANTS, THE

The Sisterhood of the Traveling Pants, a series of young adult novels penned by Ann Brashares (1967–), focuses on the close friendship shared among four young girls—Carmen, Lena, Bridget, and Tibby—as they traverse high school and their freshmen year of college. The title comes from a pair of "magical jeans" that one of the characters purchases at a thrift store. Even though all four girls have different body shapes and sizes, the jeans fit each of them perfectly. The series is arguably a response to the negative and combative proliferation of "mean girls" media that rose in popularity during the 2000s. Rather than characters that are "frenemies" who are out for only themselves, no matter the cost, the girls put their sisterhood above all else. Each of the four main characters find themselves separated for the first time ever and must contend with how this separation will enable them to potentially grow and mature.

The books and film were marketed as multicultural because of the various ethnicities and backgrounds of three of the four characters: Carmen (America Ferrera) is Latin American, Lena (Alexis Bledel) is Greek American, and Bridget (Blake Lively) is Dutch American. Even the white character, Tabitha/Tibby (Amber Tamblyn), is given a different sort of cultural differentiation to deal with; although raised as a child in an unconventional ("hippie") household, her family eventually settles into a middle-class existence that forces her to reevaluate things in terms of her own identity.

In the first novel, Carmen deals with cultural issues when her father and mother divorce, and her father remarries a white woman, causing Carmen to grapple with her own identity since her mother is Puerto Rican. Lena experiences romantic attraction to a Greek boy, Kostas, but then discovers that an age-old feud between their grandparents will keep them apart. Tibby is friends with a young girl named Bailey who has leukemia and is devastated when Bailey dies; the realization that the "magic pants" can't cure cancer forces her to view life differently than she did before. All of these story lines speak to painful issues that many adolescents face and resonate among teenagers who are struggling with mixed families, increased awareness of death, blossoming romances, and other coming-of-age issues.

Writing about young adults and sexuality can be rocky terrain to navigate. Although the teen years are often ripe with sexual awakening and exploration, sex still remains a controversial topic for some. The loss of a young woman's virginity has been written about in countless books, and the tone and themes around this vary widely from author to author. The character of Bridget is especially interesting to examine in this light. She is arguably the most physically attractive of the group, and she exudes confidence in her athletic abilities. After arriving at soccer camp, she finds herself attracted to a college-aged coach named Eric. The two end up having sex, which causes Bridget to suddenly doubt her abilities and self-worth when she realizes the relationship can go no further. More dramatically, the aftermath of the act causes her to revert back to the feelings of helplessness and despair that originated when her mother committed suicide. She loses her self-confidence and ultimately seems broken.

It's not unusual for a serious event in a work of fiction to prompt character growth and development. After all, compelling storytelling relies on dramatic arcs in order to connect with audiences. The author of the novel indicated that she included this "wound" with Bridget as just that—a catalyst for character development. It can be argued, however, that this portrayal feeds into stereotypes about the repercussions of sex for young girls. How else can the devastating effect it has upon a character that was known for her strength and self-confidence be explained? In short, Bridget is punished for her sexuality. Her swift and significant decline after sexual activity reiterates stereotypical messages about teens and sex, specifically about teenage girls and the belief that they are not as prepared to deal with the emotional element of sex that their male peers apparently are.

This, of course, is an oppositional reading of the text. The preferred reading of it is that Bridget was not emotionally prepared for sex and yet indulged regardless of possible outcomes. The "mistake" that she made cost her quite a bit in the short term but allowed for long-term introspection.

The overarching theme of friendship and personal growth resonated with readers and viewers who longed for a more positive portrayal of young female relationships. The 2001 novel was a *New York Times* best seller and received overall positive reviews from critics, notably *USA Today* and *Publishers Weekly*. The 2005 film adaptation of the original book in the series was a mild box office success and garnered mixed reviews. While many critics applauded its unifying theme of sisterhood and girl power, others felt it was a missed opportunity that could have been stronger and more challenging for its audience. It was nominated for nine Teen Choice Awards but failed to win any. The sequel, *Sister of the Traveling Pants 2*, was released in 2008, and a third film in the series is planned.

See also: 1960s: *Patty Duke Show, The*; 1970s: Blume, Judy; 1980s: *Dirty Dancing*; *Sweet Valley High*; 1990s: *Clarissa Explains It All*; 2000s: *Gossip Girl*; *Mean Girls*; *One Tree Hill*; *Pretty Little Liars*

Further Reading

Brashares, Ann. 2001. *The Sisterhood of the Traveling Pants*. New York: Random House.
Carlin, Shannon. 2017. "'Sisterhood of the Traveling Pants 3' Shouldn't Be a Teen Movie, if It Ever Happens." *Bustle*, June 23. https://www.bustle.com/articles/168595-sisterhood-of-the-traveling-pants-3-shouldnt-be-a-teen-movie-if-it-ever-happens.
Simon, Jenni M. 2017. *Consuming Agency and Desire in Romance: Stories of Love, Laughter, and Empowerment*. Lanham, MD: Lexington Books.

SPEARS, BRITNEY

Britney Spears (1981–) is one of the most popular and successful female singers of all time. With a background in entertainment that started when she was a small child, Spears has enjoyed phenomenal success within the pop music industry. She burst onto the music scene in 1999 with the release of her album . . . *Baby One More Time*. That and her follow-up album, *Oops! . . . I Did It Again*, sold millions of copies that contained defining hits that have helped define her career.

The music video for ". . . Baby One More Time" was considered provocative upon its release. Spears appears in the video dressed in a traditional parochial school girl outfit: short plaid skirt, crisp white collared shirt (cinched at the waist in the video), and cardigan sweater. The video features other high school "students" that include male athletes and female onlookers. Though there is nothing particularly racy about the video, there was something about a teenage girl dressed in garb that is commonly associated with male sexual fantasies that garnered a lot of media attention.

The follow-up music video for the titular single off of *Oops! . . . I Did It Again* made it clear that the sexual imagery wasn't going away. In the video, Spears is dressed in a red latex jumpsuit, enticing an astronaut and his communicator at Mission Control back on Earth. As with many pop videos, the story line is non-existent or nonsensical, but the optics are handled with laser-like precision. This persona of sexual provocateur continued through much of Spears's musical career, notably in the 2009 music video for "Toxic" where she capitalizes on two popular sexual fantasy roles: a stewardess/flight attendant and a secret agent. Additionally, at the 2001 MTV Music Video Awards, Spears performed her hit "I'm a Slave 4 U" with a giant yellow snake wrapped around her.

While sexuality and titillation are nothing new in popular music videos nor are lyrics peppered with innuendos, there is something noteworthy in the backlash that Spears has experienced throughout her career. Most surprisingly, a fair amount of the vitriol has come from her target teen audience. A study was conducted on the heels of Spears's breakthrough success in 1999 after the release of her initial album. It focused on the responses and reactions of two focus groups that consisted of adolescent girls who listened to Spears's music and were familiar with her background and story. The researcher chose a more relaxed format (focus group) instead of a formal one (interview) in an attempt to elicit feedback in a relaxed atmosphere that encouraged conversation and interaction. When Spears's name was mentioned, the researcher was struck by how vocal and venomous some of the reactions were. Spears was called a "whore" and a "slut," and other unflattering terms by many of the participants.

On further discussion and analysis, the researcher gleaned where much of this was originating from: a perceived dichotomy between the wholesome image of the singer featured in some teen-centered magazines (and even in some of Spears's own work) versus a fully sexualized being as evidenced in her hit songs and videos. Spears had appeared in both *Teen People* and *Rolling Stone* magazine. The photos and stories from each seemed to come from two different universes. In *Teen People*, Spears was portrayed as "the girl next door," a relatable young woman still enjoying adolescence; in *Rolling Stone*, the singer was portrayed as a vixen, a fully sexualized being. This, of course, goes deeper and stems from several issues that include a dominant male culture, sexual packaging and promotion of young women, and gender inequalities between how male and female artists are produced and marketed. The music industry is run primarily by men. They operate within their frame of reference and inherent and/or inherited biases and notions of gender differences. They also rely on proven techniques to create and sell products, and sexuality is most often an easy sell.

The apparent confusion and frustration vocalized by the young girls in the focus groups mirrors a larger disconnect beyond Britney Spears's audience. Who is the "real" Britney Spears? The naive young girl asking her boyfriend to delay intercourse in the song "Sometimes" or the teenage Lolita strutting the halls of her high school in ". . . Baby One More Time?" The answer, of course, requires emotional intelligence and the ability to realize that they are not necessarily mutually exclusive.

The singer-actress has had several public meltdowns that have contributed to tabloid fodder over the years. Given the level of success that she enjoyed at an early age and the significant media attention cast upon her, it isn't surprising. Few artists at that life stage are adequately prepared for the media scrutiny and criticism that their popularity typically brings. Activities that would be considered uneventful for noncelebrities are analyzed and dissected by entertainment and gossip reporters, and assigned meaning many times without context or even vetting, which can cause a great deal of stress.

Spears has sold millions of records and won numerous Billboard Music Awards and MTV Video Music Awards, and continues to write and record music. She is included in the top 10 list of best-selling female artists of all time, and she has a star on the Hollywood Walk of Fame. She enjoyed renewed popularity and success from 2013 to 2015 when she performed hundreds of shows in Las Vegas at Planet Hollywood Resort and Casino.

See also: 1960s: Joplin, Janis; Rolling Stones, The; 1970s: Summer, Donna; 1980s: Blondie; Gibson, Debbie; Lauper, Cyndi; Madonna; MTV; 1990s: Morissette, Alanis; 2000s: Cyrus, Miley; Rihanna; Swift, Taylor

Further Reading

Dennis, Steve. 2009. *Britney: Inside the Dream—The Biography.* London: HarperCollins.
Orenstein, Hannah. 2015. "Is Britney Spears the Ultimate Feminist Icon? I Attended a Class to Find Out." *Cosmopolitan,* April 1. http://www.cosmopolitan.com/entertainment /celebs/a38424/britney-spears-feminist-icon/.
Petrusich, Amanda. 2016. "The Sexual Innocence of Britney Spears." *New Yorker,* August 25. https://www.newyorker.com/culture/cultural-comment/the-sexual-innocence-of -britney-spears.

SWIFT, TAYLOR

No other female recording artist in history has captured the attention of bloggers, gossip columnists, and fans quite like Taylor Swift (1989–). Born and raised in Pennsylvania, Swift showed a strong interest in music as a young child. Her father, a successful investment banker, moved the family to Nashville when she was a teenager in an effort to make connections within the country music industry and hopefully help her begin a career as a recording artist. It didn't take long for success to become a reality. Her first album, the self-titled *Taylor Swift,* reached number five on the Billboard charts, and the single "Our Song" is noteworthy because it is the first song to top the Hot Country chart by an artist her age. The second album, *Fearless,* was the best-selling album of 2009 and won four Grammy Awards. Swift is the youngest artist ever to win the coveted Album of the Year Award. Proving that her success wasn't a fluke or a short-lived event, her third album, *Speak Now*, debuted at number one and a single from the album won two Grammys.

Swift's career, while financially successful, has come with a lot of baggage and personal drama. Many of her songs revolve around failed relationships—nothing particularly noteworthy about that; however, because so many of her romances have played out in the public eye, each song brings with it an abundance of speculation. Who is this one about? What clues does she leave in this song to tip us off? Some might even argue that the songs themselves are sometimes eclipsed by the guessing games they trigger with each playing. She has dated numerous celebrities including singer-musician John Mayer and actor Jake Gyllenhaal. This focus on romantic relationships and breakups in her music has special resonance with teen fans and makes Swift more relatable to them.

In addition to being a consummate songwriter and performer, Swift is known as being a savvy businessperson. Producers who have worked with her are impressed by her confidence and ability to be direct when necessary. Although some artists defer to their producers when it comes to selecting final track versions for production, Swift doesn't hesitate to share her opinions on the quality of specific tracks and possible edits or rerecordings that she feels are necessary for the sake of quality. She has a lot of power for someone so young.

Swift previously pulled access to almost her entire catalog of music from the popular streaming service Spotify. Although many fans were apparently shocked by this move, Swift had written an op-ed piece about her feelings on the issue in the *Wall Street Journal*. She made the argument that, due to a lack of categorization of levels of service on Spotify, her work was being devalued. Specifically, she pointed to other similar online services that charge members a premium fee to access her work among others, but Spotify's model didn't, and this therefore excluded her and her label from potential revenues. Her business acumen is remarkable in an industry that is still male-dominated, and her self-confidence with respect to her talent and worth is in sync with her image of female self-empowerment. She is a strong female role model for young girls.

Swift connects on such a deeply personal level with her fans because of a combination of factors. She is a follower but also an influencer with fashion. Both *Vogue* and *People* magazine have listed her among Best Dressed celebrities. She has millions of followers on social media, but, more importantly, she interacts with them more than the average celebrity. She selects some of them to attend events at which she performs, and she has showered fans with gifts both in person and through surprise mail deliveries. Many female teen fans have developed a parasocial relationship with the star. Her ability to come across as authentic even while being a pop superstar makes her relatable and approachable.

Swift officially retired her country-western persona with the release of her album, *1989,* which was released in 2014 to massive hype and sales. The album debuted at number one on Billboard and sold more than 1.25 million units its first week of release. Out of the seven singles released from the effort, three reached number one on the charts: "Shake It Off," "Blank Space," and "Bad Blood." All of the other songs except one hit the top 10. Swift's album *1989* won Grammys for both Album of the Year and Best Pop Vocal Album. The album became a cultural phenomenon with its catchy singles, extensive marketing and advertising campaign, promotional tie-in with mass retailer Target, and widely hailed critical reception. In addition to appearing on several music critics end of year "best of" lists, *1989* went on to become the best-selling album of 2014.

As with her romantic interests, Swift also is known for some high-profile feuds and controversies. Rapper Kanye West infamously interrupted her acceptance speech at the 2009 Video Music Awards, ranting about how competitor Beyoncé had the better album. The incident sparked immediate and vitriolic reaction not just among Swift fans but among the general public. The story became so far reaching and prolific that even President Barack Obama weighed in, referring to West as behaving like a "jacka**." The feud continued when West released a song in 2016 called *Famous* in which Swift is referred to as a "b****" that he made famous. Much online drama ensued from both camps; with West's wife Kim Kardashian eventually weighing in with claims that Swift not only knew about the song before it was released; she approved of it. This type of melodrama that is played out on social media and within entertainment media is followed closely by teen fans.

In an era of social media inundation and fierce competition for the dollars and loyalty of music fans, Swift has managed to remain popular, successful, and committed to her craft. Whether she continues to be adept at managing public perceptions about her remains to be seen as she continues her music career in the public eye.

See also: 1960s: Joplin, Janis; Rolling Stones, The; 1970s: Summer, Donna; 1980s: Blondie; Gibson, Debbie; Lauper, Cyndi; Madonna; MTV; 1990s: Morissette, Alanis; 2000s: Cyrus, Miley; Rihanna; Spears, Britney

Further Reading

Cullen, Shaun. 2016. "The Innocent and the Runaway: Kanye West, Taylor Swift, and the Cultural Politics of Racial Melodrama." *Journal of Popular Music Studies* 28 (1): 33–50.

Dickey, Jack. 2014. "The Power of Taylor Swift." *Time,* November 13. http://time.com /3583129/power-of-taylor-swift-cover/.

Perone, James E. 2017. *The Words and Music of Taylor Swift*. Santa Barbara, CA: Praeger.

Yoder, Katie. 2017. "Feminist Attacks on Taylor Swift Reveal Something Very Ugly about the Movement." *Washington Post*, November 9. https://www.washingtonpost .com/news/posteverything/wp/2017/11/09/feminist-attacks-on-taylor-swift-reveal -something-very-ugly-about-the-movement/?utm_term=.2df30df30b45.

TEEN MOM

Teen Mom (2008–2012) is a spin-off of an earlier show on the network entitled *16 and Pregnant*. This MTV series ran for four initial seasons before a relaunch of the show was announced for 2015. Both shows focus on four teenagers: Farrah Abraham (1991–), Maci Bookout (1991–), Catelynn Baltierra, née Lowell (1992–), and Amber Portwood (1990–). *16 and Pregnant* focuses on the girls when they are approximately halfway through their pregnancies, with the conclusions of the episodes showing them as mothers with their infants. *Teen Mom* examines a variety of issues that include the effects of young motherhood on family dynamics, financial struggles, and personal upheaval with the parents of the children.

The show received a lot of criticism when it aired, most notably from socially conservative groups who felt the series glorified teenage pregnancy. These groups cited studies that showed less than half of these mothers ever graduate from high school and that close to 70 percent of these families lived at or below the poverty level. Other media groups felt that the show served as a cautionary tale about the dangers of unprotected sex and unplanned pregnancies and their aftermath.

Research conducted by Melissa S. Kearney and Phillip B. Levine seems to indicate that teen pregnancies dropped in geographic areas where more teens were watching MTV programming than in areas with lower viewership. The researchers compared the pregnancy rates with Nielsen ratings of the network in these areas to draw their conclusions. What wasn't known, of course, is what, if any, direct effect *Teen Mom* had on behavior. While it's possible, for example, to imagine that the negative outcomes shown on the series may have prompted more teens to practice safe sex, thereby reducing the likelihood of unwanted pregnancies, this is an unknown. All studies have limitations, and this one is no exception.

Anecdotal data indicates that social media chatter and web searches about contraception spiked when *16 and Pregnant* was aired, leading some to believe that the show's topic had a positive impact in creating awareness. Regardless of the causes, teen pregnancies have been in decline for the past two decades. In 1991, 62 teen girls out of every 1,000 gave birth, while that number declined to 29 out of every 1,000 by 2012.

Were these "teen moms" exploited for network profit? Does the show serve as a socially conscious lesson about the pitfalls of "kids having kids" or is it merely a vehicle to market products to its target demographic? Or is it both? When asking questions like these, it's always important to identify who benefits. For example, MTV is a youth-oriented network. Its shows feature and cater primarily to teens and twentysomethings. Since it is a for-profit entity, it makes money primarily from advertisers. These advertisers must see a solid return on their investment or they will no longer buy media time with a specific show or series. It's arguable, then, that the content or focus of the show would change if it were produced and aired, for example, on PBS, a nonprofit organization.

The stars of *Teen Mom* gained fame and notoriety from the show. Although they were not celebrities before the show, that changed very quickly once the show aired and became popular. It is hard to argue that the show didn't create or feed celebrity and consumer culture when the stars of the show were routinely featured in magazines like *People* and *Us Weekly*. What message is sent to other young women when they see teen mothers covered in the media the same way that an actress or female singing artist is? The stars of *Teen Mom* are famous not for a demonstrable skill or talent such as acting or singing but for having an unplanned pregnancy and then becoming mothers at a very young age. If not for this TV show, would they be on the cover of any magazines? Of course, this question can be extended to other noncompetition based reality TV shows as well.

This glamorization of teen pregnancy can also be viewed through the media exposure and financial gain enjoyed by someone like Bristol Palin, daughter of former Alaskan governor Sarah Palin and vice presidential running mate Senator John McCain, who ran against President Barack Obama in 2008. Bristol Palin also appeared on her own reality show entitled *Life's a Tripp* (her firstborn son's name), competed on the TV contest series *Dancing with the Stars,* wrote a book entitled *Not Afraid of Life,* and received lucrative fees from colleges for her speaking engagements on abstinence. Had her mother not been a famous politician catapulted to national recognition during the 2008 presidential race, would any of these opportunities have existed? There seems to be a significant disconnect between what the average teen dealing with an unplanned pregnancy experiences and what ones featured within popular media do.

Exploits of a few of the show's stars have often eclipsed its intended message. In 2013, a sex tape was released of Farrah Abraham and male porn star James Deen; she was allegedly paid $1.5 million by the distributors of the tape. Amber Portwood, perhaps the most notorious cast member, has been arrested for drug possession and failure to comply with an order for drug rehabilitation. She has also been charged with domestic violence against her daughter's father, Gary Shirley. The other cast members seem to be faring better: Maci McKinney returned to school and hopes to write a book about her experiences after she completes her journalism degree, and Catelynn Baltierra is now married and has a second child.

Teen Mom, now airing new episodes under the title *Teen Mom OG*, created two spin-off shows, *Teen Mom 2* and *Teen Mom 3*, both of which air on the MTV network.

See also: 2000s: *Juno*

Further Reading

Henson, Melissa. 2011. "MTV's 'Teen Mom' glamorizes getting pregnant." CNN, May 4. http://www.cnn.com/2011/OPINION/05/04/henson.teen.mom.show/index.html.

Kearney, Melissa S., and Phillip B. Levine. 2015. "Media Influences on Social Outcomes: The Impact of MTV's 16 and Pregnant on Teen Childbearing." *National Bureau of Economic Research Working Paper*. doi:10.3386/w19795

Lowery, Annie. 2014. "MTV's '16 and Pregnant,' Derided by Some, May Resonate as a Cautionary Tale." *New York Times*, January 13. https://www.nytimes.com/2014/01/13/business/media/mtvs-16-and-pregnant-derided-by-some-may-resonate-as-a-cautionary-tale.html.

TWILIGHT

As with *The Hunger Games* and *Harry Potter*, the *Twilight* series enthralled young adult readers and created a pop cultural sensation that lasted through the release of the final book in the series and the film adaptations that followed. *Twilight* (2005) tells the story of Bella Swan, a Washington State transplant who relocates to the town of Forks with her parents due to a job opportunity for her stepfather. At school, Bella encounters the brooding and sullen Edward Cullen, a vampire who is more than 100 years old. He lives in town with his family, a group of vampires who drink animal blood rather than human blood. Although Edward is moody and unfriendly, Bella is drawn to him and soon finds herself embroiled in drama and physical danger due to the burgeoning romantic feelings that the two feel for each other. Twilight is the first of four books in the series. The subsequent titles are: *New Moon, Eclipse*, and *Breaking Dawn*.

Author Stephenie Meyer (1973–) has received significant criticism surrounding the two main characters, Bella and Edward. Detractors of the *Twilight* series consistently zero in on the overly dependent nature of Bella on Edward. Although she realizes the danger that she places herself in by associating with him and his family, Bella continues to be drawn to him and puts herself in situations where can be harmed. She rationalizes this by his "protection" of her, never realizing or acknowledging that the relationship itself is the source of the danger. In multiple passages within the books, Bella excuses Edward's overly dominating and controlling personality and actions by focusing on his magnetism, power, and physical attractiveness.

More tellingly, Bella quickly distances herself from family and friends and ignores their concerns about Edward. Incrementally, she allows herself to become so obsessed with him and so dependent on his presence in her life, that eventually, her identity is completely dependent on her being with him. She literally cannot imagine a life without him. While this relationship dynamic may seem romantic on the page or screen to a teenage girl, it perpetuates dangerous and damaging myths and stereotypes about gender roles within our culture.

While Meyer may not have set out to communicate this message of domination and submission that falls strictly along conventional gender lines, the theme is embedded in the text deeply and

Actors Robert Pattinson, Kristen Stewart, and Taylor Lautner from the *Twilight* film series. Although the novels and film adaptations were hugely popular with teens, many critics viewed the issues of dependency and co-dependency within the material as negative and even damaging to gender roles among young women. (Carlos Alvarez/Getty Images)

consistently. In *New Moon*, when Edward leaves Bella, she becomes so depressed that she cannot function. Her sense of self and happiness has become so inextricably linked to him that she becomes almost catatonic.

One question worth asking about this relationship is "Who is Bella without Edward?" What are her ambitions, dreams, and goals outside of that relationship? Are there any?

Critics have also noted that, although there is no explicit sex in the books, Meyer masterfully taps into the mind of the average tween and teenage girl regarding notions of sex and romantic love. An undue emphasis is placed upon Edward's looks. When Bella is with him, she at times literally loses track of what she is saying or doing because she is so flustered in his presence. Although this may reflect the growing sexuality of young women, the degree to which she loses herself in him is not healthy.

In terms of the genre, Meyer is able to avoid some of the inherent gore that often comes with vampire lore. Having the Cullens be non–human killing vampires allows the reader to sympathize or at least empathize with them. She takes some other liberties with the legends such as having the vampires sparkle in the sunlight as opposed to disintegrating. Last, they don't have fangs but rather sharp teeth. This approach increases the likelihood that the target audience—teenage girls—will engage in the story and not be repelled by the bloody violence that peppers most vampire tales.

As with any romance, there must be an identifiable threat to the couple. The *Twilight* series has several, most notably James, another vampire who is intent on killing Bella. There is also Jacob Black, a shape-shifting werewolf who falls in love with Bella in Edward's absence. Love triangles are always a reliable element that can disrupt the predictability of a fictional couple, and young female readers especially are intrigued by this dynamic. It heightens the dramatic tension and raises the stakes for the heroine.

There are other foes to fight and defeat, but one could argue that the most significant threat to Bella and Edward might be themselves. Edward is so controlling that he watches Bella while she sleeps; she finds this comforting rather than disturbing. He monitors her every move under the guise of protection, and she happily goes along with this and confesses to feeling completely debilitated when he is not around.

The books received unwanted attention when it was noted that the relationship between Bella and Edward met the definition of an "abusive relationship" as outlined by the National Domestic Violence Hotline. Young fans of the series probably weren't tapping into this but were instead mesmerized by the romantic nature of the relationship. These criticisms didn't affect sales of the books or box office receipts for the film adaptations. More than 120 million copies of the books have been sold and they have been translated into almost 40 languages.

The series of five films (the last book was split between two full-length features) grossed almost $3.5 billion despite mixed reviews. All of the films enjoyed record advance sales and propelled the careers of both Kristen Stewart (Bella) and Robert Pattinson (Edward) forward. Adding to the buzz surrounding the films, Stewart and Pattinson began an offscreen relationship that provided limitless fodder for gossip magazines and websites.

The fandom surrounding both the novels and the films of the series is impressive. Many mothers and daughters read the books simultaneously and attended viewings of the films together. Meyer wrote *The Short Life of Bree Tanner* (the story of Edward and Bella's supernatural baby) in 2010 and released it on her website at no charge.

See also: 1990s: *Harry Potter*; 2000s: *Divergent*; *Hunger Games, The*; *Vampire Diaries, The*

Further Reading

Ashcraft, Donna. 2012. *Deconstructing Twilight: Psychological and Feminist Perspectives on the Series.* New York: Peter Lang.

Borgia, Danielle N. 2014. "Twilight: The Glamorization of Abuse, Codependency, and White Privilege." *Journal of Popular Culture* 47 (1): 153–173.

Click, Melissa A., Jennifer Stevens Aubrey, and Elizabeth Behm-Morawitz. 2010. *Bitten by Twilight: Youth Culture, Media, and the Vampire Franchise.* New York: Peter Lang.

Fetters, Ashley. 2012. "At Its Core, Twilight Is about _____." *The Atlantic*, November 15. https://www.theatlantic.com/entertainment/archive/2012/11/at-its-core-the-twilight -saga-is-a-story-about/265328/.

VAMPIRE DIARIES, THE

Vampire stories have enjoyed a surge in popularity over the past decade. The phenomenal success of the *Twilight* series of books and films, coupled with the well-received cable hit, *True Blood*, has enabled other readings of vampire mythology to make their way into popular media. *The Vampire Diaries* (2009–2017) aired on the CW, a network whose primary target market is teenagers. When the pilot episode was shown in 2009, it garnered the largest viewing audience the network had seen (this has subsequently been surpassed by the series *Arrow*). Just as with *Twilight* and *True Blood*, the show's source material is a popular series of books, penned by L. J. Smith. The series focuses on three main characters: Elena Gilbert (Nina Dobrev), Stefan Salvatore (Paul Wesley), and Damon Salvatore (Ian Somerhalder). Elena initially is in love with Stefan, but after Damon becomes involved in their lives, her feelings are conflicted and a love triangle ensues. Throughout its eight seasons, alliances shifted as Elena and Damon joined forces to save Stefan after he reverted to his blood lust. Other characters complicated their lives as well; including a vampire doppelganger of Elena's named Katherine Pierce. The show included elements of horror mixed with melodrama, and as the seasons and story lines evolved, some critics felt the show improved with respect to character and plot development.

The show was incredibly popular, and many critics felt that it provided a relatively innocuous hybrid of *Twilight* and *True Blood*. Where *Twilight* was heavily criticized for its dilution of vampire mythology (e.g., sunlight doesn't destroy vampires—it just makes them sparkle) and *True Blood* was ultragory and hypersexualized, *The Vampire Diaries* strikes a moderate balance of thrills and romance without excessive violence or overt sexual activities. Given that the show aired on network television, it was important to adhere to existing programming guidelines and rules relative to content.

Where the traditional vampire mythology is steeped in legend and an uncomplicated portrayal of vampires as villains, the reimagined world of vampires as evidenced in *Twilight* and *The Vampire Diaries* depict the vampire as an angst-ridden teen who many times is experiencing guilt and remorse over their identity and actions. In this modified vampire universe, lines between good and evil are murky at times. Rather than relying upon a one-dimensional characterization of the vampire, these new stories portray conflicting emotions and internal struggles within supernatural beings.

The *Vampire Diaries* was developed by Kevin Williamson and Julie Plec. Before this show, Williamson had already mined the teen landscape in the hit horror film *Scream* and the popular CW series, *Dawson's Creek*. In those vehicles, he proved to be adept at creating teen characters that resonated with their audiences. When initially approached about *The Vampire Diaries*, Williamson allegedly was reluctant to attempt it given the overwhelming success of *Twilight*. He felt that the material had been depleted and that there was probably little desire to go over this familiar terrain again. One element of the show that especially reflects the influence of Williamson is the insider references to other media presentations. In one episode, a character is reading *Twilight* and expresses confusion over the appeal of the central character, Bella. There is also a mention of author Anne Rice, who wrote the popular Lestat series of vampire novels. Even in this fictional realm, there are hierarchies of importance and quality with respect to vampire literature. It also adds to the hipness factor of the show and its characters.

Though the show has a central supernatural element to it, many of its elements and themes are relatable to its coming-of-age audience. The death of Elena's parents has a significant effect on her mood and behavior. Activities that once brought her joy and fulfillment no longer do, and she finds herself no longer romantically drawn to her boyfriend. This emptiness fuels her search for something to fill the void and makes her more open to an unconventional romance. Teen viewers connect with issues or themes involving missing or dead parents; it's a deeply psychological issue that is both scary and intriguing.

The vampire mythology through all of its various reincarnations and modifications can be seen as reflective of our culture at a given point in time. Stefan fights his impulses to feed on humans and chooses instead to feast on animals. Damon points to the ultimate futility of this resistance, pointing out that when extreme measures are taken to avoid one thing, it's inevitable that a breaking point will occur, thus resulting in a "binge" activity. This proves to be true and can be read as emblematic of any number of vices that humans struggle with on a regular basis. The fears and concerns of the supernatural characters can indicate what fears and concerns are prevalent within our society: fear of being alone, fear of being different or "other," and concerns over what our legacies might be once we are gone. The theme of "otherness" is always identifiable to an adolescent audience as it mirrors their experiences as they are transitioning into adulthood and dealing with confusion and alienation among peers and adults.

Critical reception to the show was mixed but generally positive overall. *The Vampire Diaries* has been nominated for multiple People's Choice Awards and Teen Choice Awards. In 2010, it won for Best New Drama at the People's Choice Awards. The show spawned a spin-off, *The Originals*, which aired in 2013 and is wrapping its final season on the CW in 2018.

See also: 1990s: *Harry Potter*; 2000s: *Divergent*; *Gossip Girl*; *Hunger Games, The*; *Pretty Little Liars*; *Twilight*

Further Reading

Fienberg, Daniel. 2017. "Critic's Notebook: When 'The Vampire Diaries' Was Good, It Was Great." *Hollywood Reporter*, March 10. https://www.hollywoodreporter.com/fien-print /critics-notebook-vampire-diaries-was-good-was-great-984917.

Gronert, Nona. 2013. "Verbal Consent to Sex and *The Vampire Diaries*." *Society Pages*, May 3. https://thesocietypages.org/socimages/2013/05/03/verbal-consent-to-sex-and -the-vampire-diaries/.

Williams, Rebecca. 2013. "Unlocking *The Vampire Diaries* Genre, Authorship, and Quality in Teen TV horror." *Gothic Studies* 15 (1): 88–99.

Index

About the Author

Donald C. Miller holds a master's degree in media literacy from Webster University and has coauthored *Media Literacy: Keys to Interpreting Media Messages* (Praeger, 2014) with Art Silverblatt. He has also written three short plays that have been produced in St. Louis, Missouri, and also contributes to a lifestyle and arts section for the *The Telegraph*, a local newspaper based in Alton, Illinois. He is currently finishing a comedic novel.